AN AUTHOR & A GARDENER

View of the Mount from the walled Italian Garden.

AN AUTHOR
& A GARDENER

The Gardens and Friendship of
Edith Wharton and Lawrence Johnston

Allan R. Ruff

WIND*gather*
PRESS

Windgather Press is an imprint of Oxbow Books

Published in the United Kingdom in 2014 by
OXBOW BOOKS
10 Hythe Bridge Street, Oxford OX1 2EW

and in the United States by
OXBOW BOOKS
908 Darby Road, Havertown, PA 19083

Hardcover Edition: ISBN 978-1-909686-46-5
Digital Edition: ISBN 978-1-909686-47-2

A CIP record for this book is available from the British Library

Printed in China by Printworks Global Ltd.

For a complete list of Windgather titles, please contact:

UNITED KINGDOM
Oxbow Books
Telephone (01865) 241249
Fax (01865) 794449
Email: oxbow@oxbowbooks.com
www.oxbowbooks.com

UNITED STATES OF AMERICA
Oxbow Books
Telephone (800) 791-9354
Fax (610) 853-9146
Email: queries@casemateacademic.com
www.casemateacademic.com/oxbow

Oxbow Books is part of the Casemate Group

Cover images

Front, main picture: Visitors in the Old Garden at Hidcote Manor Garden, Gloucestershire, c. National Trust, 184356; *Inset*: Serre de la Madone, the main axis looking towards the house, flanked by new extensions on either side of the old farmhouse.

Back: The herbaceous borders at Hidcote, c .1929.

CONTENTS

ACKNOWLEDGEMENTS

This book had its origins in research undertaken for the Certificate Programme in Landscape and Garden History at the Centre for Continuing Education, University of Manchester. I am indebted to former staff for their support. Researching the book has been a journey: literally, with visits to Lenox and Boston, to the French Riviera and Paris, and to the Cotswolds and Northumberland in England; metaphorically, into a dimly perceived world of high society and privilege. Its focus throughout has remained a search for the character and presence of two people who made five stunningly beautiful gardens. Along the way, many people offered helpful information, advice and resources that have made possible the outcome of this project.

I am especially grateful to Glyn Jones and Mike Beeston, Head Gardener and Property Manager respectively at Hidcote, who were most helpful in providing information about Lawrence Johnston and the garden. Appreciation is also due to Marguerite Bell, the Forrest family, Peter and Sarah Lindsay, Georgina Ratcliff and Ursula Westbury, Peter Renfrew, William Waterfield and Charles Whitbread for their assistance and making materials available; also to Tim Aspden for preparing the maps. Staff members of several libraries and museums were of considerable assistance and deserve special thanks: Leonie Patterson of the Royal Botanic Garden, Edinburgh; Roberta Twin of Discovery Museum, Newcastle upon Tyne; Jonathan Swift of Trinity College, Cambridge; Brent Elliott and the staff of the RHS Lindley Library in London, James Collet-White of the Bedfordshire and Luton Archives and Records Service; also the staff at the Society for the Preservation of New England Antiquities, Boston, and The Mount, Lenox, Massachusetts.

The librarians, archivists and staff at the following institutions were also most helpful in providing photographic materials: the Beinecke Library, Yale University; the Lilly Library, Indiana University; the Watkins-Loomis Agency Archives; the Library of Congress Prints and Photographic Division; the MacCormick Library of Special Collections, Northwestern University; the Environmental Design Archives, University of California, Berkeley; the American Academy of Arts and Letters, Washington; the Knickerbocker Club, New York; the Northumberland Museum Archives; the National Portrait Gallery and the Imperial War Museum, London; the Maritime Museum, Greenwich; also the picture libraries of *Country Life*, the National Trust, Peter Owen Limited and Thames & Hudson.

A special thank-you is due to James Mitchell for his helpful comments on an early draft of the manuscript, and to my editor, Michael Packard, whose tireless work over many months has finally brought this book to publication. A final word of thanks must go to my wife Mollie, who has been my travel companion in my searches and a constant source of encouragement.

A.R.R.

INTRODUCTION

In August 1937 a small group of Edith Wharton's intimate friends gathered to pay their last respects at a cemetery in Versailles to the west of her home, the Pavillon Colombe in Saint-Brice-sous-Forêt, north of Paris. Her long-standing agent, Alfred White, described it as 'a simple funeral full of dignity', as befits a great lady. 'She was,' he added, 'surrounded by loyal friends and flowers.' Among that small group of people was her friend for many years, Lawrence 'Johnnie' Johnston, the creator of two famous gardens, at Hidcote Manor, Gloucestershire, in England and Serre de la Madone, Menton, on the Côte d'Azur in the south of France. Wharton and Johnston shared not only a love of nature and gardens but something deeper and perhaps more profound – which could be called a shared experience of life. Both were private people who had had very similar childhoods, experiencing the loss of their fathers at an early age. Yet there was one aspect of their lives in which they were very different.

Wharton, the writer, constantly described her cultural environment and chose to expose her innermost thoughts and feelings; and as someone in the public eye, she was continually photographed. Johnston, however, wrote nothing about his gardens, hardly permitted photographs of himself or his gardens and, though he kept an engagement diary, these, with two exceptions, have not survived. As a result Johnston remains a shadowy figure upon whom light occasionally falls from within the diaries kept by Edith Wharton. Her diaries also provide an illuminating insight into both her gardens at St-Brice, and at Hyères, in the south of France.

Wharton was a passionate gardener; early in her life after she had made her first garden at The Mount, at Lenox, Massachusetts in the United States, she claimed she was a better landscape designer than novelist. Most biographers, while making some reference to her gardens, have understandably concentrated on her life and work at the centre of an intellectual powerhouse: friends such as the author Henry James, and those to whom she referred as her 'Inner Circle'. Lawrence Johnston was not part of that group of like-minded people though he shared many of their beliefs and hopes. But as fellow gardeners, Edith and Johnnie spent many hours together visiting each other's gardens, staying as house guests, plant-collecting in the Haute Massif and travelling by car to nurseries and gardens throughout England and France.

So it is Wharton and her gardening friend Johnnie Johnston who are the subjects of this book, surrounded as they were by an upper-class world of house parties and plenty of money. By delving into diaries, many biographies and the numerous articles that Wharton wrote describing her gardens, it has been possible to assemble a clearer picture of their horticultural activities and influences, and to throw light on the apparent enigma that was Major Lawrence Johnston.

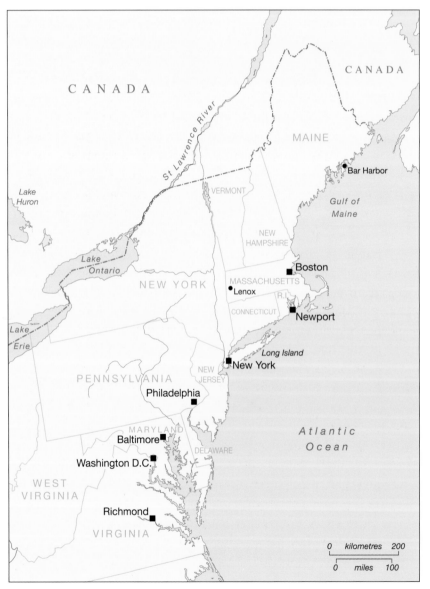

Map 1 The Northeastern seaboard of the United States. Readers will note that the main centres of wealth after the Civil War in 1865 to the early 20th century centred on the main cities and towns of Baltimore, Philadelphia, New York, Newport and Boston. This book concentrates on the wealthy inhabitants of these places; some of their summer 'colonies' were located at Bar Harbor, Maine, and Lenox, Massachusetts.

CHAPTER ONE

THE NEW YORK BEGINNINGS

The early lives of Edith Wharton (née Jones) and Lawrence Johnston followed a similar pattern. At a first glance, the later friendship between such a distinguished author and a reclusive gardener may seem unlikely, but the foundations were laid in the drawing-rooms of New York, among the gentrified society to which they both belonged.

THE JONES FAMILY OF NEW YORK

Edith Newbold Jones was born on 24th January 1862, during the American Civil War (1861–5), in what was then uptown New York City. Her mother, née Lucretia Rhinelander, had grown up in genteel poverty before making a successful marriage to George Frederic Jones, a member of the prosperous Jones family. The Jones clan was one of the larger and more socially prominent families in mid-nineteenth century America. Their wealth had come from real estate; even so, they were not as affluent as the nouveaux riches, such as the Vanderbilts and Rockefellers, whose prominence emerged in the latter part of the century. Nevertheless, George Jones did not feel the need to work after he graduated from Columbia College (named Columbia University in 1896), for his family, like the rest of New York's *haut monde*, was distinguished by its 'commitment to leisure and consumption, not for professional ambition, military prowess or social responsibilities'.[1] The Rhinelanders could trace their origins to seventeenth century huguenots, who had a 'history of lucrative and probably ruthless New York dealings in sugar, ships and tenement rentals'.[2]

Edith was a late addition to the Jones family, and therefore suffered from being raised as an only child of elderly parents. Her brothers, Frederic ('Freddie') then aged 16 and Henry ('Harry') aged 11, were often away at school, and since she had little intimate contact with her parents, her early life was a lonely world of nannies and governesses. From them she learnt French and German, and 'whatever else, in those ancient days, composed a little girl's curriculum'. She was taught Italian in Florence, which came as naturally to her as breathing, and later was to be a great source of pleasure. Describing her childhood in her autobiography, Edith observed that 'the child of the well-to-do, hedged in by nurses and governesses, seldom knows much of

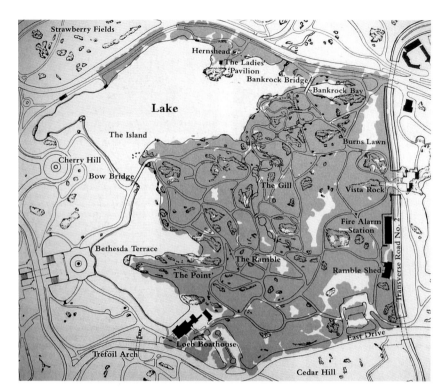

Figure 1a Plan of part of Central Park, New York, showing the location of the Ramble.

its parents' activities'.[3] However, among her earliest memories were frequent drives with her mother and, after the usual afternoon round of leaving calling-cards, the opportunity to walk in Central Park. The park was completed in the year Edith was born, and had been designed by Calvert Vaux and Frederick Law Olmsted with the intention of bringing the countryside to the people, a *rus in urbe* at the heart of Manhattan (Fig.1a). In these rural surroundings, Edith said she could 'hunt for violets and hepaticas in the secluded dells of the Ramble'. This was a 38-acre (*c.* 17 hectares) 'wild garden' sculpted out of a wooded hillside,[4] where Olmsted wanted to create, in microcosm, a forest garden full of native trees – sweet gums, tulip trees, red maples and azaleas – replicating the experience of walking in the Adirondack mountains.[5] His detailed design notes for The Ramble reveal a passionate dedication to 'picturesque' landscape composition, and Olmsted drew heavily on the influence of Uvedale Price[6] and William Gilpin[7]. He was even said always to have kept a copy of Gilpin's *Forest Scenery* in his back pocket. There were no carriage-ways, so Edith and her mother would follow the winding footpaths on foot. Olmsted had described these paths as 'exceedingly intricate and interesting',

Plate 1 Part of the Ramble
in Central Park, New York
c.1905; Olmsted's 'wild
garden' with rock cliffs and
winding streams, and planted
with native trees, shrubs and
flowers.

for they wound through a constantly changing landscape of rocky outcrops, secluded glades and tumbling streams – each step revealing a carefully planned sequence of scenic views (Plate 1). Memories of The Ramble may have stimulated Edith's early interest in wild flowers and garden-making.

These common-place occurrences stirred Edith's imagination. She never cared much for fairy tales in her early childhood but her imagination, which 'lay coiled and sleeping, a mute hibernating creature', could be aroused at the least touch of 'flowers, animals, words, especially the sound of words ... it stirred in its sleep and then sank back into its own rich dream'. Yet one fairy tale always thrilled her: 'the story of the boy who could talk with the birds and hear what the grasses said'. In her memoirs Edith wrote that 'very early, earlier than her conscious memory could reach, I must have felt myself akin to that happy child'. And though she could not recall the first time the grasses spoke to her, Edith remembered a long, spring day a few years later, spent with one of her many uncles and little cousins, in marshy woods near Mamaroneck, in Westchester County overlooking Long Island Sound; 'where the earth was starred with pink trailing arbutus, where pouch-like white and rosy flowers grew in a swamp, and leafless branches against the sky were netted with buds of mother of pearl'.[8]

A less favourable memory of those early years was the sight of her father bent over his desk in 'desperate calculations', attempting 'the vain effort to squeeze my mother's expenditure into his narrowing income'.[9] The Civil War and its aftermath, dating from 1865, had caused a monetary collapse in the country, and a preoccupation with dwindling financial resources was common to all but the very wealthy. In one way or another, money and its management, was to leave an indelible mark on both Edith (Jones) Wharton and Lawrence Johnston, and the need 'to balance the books' became a recurrent theme throughout their lives. For Edith this imprint began soon after the end of the Civil War, though its effects at this time were far from negative. On the contrary, they made an important and positive contribution to her appreciation of the world around her. When Edith was aged only four, the Jones family decided to leave New York for Europe. In the late 1860s, and on into the early years of the following decade, many upper-class American families were obliged to travel in Europe to maintain their standard of living. So for six years the Jones family moved from one watering-place to the next – Paris, Nice, Rome and Florence – living in hotels, going to the American church and only mixing with other Americans. These 'economic migrants' from New York did not cultivate European friendships for fear of being snubbed by old-world aristocrats, who might fail to recognize their gentle status within New York society.

This peripatetic existence further intensified Edith's sense of isolation, though it did have its compensations, and later she called the economic depression that necessitated these trips, a 'happy misfortune', one that gave her 'a background of beauty and old-established order' which endured for the rest of her life. During these years her playground became the Italian Renaissance villas and their gardens, such as those on the Palatine Hill in Rome, where Edith and her mother would stroll through the parkland of the Villa Doria-Pamphili [10] and among the stone pines of the Villa Borghese[11] (Plate 2). Through leisure Edith developed her appreciation of architecture, landscape and nature, as she noted in her memoirs: the 'European background [was] everywhere preparing my eye and imagination to see beauty and feel the riches of a long historic culture. All unconsciously, I was absorbing it all.' But even stronger than her love of beauty was a fear of ugliness, both of ugly places and ugly people which developed, she believed, even before her love of beauty.[12]

Plate 2 Stone pines in the Piazza di Siena, Borghese Gardens.

These feelings made a return to New York in 1872 all the more difficult for her to endure; the ten-year old Edith could not understand how 'people who had seen Rome, Seville, Paris and London' could come back and live contentedly between Washington Square and Central Park. She saw New York as a 'city of narrow, dark, brownstone houses, offensively decorated with smug and suffocating upholstery'.[13] The Jones family occupied a typical brownstone house on West 23rd Street, and Wharton described the fixtures and fittings of her childhood as collections of solid objects, strong colours and thick textures. In particular the 'voluminous purple satin curtains festooned with buttercup yellow fringe' of her mother's drawing room which kept those inside hidden from view whilst allowing them to watch the comings and goings outside (Plate 3). The brownstone was her home for the next eight years, and the extent to which she absorbed the lives of the city and its society during this time is apparent from her novels. But Edith never felt comfortable in New York – or America. Throughout her life she frequently said that she never felt other than an exile, and as a child dreamed of returning to Europe. After waking from such dreams in a state of exhilaration, the numbing reality of her surroundings would send her into a deep depression.

During the summers of her childhood, the Jones family moved to 'Pencraig', their 'cottage' in Newport, Rhode Island, where Edith was free to enjoy the simple pleasures of the country. In her autobiography,

Plate 3 The living room of the Jones' brownstone house on West 23rd Street, c.1884, with all the fussy detail that Edith Wharton came to despise.

there is no detailed mention of the interiors of Pencraig, which she merely described as roomy and pleasant, but of the exterior she recalled that 'the house was surrounded by a verandah wreathed in clematis and honeysuckle, and below it a lawn sloped to a deep daisied meadow, beyond which were a private bathing-beach and boat landing'.[14] There Edith could romp with her dog, fish for 'scuppers', ride her pony and swim in a sheltered cove. On Sundays, she would join other children in a weekly walk with their neighbour, 'Mr Rutherford',[15] over what they called the rocks. It was during those walks that Wharton discovered her deep, transcendental feeling for nature:

> ... my secret sensitiveness to landscape – something in me quite incommunicable to others that was tremblingly and inarticulately awake to every detail of wind-warped fern and wide-eyed briar rose, yet more profoundly alive to a unifying magic beneath the diversities of the visible scene – a power with which I was in deep and solitary communion whenever I was alone with nature. It was the same tremor that had stirred in me in the spring woods of Mamaroneck, when I heard the whisper of arbutus and the starry choir of the dogwood; and it has never left me since. [16]

The Johnston and Waterbury families

No letters or other documents describe Lawrence Johnston's early life. His father Elliott was born on 1st May 1826 into a prominent stock-brokerage and banking family in Baltimore, Maryland. There is, however, some confusion about the sequence of events in Elliott's early life. He seems to have turned his back on banking, and at some period spent 12 years as a planter on the eastern shore of Virginia. He also enlisted in the United States Navy[17] first as a midshipman progressing to first lieutenant, having attended the Naval Academy at Annapolis, Maryland, but it is unclear whether this was before he farmed. What is clear is that as a volunteer at the onset of the Civil War in 1861, Elliott Johnston joined the Confederate forces as a Lieutenant on the staff of Brigadier General Robert B. Garnett. The war was to divide the loyalties of the inhabitants of the State of Maryland, setting families against families and even brothers against brothers. Maryland bordered the capital city of Washington on the northern side, with staunchly Confederate Virginia on the other. An army of occupation forced the State of Maryland to declare for the Union, though there were people who still supported the secessionist Confederacy, and many young men were prepared to fight for the latter cause. One must assume that Elliott's banker brothers, Henry and Josiah, remained neutral, but his sister Bessie was an ardent Confederate. In the spring of 1862, the Confederate Army had foiled the attempt of Major General George B. McClellan and the Union forces to capture Richmond, Virginia, the centre of the Confederate Government. In July, Elliott wrote to Bessie from Richmond, where he was based:

> I do not know how long the North can hold out in this area, but be assured that we can never be subdued. The South is one bristling field of bayonets – oh we so chuckled over the *Heralds* 'onto Rich'd'[,] the last gasp of the Rebellion[,] 'the Rebellion crushed out' ... That we suffer many privations is indisputable. Coffee & tea I have not seen for months. A uniform we have scarcely a vestige. Many & many a wife and sister cut up calicoes for a shirt for the troops. We are almost shoeless but you see the troops – line after line extending for miles of muskets ... We expect a struggle for Rich'd again in a few weeks. It will not

be as hard as before but many a brave heart will be laid low – I have lost many friends in these battles. I will write often now, as frequent opportunities occur of sending letters. Give my love to all[.] I am glad to see you are still true; be sure I never doubted you.[18]

Johnston remained at the centre of the action until, in September 1862, he lost a leg in the vicious fighting at Antietam, and was taken prisoner.[19] Even so, in October, his brothers received permission from Major General McClellan to remove Lieutenant Elliott Johnston to Baltimore, after which and despite his setback, Johnston still remained loyal to the Confederate cause. He returned to war on the staff of Lieutenant General Richard Ewell, Assistant Adjutant General to General Robert E. Lee, at the Battle of Gettysburg in July 1863. In his report of the battle, General Ewell specifically mentioned Lieutenant Elliott Johnston and his 'valuable service during the campaign'.[20] Johnston was promoted to Captain, and then finally retired to the Invalid Corps with the rank of Major on 14th November 1864.

A year after the war ended in 1865, Johnston's brother Henry married Harriet Lane, who had acted as First Lady to the unmarried President James Buchanan (1857–61). This undoubtedly brought the family considerable social distinction, though it was something in which the Confederate veteran, Elliott, may not have shared.

Two years before the Jones family returned to New York in 1870, Elliott Johnston married Gertrude Cleveland Waterbury, the daughter of a wealthy northern industrialist whose family had fought on the Unionist side, though no grudges seem to have been borne between the families. The Waterburys were descended from a founder of Connecticut, John Waterbury, who had been born in England at Sudbury, Suffolk, and baptised in 1621. The family eventually settled in Stamford, Connecticut, where John Waterbury became a substantial landowner. A later ancestor served on George Washington's staff during the War of American Independence (1775–83), and Gertrude's grandfather was a founder of the First National Bank of Brooklyn. Her father, Lawrence, was the proprietor of Waterbury and Co., Brooklyn, manufacturers of cordage of all kinds. After inheriting this modest rope-works from his father in 1844, he expanded the enterprise and, with the product much in demand during the Civil War, the business prospered, making Lawrence Waterbury into one of the wealthier men in New York. Like many of the patrician class, the Jones and Waterbury families also derived a considerable income from municipal real estate, especially when rents rose steadily in New York during the second half of the nineteenth century.

Elliott Johnston, by then aged 44, married Gertrude Waterbury in October 1870, at St. Peter's Church, Westchester Square. She was 19 years younger than Elliott, and one wonders why she was attracted to him. Her address was given as the family home, 'The Plaisance', on Pelham Bay, in the New York district of Eastchester. The Plaisance was a three-storey mansion overlooking Eastchester Bay, built by her father on twenty-seven and a half acres (approximately 11 hectares) of land he had acquired in 1863. By then Westchester had become a wealthy suburb attracting entrepreneurs who had made their fortunes in the Civil War, among them the Waterburys.[21] Her father Lawrence had established himself as a prominent member of the community; he was a trustee of St. Peter's Church and a founder of the Country Club of Westchester[22] whose main purpose was to show New York society that country living need not be boring. For his part, Waterbury owned a number of trotting horses and was a well-known horseman; his love of horses was something he would pass on to his children.

After the wedding, Johnston and his bride went to France for an extended honeymoon, though not unlike the Jones family, this was probably due to economic circumstances. It was an unpropitious time to be taking a new bride to Europe, and especially to Paris which was in the throes of the Franco-Prussian war (1870-1). This was the very event that had caused the Jones family to leave the city and return to New York.[23] During the Siege of Paris and the uprising that followed, the Palace of the Tuileries (Plate 4), the Palais Royal, the Hôtel de Ville, the Palais de Justice and the police headquarters had been burnt down, and 'the once beautiful Bois de Boulogne was a scene of desolation' after many large trees had been felled to make barricades and fortifications.[24] Undeterred, parties of British and American tourists came to visit the smoking ruins. Perhaps Elliott Johnston and his wife were among them, for five months after these traumatic events, their son Lawrence Waterbury Johnston was born in Paris on 12th October 1871, eight days before their first wedding anniversary.

The Johnstons must have followed the same peripatetic lifestyle as other members of the upper-class American diaspora. Two years later a second son, Elliott, was born in Switzerland and in the following

Plate 4 The Tuileries, Paris, in 1871, showing the damage after the Paris Commune and Siege, at the time when Lawrence Johnston was born in the city.

year, a daughter Elizabeth was born in Nice, though, sadly, she died of whooping cough six months later. In 1875 the Johnstons returned to New York,[25] and after the sunny climes of the Côte d'Azur and the experiences of Europe, the shock of the fast-expanding city was perhaps as great for Lawrence and his brother as it had been for Edith Jones. The Johnstons moved into the Murray Hill district and occupied a three-storey brownstone house on 35th Street, at the heart of fashionable uptown New York.[26]

NEW YORK'S MURRAY HILL

Throughout the nineteenth century, New York was in a state of constant flux, its buildings spreading northwards at the rate of one mile a decade, though by the 1880s it extended only as far as 42nd Street. To the north there was still farmland, with the long finger of the new Central Park pushing south (Fig.1b). From mid-century onwards the elite of New York society had built their brownstone villas along Fifth Avenue and Park Avenue creating, what Edith described in *The Age of Innocence*, as an overall effect of houses coated in 'cold chocolate sauce'.[27] Fifth Avenue in the 1880s, though much narrower than today's thoroughfare, bustled with horses and carriages belonging to fashionable ladies and gentlemen and, much to Gertrude Johnston's delight, the ladies' shops displayed the very latest Parisian fashions (Plate 5).

Central Park

Murray Hill

23rd street

Figure 1b New York City on the Island of Manhattan in 1883. By 1859 the city had been built up as far as 23rd Street, where the Jones family went to live in 1872. Broadway, as its name implies, can be seen running north; it had been described by J. Henri Browne in 1869 as the great thoroughfare of the world, and the artist has shown it crammed with traffic. By 1872 Battery Park, at the southern tip of the island, had been extended to 10 acres, and Brooklyn Bridge was under construction (Brooklyn on Long Island is bottom right). The Equitable Life Building (1870) on Broadway was the work of George B. Post, pupil of the foremost Beaux-Arts architect of the Gilded Age, Richard Morris Hunt, whose synthesis of English and French styles gave the city's architecture a quality it previously lacked. Beyond it the streets were lined with chocolate-brown-fronted houses, including those of the Murray Hill district where Elliott Johnston lived with his family. Far to the north the green finger of Central Park pushes into the city. Westchester is in the green countryside top right.

After the very wealthy and 'queen' of New York society, Mrs Caroline Schermerhorn Astor, settled at the corner of Fifth Avenue and 34th Street, an address on the surrounding streets became expensive but highly desirable for the upper middle-class doctors, lawyers and other professionals.[28] Each house on Murray Hill had a classic brownstone front, and was 23 feet wide (*c.* seven metres), three storeys high with a basement. Each household included at least one servant, usually a woman, and often a boarder. The Johnstons were no exception but their servant, James Hoffman, was young and black; both the Confederates and New York City's inhabitants had opposed emancipation during the Civil War, and such servants received low wages. Their boarder was

Maria Franz, a widow aged 22, born in France. She may have assisted with the young boys who were both at school, and even helped as a seamstress for Gertrude – such a person was regarded as an essential part of any upper middle-class home. It is not known whether the Johnstons, in the same way as other wealthy New Yorkers, had a country house where they could escape from the city's summer heat, though it is more than likely. In any case, across the East River, in the rural surrounds of Westchester, there lived many relatives of the Waterbury clan. In 1879 her father died leaving Gertrude comfortably off, and her brother James, who had inherited the cordage business interests, was now living at The Plaisance with his wife, four children and eight servants.

DEATHS OF THEIR FATHERS

Earlier, with the death or disappearance of their fathers, the childhood experiences of both Edith and Lawrence became even more similar. Edith's father George Jones became ill in 1880, and as it was feared he would not survive another New York winter, the family left again for Europe, much to Edith's delight. They stopped first in London before spending the winter in Cannes and when, by the following spring George Jones had recovered, the family returned to Italy. Edith's father had given her John Ruskin's books, *Stones of Venice* and *Mornings in Florence* and, armed with these as guides, she explored the city, sometimes with her father but more often alone. Ruskin influenced her greatly, both as a teacher and as an adversary *in absentia*, for she would sometimes disagree strongly with his opinions. 'Ruskin,' she said, 'awoke in me the habit of precise observation.' But even more, as Vivian Russell has observed, Ruskin showed her how to respond with informed intelligence to beauty of all kinds. She referred to the emotion such aesthetic experiences awoke within her, as a 'sensation'. It was a word she often used to describe her most thrilling moments, and 'sensation' provided the impetus for her travels and sustained her in troubled times.[29] But, early in the spring of 1882, Edith's father died in Nice. It was a deeply disturbing event for her, for she 'had lost the companion who had taught her to read, who had taken her to church, the theatre, and been with her in all the important places'.[30] Her loss was even more than that of a father: she wrote later that there had been little communication between her parents, and it was she herself who became her father's soul-mate. Her mother in contrast, did not encourage any cultural thoughts or artistic activity, either by her husband or Edith, who in turn was forbidden to read contemporary novels until after she married.

There is considerable mystery surrounding the demise of Elliott Johnston. It appears from the census records that by the mid-1880s Gertrude and Elliott were no longer living together. The New York Register lists Mrs Gertrude Johnston as living there with her two sons, while her husband seems to have disappeared from the scene. There are two possible explanations for this puzzle: first, Elliott's death, possibly hastened by his wounds received in the Civil War, or second that they had separated. The New York legislature had authorized divorce by that time, but only for adultery, which in turn was so tinged with scandal, that many couples separated and remarried without the knowledge of the law – and often with at least one partner moving to another State.[31] Since no formal record of the dissolution of the Johnstons' marriage has been found, separation seems the most likely explanation for Elliott's disappearance, especially as Gertrude was determined to remain part of New York's social scene. Elliott probably moved to another State.[32] There is no way of knowing how close Lawrence was to his father, though later he sought to emulate his father's military achievements, perhaps as a way of escaping from his mother's cloying grasp. But what is beyond doubt is that, as a result of the loss of her husband, his mother became firmly attached to her surviving son. For the rest of her life Gertrude was loath to let 'Laurie' out of her sight.

The loss of their fathers meant that Edith and Lawrence were to be dominated by their mothers' strong personalities and tastes. The absence of a father, caused by death or divorce, can have a traumatic effect on the surviving children. The author Ethne Clarke, in her account of Hidcote, points out that the grief of such a loss and the isolation which follows, can persist throughout a person's life. Adult development can be crippled by the fear of repeated loss, but the sense of isolation can become a source of considerable energy, and be used to fashion the security of a private world – an escape which could be bolstered by the creation of novels and gardens. Isolation and childhood experiences left Edith and Lawrence with a lifelong shyness, a dislike of being in the public eye, so much so that both were regarded by many as reclusive. Clarke observed that even 'people who knew him [Johnston], never knew him at all. He was diffident, eschewed celebrity and always maintained a solitary distance between himself and those who came within his orbit'.[33] It was something also noticed by friends of Edith Wharton. Lawrence often declined to be photographed, something Edith could not avoid, either as young girl entering society or as an increasingly successful author.

ENTRY INTO SOCIETY

After the prescribed period of mourning for her father (usually a year), Edith and her mother returned to the customary social round of visiting, and of parties and balls. Before her father's death, however, Edith's parents had been alarmed by her growing shyness and passion for study, and they decided to launch her into society in 1879, at the tender age of seventeen. The 'initiation rites' included the tedious chore of making afternoon visits to all her mother's acquaintances, probably in excess of a hundred people, and may have included Johnston's mother, Gertrude. In spite of her shyness, Edith was an immediate social success; she mixed freely with the friends of her elder brothers and, after her return from Europe, she continued as before. In a portrait of her, painted when she was nineteen, there is perhaps a hint of shyness, but there is also an inner confidence and the look of a keen observer (Plate 6). During those years Lawrence Johnston may have seen Edith in New York, when she was accompanying her mother on

Plate 6 A portrait of Edith Jones, *c.* 1881.

the endless round of visiting or during their walks along Fifth Avenue – but it has to be remembered that he was a shy twelve-year-old schoolboy, and she was nineteen and a gay debutante.

This new life of balls and parties did not lessen Edith's emerging passion for writing; rather it was her acute observation of high society and all its foibles that later became the subject of her novels. In her book *The Age of Innocence* (1920), Edith provides a picture of New York society in the 1870s, the one occupied by the Jones, Elliott and Winthrop families. At the time, the old New York establishment was being overwhelmed by ever-increasing numbers of the newly-rich railroad barons, mining kings and industrialists from the Mid-West. America was entering what Mark Twain derogatively called the 'Gilded Age'.[34] Edith dramatised this conflict in *The Age of Innocence*, and, according to her perspective, at the heart of this society was a private sphere populated to a great degree by female rather than male characters. It was the women, occupying the ballrooms, the living and dining-rooms and the privacy of their own opera boxes, who were most often portrayed as strong personalities, despite their sufferings. By contrast the men were socially weaker, paler and more passive.

The self-styled queen of New York (and Newport) society at this time, Mrs Astor (Edith's first cousin once removed) was anxious to maintain the traditions and heritage of her native New York against the *arrivistes*. She was dedicated to determining who was acceptable among them, and attempted to codify proper behaviour and etiquette. To keep these nouveaux riches out, Mrs Astor, assisted by her social arbiter Ward McAllister (an Astor by marriage), had prepared for the social season of 1872–3 what eventually became her 'list of 400' acceptable members of society. The number was reputed to be derived from the capacity of her ballroom, but McAllister said that there were only 400 people who could be counted as members of Fashionable Society. The list represented the pinnacle of New York society, and was restricted to those whose social prominence was supported by inherited wealth and ancestry. No one knew who was on the list in 1872, as it remained undisclosed until 1891–2, at which point McAllister passed it to the *New York Times,* and society's sacred inner circle of the Gilded Age was finally revealed. At that time the list included the Jones family, whose members were in the front rank of society. By 1891, however, Edith (Jones) Wharton had married and moved to Newport, Rhode Island. Her brother Freddie and his wife Mary Cadwalader ('Minnie'), were both shining examples of New York high society, as was their daughter, Beatrix. James Waterbury and his wife were also on the Astor list, but Gertrude and Lawrence Johnston, having returned to Europe, were not.

Escape from New York

Despite this social background, the future for both Edith and Lawrence no longer lay in New York. Both also needed to emerge from the over-protection of their mothers. Edith, in particular, could not have become a successful novelist without displaying her own strength of character, which meant escaping from the confines of New York society and establishing herself as an independent-minded woman on her own merits. Her means of escape came through marriage to a man thirteen years her senior, who was ultimately to display all the characteristics of male weakness described in *The Age of Innocence.* Edith Jones met Teddy Wharton, a friend of her brother Freddie, in 1883, and two years later married him (Plate 7). She was perhaps attracted to him initially because he was a handsome, easy-going sportsman, a good club man with an eye for a good picture, a palate for a good wine and a taste for lively people. Although her husband was well off rather than rich, the marriage allowed Edith to escape from her mother, something of the utmost importance to her. In the first three years of their marriage (Plate 8), the Whartons avoided the social life of New York and divided their time between Newport and Europe. At last Edith was able to submerge herself 'freely and entirely in delicious Italy'. Every February the Whartons would travel to Italy and spend several months exploring a different region on each trip.[35] But it soon became apparent that this arrangement

Plate 7 Edward 'Teddy' Wharton with the dogs.

Plate 8 Edith Wharton riding 'Fatty' shortly after her marriage to Teddy Wharton in 1885.

was not working. The two were fundamentally mismatched; he loved the country life of sportsmen and easy-going people, and she cared for books, European sights, scholars or, failing them, dilettantes. It became increasingly impossible for Teddy Wharton to live with a woman so much his intellectual superior and one who could never keep herself from showing it.[36] Even so the marriage was to last for 20 years, until it ended in divorce in 1911, during which time Teddy's mental health gradually deteriorated. Edith Wharton's health also suffered and she was to say later that 'for twelve years I seldom knew what it was to be, for more than an hour or two of the twenty-four, without the intense feeling of nausea, & such unutterable fatigue that when I got up I was always more tired than when I lay down'. She identified her problems as 'neurasthenic', regarded at the time as a debilitating mental condition of the middle classes brought on by the complexities of modern life: in modern parlance, stress. One of the prescriptions advocated by reformers was a simple life, spent in direct contact with nature – which included gardening – some doctors even recommended homesteading.

Gardening was indeed a part of the course of self-help Edith followed successfully during those years from 1885 to 1897, but in essence Wharton's problems stemmed from the fact that she was a round peg in a square hole. In his biography of Wharton, Louis Auchincloss pointed out that New York society comprised not one but two interlocking circles, the one disdaining the other. On one side was the intellectual group, whose number included the family of the writer Henry James (see Chapter 5), in which generations were united by a love of the arts and sciences, and offered encouragement to those who wished to pursue interests in those fields. On the other was the fashionable group, to which the Jones family belonged, in which a passing acquaintance with the arts was all that was necessary. In her early twenties Edith found herself marooned between the two, and even after her writing was published, she became a mild embarrassment to her family. She later wrote in her autobiography that in Boston, the home of her husband, 'I was considered too fashionable to be intelligent and in New York, too intelligent to be fashionable'. These formative years had left Wharton determined to find her own identity, which ultimately she would come to express in her books and magazine articles. For Johnston the future was much less certain, because he was still dominated by his mother, though it was that circumstance which would determine his future.

NOTES AND REFERENCES

1 Lee, H., *Edith Wharton*. Chatto & Windus, London, p. 19. In her autobiography, *A Backward Glance*, Wharton mentions that even acquiring wealth had ceased to interest the closed society into which she was born. Extremely wealthy families, such as the Astors, had earned their great fortunes by judicious investment and prudent administration rather than by feverish money-making on Wall Street, or in railway, shipping or industrial enterprises.

2 Ibid, p. 19.

3 Wharton, E., *A Backward Glance*. Constable, London, p. 57.

4 In construction The Ramble was almost entirely artificial; even the water in the stream was turned on and off by a tap.

5 Rogers, E. B., *Rebuilding Central Park*. MIT Press, Cambridge, Massachusetts, p. 118.

6 Sir Uvedale Price was an English landowner best known for his *Essays on the Picturesque* (1747–1829). His highly influential work discussed the picturesque as an aesthetic experience, distinct from the sublime and beautiful. His ideas were put into practice on his estate at Foxley, Herefordshire, where he planted, pruned, made clearings and opened vistas to distant views. He and his close friend Richard Payne Knight (1750–1824) strongly opposed the bland landscapes of Lancelot 'Capability' Brown.

[7] William Gilpin (1724–1804), an English clergyman and artist, was the originator of the 'Picturesque', later developed into an abstract theory by Uvedale Price. His *Remarks on Forest Scenery* (1791), written after he moved to the New Forest in 1778, advocated the natural form of trees, exposed roots and broken banks, in preference to the stylised scenery created by Brown and disciples of the landscape movement.

[8] Wharton, op. cit., p. 4. She adds that it was the day when Foxy, a white Spitz puppy, was given to her, when she learnt 'what the animals say to each other, and to us'. From then on Edith Wharton would always be associated with dogs.

[9] Lee, op. cit., p. 26.

[10] Villa Doria-Pamphili had been the home of this Roman noble family since the 17th century; in 1750, a vast park was laid out by Alessandro Algardi, but a century later this was redesigned in the English romantic style.

[11] Villa Borghese was laid out after 1605 for Cardinal Scipione Borghese with extensive plantings of trees in many varieties, including umbrella pines, intersected by allées with statues, grottoes and lakes. Early in the 19th century it was redesigned in an English romantic style.

[12] Wharton, op. cit., p. 55.

[13] Ibid., p. 55.

[14] Ibid., p. 45.

[15] Lewis Morris Rutherford was an American lawyer and astronomer who made the first detailed photographs of the moon.

[16] Wharton, op. cit., p. 55

[17] Pearson, G., *Hidcote – The Garden and Lawrence Johnston.* National Trust Books, London, p. 10.

[18] Extract from a letter to Bessie Johnston from Lieutenant Elliott Johnston, 21 July 1862. Gresham family papers, 1825–1940; collection number MS 699-096, at Virginia Tech, Blacksburg, Virginia.

[19] Some 23,000 soldiers were killed or wounded in the battle, which remains the bloodiest single-day engagement in American history. Johnston's return to the battle after losing a leg followed the example of his commander, General Ewell, who lost a leg at Graveton in August 1862, was given a wooden leg, and was back on active duty by 23 May 1863. Johnston later travelled to Europe, it was said, in search of an improved prosthesis.

[20] Report of Lieutenant General Richard S. Ewell, Commanding Second Army Corps during the Gettysburg campaign, 3 June to 1 August, to Colonel R. H. Chilton, Adjutant and Inspector General.

[21] Lawrence Waterbury had moved from the family's former mansion on the waterfront in east Brooklyn.

[22] The Country Club of Westchester is not to be confused with the more prestigious Westchester Country Club.

[23] In the winter of 1870 the Prussians laid siege to Paris, and many Parisians were to suffer from starvation, bombardments and disease, whilst their only means of communication with the outside world was by balloon or pigeon post. After the lifting of the siege in March a bloody civil war followed, when the Paris commune fought with troops of the Versailles government. By the time the uprising was crushed in May, some 20,000 to 30,000 communards had been killed and as many arrested and deported.

[24] Allan, M., *William Robinson 1838-1935.* Faber, London, p. 120.

[25] Pearson, op. cit., p. 10.

[26] Murray Hill was named after Robert Murray, a quaker, who built his country home there in the 1760s. He was a loyalist and had been forced after the War of Independence to flee to England where he lived the remainder of his life in York. It was perhaps an appropriate address for the young Lawrence, given that he was to become such a complete anglophile.

[27] Wharton, E., *The Age of Innocence.* Virago, London, p. 76.

[28] These were the professions of Johnston's neighbours, as recorded in the 1880 New York census. Elliott was entered as a 'gentleman', and his age recorded as 40, which does not accord with his date of birth.

[29] Russell, V., *Edith Wharton's Italian Gardens.* Frances Lincoln, London, p. 11.

[30] Dwight, E., *Edith Wharton – an extraordinary life.* Abrams, New York, p. 30.

[31] According to the New York Genealogical and Biographical Society.

[32] Pearson, op. cit., p. 10, maintains that Elliott and Gertrude divorced, but her Obituary in the *New York Times* of 14 March 1926, reported that she remarried, five or so years later, after the death of her first husband. Ethne Clarke, in her 2009 revised edition of *Hidcote* (Norton, London), p. 27, notes that Elliott Johnston is recorded in the 1900 Federal Census as the head of a household in Pungoteague, Accomack County, Virginia. His age is recorded as 74, and that he had been married for 13 years to 'Alice M.', aged 33, which meant that he would have tied the knot a second time in 1887.

[33] Clarke, E., (1989) *Hidcote.* Michael Joseph, London, p. 12.

[34] Mark Twain coined the term, the 'Gilded Age', in an effort to illustrate the outwardly showy, but inwardly corrupt nature of American society during the Industrial Revolution (1870-90). In New York, the opera, the theatre and lavish parties consumed the ruling classes' leisure hours.

[35] Russell, op. cit., p. 12.

[36] Auchincloss, L., *Edith Wharton – a woman in her time.* Michael Joseph, London, p. 49.

CHAPTER TWO

THE ARBITER OF TASTE

THE EDUCATION OF EDITH JONES WHARTON

The strictures of Edith's mother had left her largely uneducated after the death of her father. She needed to metamorphose into a 'creative artist', and the person who helped her to discover her true self, and 'to pass into the warm glow of cultivated intelligence'[1] was Egerton Leigh Winthrop (Plate 9). Winthrop was the kind of cultured aesthete Edith needed: an ardent bibliophile and a discriminating collector of art.[2] In the role of 'paternal' mentor, he provided guidance and instruction in both the arts and sciences. He introduced her to the 'wonder world of nineteenth century science'[3] and the likes of Charles Darwin and the *Origin of Species*, as well as modern philosophy, contemporary French novelists and literary critics of the day. In so doing Winthrop 'taught my mind to analyze and my eyes to see'.[4] He taught her how to read critically; to mark passages that were important, to re-read them and to return to those she could not understand.

Plate 9 Egerton Leigh Winthrop, a portrait by John Singer Sargent, c. 1901. He was the debonair President of the Knickerbocker Club, and Edith (Jones) Wharton's mentor and close friend.

Edith developed an insatiable capacity for learning in all intellectual fields of science, philosophy, history, the arts; and to this list has to be added gardening and architecture. One book she read closely and marked at this time was Andrew Jackson Downing's *Treatise on the Theory and Practice of Landscape Gardening*, published in 1841 (see Appendix 1). Although his notion seems far-fetched today, Downing wrote that it was 'horticulture' that would counter the American tendency toward materialism: by contemplation of God's works, a gentleman would come to an 'appreciation of divine beauty and perfection thus purifying his soul and refining his sensibilities'.[5] Edith was not a religious person, but this phrase must have resonated with her, for it encapsulates her lifelong personal philosophy. After the Civil War, attitudes towards horticulture changed in America – the art of gardening was no longer regarded as the antidote to the particular male vices of greed and ambition – but Downing's *Treatise* still exerted its influence. It became central to a vigorous debate about the design and function of gardens in the wider landscape. Prior to the Civil War, American women had been excluded from 'horticulture', but afterwards they were free to take part in the debate, and Edith, together with her niece Beatrix (Jones) Farrand, took an active part.

Her treasured possession was the sixth edition of Downing's *Treatise*, published in 1859, which included a supplement written by Henry Winthrop Sargent, designed to appeal to the affluent new leaders of the Gilded Age (now generally accepted as the period 1870 to 1890). In continuing Downing's emphasis on the value of 'Rural Pursuits' as part of the democratic spirit of the Founding Fathers, Sargent noted that:

> In the United States, it is highly improbable that we shall ever witness such splendid examples of landscape gardens as those abroad. Here the rights of man are held to be equal; and if there are no enormous parks, and no class of men whose wealth is hereditary ... there is a large class of independent landowners who are able to assemble around them, not only the useful and convenient, but the agreeable and beautiful, in country life.[6]

Sargent, who had travelled widely in Europe, no doubt had in mind the extensive landscaped parks associated with country houses in England. By comparison his own estate at Wodenethe on the river Hudson was small, though, as his friend Downing pointed out, it was 'a bijou full of interest for the lover of rural beauty'.[7] Even so, the garden was beyond the means of the modest citizen envisioned in Downing's idealism. Concern for how city people might enjoy the sights and sounds of nature, in a country where 'the rights of man are held to be equal', had led to Frederick Law Olmsted, a friend and admirer of Andrew Downing, being dispatched to Europe in 1850 to look at urban parks. His mission was part of a moral debate among young radical idealists in New York preoccupied with the questions of how to plan a modern industrial city in the spirit of the Founding Fathers. Soon after his arrival in Liverpool, Olmsted was impressed by Birkenhead Park designed by Joseph Paxton,[8] not so much for its design but for its inherent democracy – the right all citizens had to enjoy its pastoral landscape. After he had returned to New York, Olmsted, together with his business partner, the architect Calvert Vaux, won the competition and with it the commission to lay out Central Park on Manhattan.[9]

In her father's library Edith also found several books on art and architectural history, among them Gwilt's *Encyclopedia of Architecture* and Ruskin's *Modern Painters* and *The Seven Lamps*

of Architecture. Another of her well-marked books was Fergusson's *History of Architecture* which she described as 'one of the most stimulating books that could fall into a young student's hands' because 'it shed on my misty haunting sense of the beauty of old buildings the light of historical and technical precision'.[10] In addition to her copious reading, Edith spent time in Europe travelling extensively and discovering Italy, with occasional visits to London and Paris, often accompanied by the indispensable Egerton Winthrop. It was in Paris that she met again the other person who was important to her intellectual and aesthetic development, the architect Ogden Codman (Plate 10). After meeting her, appropriately in the gardens of Versailles, Codman reported to his mother that Edith was not very strong, but together they shared a love of Europe's wonderful palaces and churches. Edith was frequently ill; as a child she suffered from asthma and later developed many bronchial complaints, as well a susceptibility to heavy colds and 'flu, exacerbated by her smoking. These complaints, however, did not stop her from being an insatiable and exhaustive traveller.

Plate 10 Ogden Codman, the young Boston architect, who was Edith Wharton's friend and collaborator in the early years.

Edith first met Codman in Boston during the summer of 1886, shortly after her marriage to Teddy Wharton, and during the early 1890s, the Whartons saw 'Coddy', as they called him, frequently.[11] Edith and Codman became close friends, sharing a similar outlook on life. In the years that followed, she often wrote to Coddy giving impressions of her travels in France and Italy. As with many of Wharton's friends, Codman was sexually ambivalent, though in mid-life he married a wealthy older woman and enjoyed a happy but brief marriage.

Codman was the same age as Edith, devoted to his mother, and coming from an old Boston family whose members had been forced to live abroad for reasons of economy. After spending his youth in France, Codman returned to Boston to study at the Massachusetts Institute of Technology, having been influenced in his choice of career by his two uncles, the architect John Hubbard Sturgis and Richard Ogden, an interior designer.[12] Sturgis was a cousin of Edith Wharton through the New York family of Newbold (Edith's other forename was Newbold), and one of his early commissions was the design of a house at Newport for a business associate of his father. Later 'Land's End' as it was called, would be the first house bought by Edith and Teddy Wharton. She turned to Codman for advice in transforming the house, giving it a certain dignity. Subsequently they collaborated in Wharton's first successful excursion into print.

'LAND'S END'

After their marriage, the Whartons lived opposite the Jones mansion in Newport, in Edith's mother's house 'Pencraig Cottage' until the early 1890s, when they bought 'Land's End', well away from maternal scrutiny. The latter was an extremely expensive house and its purchase had only been made possible by a substantial legacy Wharton received from a reclusive millionaire cousin, Joshua Jones. The legacy also made it possible for her to buy a small house on Park Avenue in New York, chosen, as she told Ogden Codman, 'on account of the bicycling' in Central Park. Wharton described Land's End as an 'incurably ugly wooden house with half an acre of rock and illimitable miles of Atlantic Ocean',[13] but in spite of this antipathy, it provided the opportunity to shape her own environment and, with the collaboration of Codman, she was soon redesigning the house, inside and out. With Codman's assistance, she began to create an Italianate garden, enclosed in front with elaborate trellises in the eighteenth-century style, set at right angles to the walls. Wharton's direct involvement with the garden is obvious from a letter she sent to Codman on 30th April 1897; 'the formal garden is blooming. The paths are partly cut, the stone steps are being put in, and on Monday I am going to put out the standard privets.' Wharton's appreciation of the rightness of design is apparent when she continues; 'with regard to the pergola, I am perfectly willing to order four columns if you think anything would be gained by doing so at once; but think the matter needs study, owing to the fact that the veranda is slightly raised above the grade of the terrace and it will perhaps be rather a nice question of how to "marry" the pergola with the hedge on the one side and the veranda columns on the other. I want to talk it over with you when you come next week' (Plate 11).[14]

While Wharton was changing the physical world around her, she was also undergoing an internal metamorphosis that would see her emerge as both a serious author and a formidable intellectual. Among the first guests at Land's End were the French writer, Paul Bourget, and his wife Minnie.[15] Bourget was one of the new friends Wharton was desperately seeking for, at first, as she said in her autobiography, she knew almost no men of letters, and the idea of entertaining a great French writer frightened as much as it flattered her. In turn, Bourget was fascinated by the contrast he found between her quiet library at Land's End, with its great windows opening to the immensity of the Atlantic Ocean, and the giddy life of the Casino with its sports, yachting, bridge, sumptuous dinners and elegant dances.[16] These pursuits were part of the daily routine for the wealthy inhabitants of Newport, and Wharton was a prominent, if not an altogether enthusiastic, participant. It summarised what Eleanor Dwight described as Edith Wharton's complex personality at this time: half socially-accomplished, post-debutante, half serious writer.

Plate 11 Land's End, Newport, Rhode Island; the house and garden remodelled by Edith Wharton in collaboration with Ogden Codman.

Under the guidance of her mentor, Egerton Winthrop, Wharton read voraciously, which led Bourget to observe that 'there was not a book of Darwin, Huxley, Spencer, Renan or Taine which she has not studied, not a painter or sculptor of whose works she could not compile a catalogue, not a school of poetry of which she does not know the principles'.[17]

Following the success of their first practical collaboration, Wharton and Codman began an even more ambitious project, by challenging the interior decoration of the American house. Wharton, influenced by Downing's *Treatise*, believed American society had become dominated by 'conspicuous consumption', which often meant 'the wholesale importing of European artifacts and styles, the rapid appearance and disappearance of gigantic, opulent private houses'. Every room in the house had become 'crammed with curtains, lambrequins, jardinières of artificial plants, wobbly velvet-covered tables littered with silver gew-gaws, and festoons of lace on mantelpieces and dressing tables'.[18] Wharton was determined to chart a new direction for American taste, in both house and garden, and collaboration with Codman led to the publication of her first book, *The Decoration of Houses*, in 1898. Their alternative blueprint was for houses to be 'simple and architectural', drawing on Renaissance models and English houses of the eighteenth century; their recommendations intended for those rich enough to model their style on Versailles or Audley End.[19] *The Decoration of Houses* ran to several editions and achieved a marked influence on house design in America, as well as in England. It was said to have killed off, once and for all, the fashion for rooms decorated in different styles within the same house.

Wharton's next challenge was to be the garden, 'overstuffed' with ornamentation and flowers, especially anything that 'weeped', and their overall lack of design. In a satire of such gardens (*Twilight Sleep*, 1927), Mrs Manford thinks, as she sees 'a flash of turf sheeted with amber and lilac. In a setting of twisted and scalloped evergreens', of seventy-five thousand bulbs: twenty-five thousand more than last year ... 'that was how she liked it to be'. Wharton had used the chaste examples of Louis XIV inside the house, and she proceeded to choose the Italian garden to make her case outside; 'there is,' she wrote, 'much to be learned from the old Italian gardens, and the first lesson is that, if they are to be a real inspiration, they must be copied, not in the letter but in the spirit'.[20] The opportunity to put these ideas into practice came at 'The Mount', the first and only house she built, where the garden was designed not from research but her assumptions about Italian gardens.

EDITH WHARTON AND THE AMERICAN RENAISSANCE

Wharton and Codman were part of what is known today as the American Renaissance in architecture, art and literature that had emerged in the 1870s and continued until the beginning of the First World War in 1914. That rebirth developed out of a strengthened sense of national self-confidence which followed the Civil War, and with it came a feeling that the United States was heir to Greek democracy, Roman law and Renaissance humanism. The art connoisseur Bernard Berenson, who later became Edith's close friend,[21] said that 'we ourselves, because of our faith in science and the power of work, are instinctively in sympathy with the Renaissance ... the spirit which animates us was anticipated by the spirit of the Renaissance'.[22] An essential part of this feeling was an awakening of national identity. In the first half of the nineteenth century Americans had been 'pioneers' in spirit and practice, valuing local traditions but unaware of their own national history. As Edith Wharton wrote: 'The American landscape has no foreground and the American mind no background'.[23] This changed with the pressure of increasing industrialisation and urbanisation which came, as usually happens in these circumstances, with a sense of nostalgia causing people to look back to their pre-industrial past for inspiration. The American Historical Association and other historical groups were formed, and illustrated articles on American history appeared in such magazines as *Harper's* and *Scribner's*, to which Edith Wharton would later contribute.

An important event in this 'renaissance' was the Philadelphia Centennial Exposition of 1876, held to commemorate the centenary of the signing of the Declaration of Independence. As well as looking to the past, the Exposition celebrated the country's emergence as an industrial nation with exhibits on mining, science and manufacturing. A vast horticultural hall was built, in tribute to the Crystal Palace of 1851 in London, with Moorish architecture and displays of the very latest plants, decoration and technology. It is not known whether the 14 year-old Edith visited the exhibition, though it is possible she went with her sister in-law, Mary, and her family, the Rawles, of 'good' old Philadelphian stock. Mary, or 'Minnie' as the family called her, was twelve years older than Edith, and had married Freddie Jones in 1870. She was instantly attracted to Edith at their first meeting in Paris shortly afterwards. Minnie became the missing 'elder sister', or 'the better mother' Edith missed,[24] and she remained one of her closer friends throughout her life. In the year after the Exposition, the Society of American Artists and the Society of Decorative Arts were founded, accompanied by specialist journals such as *Art Review* and the *American Architect and Building News*, which reported developments in American art and architecture. Edith later subscribed to both magazines.

Some architects and artists also looked to their European heritage for inspiration; some believed that, since America possessed the democratic ideals of the ancient Greeks, its architecture, art and gardens should reflect those ideals, and their extension into the Italian Renaissance. Towards the end of the century a new generation of millionaires, who had made their fortunes in minerals, steel, oil, banking, newspapers, textiles and much besides, were clamouring to have their new residences designed in imitation of European models. Fifth Avenue became a virtual architectural competition, when old houses were torn down and replaced by a motley collection of styles. W. H. Vanderbilt spent $2 million of the $90 million he had inherited from his father on his New York 'palace', while his son spent $3 million on 'Biltmore', a vast French-style chateau in North Carolina. The gardens of the chateau were designed by Frederick Law Olmsted and rather enjoyed by Edith, though she satirised the lack of taste among most of the nouveaux riches. In her first major novel, *The House of Mirth* (1905), Edith had van Alstyne mock the new buildings on Fifth Avenue: 'That Greiner house, now – a typical rung on the social ladder ... His façade is a complete architectural meal; if he had omitted a style his friends might have thought the money had given out'.[25] Others of this new social elite were more discerning and saw it as their duty to enrich the city with the best possible demonstrations of American architecture and design, and in doing so contributed to a great upsurge in the decorative arts after 1880.

The Philadelphia Exposition led directly to the 1893 World's Columbian Exposition held in Chicago. This marked the coming of age for the arts and architecture of the American Renaissance and the establishment of the Beaux-Arts tradition[26] that would dominate

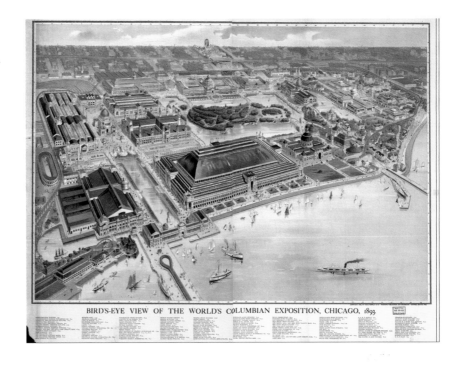

BIRD'S-EYE VIEW OF THE WORLD'S COLUMBIAN EXPOSITION, CHICAGO, 1893.

American architecture and the design of gardens for the next twenty-five years. Though, as Isabelle Gournay commented, the major pavilions at the World's Columbian Exposition, were some of the best-known and most ridiculed examples of the style.[27] However, the Exposition did see a fusion between the twin styles in garden design that had developed since the 1870s. The massive residences that had become popular in the 1880s and '90s required more of a geometrically arranged setting than the Gothic cottages designed previously by Downing and Vaux. In response many architects such as Stanford White,[28] who greatly interested Edith Wharton, began to lay out formal gardens around their houses. At the Colombian Exposition Frederick Law Olmsted, with his partner Henry Sargent Codman,[29] successfully juxtaposed his own picturesque approach with this formal treatment (Plate 12). But Olmsted Senior was in a minority, and seven years later, in 1900, his son John Charles, who had been involved in the Beaux-Arts extravaganza, declared in an address to the American Institute of Architects that America's architecture and its landscaped settings must conform to the new classicism. They must be 'strongly formal whether they are perfectly symmetrical or not, and this formal quality ought to be recognized in the plan of their surroundings if the total effect is to be consistent'.[30]

By the time of the Columbian Exposition many of the historians, philosophers and writers leading this resurgence of interest in art, architecture and literature of the classical past were among the wide circle of friends Edith had gathered around her. There were men such as Henry Adams, who had travelled extensively in Europe,[31] and who published the first of his nine volumes on the *History of the United States 1801–17* in 1889. Not unsurprisingly Wharton's own appreciation of America's European heritage came from her frequent travels to Italy, which had begun in childhood, and continued with her studies of European art and architectural history. She became so enamoured with Italy that she came to feel more worthy of its landscape and history than the Italians; 'I think sometimes that it is a pity to enjoy Italy as much as I do, because the acuteness of my sensations make them rather exhausting when I see the stupid Italians I have met there, completely unsensitive to their surroundings and ignorant of the treasures of art and history among which they have grown up, I begin to think it is better to be an American, and bring to it all a mind & eye unblunted by custom'.[32] Though Edith's ultimate response to Italy was to be her own, she was strongly influenced by Charles Eliot Norton, who had been Harvard's first Professor of Art History from 1875 to 1898.[33] His interests were not confined to the history of art; rather, his appreciation of art was strongly influenced by a deep understanding of the land and the peoples who had shaped the landscape. In his teaching, Norton saw his mission as quickening 'so far as may be, in the youth of a land barren of visible memorials of former times, the sense of connection with the past and of gratitude for the efforts and labors of other races and former generations'.[34] When Edith first met him, Norton was regarded as one of the grand old men of American culture and, not surprisingly, he immediately became a father-figure for her and an intellectual guru. Long after Norton's death, she remained a devotee of his vision of a present, whose meaning, richness and very reality elusively resided in the past: 'it was he who opened my eyes to everything worthwhile'.[35] His daughter Sara became another of Edith's close friends with whom she regularly corresponded, confiding some of her innermost thoughts. In the following decade Edith Wharton absorbed the ideas and ideals of the American Renaissance in her forays into architecture and gardening, which took both literary and practical forms. As a result, she emerged as one of the significant arbiters of American taste.

Notes and References

1. Wharton, E., *A Backward Glance*. Constable, London, p. 94.

2. Egerton Leigh Winthrop (1839-1917) was a distinguished member of an important New York family. He was directly descended from John Winthrop who became Governor of the Massachusetts Bay Company and, during 1630, headed the great immigration to America. Egerton was a lawyer, who inherited a considerable fortune on the death of his father. Edith Wharton met Winthrop when she was 26; he was 46 and was a married, family man. Hermione Lee observed that he 'sounds more like one of the bisexual or homosexual male friends with whom Wharton had some of her most satisfactory relationships' (Lee, H., *Edith Wharton*. Chatto & Windus, p. 68). He was certainly shy and awkward in company and preferred to be with small gatherings of friends.

3. Wharton, op. cit., p. 94.

4. Ibid.

5. Massachusetts Horticultural Society, *Keeping Eden*. Bullfinch Press: Little, Brown and Company, London, p. 191.

6. Ibid., p. 65.

7. Ibid., p. 17.

8. Joseph Paxton (1803–65) was from 1826 Head Gardener for the 6th Duke of Devonshire at Chatsworth, with whom he became a great friend. He was allowed to undertake many outside commissions that included the design of several public parks, of which Birkenhead was England's first (commissioned in 1843); it was a highly original concept owing little to the 18th century landscape tradition. Paxton is perhaps most famous for his design of the Crystal Palace in London, built for the Great Exhibition of 1851, and for which he was knighted.

9. Olmsted saw the park as a great democratic institution that would have an influence on the moral health of the citizens. Though influenced by Birkenhead Park, he wanted Central Park to have a picturesque quality all its own, but of New England in its association. However, the circulatory system used at Birkenhead was reproduced, in a modified form.

10. Wharton, op. cit., p. 91.

11. He called her 'Mrs Pussy', a reference to her childhood nickname; together they called themselves 'Mr and Mrs PussCod'. On one occasion Wharton said it would be her fate to marry him, to which he replied that first she would have to marry someone rich, something, he said, 'she did not quite like' (quoted in Lee, op. cit., p. 125).

12. Codman started his own practice in Boston and Newport in 1891, and established a flourishing business before moving to New York.

13. Wharton, op. cit., p. 106.

14 Letter to Codman, 7 April 1897; quoted in Dwight, E., *Edith Wharton – an extraordinary life*. Abrams, New York, p. 49.

15 Paul Bourget (1852–1935), French novelist and critic. Wharton equally admired his wife Minnie, 15 years his junior, describing her as 'a rarer being'.

16 Benstock, S., *No Gifts for Chance*. Scribner, New York, p. 75.

17 Herbert Spencer (1820–1903), English philosopher, who first used the term 'survival of the fittest' in *Principles of Botany*, 1864; Ernest Renan (1823–92), French philosopher; Hippolyte Taine (1828–1923), French literary critic and historian, who argued that literature was largely the product of the author's environment.

18 Quoted in Lee, op. cit., p. 129.

19 Ibid., p. 133.

20 Dwight, op. cit., p. 110.

21 Bernard Berenson, born Bernhard Valrojenski in what is now Lithuania (1865–1959), moved with his family to Boston in 1875. He became a pre-eminent authority on Italian Renaissance art and played a pivotal role as advisor to several important American collectors, among them Edith Wharton's friend Isabella Stewart Gardiner. After Wharton moved to France in 1920, she became close friends with the Berensons, often staying as guest at their home 'I Tatti', near Florence.

22 Quoted by Jeffrey Morseburg in *The American Renaissance*. Morseburg Galleries, Hollywood, California.

23 Quoted in Lee, op. cit., p. 156. Edith Wharton wrote these words when she was becoming disillusioned with the United States, and more attracted to Europe and, in particular, France.

24 Quoted in Lee, op. cit., p. 39.

25 Ibid., p. 49.

26 *The Grove Dictionary of Art* (1996) defines the Beaux-Arts style as a term applied to a style of architecture found particularly in France and the USA that derived from the academic teaching of the École des Beaux-Arts, Paris, during the 19th and early 20th centuries. The style was characterized by formal planning and rich decoration.

27 Isabelle Gournay, Associate Professor at the School of Architecture, Planning and Preservation at the University of Maryland, was author of the Grove definition of the Beaux-Arts style.

28 Stanford White was a partner in the leading Beaux-Arts firm of architects, McKim, Mead and White, and designed many houses for the wealthy, embodying the principles of the American Renaissance.

29 Henry Sargent Codman was the father of Wharton's friend Ogden Codman. At the time he was in partnership with Olmsted, and together they drew up the master plan for the Chicago Exposition. He died before the opening of the exhibition.

30 Massachusetts Horticultural Society, op. cit., p. 30.

31 Henry Adams was appointed Professor of Medieval History at Harvard in 1870, a post he held briefly until his early retirement in 1877 at the age of 39.

32 Letter to Margaret Chandler, 8 March 1903, quoted in Lee, op.cit., p. 93.

33 Charles Eliot Norton's influential lectures on Italy followed the line of his friend and mentor John Ruskin, by excluding everything after the late medieval period.

34 Quoted in Goodman, S., *Edith Wharton's Inner Circle.* University of Texas Press, Austin, p. 44.

35 Wharton, op. cit., p. 154.

CHAPTER THREE

'The Mount' and Italian Gardens

By the turn of the century, Edith Wharton was finding Newport, as well as New York, intolerable, and her doctors advised that it was making her 'neurasthenic' condition worse. By then the Whartons were making regular visits to the Berkshire Hills, staying at Lenox, Massachusetts, where Teddy's mother had a summer residence. Her mid-nineteenth century house was heavily furnished and full of the nooks and beams Edith had come to dislike, but in 1899 she spent the summer in Lenox, while Teddy and his mother were in Europe. Wharton found the countryside and views more picturesque than in Newport. By the late 1890s, Lenox had become popular among the wealthy, though it had an even earlier history of being home to the intelligent and the cultivated: Nathaniel Hawthorne, Herman Melville and Henry Longfellow were among the artists and writers associated with it. Now Wharton wanted to join that list and, in August 1900, wrote and told Codman that she was 'in love with the place – climate, scenery, life and all – and when I have built a villa on one of the estates I have picked out, and have planted my gardens and laid out paths through my *bosco*, I doubt if I ever leave here – expect [sic] to go to Italy.'[1]

In 1900 the Whartons rented a house and began looking for a property to buy. In June the following year Edith bought Laurel Lake Farm from the Sargent family,[2] which included 113 acres (c. 46 hectares) of farmland, wetland and forests of maple, birch, oak and pine. Looking over the landscape from a ridge of hills, Wharton believed the foreground of fields, the middle ground of woods and lakes, and background of blue hills and mountains, could all be assembled into pleasing, picturesque images. So with her inheritance and profits from the sale of Land's End, she set out to create a splendid residence that would express the ideas laid out in *The Decoration of Houses* and draw on her knowledge of European villas and palaces. Although Edith's mother had died in Paris, the terms of her will led to a bitter family quarrel that persisted into Wharton's old age and even after her death.[3] It was not unusual in Victorian and Edwardian times for sons only to inherit their parents' money after they died, and for the daughters to have their bequests put in trust. This was supposedly so that daughters' inheritances would not leave the family by being taken over by greedy husbands, for menfolk were meant financially to look after their wives. Lucretia Jones indeed left cash bequests to her sons Frederic and Henry, but Edith's money was placed in a trust fund and, as had happened with her father's legacy earlier, she was unable to use the capital in her lifetime; and which would revert to Frederic if she died without children. It was a frustrating position for Edith and, though she challenged the terms of the will, she never received the full share of her inheritance. Fortunately income from her writing soon augmented her finances.

'The Mount', named after the home of Edith's patriotic military ancestor in Astoria, New York, was to have been Wharton and Codman's next collaborative project, but they parted company following a dispute over fees. In Codman's place Wharton commissioned Francis L. Hoppin,[4] who was best known for designing country and city houses which displayed his interest in Adam and Georgian styles. This was much in keeping with the style Wharton preferred for American houses. Five years before she commissioned Hoppin and Koen to be the architects for The Mount, she had written an article for the *Newport Daily News* extolling the virtues of the Georgian style:

> The true Georgian house is rectangular, thus providing more accommodation in any given space than any of the gabled and pinnacled structures which at present adorn our streets. Relying for its effect upon the proper adjustment of its parts, it requires far less outward adornment than the wilfully irregular house, which can only be saved from looking like an aggregation of woodsheds around a central cow-barn by a liberal display of expensive ornamentation.[5]

Wharton's outspoken critique of the prevailing fashion would not have made her popular with her wealthy neighbours, who had built their large 'cottages' on the hills around Lenox in a wide variety of styles. Changing fashion had seen the earliest shingle-faced houses replaced by over-large Colonial Revival mansions, which in turn were superseded by palaces in brick and marble, and even a Scottish baronial castle and a house modelled on the Petit Trianon in Paris. Confronted by such ostentatious display, Wharton believed that the English Georgian style was most suited to the American landscape, for it was 'above all

Plate 13 Belton House,
Lincolnshire (above), the
English house reputedly
designed by Christopher
Wren. It was admired by Edit
Wharton and taken as an
inspiration for The Mount
(left), seen here in the summe
of c. 1910 from the corner of
the flower garden.

sincere. It does not affect to be a castle, a fortress or a farmhouse'.[6]
At The Mount, Hoppin used the Georgian style exemplified at Belton
House in Lincolnshire, reputedly the work of Christopher Wren, as
the model for his design. It was a house much admired by Wharton
during her visits to England, though it may have been Codman's idea
to imitate Belton (Plate 13).

THE MAKING OF 'THE MOUNT'

Work began at Lenox in the summer of 1902 and continued until
September the following year, when the Whartons moved in. The
house was built into the side of a hill and made of white stucco over
a wooden frame with black shutters at each of the hundred windows,
a common motif of nineteenth-century New England houses. At the
rear, a large striped awning over the centre of the terrace reinforced
the American Colonial style, though the house drew on a great
mixture of other motifs and sources – French, Italian and English
(Plate 14). The H-shaped layout, with a double Palladian staircase and
dominating cupola as its central feature, was taken from Belton House.
The grotto-like entrance hall, complete with dripping water effects on
the stuccoed walls, a fountain and a statue of Pan, was reminiscent
of Italy, as was the long gallery on the *piano nobile*. Running parallel
with the terrace, the gallery had vaulted ceilings, terrazzo floors, statues
and Italian furnishings. The arrangement of the main rooms on the

first floor in a connecting row – dining room, drawing room, library, den – was French in feeling. These opened on both the gallery and the terrace, so they could be entered without having to go through from one to the other. Fortunately, Wharton and Codman reconciled their differences in time to design the interior in accord with ideals they had set out in *The Decoration of Houses*.

Though Edith consulted Codman before his dismissal and collaborated with her architect Hoppin, the ideas behind the design of The Mount were generally her own. They reveal a great deal, not only about her architectural ideas but about Wharton herself. Her intention was to articulate and arrange a series of different kinds of space; for social relations (the first floor has a large hall dividing service rooms on the right from the long gallery running most of the length of the rest of the house connecting the den, library, drawing room and dining room); for privacy (the second floor where Edith Wharton's suite of rooms in the eastern corner, her husband Teddy's smaller rooms and three guest rooms are all separated by a long corridor). These spaces were arranged in such a way that social interactions were carefully planned, controlled and organized. What emerges from this is a sense of order, a careful symmetry allowing no unexpected mingling of servants and masters, no penetration of guests into private quarters, no romantic trysts in the garden, for Wharton carried the same principles into the outdoor spaces. In her private life Wharton demanded the same sense of order and symmetry, expressed in a well-established routine both for herself and visitors to The Mount. Above all, she believed in 'harmony and proportion' in human and domestic relationships, and in artistic expression. 'If proportion is the good breeding of architecture, symmetry, or the answering of one part to another, may be defined as the sanity of decoration. The desire for symmetry, for balance, for rhythm in form as well as in solids is one of the most inveterate of instincts'.[7]

Plate 14 A mixture of styles: the front entrance to The Mount, taken in 2008, from where the Whartons would set out in their motor car to explore the local countryside and 'the mystery beyond the blue hills'.

Stepping on to the Italianate terrace from one of the principal rooms – library, drawing room, dining room or den – was the dramatic climax of a promenade through the architecture of the house. From the terrace visitors could gain their first glimpse of the vista across the gardens to the Laurel Lake framed by American elms, and beyond to the distant Berkshire Hills (Plate 15). As one visitor described it, there was a 'magnificent view of nearer and farther hills, with half a dozen lakes flashing in the sun', and in the foreground '... on one side a rock garden of great beauty, and the shrubbery, curving like an approaching wave, edges the lawn nobly. But it is the double sunken garden, set down into the hill, that is, the distinction of the place. Each has its central fountain, surrounded by the geometrically shaped beds separated by narrow gravel paths and planted with brilliant flowers of contrasted hue. At their lower edge stand marble walls in the Italian style, with openings that permit exquisite glimpses of the view, and, at the same time, form a lovely background for a few of the taller flowers and some choice rose trees'.[8]

A Palladian staircase led down from the terrace to a path covered in marble chips (Plate 16), and then more steps descended through a series of parterres, bordered by arborvitae (thuja) and hemlock hedges, to an allée flanked by pleached lindens (lime trees). This ran parallel to the rear elevation of the house. At the south-west end it opened to a walled Italian garden with a lion's head rock fountain, designed by Francis Hoppin (see Frontispiece). The minimalist planting of emerald-green ferns (*Osmunda regalis*) and a ring of white impatiens provided in Wharton's words, 'a charm independent of the seasons'. The east side of the walled garden was breached by arched openings

Plate 15 A view of Laurel Lake c. 1910 (left), compared with the scene in 2008 (right). Since Wharton's time the open landscape of Massachusetts has reverted to woodland, and the view of Laurel Lake and the distant Berkshire Hills has all but disappeared.

Plate 16 A view of The Mount, taken in 2008, looking back towards the terrace and Palladian staircase from the rising ground where Edith and Teddy Wharton first viewed the estate.

framing views towards the lake and hills. In contrast, at the other end of the walk was a flower garden with a profusion of annual flowers – petunias, phlox, snapdragons, stocks, penstemons, and hollyhocks arranged around a dolphin fountain (see Plate 13). This tableau could be viewed from Wharton's bedroom on the north-east corner of the house, and Edith took pleasure in constantly planning new colour arrangements for the garden. Just beyond the flower garden was Codman's arched trellis niche, as designed for Land's End, and transferred to The Mount. Completing the ensemble was a rock garden and native varieties of sweet ferns (*Comptonia peregrina*) which Wharton collected from the surrounding countryside. Clipped hedges and trees provided a gradual transition from these formal plantings to the landscape beyond, following Wharton's principle that 'each step away from architecture was a nearer approach to nature'.[9] The woodland paths featured rugged outcrops of limestone, blanketed with moss, lichen and the delicate nodding flowers of red columbine (*Aquilegia canadensis*). Wharton was keenly interested in the native flora of every region in which she lived, and at The Mount the New England landscape permeated throughout. Many wild flowers and ferns were introduced to the gardens, including wake robin (*Trillium erectum*) and the ostrich fern (*Matteucia struthiopteris*) which forms drifts along the entrance drive (Plate 17), as well as bloodroot (*Sanguinaria canadensis*), ginger plants (*Asarum canadensis*) and New England purple asters, flowering in the autumn.

COLLABORATION WITH BEATRIX (JONES) FARRAND

At The Mount, Wharton was assisted greatly by her niece Beatrix Jones (later Farrand), who was on hand to discuss and advise on the layout of the gardens and estate. Beatrix was ten years younger than Edith, but regarded her aunt as an elder sister with whom she shared her passion for gardens and gardening. It is a remarkable coincidence that at this crucial moment in the developing art of garden design in America, two of its leading figures – one the country's arbiter of taste and the other soon to become one of its leading exponents – were not only related but close friends able to exchange ideas on the new style of garden design. Like Wharton, Farrand had experienced great difficulty in convincing her parents that she did not wish to be 'a lady of high society' but preferred instead to become a professional garden designer – an activity largely undefined yet considered very unladylike in the 1890s. Fortunately for Beatrix attitudes began to change after the publication in 1893 of a book by Mariana Griswold van Rensselaer, the *Art Out-of-Doors: Hints on Good Taste in Gardening*. Van Rensselaer was a highly respected member of New York society, a close friend of Minnie Jones and a member of Wharton's social group. She was also a frequent guest at The Mount, with her husband Schuyler. In design, van Rensselaer preferred the natural to formal gardens and, like Olmsted, wanted architecture to be moral. She was a critic of self-assertion in contemporary architecture and landscape design. She also argued for gardening to be considered an art, and the landscape gardener to be in part 'a gardener, an engineer and an artist, who like an architect considers beauty and utility together' – something that Beatrix Farrand would exemplify. The book 'brought aristocratic recognition to the gardening arts'[10] and helped encourage the notion of garden and landscape design as a new profession, suitable for women, and one quickly embraced by Beatrix Farrand, with encouragement from her aunt Edith.

Plate 17 Designed by Beatrix Jones Farrand, the entrance drive to The Mount leads through a copse of hemlock, white pine and maples. In spring the dappled sunlight plays on the under-planting of ostrich fern (*Matteucia struthiopteris*) and other New England plants. (Photo taken in 2008.)

The turning point for Farrand came when she was introduced to the wife of Charles Sprague Sargent, who was Dean of American Horticulture and founder, as well as first Director, of the Arnold Arboretum, just outside Boston. Sargent, a cousin of Henry Sargent, was already known to Wharton, and Beatrix, then twenty years old, was persuaded to spend a year at the Arnold Arboretum studying botany, horticulture and the basic concepts of landscape design. During this time she lived with the Sargents at 'Holm Lea', their estate outside Boston, regarded by contemporaries as among the best interpretations of the English Picturesque in America. The naturalist John Muir, who was more at home in the wild landscapes of Yosemite, visited Holm Lea and noted that 'this is the finest mansion and grounds I ever saw. The house is 200 feet long with an immense veranda trained with huge flowers and vines and stands in the midst of acres of lawns, groves, wild woods of pine, hemlock, maple and beech hickory. There are all kinds of underbush and wild flowers, acres of rhododendrons 12 feet high and a pond covered with lilies. All the ground, hill and dale, [are] waves clad in the full summer dress of the region and is trimmed with exquisite taste'.[11] The garden's subtle management allowed nature to appear unconfined, and Sargent instilled in Beatrix the idea that the 'plan' must always fit the ground and the ground should never be changed to fit the plan.

Sargent also encouraged her to travel as much as possible, and in 1895 she went to Europe with her mother, spending a year studying gardens, landscape paintings, and analysing natural beauty. In England Farrand stayed with Henry James at Lamb House, Rye. James was not a gardener and had engaged Susan Muir-Mackenzie, a friend of Gertrude Jekyll, to look after the garden. Farrand greatly admired Jekyll, and Muir-Mackenzie arranged a visit to Munstead Wood but, unfortunately, their meeting was not a success. Farrand remained an admirer and was greatly influenced by the intense emphasis Jekyll placed on the value of nature and her use of native materials, as well as her subtle use of colour ; 'I am strongly for treating garden and wooded ground in a pictorial way', Jekyll wrote in *Some English Gardens* (1904). On her return to New York in 1897, Farrand began her practice as a landscape architect and opened an office on the top floor of her mother's brownstone house[12] (Plate 18). Wharton recommended her niece to cousins and influential friends such as Emily Vanderbilt, and very soon Beatrix was receiving important commissions in Lenox and Newport. Over the next fifty years, Farrand proceeded to design many important private gardens, in what she termed a 'country-house style' – a 'middle way' between 'American naturalism and European classicism'[13] to which, 'Robinson-inspired naturalistic areas' were added.[14]

Plate 18 A photograph of Beatrix (Jones) Farrand taken at the beginning of her career as a landscape gardener.

The extent of Beatrix Jones Farrand's collaboration with her aunt at The Mount is not known. The Mount's historian, Cynthia Zaitzevsky, believes that Wharton, who was not a trained landscape architect but rather a designer of just her own gardens, must have worked closely with her niece. Farrand's 'excellent eye and instinctive sense of how to work a garden into the landscape, worked well with her aunt's own grasp of spatial relations'.[15] Against this, Stephanie Copeland, the former Director of the Edith Wharton Restoration, considers it unlikely that Beatrix would have told her aunt what to do; also there is no documentation other than the drawings. This situation can be explained partly by the fact that Farrand, in an attempt to conceal her shame at her parents' divorce in 1896, felt compelled afterwards to destroy most of her papers and letters.

Farrand numbered all her drawings and the highest number for The Mount is 27 and, as only five drawings survive, it can be assumed that at least 22 have been lost. The first drawings for a large kitchen garden 250 yards (228 metres) long and 175 yards (160 m) wide, were produced in July, a month after the purchase of Laurel Lake Farm. A few days later came a 'lost' plan for the 2000 foot (610 m) driveway, which leads to the front of the house through a sequence of glades. Beginning with an 800 foot (244 m) straight section through a sugar maple allée, it passed the gatehouse, kitchen garden and stables, before turning downhill through the woods, finally curving up to the forecourt. The way the shady stands of hemlock, white pine, ash and maple reveal the glistening, elegant, white house and its forecourt, is reminiscent of Italy, where narrow, dark streets spill on to an open piazza and church.[16] The stream which crossed and re-crossed the driveway was culverted under the formal gardens and re-emerged in the meadow below the house (Fig.3a). The approach to The Mount shows Edith and her niece working together within the landscape; in Wharton's words, 'adapting nature without distorting it'. After designing the approach drive in 1901, it seems that Beatrix did not revisit the house, despite Edith's pleas for her to come.[17]

REACTION TO THE MOUNT AND ITS GARDEN

Approval of The Mount and its garden was mixed, and not everyone appreciated its assemblage of styles. The distinguished New York lawyer Joseph Choate, who had extensive knowledge of European gardens, visited soon after it was finished, and was said to have stepped on to the terrace and remarked 'Ah, Mrs Wharton, when I look about me I don't know if I'm in England or in Italy'.[18] This could be taken as both praise and disparaging comment; certainly the garden historian, Jane Brown, considered it to be the latter, and described the mix of styles and inspirations at The Mount as a 'designed disaster'.[19] However, the American garden historian, Alan Emmet, has said this comment

Figure 3a A plan of The Mount, Lenox; the entrance is at bottom left, and the straight drive passes the kitchen garden, and then winds up to the house with its terrace beyond. The drive was conceived as an unfolding and carefully modulated sequence of open and enclosed, formal and informal, natural and pastoral landscapes.

overlooks the significance of the view and the setting of the house. For it was the view from the house that had meaning for Wharton, and her 'keenly developed visual sense, her self-confident taste and her years of studying gardens in Italy', allowed her to combine 'the house and landscape into one felicitous whole'.[20] For Wharton, the rapture of the distant Berkshire hills could only be complete when the natural scenery was contrasted with the geometry of a formal garden in front of a terrace; though the hills of Tuscany were far away, The Mount nevertheless had to reflect the virtues of a Tuscan villa. In Wharton's first successful novel *The House of Mirth* (1905), written soon after her arrival at The Mount, the doomed heroine Lily Bart wanders off during a house-party weekend, and leans pensively against the balustrade of a broad terrace overlooking 'a landscape tutored to the last degree of rural elegance. In the foreground glowed the warm tones of the garden. Beyond the lawn with its pyramidal pale-gold maples and velvety iris, sloped pastures dotted with cattle; and through a long glade the river widened like a lake under the silver light of the moon'.[21] This is a description of the scene that spread out before Wharton as she wrote, though her writing always took place in the morning.

Others found the very perfection Wharton sought to be the garden's undoing. Hildegarde Hawthorne, the granddaughter of Nathaniel, in her book *Gardens of New England* (1911), complained that Mrs Wharton's garden lacked 'intimate charm ... the sense of personal and loving supervision'.[22] While the sister of Edith's friend Sara Norton found the garden quite chilling: 'her house, her garden, her appointments were all perfect – money, taste, and instinct saw to every detail; yet the sense of a home was not there'.[23] Edith indeed was neither a home-maker in the sense of cosiness, nor did she have children to knock the corners off her sense of order and control. She was impervious to any criticism and flushed by the success of her efforts, she later wrote to her lover Morton Fullerton, 'Decidedly I am a better landscape gardener than novelist, and this place, every line of which is my own work, far surpasses *The House of Mirth*'.[24] The success of her first major novel had made it possible for Wharton to complete the sunken Italian garden in 1905, creating what was, in effect, a *giardino segreto* (see Frontispiece).

PEACE AND CONTENTMENT

The Mount was a great success personally for Edith Wharton, for at last she was able to partake of both her social and creative worlds without conflict. Her writing was done early in the day and 'by eleven o'clock she was ready for friends and engagements, for walking or garden work'.[25] Wharton was now in her forties (Plate 19), and had achieved the equilibrium in her life she had so fervently desired. Whilst she devoted her time to writing, horticulture and her friends, 'Teddy looked after the farm and business management of the house, rode, fished, hunted and later drove'.[26] With her new routine established, Wharton was moving further away from the world her mother had known. She avoided taking part in New York social life, and at Lenox she shunned the social merry-go-round, which of course did not endear her to her neighbours. She was even said to have been rude to Mrs Sloane, the 'Queen' of Lenox society. It was not that Edith was a recluse, but her writing set her apart from her neighbours and she preferred to

Plate 19 Edith Wharton aged 40, photographed after her move to The Mount; first published in *Women Authors of Our Day in Their Homes*, 1903.

choose her own companions, entertaining only small groups of people at The Mount. But, although social activities disturbed her writing, the one event she relished was the annual flower show, a highlight of the Lenox season. Wharton assisted the organizing committee of the Lenox Horticultural Society, fretting over her own entries, tying and labelling the bunches of flowers (Plate 20). In 1905 she received seven prizes: a first in the class for twenty-five annuals, hollyhocks, penstemons and carnations; second prize for sweet peas, Shirley poppies as well as her double poppies; and a third for her lilies.[27] She noted the number of prizes in her diary, and on the next page, the number of weeks that *The House of Mirth* had been the best-selling book in New York. Edith Wharton was intensely competitive and anxious to do well in every aspect of her life, and almost certainly she took as much pleasure in her success at the flower show as she did later in winning the Pulitzer Prize for Literature.

With her growing reputation as a novelist, Wharton began to make many new literary and academic friends, and during her long visits to

Europe she was beginning to meet people of her own kind – people with the understanding and sympathy she needed and who in time would become her long-standing friends. In England these centred on the house of Howard Sturgis, 'Queens Acre', abbreviated to 'Qu'Acre', in Windsor (see Chapter 5). Sturgis, the brother of John Hubbard Sturgis,[28] was son of an American banker and who had been educated in England. It was through him that Wharton came to know Percy Lubbock, novelist and critic, as well as Gaillard Lapsley, an American-born Cambridge don. Another intimate friend was the author Henry James (also see Chapter 5), whom she 'adored, cultivated and pursued'. She had known James since the 1880s and finally 'co-opted' him as a friend following a lunch in London, but the staid bachelor was somewhat ambivalent about their friendship. He regarded her as the 'angel of devastation' for the way she would descend upon him at Lamb House in Rye and whisk him away to tour the countryside and visit gardens.

TRAVELS IN ITALY

Edith Wharton had become an established authority on seventeenth and eighteenth century Italian architecture. In the late 1880s she became aware that 'everybody behaves – the historians as well as the art critics – as if Italy had ceased to exist at the end of the Renaissance'.[29] Thereafter Wharton devoted her holidays to a deeper study of eighteenth century art and architecture in Italy. An important influence on her appreciation of Italian art and culture was the author Vernon Lee, the pen name of Violet Paget.[30] 'Lee' was a tall, masculine woman, a tremendous talker, outspoken and witty, who lived in Florence from 1889 until her death in 1935. Wharton had been introduced to her in Italy by Paul Bourget in 1884. Afterwards Wharton wrote that Lee 'was the first highly cultivated and brilliant woman I had ever known'.[31] After reading Vernon Lee's *Studies of the Eighteenth Century in Italy* (1880), she often told the author that 'your eighteenth century studies were letting me into that wonder world of Italy which I had loved since childhood without having the key to it'.[32]

Wharton's Italian travels provided the background to her first novel *The Valley of Decision* (1902). A year later she was invited by *Century Magazine* to write a series of articles on Italian villas and gardens. The publishers saw the essays as a vehicle for a series of watercolours by the immensely popular American artist Maxfield Parrish, but Wharton was reluctant to play 'second fiddle' to someone she regarded as a fairytale illustrator whose paintings of Italian gardens were sentimental, more evocative of 'moonlight and nightingales' than illustrations for a serious technical and historical analysis of the gardens. Nevertheless, Wharton accepted the assignment which was very timely. As we have seen, the garden at The Mount had been created from her assumptions about Italian gardens, but now she had the opportunity to make a deeper study of those gardens, many of which she had known since childhood. She began enthusiastically to research old books, in four languages, as well as drawings and plans, in preparation for the trip – she always regarded herself as an academic and critic rather than a dilettante. Her intention was to write, not as though she was 'a young lady from the west', as had been requested by her publisher, but to try to understand the Italian garden in its entirety.

Armed with this commission, she set out for Rome in the winter of 1903 with Teddy, who had been advised to travel to Italy for his health, which was causing increasing problems. On arrival in Italy Wharton turned to Vernon Lee for help in researching the book. Lee had earlier spoken favourably about Wharton's novel *The Valley of Decision*, and now proved to be most generous in her help – 'her long familiarity with the Italian countryside, and wide circle of her Italian friendships made it easy for her to guide me to the right places and put me in relation with people who could enable me to visit them'.[33] Very little had been written about Italian villa and garden architecture, and what had been published was confined to the most famous places. Wharton's intention was to make known the simpler and less familiar types of villa. Vernon Lee also took the Whartons to the villas Edith wished to see near Florence. As Hermione Lee observed, everyone who met Lee said how wonderful it was to be shown Italy by her.[34]

In her essay, *Old Italian Gardens* (1897), Vernon Lee had provided an account of the phases of Italian garden design, but Wharton wanted to study the garden in relation to the house, and both in relation to the landscape. 'How is it,' she asked, 'that the garden and the landscape seem to form part of the same composition? How did nature and art become fused in this way?' The answer, Hermione Lee reminds us in her biography of Wharton, could only be found by looking at the history and the techniques of compositions used by garden architects of the sixteenth to eighteenth centuries, and in working out the components that made up their 'deeper harmony of design'. It was not just the materials, hard and soft; it was the 'grouping of the parts', the care taken with transitions and contrasts and 'the relation of the whole composition to the scene about it', which had to be judged. It was this relationship to their surroundings that gave gardens such as Caprarola or the Villa Lante a quality of inevitability about them – 'one feels of it, as of certain great verse, that it couldn't have been otherwise, that in Vasari's happy phrase, it was *born* not *built*' (Plate 21).[35] This quality of 'inevitableness' became her criterion for judging the success of a garden; added to which, each Italian villa garden needed to be appreciated for its 'essential convenience and livableness'. Design was always at the service of utility; 'The old Italian garden was meant to be lived in.'[36] In encouraging her American readers to look at Italian gardens in this way, 'with their history and function in mind', Wharton used them as an exemplar of what she believed was the way forward for the new American garden; a way to replace 'overstuffed' ones which had lost all sense of design with carefully planned and functioning gardens.

Between January and June 1903, the Whartons visited more than 70 villas and gardens, which resulted in six articles by Edith, and by the time *Italian Villas and Their Gardens* was published in 1904, the

Plate 21 Caprarola – the Catena d'Aqua, similar in design to the cascade at the Villa Lante, leads up to the Casino Villino. Wharton found this garden enchanting: its 'huge sylvan figures half emerging from their stone sheaths, "seems born not built"'.

drawings by Maxfield Parrish had become an embellishment (Plate 22), to which she added her own photographs. Wharton wrote to Parrish telling him what villas she wished him to visit: of Caprarola she explained that the gardens are 'impossible to get in … If you know an ambassador … he can get you in'. Wharton sent Parrish photographs of the villa, mistakenly including herself in a summer dress in one photograph, for which she apologized at the end of the letter. Parrish discussed the idea of using a painted photograph of Caprarola with the art department at *Century* magazine; consequently the first edition of *Italian Villas and Their Gardens* featured a picture of the Villa Caprarola described as 'retouched photography by Maxfield Parrish'. One of the early readers of the book, according to Vivian Russell, was Egerton Winthrop's cousin by marriage, Lawrence Johnston, and the book influenced his ground-breaking English garden at Hidcote.[37]

A spate of books written about the Italian garden followed this publication, most notably *The Art of Garden Design in Italy* (1906) by H. Inigo Triggs. This was a comprehensive study of Italian gardens, about both their history and design, with 27 lithographic plans accompanied by 150 photographs. It was exactly the kind of book Edith Wharton had hoped to produce. She believed that till then the subject had

Plate 22 Maxfield Parrish's illustration of the Villa Gamberaia in *Italian Villas and Their Gardens* (1904); Wharton called this garden ' the most perfect example of the art of producing a great effect on a small scale'.

been treated in the most amateurish fashion, and was bitterly disappointed that *Century Magazine* would not use the historical garden plans she had found during her research. The publication of Triggs's book rectified this oversight and did much to influence the Italianate approach to arts and crafts gardens, seen in the work of designers such as Harold Peto (1854–1933).

TRAVELS BY CAR

One development during her time in Italy helped to transform Edith Wharton's mode of travelling and her experience of the landscape for ever. Her visits to the gardens had been made almost entirely by train and carriage, and it was hard work. She spoke of long dusty drives to some of the more remote places, and the frustration of either rushing through villas in order not to miss the train, or else, 'the villa exhaustively inspected, kicking our heels in some musty railway station'.[38] But on one occasion her friend, the United States Ambassador in Rome, offered to provide a car for her visit to Caprarola, the sumptuous villa designed by Vignola for the red cardinal, Alessandro Farnese.[39] The car was one of the more luxurious and fast types of the day, though it was without hood or screen, and Edith Wharton had to sit on as high a seat as a coachman's box. 'In a thin spring dress, a sailor hat balanced on my chignon, and a two-inch tulle veil over my nose, I climbed proudly to my perch and off we tour across the Campagna, over humps and bumps, through ditches and across gutters, windswept, dust enveloped, I clinging to my sailor's hat.'[40] One is reminded of Gertrude Jekyll's excursions around the Surrey landscape with Ned Lutyens, perched on the fly, but Wharton thought it the most beautiful excursion she had ever made. Since her childhood experiences in Italy, Wharton had experienced an almost transcendental response to the beauty of landscape and nature, and now, perched high on her seat, she could look down on the landscape and see it unfold not unlike one of Turner's Italian visions. She spent the next day in bed fighting acute laryngitis; motoring for Wharton would not become an 'unmixed joy' until the invention of the wind-screen.

Soon after that experience, Edith Wharton bought the first of a succession of cars in which she could tour the countryside in style, both in Europe and around Lenox, driving in what she described to Sara Norton as 'a little spluttering shrieking American motor'.[41] In July 1904, *The Berkshire Resort Topics* reported that Mr Edward R. Wharton had purchased a very handsome Pope-Hartford light touring car of ten horse-power, with removable tonneau and brass fittings (Plate 23). Soon the Whartons and their guests were taking tours to eastern Massachusetts, Newport, Rhode Island, and the Hudson River area of New York made famous by painters such as Frederic Church. With the arrival of the car, Wharton's fervour for the intense beauty of the region grew stronger. She wrote lovingly to Sara Norton of the naturalistic areas around Lenox, of what she called 'the texture of the surrounding woodlands' and 'the perfume of my hemlock woods'. As she explained in her autobiography, 'the range of country-lovers like myself had hitherto been so limited, and our imagination so tantalized by the mystery beyond the next blue hills, that there was inexhaustible delight in penetrating to the remoter parts of Massachusetts and New Hampshire, discovering derelict villages with Georgian churches and balustraded house fronts, exploring slumbering mountain valleys, and coming back laden with a new harvest of beauty'.[42] The car restored for her the romance of travel (see *A Motor Flight Through France*, 1908); she not only enjoyed travelling, it restored her mentally. It allowed her to see the

Plate 23 (left) An advertisement for the Pope-Hartford motor car purchased by Teddy Wharton in July 1904.

(right) Motoring at The Mount, 1904: the 'spluttering shrieking American' Pope-Hartford. Edith Wharton and Henry James are in the back, while Teddy waits with the Pekingese dogs.

countryside in an entirely new way, an elevated and sequential view of the landscape. In the car Wharton enjoyed 'a quick but direct look at the landscape, leaving her with a constantly shifting vista and scenes to observe – a fantastically efficient way to collect mental pictures'.[43] One of the Whartons' first excursions in their new car was to the south of France in January 1904. It made Wharton extremely happy: 'our long flights across the hills and along the shore take us into the heart of the country, and steep us in warm bright air'.[44] After this experience, France became the new European destination of her heart and, later, impressions of the unfolding countryside would provide inspiration for the landscape in her novels.

BACK TO THE MOUNT

After she returned from Italy, Wharton found the garden at The Mount in disarray. A drought of two months had reduced the countryside and the estate to desolation: dust everywhere, the grass parched and burned, flowers and vegetation stunted. Even worse, the head gardener had neglected his duties while they were away, and there was little to show for all the money previously spent on the garden.[45] Her frustration was overcome by engaging an admirable replacement, Thomas Reynold. The improvements following his arrival encouraged Edith to immerse herself in the garden during that summer and the next. In the crudest terms, the 'gardening bug' had infected Wharton; so much so that at the end of June 1905, when rain prevented her from travelling to Williamstown to see her friend President Theodore Roosevelt receive an honorary degree, she wrote to Sara Norton to say that she was far from upset as 'the flowers come easily first, I am growing besotted by gardening'. She invited Norton to come and see the red garden; 'it is really what I thought it never could be – a mass of bloom.' There are 'ten varieties of phlox, some very gorgeous, flowering together, and then the snapdragons, lilac and crimson stocks, penstemons, annual pinks in every shade of rose, salmon, cherry, and crimson. The white petunias which now form a perfect hedge about the tank – the intense blue *Delphinium chinensis*, the purple and white platycodons, etc. – really with a background of hollyhocks of every shade from pale rose to dark red it looks, for a fleeting moment, like a garden in a civilized climate'.[46] By a 'civilized climate' Wharton was referring to England and gardens she had seen on a recent visit to Cambridge.

The climate at The Mount was far from conducive to gardening, with frosts before the end of September and winter temperatures falling to 20 degrees below zero Fahrenheit (Plate 24). Wharton had told Sara Norton on one occasion that the garden was advancing in a reluctant New England way. In her gardening Wharton, like her niece Beatrix Farrand, was strongly influenced by Gertrude Jekyll, having purchased *Lilies for English Gardens* and *Roses for English Gardens* when they were first published in 1901 and 1902. She had already acquired William Robinson's *Wild Garden* in 1888

Plate 24 The Mount, Lenox *c.* 1906; the gardens in winter, a time when the Whartons often travelled to Europe.

and had a 1901 edition of the *English Flower Garden and Home Grounds* (Appendix 1). These were the same gardening books that inspired Lawrence Johnston, her good friend of later years. Unfortunately, a visit to Gertrude Jekyll, the great English designer, was as unrewarding as that made by her niece: 'On that long desired day I had a hundred questions to ask, a thousand things to learn. I went with a party of fashionable and indifferent people, all totally ignorant of gardens and gardening: I put one timid question to Miss Jekyll, who answered curtly, and turned her back on me to point out a hybrid iris to an eminent statesman who knew neither what a hybrid nor an iris was; and for the rest of the visit she gave me no chance of exchanging a word with her'.[47]

Another passion, later shared with Lawrence Johnston, was for phlox, and in August she announced that she had 32 varieties. In an horticultural exchange with her friend George B. Dorr, she told him: 'what you say of the phloxes makes my mouth water, for I have tried to get as many good varieties as possible, and am especially keen for new colors. If there is any really good novelty, wd. you not ask your manager to send me the name and color ?' [48]

Edith Wharton was always keen to gain advice from others when making her gardens and George Dorr, who had been involved in the efforts to create the Acadia National Park on Mount Desert Island in Maine, was also consulted on landscape design matters.[49] Having taken his advice Wharton wrote in September 1904 to say, that 'your path is finished, and the task of planting its borders now confronts me; and we are just about to attack the laying out of the path from the flower garden to the little valley which is to be my future wild garden'[50] – a reference to the style made popular by William Robinson. Another friend was Daniel Chester French, a neighbour who was an artist and sometime garden designer, who visited her with his wife Mary. They appreciated Wharton's artistry at The Mount and, according to Mary, the place, with its view 'like an old tapestry', was among the most exquisite to be found anywhere in the Berkshires. She said that her husband and Edith Wharton would wander about the grounds exchanging ideas; she courteous enough to ask his advice, but artistic enough to need little help from anyone.[51] The Frenchs' believed that The Mount was an example of what could be done in landscape gardening by developing every little natural beauty, instead of starting with preconceived ideas and trying to make it like some other beautiful place, to which the lie of the land bears no resemblance whatsoever. In so doing, Wharton was going against the prevailing Beaux-Arts tradition, preferring instead to follow the examples set by Olmsted at Central Park, and by the lessons her own niece Beatrix Farrand had learnt from the Sargents at Holm Lea.

FAREWELL TO THE MOUNT

By the winter of 1906–7, Edith Wharton had outgrown the parochialism of American society. As Eleanor Dwight wrote, that particular winter was the beginning of her life as an expatriate. Gradually she was to consign New York and Newport, even Lenox and The Mount, to the background, and create a new life for herself in France.[52] Up to that point, Europe had been a place for holidays, with endless explorations of Italy and France, but Wharton now believed Paris offered her a *milieu* 'where ideas could be freely and continually exchanged', and where that 'exchange was regulated by rules of good taste and good manners ... order was everywhere: in the chateaux, in the flower borders, in the design of towns, and above all in the thinking'.[53]

She spent the winter with Teddy, in the apartment of George Vanderbilt on the rue de Varenne, in the Faubourg St. Germain (part of the 7th Arondissement). In 1907 Paris was in the midst of what the French call 'La Belle Époque' – equivalent to the 'Gilded Age' – a term characterized by 'elegantly attired aristocrats and gowned, if suspect, ladies gathering after midnight at Maxim's in the rue Royale; bearded gentlemen wearing dark clothes and top hats in winter, white linen and Panama hats in summer; women wearing long, flowing, brightly coloured dresses and hats with plumes and artificial fruits and flowers, bosoms accentuated by hidden supporters, waists held in by tight belts and worldly salons of the idle nobility along the Champs-Elysées.'[54] Historically the Faubourg St-Germain was the locality for the town houses of the French nobility, slowly being penetrated by bourgeois artists and intellectuals. Through the centre of the district ran the narrow, tree-lined rue de Varenne, its imposing line of stony façades concealing a world Wharton craved. Beyond the entrance was a complex of service buildings off-set by courtyard gardens, with shrubs and parterres, where she could take tea. A curving staircase swept up from the entrance towards the *piano nobile* where the rooms were decorated in the style of Louis XV or XV1, their ambience reflecting the perfectly arranged rooms Wharton and Codman had so enthusiastically described in *The Decoration of Houses* ten years before. She described her new home in a letter to Sara Norton, and the delight she took in rooms with their 'charming old furniture, old Chinese porcelains and fine bronzes'.[55]

Once installed, Wharton set about the task of establishing a pleasing round of dinners, teas, luncheons, theatre, motor excursions to nearby towns with her new friends, and of course writing. Her ambition was to establish herself at the centre of an intellectual and cultural circle of writers, artists and expatriates, in the tradition of the European salon. She soon gathered a circle of male friends, which included Henry James and the art critic Bernard Berenson; also Jacques-Émile Blanche, the most fashionable French portrait painter of the time, who lived in a seventeenth century manor house among the 'leafy quiet' of Offranville, near Dieppe. Later Wharton often visited there, giving Blanche and his wife advice about laying out their gardens and the planting of trees, something Jacques-Émile would reciprocate during the next phase of Edith's gardening career. For now the Blanches accompanied Wharton on her excursions to old chateaux in Normandy, introducing her to the eccentric aristocrats who occupied them. Though Wharton was a snob, her snobbery was in part historical curiosity and integral to her creative imagination. But she was anxious to include more French intellectuals, artists and conversationalists in her circle, and sought out those 'people who shared her tastes, rare people who had the "ineradicable passion" for good talk'.[56]

In the spring of the previous year Wharton had met Morton Fullerton (Plate 25), whom it might be said, was the third and final man to shape her life, though this time it was of her emotional self rather than her intellect. Fullerton was the *Times* correspondent in Paris, though he often exaggerated his importance. He was an attractive, expatriate American who was also bisexual and a serial philanderer – in P. G. Wodehouse's words, a cad – though Wharton did not discover this fact until later in their relationship. In October 1907, Fullerton visited The Mount, and on the day he was leaving they took a drive along the snow-dusted roads of the Berkshires. When the car had to stop so that chains could be fitted to the wheels, they sat on the ground and smoked. Suddenly Wharton noticed a witch hazel blooming on a wet bank; in folklore the hazel (*Hamamelis virginiana*), which only begins to flower when all other plant-life is dying, is sometimes called the old woman's bloom. Seeing the wispy yellow flowers seemed 'to unexpectedly quicken Edith's 45 year-old life and Fullerton shared the feeling'.[57] After Fullerton's departure she wrote in a long-discarded diary, 'if you had not enclosed that sprig of wych-hazel [sic] in your (thank-you) note ... the note in itself might have meant nothing. The sprig of wych hazel told me that you knew what was in my mind when I found it blooming on that wet bank in the woods.'[58]

After she returned to Paris, she began to see Fullerton constantly and, for a brief period, her infatuation with him merged with her love of France. Meanwhile Teddy Wharton's health was deteriorating, and after their arrival in Paris he fell into a 'nervous depression'. Edith did not understand until later what was already becoming apparent to her friends, that the new life she was creating for herself was anathema to her husband. The salons of Paris, Edith's growing fame and wealth, not to mention his total financial dependence on her, was stifling the 'easy going lover of fishing and the looser amenities of American social gatherings'.[59] Then there was Morton Fullerton. While the presence of the elderly Egerton Winthrop and Ogden Codman had posed no threat, it was obvious that this relationship was altogether different. In

Plate 25 The enigmatic and alluring Morton Fullerton.

March Teddy returned to America for treatment, and at around the same time Edith Wharton and Morton Fullerton became lovers; it would be the only intimate experience she would ever enjoy, or allow.

In May 1908 Wharton returned to The Mount, and though the relationship with Fullerton continued after her return to Paris at the start of 1909, 'everything was different, she had lost confidence'.[60] Fullerton too had been having an affair with his half-sister in Edith's absence. In March the Whartons moved into the Hôtel Crillon, but Teddy was in a very poor state and, after a disastrous motor journey to the south of France, he returned to the States. Wharton spent the entire summer in Europe, the first time for three decades. She was looking for a permanent home in Paris, and in late spring her brother, Harry Jones, found another apartment on the rue de Varenne, available for an indefinite lease. That summer she

Plate 26 Paris, 53 rue de Varenne; the grand entrance to Edith Wharton's home from 1910 to 1920, photographed in 2007.

spent a few weeks in England, dividing her time between Rye, the home of Henry James and Qu'acre, Windsor, that of Howard Sturgis. By the end of 1909, her relationship with Teddy had deteriorated further. In the summer he had been diagnosed as neurasthenic, and at the end of the year he told Edith that whilst in America, he had been speculating wildly with her money and been unfaithful to her.

In January 1910, Edith Wharton moved to 53 rue de Varenne – the grandest apartment building in the block – which became her Paris home until 1920 (Plate 26). Having created the 'European style' for the decoration of houses in America, Wharton now moved into the authentic version of what she had so long admired. Although the apartment was not much older than The Mount, the eighteenth century decor had been carried into that of the late nineteenth century by wood-panelled walls and ceiling dadoes decorated with elaborate swags and cherub motifs in Louis XVI style. At the back of the house the main rooms overlooked a large courtyard and, from the long windows, Wharton could see the gardens of the Hôtel Doudeauville stretching far into the distance. So, although the apartment had no garden, the impression was of living in a country park (Plate 27). Soon her apartment on the rue de Varenne became a great place of entertainment, not just for her new French friends, but for those Americans she had known since childhood, when the Jones family had lived in Nice. Her friend Henry Adams said of the American group in Paris: it was 'more closely intimate and more agreeably intelligent, than any left to me in America' and 'Edith Wharton is at the centre of it'.[61]

Though the affair with Fullerton ended in the summer of 1910, the experience would have a lasting effect on her writing. She was able to 'describe strong, vital relationships, and all the feeling associated with love – possessiveness, jealousy, sadness, rejection, and bliss',[62] with insight and understanding. These crowded years in Paris were some of the most productive in Wharton's literary life. On 24th June 1911, Edith Wharton sailed for New York, having written to promise Teddy that she would have their Lenox home ready for him when he returned from his fishing trip. After a three-year absence, Edith returned to The Mount on 8 July during a heat-wave. She was delighted to find how lovingly the gardens had been kept up, though it was uniformly green and her clematis had died. She did not feel there was anything to compensate 'in this grim New England country', for 'the complete mental starvation'.[63] But by nightfall she was surrounded by her 'inner circle' of friends, Henry James, John Hugh-Smith,[64] making his first visit to the United States, and Gaillard Lapsley. The Mount and its gardens had never seemed more beautiful and, with the moon reflecting on Laurel Lake, the four friends sat on the terrace, talking long into the warm July night. After the departure of Hugh-Smith and Lapsley three days later, Wharton and James were walking in the grounds, discussing her domestic difficulties. Wharton had already considered selling The Mount, and James was of the opinion that she should leave and no longer live with Teddy, whose behaviour was becoming intolerable. Edith was yet to be fully convinced, but on his return from his fishing trip, Teddy was violent and abusive to her; his manic depression was making him impossible to live with.

That year, 1911, she spent the entire summer in the garden, but Edith realized her idyllic days at The Mount were numbered. The house was becoming too expensive to maintain and, though she still hoped for some reconciliation with Teddy, a divorce seemed increasingly likely. For those in the Gilded Society divorce was unacceptable, but more than that, Wharton disliked the idea of disorder and the sexual infidelity it implied. In September she sailed for France leaving Teddy in total control over the future of The Mount. There had already been a good offer for the house, and in November Teddy agreed a sale which was completed the following June, so bringing Edith Wharton's American life to an end. The wrench of leaving The Mount must have been considerable: it had been after all her first real home and the only one she had built; also, it had embodied that sense of good taste of which she had been one

Plate 27 Paris, 53 rue de Varenne; the balcony windows at the rear from which Edith Wharton could view the gardens of the Hôtel Doudeauville, photographed in 2007.

of the arbiters in American society. In the years to come she would repeatedly return to the United States, but never to The Mount, crossing the Atlantic a remarkable 60 times in the years up to 1924. But now France had become her adopted home. For the next 13 years, Edith Wharton's world became one of apartments and hotels. Any experience of gardens would be second hand; visiting historic gardens in France and Italy with friends, or their gardens where she would often be asked for, or at least, proffer her advice. For two years she struggled on with her husband, but Teddy's increasingly irrational behaviour, financial irregularities and adultery brought the inevitable realization that their marriage was over. On 16 April 1913 a divorce decree was granted in the Tribunal de Grande Instance de Paris. Edith was allowed to retain the name Mrs Wharton to avoid undue publicity.

Notes and References

[1] Wharton letters to Codman. Archives of Historic New England, Boston. Quoted in Lee, H., *Edith Wharton*, Chatto & Windus, London, p. 135.

[2] Laurel Lake Farm was purchased on 29 June 1901 from Georgiana Sargent, a distant relative of the painter John Singer Sargent, for $40,600.

[3] Lee, op. cit., p. 115.

[4] Francis L. Hoppin of Hoppin and Koen, had begun his architectural career as an apprentice with McKim, Mead and White.

[5] *Newport Daily News*, 8 January 1896. Reprinted in Wegener, F., ed., *Edith Wharton: The Uncollected Critical Writings*. Princeton University Press, p. 56.

[6] Ibid., p. 56.

[7] Quoted in Fryer, J., *Felicitous Space*. University of North Carolina Press, Chapel Hill, p. 71.

[8] Quoted in Dwight, E., *Edith Wharton: An Extraordinary Life*. Abrams, New York, p. 112.

[9] The quotation was originally from Wharton's *Italian Villas and their Gardens*; and was a guiding principle for the recent restoration: 'The Mount, Edwardian Promenade', *Chicago Sun-Times*, 2 June 2002.

[10] Tankard, J., *Gardens of the Arts and Crafts Movement*. Abrams, New York, p. 179.

[11] Quoted in 'Ignatius Sargent and the Arnold Arboretum', *Jamaica Plain Gazette*, 13 August 1993.

[12] Farrand was a founder member of the American Society of Landscape Architects, though she preferred to call herself a landscape gardener, because she believed it brought her closer to plants, the fundamental basis of her designs. She married the academic historian, Max Farrand, in 1913.

13 Lee, op. cit., p. 122.

14 Tankard, op. cit., p. 186.

15 Dwight, op. cit., p. 94.

16 Sharp, H., A Garden Reawakened. *Berkshire Week*, July 2003.

17 Emmet, A., *So Fine a Prospect: Historic New England Gardens*. University Press of New England, Lebanon, New Hampshire, p. 214.

18 Choate knew a great deal about gardening and European gardens; he lived in a McKim and Mead 'cottage', Naumkeag, designed by Stanford White in 1884. Each room in the house was designed in a different style ranging from Jacobean to Neoclassical and Colonial Revival and decorated accordingly. Nathan Barret organized the formal gardens, with shaded walks, formal parterres and rose gardens, on a steep hillside overlooking Monument Mountain.

19 Brown, J., *Beatrix – the gardening life of Beatrix Jones Farrand*. Viking, London, p. 80.

20 Emmet, op. cit., p. 214.

21 Quoted in Brown, op. cit., p. 79.

22 Quoted in Emmet, op. cit., p. 214.

23 Ibid.

24 Lewis, R.W.B., and Lewis, N., eds., *The Letters of Edith Wharton*. Scribner, New York, p. 242.

25 Quoted in Dwight, op. cit., p. 101.

26 Lee, op. cit., p. 151.

27 Quoted in Dwight, op. cit., p. 113.

28 Howard Overing Sturgis (1855–1920) was the brother of the architect, John Hubbard Sturgis, who had designed Land's End, and was married to Frances Anne Codman, aunt of Ogden Codman.

29 Wharton, E., *A Backward Glance*. Constable, London, p. 102.

30 Vernon Lee had been a childhood friend of John Singer Sargent; their parents were neighbours in Nice; later she was a close friend of Henry James.

31 Dwight, op. cit., p. 75.

32 Lee, op. cit., p. 97.

33 Wharton, op. cit., p. 134.

34 Lee, op. cit., p. 99.

35 Dwight, op. cit., p. 104.

36 Lee, op. cit., p. 117.

37 Russell, V., *Edith Wharton's Italian Gardens*. Frances Lincoln, London, p. 17. Egerton Winthrop's second cousin, Charles Francis Winthrop married the 'widowed' Gertrude Johnston in 1887 (see Chapter 4).

38 Wharton, op. cit., p. 136.

39 In 1559 Cardinal Alessandro Farnese commissioned the architect Giacomo Vignola (1507–73) to transform the existing country estate into a palace for the Farnese family. Among the most well-known artists of the day who worked on its decoration were the Zuccari brothers (Tadeo 1529–66 & Federigo 1543–1609), who painted a famous series of frescoes depicting the feats of the Farnese family.

40 Wharton, op. cit., p. 137.

41 Letter to Sara Norton, 24 January 1904.

42 Wharton, op. cit., p. 153.

43 Dwight, op. cit., pp. 135-6.

44 Lee, op. cit., p. 534.

45 Lewis, R.W.B., *Edith Wharton: a biography*. Constable, London, p. 120.

46 Quoted in Craig, T., *Edith Wharton: a house full of rooms, architecture, interiors and garden*. Monacelli Press, New York, p. 122.

47 Wharton, op. cit., p. 250. In her autobiography, Wharton refers to Miss Jekyll's famous garden at Great Warley, rather than Munstead Wood: a confusion with Warley Place the home of Ellen Willmott, another famous gardener, whom Wharton would also visit.

48 Letter to George Dorr, 3 September 12 1904.

49 Dwight, op. cit., p. 116.

50 Letter to George Dorr, op. cit.

51 French, M., *Memories of a Sculptor's Wife*. Houghton Mifflin, Boston, quoted in Emmet, op. cit., p. 214.

52 Dwight, op. cit., p. 141.

53 Auchincloss, L., *Edith Wharton – a woman in her time*. Michael Joseph, London, p. 108.

54 Lewis, op. cit., p. 174.

55 Ibid., p. 184.

56 Dwight, op. cit., p. 143.

57 Ibid., p. 144.

58 Ibid.

59 Lewis, op. cit., p. 192.

60 Lee, op. cit., p. 330.

61 Lewis, op. cit., p. 214.

62 Dwight, op. cit., pp. 166-7.

63 Lee, op. cit., p. 386.

64 Edith Wharton spelled his surname with a hyphen, which was perpetuated by Lewis, but not by other writers.

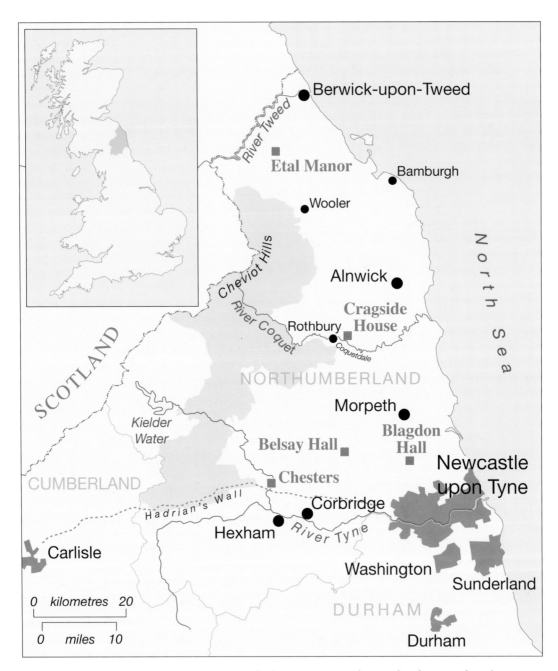

Map 2 Northumberland in north-east England where Lawrence Johnston lived as a student farmer after graduating from Cambridge University. The houses and gardens of his influential friends and acquaintances are shown, together with the county boundaries of Johnston's time. The features of the Northumberland National Park (in darker green), designated in 1956, and Kielder Water, the reservoir constructed between 1975 and 1981, will help to orientate the modern reader, as will the medieval village of Washington which steadily increased in size till it was redeveloped into a 'New Town' in 1964, and which is now a suburb of Sunderland.

CHAPTER FOUR

THE MAKING OF A GARDENER

On 5th November 1887 Gertrude Johnston remarried in London at St. James's Church, Westminster, with her son, Lawrence, in attendance.[1] Her second husband was the wealthy bachelor, Charles Francis (Frank) Winthrop, who was descended from the same patrician family as Egerton Leigh Winthrop, Edith Wharton's close friend and mentor, who was Frank's second cousin once removed. Eighteen years older than Gertrude, Frank Winthrop had been prominent on Wall Street.[2] He fought in the Civil War with the 5th New York Infantry Regiment. In 1868, when he was forty, Winthrop retired from business, and ten years later went to live in Paris. A witness at the wedding was French Ensor Chadwick, who also had served in the war, though in the New York Naval Militia and later became a leading officer in the US Navy, and who may have been acquainted with Gertrude's first husband Elliott Johnston. Indeed, given the nature of New York's small, exclusive and closely-knit high society, Gertrude may have met Frank Winthrop when still married to Elliott Johnston. As has been mentioned, an important element of this society was for gentlemen to be considered 'clubbable'. Both Johnston and Winthrop were members of the same New York club – The Union – as were Gertrude's father, uncle and brother. Among other New York clubs to which they all belonged was the Knickerbocker Club, which included among its members Teddy Wharton and Egerton Winthrop, a former President of the club. At the time of his marriage Frank Winthrop's residence was given as New York, though he lived mostly in Paris where it is assumed he returned with his new bride and stepson. Marriage, however, did not curtail Gertrude's social life, and she was constantly moving between engagements back in New York, New Jersey, Rhode Island and Maine where she liked to join the summer colony at Bar Harbor. Frank Winthrop, who did not share his new wife's enthusiasm for the high life, remained mostly in Paris.

Lawrence said later in a letter, that he received most of his education in France and, although nothing is known of his schooling, it is likely that he had a private tutor. During this period he converted to Roman Catholicism, much to the annoyance of Gertrude, who was a staunch New England Protestant. It has been suggested that his conversion was influenced by his tutor and, while this is most likely, he may have been encouraged by his cousin Anna (Nan) Hope Hudson, who was in Paris at this time (Plate 28). It is difficult to establish the family connections between Lawrence Johnston and Nan Hudson, but the Holly family, on Hudson's maternal side, was one of the original Connecticut families who settled in Stamford and intermarried with the Winthrops. Nan was two years older than Lawrence and, though coming from a Protestant family, she had been raised a Catholic, and after receiving an inheritance from her mother, travelled to Paris intent on becoming an art student. There she met fellow artist Ethel Sands, who became her lifelong companion. For the next sixty years they divided their time between houses in England and France.[3]

During these years Johnston also developed an enduring passion for lawn tennis,[4] and he soon showed his capabilities as a player. In 1893 he returned to England, and it was said by friends that he came for a tournament and, finding the country to his liking, decided to stay. But by now Johnston must have been facing a crisis of identity for, at the age of twenty-two, he was a young man without any sense of belonging. Edith Wharton had expressed the same sense of detachment, also felt by most peripatetic Americans, when she returned to the States from Italy in 1903: a perception of envy and a desire to belong. Writing to Sara Norton, she said 'we are none of us Americans, we don't think or feel as the Americans do, we are the wretched exotics produced in an European glasshouse, the most *déplacé* and useless class on earth'.[5] Johnston may also have shared something of Newland Archer's feelings, expressed in Wharton's novel *The Age of Innocence*. This fictional character felt oppressed by New York society and loved solitary reading, fantasizing about travelling to exotic places and, though appearing to play along with convention, longed to be free. It must have been around this time that Lawrence and his mother decided his future was to become an English gentleman, a country squire. In a similar way to the custom of other wealthy young men wishing to enter the upper echelons of English society, Johnston's first step was to gain admission to Cambridge University and to study for a 'safe' degree.

EDUCATION AT CAMBRIDGE

Johnston's education in France left him ill-prepared for the entrance examination to an English university, and so in August 1893 he

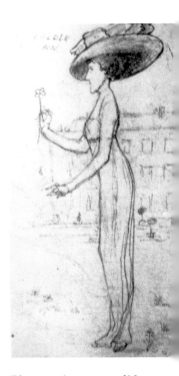

Plate 28 A cartoon of Nan Hudson, Johnston's cousin, at Newington Manor, Oxford.

Plate 29 Trinity College, Cambridge University, c. 1890s: students leaving the Great Hall attired in the caps and gowns favoured by the College.

boarded at the 'crammer' run by a former Cambridge don, John Dunn, at his home in Little Shelford, near Cambridge. Dunn's specialist subjects were Latin, Greek and Mathematics, and with his son Arthur, a Tutor at Trinity College, he was highly successful in preparing young hopefuls for their entrance exams. While at Little Shelford, Lawrence became friends with Vandeleur Bright-Smith, who was courting Ethel Dunn, the daughter of his tutor. Bright-Smith, the son of the Reverend George Bright-Smith, had been a 'pensioner' at Trinity College, graduating in 1890,[6] and at the time he met Johnston, was preparing to take up farming. This may have directed Johnston's thoughts in a similar direction. In May 1894 Johnston attended the oral examination for entrance to Trinity College, and in October was admitted as a pensioner. Edith Wharton's younger brother Harry had been at Trinity earlier, where he had made a rather desultory study of Civil Law. At this time it was customary for undergraduates to live outside college, and Johnston took lodgings in Portugal Street, a stone's throw from the College itself, one of the more gracious of the

Cambridge colleges.[7] On entering the Great Court at Trinity, attired in the cap and gown favoured by the College (Plate 29), Johnston would instantly have been aware of its great antiquity and soon was following the daily routine of the undergraduate:

> The mornings in Cambridge are for books, the afternoon for exercise, and the evening for social intercourse. So, at least, the majority of the undergraduate members of the University regard them, and sometimes throw in an extra hour or two for work between tea and dinner. Of course there are those who work all the evening as well as all the morning, and there are others who do not work at all; but the morning for lectures and books is a general rule, and one that has few exceptions, however squeezed up the morning may be between late breakfast and early luncheon. If you go into the Great Court of Trinity, let us say about ten minutes to eleven in the morning, you will find it, comparatively speaking, deserted. Quite deserted it never is, unless in the dead hours of night, and not always then; but now its chief occupants appear to be the bed-makers, who empty their pails down the gratings, or stand for a few minutes' gossip by their respective staircases ... But of the undergraduate life which is so busy in the courts of a college at other times of the day there is very little, for most undergraduates are listening to lecturers or coaches, or reading in their own rooms.[8]

Johnston would have enjoyed life at Cambridge, even though he was naturally reserved and had a minor speech impediment which caused him to pronounce all his 'r's as 'w's, with a slight French accent. He was artistic and was a competent water-colour painter and piano-player. At the sporting level, he was a good tennis player and, throughout his years at Trinity, belonged to the college Rifle Club, serving as its treasurer from 1895 to '97. There are no records of his studies yet, consistent with a desire to become an English gentleman, his courses did include English Constitutional History, as well as (probably from his personal interest) the History of the Papacy. Johnston graduated with a modest second-class degree in history but, perhaps more important to his future, were the friends and acquaintances he had made at the university. Many of them were to remain in touch throughout his life and play an important part in his future.

MR. REGINALD CORY.

One of these friends was Reginald Cory (Plate 30), a law student entering his final year at Trinity in 1894.[9] They shared many interests; both played the organ and piano, collected porcelain, could draw well and were good athletes, Cory being a more than capable oarsman. But Cory had already discovered his passion for plants and horticulture, and had begun a lifelong association with the University's Botanic Garden. His father, Sir John Cory, was the millionaire founder of Cory Brothers, a shipping, coal and oil conglomerate in Cardiff. After completing his degree, 'Reggie' chose not to take an active role in the company, preferring instead 'to develop his wide-ranging interests and artistic tastes'.[10] The year before Cory had gone up to Cambridge, his father had bought the Dyffryn estate near Cardiff, and after university 'Reggie' devoted his time to making it one of the more important gardens in the country. In so doing Reginald Cory achieved the distinction of being a leading horticulturist too.

Another of Johnston's friends in that final year was the Hon. Bill Barrington, heir to titles in Ireland,[11] who had no interest in gardens and was no scholar. Rather, his time at Cambridge was devoted to cricket, athletics and shooting, whilst avoiding any attempt at gaining a degree.[12] Barrington would later become one of a group of Johnston's closest friends, although his interest in gardening took time to develop (and then under the influence of a very forceful woman – see Chapter 8).

After finishing his studies in 1897, Johnston returned to Little Shelford in time for the wedding of Vandeleur Bright-Smith and Ethel Dunn. Lawrence was now at a crossroads in his life; nothing had prepared him for serious work, and he remained dependent on his mother for an income, as he would throughout his life. Many graduates planned careers in law or the City after leaving Trinity. One such was Claud Biddulph of The Park, Ledbury in Herefordshire. He was the same age as Johnston, and had been a boarder at Little Shelford two years before Johnston arrived,[13] and admitted to Trinity College in 1889.[14] On graduation Biddulph's father gave him the

Rodmarton estate, near Cirencester in Gloucestershire and, after his marriage, Claud commissioned the Arts and Crafts architect, Ernest Barnsley, to build a country retreat at Rodmarton. Unfortunately, Lawrence had no aptitude for either the law or the City, and in spite of his experience with the Rifle Club, his mother regarded him as incapable of managing his financial affairs. Then in February 1898 Frank Winthrop died in Paris,[15] leaving his wife as a very wealthy widow. She was now even more possessive of her son, and they probably agreed that Gertrude would purchase a suitable property where they might live together. No doubt she hoped that her beloved 'Laurie' would settle down as a gentleman farmer, marry into a respectable family and have children, though it would be 'events' that would determine Johnston's future, rather than his mother's machinations (Plate 31).

Some time after 1896, Johnston met George Laing, who was the son of Sir James Laing, the chairman of a Sunderland ship-building company and a wealthy landowner. George managed the family farm at New Etal Manor near Cornhill-on-Tweed, Northumberland. Johnston may have been introduced to Laing by his friend Vandeleur Bright-Smith, who in turn had family connections with the Thompson family, another of the leading ship-builders in Sunderland. It seems likely that this network of connections, led to

Plate 31 Lawrence Johnston and his mother, Gertrude Winthrop, photographed in the 1890s.

Plate 32 New Etal, Northumberland, in 1910; the village street with cottage gardens, and Elcho Castle in the background.

Johnston being able to move into Grange Farm on the Laing estate in October 1898, as a pupil farmer. The move, of course, permitted him to get away from his mother, not unlike Edith Wharton's escape to Lenox. New Etal is an estate village located near the Scottish border in the most distant part of England (Plate 32). Sir James Laing lived in the fine Georgian Manor house, and the estate offered excellent fishing and shooting – as the sale catalogue later stated after his death. There were three packs of foxhounds in the district, the Master of one of them being Lord Elcho. In one of several coincidences surrounding Johnston at this time, it is possible that he met Lord Elcho through hunting, before his eventual move to Hidcote when he became friends with Elcho's family at Stanway.[16]

THE SECOND BOER WAR

Johnston fitted easily into life as a pupil farmer at Grange Farm, when Mary Laing described him as 'a gentleman of great respectability and excellent character'.[17] Yet he had hardly time to settle at New Etal before world events sent his life in an entirely new direction. In 1899 Britain was gripped by war fever, and leading imperialist newspapers were pressing for a second war against the Boers in South Africa. The Boers, the descendants of Dutch and Huguenot settlers, had first rebelled against British expansion in 1880. They succeeded in gaining self-rule in their own territories in 1881, though Britain retained overall control of southern Africa. But in October 1899, the Boers pushed for complete independence from British Imperial rule, and started a second war, fighting under the maxim, 'the key to a good defence is a good offence'. They quickly invaded Natal and Cape Province, before laying siege to Mafeking and Ladysmith. Unfortunately the British response, despite a few victories, ground to a halt due mainly to insufficient numbers of cavalry. Without mounted soldiers, the Imperial Army could neither match the manoeuvrabilty of the Boers, nor outwit them. The War Office rushed in cavalry from the regular Army and from around the Empire, but the numbers were comparatively small, resulting in the Government being forced to turn to the part-time soldiers of the county Yeomanry.

When the serious state of the Boer War became apparent, a certain Henry Scott wrote a letter to the local press in Northumberland highlighting the fact that there were many patriotic young men in the county who could ride and shoot, and who were anxious to place their services at the disposal of the country in its time of need. Moreover those unable to leave the country had the financial resources to assist these volunteers. He concluded that the War Office should be asked to allow the enrolment of suitable young men and the raising of a fund for the provision of horses (a not insignificant request, since a good cavalry horse cost £40-0-0). Mr Scott donated £1000 and no doubt Sir James Laing as a deputy lieutenant of the county made his contribution; altogether £33,000 was donated by officers of the Northumberland Hussars. Similar letters were printed in the press around the country. On 21st December 1899, a War Office circular instructed the Commanding Officer of each regiment of yeomanry to enlist recruits for active service. It was expected that a company of around 121 men could be mustered locally, consisting of 115 rank and file and five officers: one captain and four subalterns, who were to be equipped with their own horses, saddlery and clothing. The dress code was woollen Norfolk jackets of neutral colour, breeches and gaiters, laced boots and felt hats; no strict uniformity of pattern was required (Plate 33).

Plate 33 An officer of the Northumberland Hussars in a uniform worn during the second Boer War.

In Northumberland, the Yeomanry (Hussars) had been raised initially in 1819 to quell a civil uprising among keelmen, dockers and miners, and was known as the Northumberland and Newcastle Volunteer Cavalry. When the threat of rebellion passed, they became more focused on national defence, and in 1876 were reformed as the Northumberland Hussars. In the years that followed, the Hussars became a popular and well-established part of Northumberland society, though they were often looked upon by the Regular Army as toy soldiers; in their Hussar uniforms with silver braid they cut quite a dash at the county fairs, but that was all. However, up to 1899 they had never seen active service, and for those not convinced of their usefulness, they were (in the vernacular):

> Blue-arsed bumblers,
> Cock-tailed tumblers,
> Fireside sowljers,
> Dor'ny gan to war.

But the Boer War was about to change both that and their image. By the turn of the year, officers and men of the Northumberland Hussars were preparing to ride off to war, with the words of their regimental song (of 1895) ringing in their ears:

> So here's to the man who fates dare defy,
> Who for Queen and Country is ready to die,
> Who, though gentle in peace, will be fearless in war,
> Hurrah for Northumbria's Yeoman Hussars.[18]

The officers were drawn usually from the squirearchy and the troopers from the rural land-workers: in some ways the Hussars were like the Boers – raised on the land and often natural riders and good shots.

JOHNSTON THE SOLDIER

The response to the War Office circular was immediate, and many patriotic young men seized the opportunity for travel and adventure for, after all, it would be over by Christmas. Among those who responded to the call were George Laing and Lawrence Johnston, who enlisted on 11th January. Little in Johnston's family history had suggested farming, but the very opposite was true about enlisting in a local militia. Both his father and his stepfather had fought in the American Civil War and, though Johnston did not realize it at the time, his enrolment was to be the start of an army career that would last for twenty years. An intense period of activity followed the call for volunteers; the Commanding Officer and his officers, had to enrol, billet, feed, equip and find horses for the men, as well as provide training for the recruits. Johnston and Laing were soon at the Yeomanry's Riding School in Newcastle,[19] where they learned the art of mounted warfare (Plate 34). But Johnston had

Plate 34 The Riding School building of the Northumberland Hussars in Newcastle upon Tyne, where recruits such as Lawrence Johnston were schooled in the art of cavalry warfare.

an even more pressing problem for, as an American, he had to apply for British citizenship. This he did on 15th January and, as one might expect, his application, coming with the support of Sir James Laing, a deputy lieutenant of the county, passed rapidly through the Home Office. It received the personal attention of the Chief Constable and, on 25th January 1900, a Certificate of Naturalisation was granted. So on 2nd February Private Johnston 3296 was able to enlist with the 15th (Northumberland and Durham) Company of the 5th Battalion Imperial Yeomanry en route for South Africa on the SS *Monteagle* (Plate 35). Sharing the journey were the cavalry horses; the Company's carpenters had made temporary horse boxes, which were lashed to the deck of the ship, but unfortunately many of the animals did not survive the sea voyage.

The Northumberland Hussars arrived on 27th February and first saw action in May. For its exploits in South Africa, the regiment was later awarded the battle honour, 'South Africa' to be displayed on pennants and regimental crests. According to his later mention in *The Illustrated Chronicle* of 27th October 1914, Johnston took part in operations in the Cape Colony, north of the Orange River, including the action at Ruidam, and also fighting in the Orange River Colony and the Transvaal.[20] The task of the Yeomanry was to track down

Plate 35 'Night send-off – departure of Imperial Yeomanry from Liverpool', February 1900; a large crowd turned out to see the SS Monteagle sail for South Africa.

and chase the elusive Boers, who had an army of about 20,000 men, across rough country frequently for long periods. Johnston's privileged background had not prepared him for the difficult conditions in South Africa. The Yeomanry had to ride long distances without food or water, and they travelled light in order to move quickly. In winter, when it was freezing cold at night, they had only a single blanket to keep them warm. The day's ration of food for the troopers was, 'Three biscuits and one-and-a-quarter pounds of fresh meat, which we generally cook ourselves ...' [21] The conditions were equally bad for the horses, which were seldom fed due to supply problems, or not cared for properly, and often were ridden to death; of the 500,000 animals used by the British, over 350,000 died. This was the fate of Johnston's own horse 'Moonbeam'. He kept a hoof as a souvenir and later gave it to his friend Mark Fenwick, a near neighbour when he moved to Gloucestershire.

A war that was supposed to be over by Christmas 1900 dragged on interminably. George Laing who had been married previously, returned home after the death of his father in December 1901, to attend to domestic duties. Johnston stayed on. Throughout the following year the war proved particularly unpleasant for those who had volunteered out of a spirit of adventure and a chance to travel. By 1901 Lawrence Johnston and his fellow officers had become seasoned campaigners, and in October he was promoted to 2nd Lieutenant. In October he was attached to the 26th Imperial Yeomanry as a Lieutenant, and subsequently commanded a troop of yeoman cavalry on active service. On one occasion Johnston led his troopers in a cavalry charge against the Boers. Under Lord Kitchener's command the army adopted a ruthless scorched-earth policy: clearing the land, burning the farms, separating women and children from the men all of whom were herded into concentration camps. Over 3000 miles of barbed-wire fences were employed to confine the Boer prisoners; the camp perimeters were patrolled, and block houses had been built every few hundred yards. The conditions within the camps were deplorable and over 20,000 captives died, most of them children. These must have been extremely harrowing for officers and men of the Imperial army. The Commander-in Chief, Kitchener, appears not to have heeded the suffering he caused in South Africa.[22] At the end of May 1902, the Boers finally surrendered and peace was signed. Johnston returned to England on board the SS *Braemar Castle* in company with

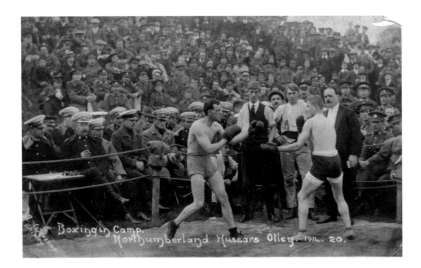

Boxing in Camp.
Northumberland Hussars Otley. 1914. 20.

151 men of the 26th Imperial Yeomanry, and landed at Southampton on 28th August. Johnston was in very poor health and instead of resuming his farming interests he returned to his lodgings in Little Shelford. While staying at Woodvale Lodge he made a rock garden and was the first person to drive a car in the village, an interest in motoring he would later share with Edith Wharton.

Lawrence Johnston's experiences in South Africa gave him some familiarity with the country's flora and landscape (he would return some years later with a more botanical interest in mind). In military terms, the South African war had shown the value of the Yeomanry, and it was appreciated that veteran officers like Lieutenant Johnston and the men they commanded, had gained valuable experience. Many would become officers during the First World War (1914–18). Reforms in the years that followed recognized this experience and, from being a fashionable frill to society, the Yeomanry became an important component in the organization of the Army.[23] For their part, the officers of the Northumberland Hussars were determined to raise standards of fitness and preparedness. Annual training was extended from eight to 16 days a year, and lessons learned in the South African campaign were applied to training. Great emphasis was placed on activities, though these usually served to underline differences in rank. The men took part in games, especially athletics and boxing tournaments (Plate 36), while the officers enjoyed equestrian sports, including riding to hounds. Photographs of the summer camps, such as the one held at Rothbury in 1902, show several officers, including Lieutenant Johnston, holding Border terriers under their arms (Plate

Plate 37 Officers of the Northumberland Hussars at the Rothbury summer camp in 1902. Lieut. Clayton is standing to the left of Major the Lord Armstrong, with Major Backhouse DSO on the right. Lieut. Johnston is seated on the left of the steps opposite Lieut. Laing, characteristically holding a dog.

37). These dogs, sometimes known as Coquetdales – where Rothbury is located – had been bred to flush foxes from below ground. Not everyone, however, was convinced about the value of this part-time army. Osbert Sitwell, himself an officer in the Yeomanry, said of these annual summer camps, that it was though 'the whole youth of the country were playing at being soldiers; farmers, colliers, seed-merchants, squires, pawnbrokers, wool manufacturers, gardeners, sweeps, iron workers, all were engaged in the delightful game of make believe'.[24]

Unlike Sitwell, Johnston showed himself to be an enthusiastic soldier, and he was often the Orderly Officer, responsible for running the camp. This meant being on duty for 24 hours supervising and inspecting the guard, ensuring meals were cooked punctually and the canteens emptied of men in good time, as well as being present in the stables during the morning and afternoon – even overseeing those in detention. During these years Johnston also pursued his training as an officer; in the first six months of 1903 he was at Aldershot, and in May passed a course of 'Instruction for Imperial Yeomanry'. In 1905 he attended a Musketry Course in Hythe and was confirmed a Lieutenant on 28 May. In July the following year it was a proud Lieutenant Lawrence Johnston, resplendent in the dark blue uniform of the Northumberland Hussars, who commanded an escort for King Edward VII and the royal procession at the opening of a new rail bridge over the Tyne. By June 1909 he had been promoted to Captain.

THE HIGH SOCIETY OF GARDENERS

The army provided Johnston with the family and close friends he had never had in his youth, and during his time in South Africa he met and became a friend of George Savile Clayton, a Lieutenant in the 14th (Northumberland and Durham) Company of the 5th Battalion Imperial Yeomanry and a fellow tennis enthusiast.[25] Such male friendships were commonplace in the manly world of the British Empire; as A. N. Wilson points out, it was a world that was 'stiflingly, overpoweringly male, whether it was the army, navy, the civil service or parliament'. Even at Cambridge during Johnston's last year at Trinity, the undergraduates and fellows had voted overwhelmingly to exclude women from entry to the university. In such a society, close male friendships were the norm, and it is pointless to think only in modern terms of homoeroticism or sexual repression.[26] It is likely that Johnston was introduced to Clayton by George Laing, whose younger brother Hugh had been a boarder at the Palmer Flatt Boarding School in Aysgarth with Clayton during the 1880s. An officers' photograph of the Summer Camp in 1902 shows the three Lieutenants, Johnston, Clayton and Laing, on their return from South Africa, relaxing together at Rothbury (Plate 37).

The Clayton family[27] lived at Chesters on the banks of the North Tyne, near Humshaugh, a few miles from Hexham, in a fine Georgian mansion which had been built for John Clayton in 1771 by John Carr of York and later enlarged by Norman Shaw in 1891. The parkland in front of the house was laid out at the end of the eighteenth century in a Reptonian style, and a large kitchen garden adjoined the house. After his return from South Africa, Johnston may have moved to be near Clayton, lodging with the landowner George Ray – though there is no evidence for this.[28] Savile Clayton almost certainly introduced Johnston to his brother-in-law Mark Fenwick, who was already another of the group

Plate 38 Mark Fenwick and his wife Molly (née Clayton) at the time of their marriage.

Plate 39 Abbotswood, Stow-on-the-Wold, photographed in spring 2008; the Cotswold home of Johnston's close friend Mark Fenwick. The rear of the house was extended by Edwin Lutyens.

of distinguished amateur horticulturists of the day, and a prominent figure in the Royal Horticultural Society. Fenwick had married Clayton's younger sister Mary Sophia (known as Molly), in 1883 (Plate 38). He had been a banker and chairman of the Consett Iron Works, but retired early, however, to devote himself to his house and its garden at Abbotswood near Stow-on-the-Wold, in the Cotswolds, which he had purchased in 1901 (Plate 39). Edwin Lutyens had been asked to make alterations to the house and surrounding terraces. He added a gazebo, a formal lily pond and a canal garden, all 'planted in the most harmonious Jekyll style' – though she had not been personally involved. The firm of James Pulham and Son was invited shortly afterwards to lay out a stream garden using their artificial rockwork (Plate 40), which was very much in vogue at the time.[29] By the time Johnston moved to the Cotswolds, and Mark Fenwick was helping him to lay out the garden at Hidcote, Abbotswood was regarded as among the finest gardens in England.[30]

Shortly after his return from South Africa, Johnston applied to join the Royal Horticultural Society, and in 1905 his name appears on the list of new members, his address being given as Little Shelford. By now his interest in architecture and garden design was beginning to develop; one of the first books he borrowed from the RHS Lindley Library was *A History of Gardening*, written in 1895 by Alicia Amherst and illustrated by Lady Victoria Manners, daughter of the Duke of

Rutland.[31] Johnston's initial borrowings from the RHS Library also show an early interest in alpine plants and bulbs. It was an interest he maintained throughout his life and one he shared with Mark Fenwick, who had a 'huge collection of rock and water-loving plants and alpines and flowering shrubs' at Abbotswood.[32] His borrowings in 1907 also included two books by Gertrude Jekyll, *Home and Garden* and *Wood and Garden*. Two years earlier he had borrowed *The Art and Craft of Garden Making* written by the leading garden designer of the day, Thomas H. Mawson.[33] In the following years Mawson's book was to become a standard source of reference for Edwardian garden-makers such as Johnston and his friends.[34]

Johnston may have had an even closer association with Mawson through his friend Reggie Cory. Cory's father had asked Mawson to prepare a master plan for the Dyffryn gardens in 1903–4 and, though the work had been largely carried out, it was 1906 before Mawson and Cory began to work on 'extensive improvements'. To the west of the central lawn, Cory and Mawson arranged a series of 'rooms' designed as small, specialist gardens, each with its own character and planting, 'separated from its neighbour by hedges of clipped English yew, or walls and arches'.[35] Mawson said of Dyffryn that 'every type of garden design has been happily welded' in the west gardens by 'Reginald Cory, an amateur landscape gardener and horticulturist of insight and ability. The credit for the success achieved in these gardens largely belongs

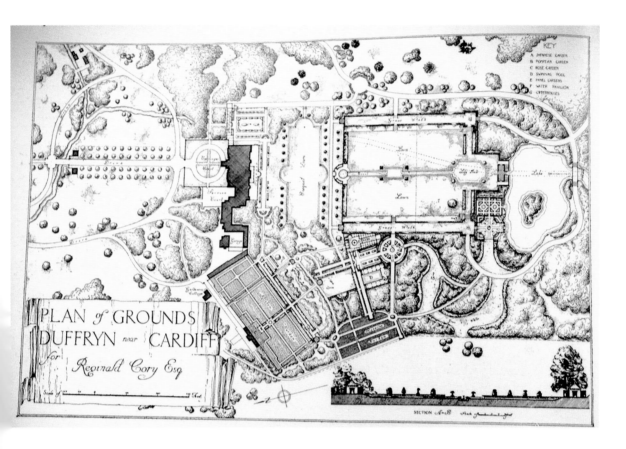

KEY

A JAPANESE GARDEN
B POMPEIAN GARDEN
C ROSE GARDEN
D SWIMMING POOL
E PANEL GARDENS
F WATER PAVILION
G GREENHOUSES

PLAN of GROUNDS
DUFFRYN near CARDIFF
for
Reginald Cory Esq

SECTION A–B

Figure 4a The plan for Dyffryn (Duffryn) by Thomas Mawson; the small specialist enclosures of the West Gardens are located on the lower part of the plan, either side of the Round Garden. The plan was eventually modified by Reginald Cory.

to him'.[36] An arboretum, with new species then being introduced to Britain, was also established.[37] (Fig.4a)

Johnston may also have been further influenced and inspired by Cory and Mawson's decision to go on an Italian Grand tour. 'Although I possessed all the books on Italian gardens,' wrote Mawson, 'Mr Cory and I felt the books were inadequate for our full education with regard to both the setting and planting of many of the best known Italian Gardens and a few of the lesser known ones. So we arranged a tour, bringing away records in the form of photographs, rough plans and sketches.'[38] Many of their visits were made on donkeys, following the same dusty roads Edith Wharton had travelled a year or so earlier. On their return Mawson and Cory built the Pompeiian Garden at Dyffryn in the ancient Roman style, with colonnades, loggias and a fountain. Fired by his enthusiasm for the style of Italian gardens, Johnston would make his own tour of the palaces and gardens of Italy a few years later, though he would travel in a more comfortable manner.

Johnston's interest in gardens would have been additionally stimulated by his fellow officers in the Northumberland Hussars, one of whom was Major the Lord Armstrong of Bamburgh, who had recently inherited the house and gardens at 'Cragside', Rothbury, from his uncle, the first Lord Armstrong.[39] Major Armstrong was known for his lavish entertainments and, no doubt, dined his fellow officers at Cragside during their annual Summer Camp. From the terrace where Edward, the Prince of Wales, had once enjoyed smoking his cigar, Johnston would have seen how the late Lord Armstrong had transformed the barren hillsides of Coquetdale, under the influence of William Robinson's *Wild Garden*, into a picturesque landscape of woodlands, lakes and walks. No doubt his friend, Lieutenant Savile Clayton, would also have taken pleasure in pointing out that the house at Cragside was largely the work of the architect Norman Shaw who had enlarged Chesters. Another Trinity alumnus was Major Miles Backhouse,[40] part of the quaker 'dynasty' of bankers and horticulturists originally from Darlington, and distantly related to the other branch of the family which had established the Backhouse nursery of York. This was among the most successful plant nurseries in England, and often visited by Johnston in later years. There was also interest in horticulture among Miles Backhouse's own family; his father Jonathan had laid out an 'elegant garden' around 'The Rookery' at Middleton Tyas in north Yorkshire. His grandfather, Edmund and his wife Juliet (née Fox) had inherited the celebrated garden at Trebah, near Falmouth in Cornwall. The 30 years of Backhouse ownership was a golden period for Trebah, when it acquired a huge collection of exotic plants and trees from all over the world, including many rhododendrons, magnolias and other 'tender' plants. Finally among his Northumbrian friends was Major Sir Matthew Ridley (see note 17), whose home at Blagdon Hall had been enlarged by the Durham architect Ignatius Bonomi in the 1830s, and set in an eighteenth century parkland.

While Johnston absorbed the features of these gardens, together with information from books and journals, he may also have built on some earlier formal architectural training. His friend Norah Lindsay certainly claimed he had, though there is only sketchy evidence to support this notion. But, as Jane Brown observed, Johnston was 'extremely, compulsively, scrupulous and thorough in everything he did', and such careful preparation can be seen in his soldiering, his farming studies and so, one might assume, in his approach to garden design.[41] Such flimsy evidence as there is suggests that Johnston was already developing an interest in architecture during his time at Cambridge. In her revised account of *Hidcote: the Making of a Garden* (2009), Ethne Clarke notes that at the time he was studying at Trinity, his name also appears on the lists of the newly formed Architecture Department of Columbia College, New York. This suggests that Johnston was uncertain about his future, as to both career and country, but the Columbia programme was designed to prepare young men for study at the École des Beaux-Arts, Paris. So although he did not graduate from Columbia, he may have benefited from some formal architectural training during this time,[42] having accompanied his mother on one or more of her many visits to America. It is quite obvious that, although he always claimed to be more interested in plants, Johnston appreciated design as a creative process, and soon would have the opportunity to put this interest into practice.

THE PURCHASE OF HIDCOTE

Lawrence Johnston was now ready to take the next step towards becoming an English gentleman, that is to say a man of leisure with a passion for gardens, albeit through the generosity of his mother. In 1907 *The Times* carried a notice for sale by auction of the Hidcote Manor estate in Gloucestershire, close to Chipping Campden. The estate was described as a valuable freehold farm comprising nearly 300 acres of land, a village of ten cottages, a blacksmith and the manor house (Fig. 4b). In addition, there was good partridge shooting on the estate, and the meets of the Warwick, North Cotswolds and Heythrop Hunts were within easy hacking distance. The sale notice stated that the farm was in a particularly healthy position, being on a spur of the Cotswolds, at an elevation of 500 to 800 feet above sea level, with fine views over the neighbouring counties. The manor house was described as 'a very substantial and picturesque farmhouse' which included three sitting rooms, eight bedrooms, two box rooms and the usual offices, with lawns in front and to the south side. There was also a large kitchen garden and, of particular interest to Johnston, an adjoining tennis lawn.

The estate had been farmed under a tenancy for 34 years by John Tucker since 1873, when it was originally owned by Captain William Thomas Freeman of Chipping Campden. Upon Freeman's death in December 1882, the estate passed to his widow, Mary Webb Freeman. In August 1893, the estate was left to her daughter, Mary Hannah

Figure 4b Sale plan of Hidcote Manor, c. 1907, which shows the house, a paddock, a nut orchard and building with a yard. In 1919, Gertrude Winthrop purchased part of Hill Farm – the small paddock and field in the centre of the lower part of the plan – which allowed the garden to be extended south.

House and garden

Shekell Freeman who, in 1906, left it to John Tucker. When probate was granted on 30 March 1907, it became apparent that there was an outstanding mortgage of £4,900 and a requirement to pay annual interest of £100 to a cousin of Mary Freeman.[43] Tucker, who was then aged 63, decided that the financial liabilities were too great, and opted to sell the estate as soon as possible. At the auction held in July, at the Noel Arms in Chipping Campden, the property failed to reach its reserve price and was withdrawn from sale when the bidding reached £6,500. Three weeks later Johnston, acting on behalf of his mother, made an acceptable offer of £7,200 for the Hidcote Bartrim estate and paid a deposit of £10.[44]

Characteristically, Mrs Winthrop had already left for America, sailing from Southampton on the *Kronprinz Wilhelm*, bent on spending the late summer season at Bar Harbor on Mount Desert Island, Maine. This was a less formal resort than Newport, though very much favoured by New York's Gilded Society. The *New York Times* reported the 'season' that year gave no signs of being a quiet one, and on 8 September 1907, Gertrude gave a luncheon at the prestigious Malvern Hotel.[45] Among her guests were Constance Cary Harrison, member of a prominent Virginian family, and the celebrated author, Mrs L. E. Opdyke, whose husband was President of the Bar Maine Improvement Society; also Mrs Louis Hassel, granddaughter of Mary Mason Jones, the formidable great-aunt of Edith Wharton. Mary Mason Jones had once been the 'queen' of New York society, and it was said that after hounding her husband to death, she built a fabulous mansion on 54th Street with his money – the phrase 'keeping up with the Jones's' is said to refer to Mary and her sister. Another luncheon guest was Mrs J. Madison Taylor whose husband was a medical specialist in the field of neurasthenics. It may be safely assumed that Mrs Winthrop's purchase of Hidcote Manor in the Cotswolds, England, was a hot topic of conversation over lunch.

Edith Wharton had earlier spent an idyllic time at Bar Harbor during the summer of 1880, exploring what was then a largely unspoilt landscape, and enjoying a flirtation which led to a brief engagement. Edith had stayed with her brother Freddie and his wife Minnie, who had 'set up a cottage' at 'Reef Point' on a few acres near the shore.[46] When Gertrude Winthrop visited Maine in 1907, this house had become the residence of the Jones's daughter, Beatrix, who used the garden as a laboratory in which to explore her ideas of garden design.[47] At that time, she was in the throes of creating gardens for the new and very expensive 'cottages' then being built at Bar Harbor for the Vanderbilts, Morgans and others of Gertrude's acquaintance. At the end of September, Gertrude returned to England to complete the Hidcote purchase arrangements, signing the documents the day after Michaelmas, the customary time for such agricultural exchanges after harvest had been gathered for the benefit of the previous owner. A month later, in October 1907, Gertrude Winthrop and her son Lawrence arrived at Hidcote, and one can only speculate about what this wealthy widow, more accustomed to the sophisticated life of New York society, thought about this rural backwater. Needless to say, she soon returned to New York for the winter season with its usual round of parties, dances and shopping.

Though the sale notice mentioned that the farm was in a good state of cultivation, it has to be remembered that Hidcote Bartrim and its manor, like the rest of rural England, would have suffered from the

Great Depression which had afflicted British farming from 1870 to the turn of the century. This had had a devastating effect on people, villages and the landscape. Many farm labourers left the land, and those who remained were often living in hovels as a result of landlord neglect. So, with declining numbers to work the land, fields often lay fallow. The situation must have been particularly acute at Hidcote Bartrim where the physical attributes of the site in reality were not conducive to profitable agriculture: the site was exposed and the quality of the agricultural land was poor. If farming was Gertrude's only consideration Hidcote Manor was not a good choice, but there was more to the purchase than mere agriculture. It was almost certainly the outcome of a deliberate and careful search, and Mark Fenwick at nearby Abbotswood may well have alerted Lawrence to the sale. However, the real reason for the purchase was the closeness of other Americans in nearby Broadway. With her son's decision to settle in England, Gertrude needed a place that could provide the social life she craved since, as Jane Brown has pointed out, one of the major reasons why Americans liked living in Europe was because they were noticed, and Gertrude liked to be noticed by her own kind.[48] With the purchase of Hidcote Manor came the opportunity to see and be seen, and she hoped it would also restore her beloved Laurie to her.

NOTES AND REFERENCES

[1] On the marriage certificate Gertrude was described as 'unmarried'. In New York, where church and state were separated, the classification 'unmarried' could include those women who were widowed, divorced or never married.

[2] *New York Times*, 17 February 1898; the obituary mentions his association with the Wall Street firm of Drexel, Winthrop and Co.

[3] Anna (Nan) Hope Hudson (1869–1957) was born in New York but brought up in Washington DC after 1870. She inherited a fortune from her mother, who died in 1879, out of which she endowed a fellowship (1895) in the Department of Philosophy, Catholic University of America, Baltimore. She had moved to Paris in 1893 to study painting. She met fellow artist and expatriate American, Ethel Sands, at an art *atelier* in Paris, and both women attended Eugène Carrière's classes in 1896. They became devoted friends and lived together in England at Newington Manor (House) near Oxford, in London and in France for over 60 years. Nan much preferred France, but Ethel became a celebrated London hostess and friend of members of the Bloomsbury set, notably Virginia Woolf, Vanessa Bell, Duncan Grant and Roger Fry; also of Walter Sickert, Desmond MacCarthy, Logan Pearsall Smith and Lady Ottoline

Morrell. Nan Hudson bought the Château d'Auppegard, near Dieppe, in 1920, where she was content to paint and garden, occasionally exhibiting in London with Sands. It is likely that she was often visited in France by her cousin, Lawrence Johnston, when he journeyed south, or with Edith Wharton when staying at St-Brice. Hudson stood in for Johnston at certain events in England, visited Hidcote and was remembered in Johnston's will. See Baron, W., *Miss Ethel Sands and Her Circle*. Peter Owen, London, for details of Hudson's character and artistic capabilities.

[4] Lawn tennis originated among the upper classes in England during the 1870s and was soon all the rage among those wealthy enough to possess a spacious lawn. Clubs were established and tournaments arranged in France, England and America. Edith Wharton joined the Newport Tennis Club, when the game finally superseded archery. Years later Edith and Johnnie would play together, with their mutual friends, in the south of France.

[5] Letter to Sara Norton, 5 June 1903, quoted in Lee, H., *Edith Wharton*. Chatto & Windus, London, p. 95.

[6] Venn, J. S., *Alumni Cantabrigienses, Part 11, Vol. IV*. Cambridge University Press, Cambridge, p. 381.

[7] The Great Court of Trinity is the largest courtyard of any Cambridge college, and was designed by Thomas Neville in 1593. The library was added later by Sir Christopher Wren. The Great Court Run takes place at noon each year, on the day of the Matriculation Dinner, when athletically-minded members of Trinity attempt to run round the 341 metres of the Great Court in the time it takes the College clock to strike twelve.

[8] From Archibald Marshall [Trinity, 1890-1894], *Peter Binney, Undergraduate* (1899).

[9] Venn, op.cit., p. 143.

[10] Day, J., 'Reginald Cory, Benefactor of Cambridge University Botanic Garden'. The Board of Trustees of the Royal Botanic Gardens, Kew, p. 199.

[11] Venn, op.cit., p. 169.

[12] Douglas-Home, J., *Violet – the Life and Loves of Violet Gordon Woodhouse*. Harvill, London, p. 51.

[13] The 1891 census enumerator described boarders at the crammer in Little Shelford, as 'visitors'.

[14] Venn, op.cit., p. 259.

[15] *New York Times*, 17 February 1898.

[16] Another strange coincidence was that Elcho Castle, in the grounds of New Etal Manor, had been owned by the Manners family, the Dukes of Rutland. In 1911, Lady Violet Manners, daughter of Henry, 8th Duke of Rutland, married Hugo Charteris the son of Lord Elcho. Her mother Madeline, the Duchess of Rutland, was the sister of Norah Lindsay who became one of Johnston's close friends.

17 Letter from the Chief Constable, Newcastle upon Tyne, 23 January 1900. The National Archives, HO144/455/B31405. Interestingly, the letter was from the Chief Constable to the Secretary of State at the Home Office, quoting a response from Mary Laing to his enquiry. The Home Secretary was Sir Matthew White – later Viscount – Ridley of Blagdon, MP for North Northumberland and later Blackpool, and a Major in the Northumberland Hussars.

18 Holmes, D., 'The Drill Hall – Northumbria University'. SGU@NU April 2007.

19 The Riding School was designed by the famous Newcastle neo-classical architect John Dobson (1787–1865); adjacent were the regimental headquarters, armoury and stores.

20 Altogether Johnston was awarded the Queen's South Africa Medal with three clasps and the King's South Africa Medal with two clasps.

21 The Worcestershire Yeomanry Cavalry, Worcester City Museums.

22 Wilson, A. N., *The Victorians.* Arrow Books, London, p. 612.

23 When the Yeomanry was reorganized in 1901, the regiment's name changed to the Northumberland Yeomanry, which was disbanded in 1908, when the regiment was renamed Northumberland Hussars (Yeomanry) and became part of the cavalry arm of the Territorial Force.

24 Sitwell, O., *Left Hand Right Hand, Vol. 3 Great Morning.* Macmillan, London, p. 144.

25 Personal communication with Ethne Clarke, 21 September 2005.

26 See Wilson, op.cit., Chapter 40, 'Appearance and Reality', pp. 548–571.

27 Members of the Clayton family had been officers in the Northumberland Hussars since 1886.

28 Clarke suggests that Johnston took lodgings with a nearby landowner, George Ray or Bay, so as to be close to Clayton and renew his farming studies but, although Ray is a familiar name in the parish, this cannot be substantiated. It is possible that Johnston returned to New Etal but there is no evidence to support the claim by Jane Brown that Johnston persuaded his mother to buy a farm at Crookham on the Ford estate.

29 James Robert Pulham, 1873–1957, had taken over the production and installation of pulhamite rock gardens. The process involved pouring cement over clinker and moulding the result into artificial rockwork with such accuracy that the results often deceived specialists.

30 Lord Redesdale of the Batsford Arboretum said that Fenwick was 'the best all round amateur gardener I know, his knowledge of plants is consummate ... he has worked at Abbotswood in such a way as to combine the formality of an Italian architectural garden with the broader wilder lines of a natural woodland scene, the one fading into the other by the skill of imperceptible graduations'. *Country Life*, Vol. 33, No. 841, 22 February 1913, 234–240.

[31] This book was among the first comprehensive, and certainly the most scholarly, studies of English gardening history, written by an author who lived at Hatfield House with access to the Cecil papers.

[32] Page, R., *Education of a Gardener*. Harvill, London, p. 18.

[33] Mawson, T. H., *The Art and Craft of Garden Making*, Batsford, London, was first published in 1901 and, such was its popularity, that a new enlarged edition appeared in 1904. This was the edition borrowed by Johnston.

[34] The title of the book gave its name to the 'arts and crafts' garden, a style pioneered earlier by Lutyens and Jekyll, and loosely based on the ideals of William Morris.

[35] Torode, S., *Dyffryn – an Edwardian Garden*. Glamorgan Record Office Publication, p. 15.

[36] Mawson, op. cit., p. 387.

[37] Plant collectors like Ernest 'Chinese' Wilson sent seeds direct to Dyffryn, including the paper-bark maple (*Acer griseum*). The specimen at Dyffryn is now considered to be among the largest in the country.

[38] Mawson, T. H., *The Life and Work of an English Landscape Architect*. Batsford, London, pp. 138-9.

[39] Major Armstrong had been at Trinity ten years before Johnston.

[40] Miles Roland Charles Backhouse had a distinguished military career and rose to the rank of Lieutenant-Colonel in the Northumberland Hussars.

[41] Brown, J. *The English Garden through the Twentieth Century*. Garden Art Press, Woodbridge, p. 182.

[42] Clarke, E. (2009), *Hidcote: the Making of a Garden*. Revised Edition. Norton, London, p. 29.

[43] 'Cotswold Chatterblog', 29 June 2007.

[44] The insurance was arranged through the Newcastle branch of the Hexham company which Lawrence used – Clarke, op. cit. (2009), p. 33.

[45] *New York Times*, 8 September 1907.

[46] Lee, op.cit., p. 58.

[47] Reef Point, Beatrix Farrand's home, gave its name to the collection of her papers and library, among which were Gertrude Jekyll's garden plans and photographs, which Farrand bought during the early 1940s, rescuing them from destruction. The Reef Point Collection was bequeathed in 1955 to the University of California at Berkeley, where it is held in the Archives of the College of Environmental Design. Farrand died in 1959.

[48] Brown, J., *Eminent Gardeners*. Viking, London, p. 49.

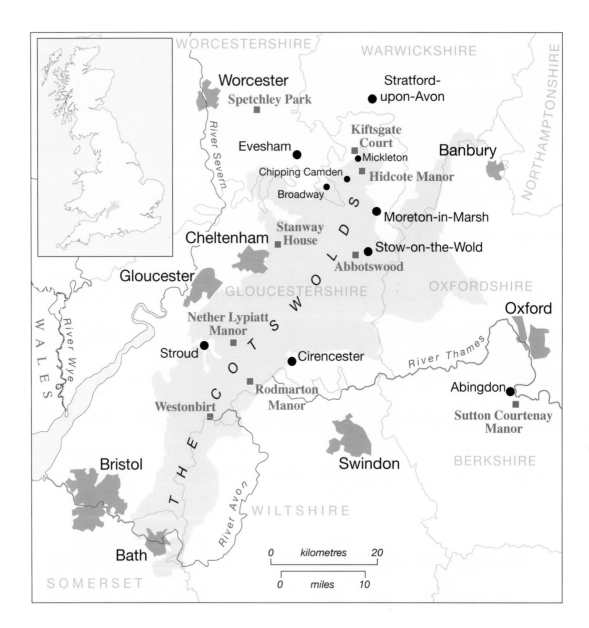

Map 3 The Cotswolds area of England showing the location of many of the gardens and houses of Lawrence Johnston's friends in particular; also the small towns where many expatriate Americans settled in the late nineteenth century.

CHAPTER FIVE

THE COTSWOLDS AND THE AMERICAN DIASPORA

Since 1885 the Cotswolds, in particular the towns of Broadway and Chipping Campden close to Hidcote Bartrim, had become very fashionable for the American diaspora and artists of the Arts and Crafts Movement; there was also a strong undercurrent of Roman Catholicism,[1] encouraged by the presence of the former actress Mary Anderson and her husband Antonio de Navarro, the Papal Privy Chamberlain of the Sword and Cape. The fascination of the area had begun when the American artist 'Frank' D. Millet played host to a small expatriate colony at Broadway. Among the Americans who came in 1885 and the following year, was another artist and Millet's good friend, Edwin Austin Abbey, who in turn brought along another exile, the portraitist John Singer Sargent, a friend of Edith Wharton whom she had met in New York.[2] The author Henry James, another of Wharton's friends, came with his colleague from *Harper's Magazine*, Alfred Parsons, the English artist who was to become 'garden designer' to the Cotswold set.[3] The Anglo-American friendship between Millet, Abbey and Parsons had begun six years earlier and was based on their shared interest in 'Englishness',[4] a familiar subject in Parsons's paintings. Edwin Abbey wanted to immerse himself in English life and had been illustrating aspects of it in *Harper's*, but it was Henry James who ensured the fame of the Cotswolds, when he wrote in the *Harper's New Monthly Magazine* (1889),[5] that 'Broadway and much of the land about it are in short the perfection of the old English rural tradition'.

In the article entitled 'Our Artists in Europe', James said that for this band of creative artists, the people were friendly, the rent was inexpensive, and the Cotswold countryside offered countless lush day-walks from nowhere to nowhere and nothing but gorgeous scenery of a 'very old English village, lying among its meadows and hedges, in the very heart of the country, in a hollow of the green hills'.[6] (Plate 41)

Plate 41 The Village Green, Broadway; an illustration by Alfred Parsons, which appeared in an article written by Henry James entitled 'Our Artists in Europe', in *Harper's New Monthly Magazine*, c. 1889.

MARY ANDERSON

The social attraction of the Cotswolds for the American expatriates was enhanced in 1889, when the popular American actress Mary Anderson settled at Court Farm, Broadway (Plate 42). She had come to England in 1883 and remained for six years, during which time she enjoyed great popularity with audiences and critics in London and Manchester, and also performed with much acclaim at the Shakespeare Memorial Theatre, Stratford upon Avon. While she was in England, she became enchanted with the Cotswolds, with its 'moss-grown farmhouses, its grey steeples, its white cottages clustering under their shadow, its tiny fields, its green hedgerows, garrisoned by mighty elms'.[7] After her return to America in 1889, Anderson collapsed on stage due to nervous exhaustion, exacerbated by hostile press reviews, and at the age of only 30, retired from the stage. Ordered to rest and recuperate, Anderson returned to the Cotswolds and settled at Court Farm, remaining there for the rest of her life with her husband, the New York lawyer Antonio de Navarro. In her autobiography she described Broadway as a 'place of complete freedom. It has no sharp conventional corners. Mental stay-lacing is unknown, and everyone is free and easy as in bedroom slippers'.[8] When Mary Anderson moved to Broadway in 1893, there were two farms on the site; the upper farm, Bell Farm, where her friend the pianist and composer Maud White lived, and the lower, Court Farm. After White left, the Arts and Crafts architect, Andrew Prentice, joined the two farms with a music room, its large elegant stone-mullioned window overlooking the garden (Plate 43).[9]

Within London society Mary Anderson had already established a reputation of being as magnetic in the drawing rooms as she was attractive on stage, and once settled in Broadway she became a noted and indefatigable hostess with a distinguished circle of musical, literary and ecclesiastical guests. 'Madam Anderson', as she became known, would have ensured that Gertrude Winthrop and her son were soon assimilated into Cotswold society, once they had taken up residence at Hidcote. 'We were a merry little colony, all friends –

Plate 42 Mary Anderson de Navarro, c.1894.

Plate 43 Court Farm, Broadway: the striking windows of the music room, designed by Andrew Prentice, overlook the garden laid out by Alfred Parsons, c.1936.

fencing, gardening, riding together'.[10] But one result of the Cotswold's popularity among the American coterie, in the twenty years after Millet, Abbey and Anderson arrived, was to make houses difficult to find and expensive to buy, as Anderson wrote in her autobiography; 'Everyone who visited wanted to live there but no houses were to be had'. So the purchase of Hidcote Manor, five miles from Broadway, was a considerable coup for Mrs Winthrop and her son.

ALFRED PARSONS

Within the Anglo-American community Alfred Parsons played a very special role as a link between American aspiration and actual realisation (Plate 44). When he met Edwin Abbey, he found that the American artist wanted to immerse himself in English life, a subject for which Parsons had already become well known. What Abbey wished to illustrate, and the readers of *Harper's Magazine* wanted to picture, was an England in which the landscape and people were untrammelled by change. Parsons provided this nostalgic vision, and even wrote in his own book that 'the peasants are the real life of a country, preserving habits, costumes, and traditions and staving off for a time the influences of railroads and steamships, which threaten to reduce man's condition throughout the world to one dull level of uniformity'.[11] For his part, Abbey wrote in his diary 'What a lucky fellow I am to drop right into a society I most enjoy and from which

I can learn so much'.[12] Parsons' great gift was to understand and possess the ability to deliver what the American market desired, and from 1885 he extended his painterly idyll of a cottagey, flower-filled garden into the gardens of Broadway and elsewhere, much to the delight of his clients in the American diaspora. Among those clients were Henry James, whose garden at Lamb House, at Rye in Sussex, Parsons designed some time after 1897, and the Navarros' garden at Court Farm in Broadway.

James believed the cottage garden to be the very essence of Englishness and that Parsons was the artist who knew exactly how the Americans would like England to appear. Commenting that garden-making was a national obsession, James suggested that 'one must have lived in other lands to observe how large a proportion of this one is walled in for growing flowers'. He felt Parsons 'had captured that peculiarly English look of the open air room, that nook quality, the air of a land and a life so infinitely subdivided that they produce a thousand pleasantries'.[13] At the heart of Parsons' work was a 'love

of the myriad English flowers', and in the paintings of his garden at Luggers Hall plants tumble out of the borders, in a profusion of flowers and colours (Plates 45 & 46). At Court Farm, whose garden Parsons designed for Mary de Navarro, could be found all the 'peacocks and roses' and 'topiary nookiness' which characterize Johnston's earliest efforts in garden design, along with coppices, orchards and formal avenues of lime trees. Perhaps an even more significant influence on the design of Hidcote, was the 'scenic approach' Parsons used to lead the eye away from the formal, old-fashioned parterres and clipped yews near the house, to the open prospect of the hillside beyond. This was in the spirit of the Aesthetic Movement's philosophy, to which Parsons subscribed, of designing the total view.[14]

ARRIVAL AT HIDCOTE

After her arrival at Hidcote, Mrs Winthrop transferred the somewhat matriarchal position she had held in New York society into the role of Lady of the Manor. She was also referred to as 'Madam', and became deeply involved with the welfare of the Hidcote staff and the spiritual well-being of the children from the hamlet of Hidcote Bartrim and the nearby village of Mickleton. Together mother and son must have been imposing, if not unusual or eccentric, figures in this rural backwater: he was always meticulously dressed, often in riding attire, and she was always swathed tightly in a long dove-grey satin dress, 'as though she was in the royal enclosure at Ascot', or perhaps more accurately, the drawing rooms of New York. Those who knew her recalled that she was very stern of manner with piercing blue eyes that could silence an unruly child at ninety paces (see her look at the photographer in Plate 31), especially when sighted through her lorgnette.

One visitor to Hidcote shortly after their arrival may have had far-reaching consequences for the gardens. In 1907 Beatrix Jones was doing the rounds of Cotswold gardens 'under the friendly and delightful Parsons wing'[15] and together they visited Court Farm to see the garden Alfred Parsons had designed for the Navarros. They also called on Johnston's new neighbour, Mark Fenwick, at Abbotswood, and social etiquette would have dictated a visit to Mrs Winthrop, a fellow member of the summer colony at Bar Harbor. Did they perhaps discuss plans for the new garden over tea, whilst Farrand explained her ideas about the American Country House garden to Lawrence? In that year Beatrix had described her approach to garden design in an article for *Scribner's Magazine* entitled 'The Garden as a Picture'[16] in which she discussed the great Italian garden artists, using the formal Medici garden of the Villa Castello as an illustration. Beatrix, like her aunt Edith, did not believe in simply copying a garden from another country and culture, but spoke of adaptation and the need for a garden to be 'in scale with its natural surroundings, as well as appropriate to them'. She sought a balance in her gardens between European classicism and American naturalism, deriving in part from Olmsted and Charles Sprague Sargent, with the additional 'picturesque' natural beauty of Robinson and Jekyll. This is what Johnston ultimately would try to achieve in making the gardens at Hidcote.

Almost before Johnston could become established at Hidcote, his mother decided she wished to sell up and find somewhere to live near Bath. After five years Gertrude Winthrop told her solicitor she wished to move for reasons of health, something she attributed to the hardness of the water, soft water being almost a mania with her. These must have been difficult times at Hidcote, for Gertrude believed her 'treasured son was growing away from her'.[17] The more she tried to protect and bind him to her, the further he withdrew not just from her but from staff and others close to him. In later years local people, who had grown up while Mrs Winthrop and her son were at Hidcote, recalled that Johnston was rarely there and, when he was present, he was rarely seen.[18] There may well have been friction between Lawrence and his mother, but it must be remembered that Johnston also had an army career, as well as friendship with Savile Clayton and a wide circle of friends with common interests in gardens and tennis. He was also an experienced horseman, dating from his time in Northumberland and South Africa, and when his cousins, James 'Monte' Waterbury – four years Lawrence's junior – and his brother Lawrence, visited England as part of the American polo team, his recreational interests would have been enhanced.[19]

Mrs Winthrop's intention to leave Hidcote was constantly interrupted during these years by her frequent visits to Europe and America; in 1910, for example, she was travelling in Italy, and in the following year she was in New York as usual for the season. Meanwhile at Hidcote it soon became apparent that Johnston's interests were not in farming, and so management of the estate was handed over to a farm bailiff, George Wheeler. It was said that Johnston used to spend his mornings on the farm after which his attention would be drawn to other interests. It is not known whether those other activities included gardening.[21] Yet for wealthy gentlemen, such as Lawrence Johnston, the years before the First World War were a time of endless leisure and frequent house parties. Hermione Lee has pointed out that there were two main models of high society on offer. 'One was that of the aristocratic, land-owning, Liberal or Tory hostess with her big houses in London and in the country, for networking, lionising, politics, hunting and adultery'. The other interconnected milieu was the 'world of writers, artists and their friends – mainly establishment figures – with their clubs and dinners and well established social rounds and their country houses'.[22] Johnston's hankering was for the former strand of society since he was after all extremely status-conscious. Likewise Edith Wharton who, though she dabbled with the latter, found their company dull and parochial, and much preferred the English aristocracy as a source of theatre and amusement.

LADY ELCHO AND THE SOULS

Johnston's introduction to local Cotswold society most probably began with an invitation to a weekend party, Saturday to Monday as was usual, at Stanway House in Broadway (Plate 47), the home of Lord and Lady Elcho, where perhaps he was renewing an acquaintance with the family he had first met in Northumberland. Lady Elcho was among the most energetic and glittering hostesses of the age, always on the lookout for wealthy, eligible bachelors to pair with suitable partners. Johnston must have seemed ideal; he not only played tennis, rode and played the piano but stood to inherit a considerable fortune; and in spite of his outward diffidence, he had a likeable sociability. For his part, Johnston would soon have fallen under what the Elcho's daughter, Lady Cynthia Asquith, described in her memoirs 'as the spell of Stanway'. The Jacobean house standing in its own grounds had 'an atmosphere of peace and calm' which 'permeated the golden Cotswold stone ... fostered by long lawns and ancient trees'.[23]

Plate 47 Stanway House.

Soon after moving to Stanway in 1883, Mary Elcho had made the house the spiritual centre of 'The Souls', a group of English aristocrats who were united in their pursuit of the aesthetic life. It was Lord Charles Beresford in the late 1880s who claimed to have first used the term to describe them, since they were always talking about each other's Soul. The original members of the group were wealthy patrons of the Arts and Crafts designers, and many were themselves talented amateur artists, sculptors and painters. 'Souls' society was dominated by women who were admired for their social gifts, beauty and a sense of fun and fantasy; but they could be intensely serious too. Their philosophy of life was based on Christianity, patriotism and the triumph of optimism, and for this reason they disapproved of the many aimless and extravagant pursuits undertaken by their social contemporaries, such as racing, hunting and card games, all of which were regarded as vulgar and extravagant. The Souls had a contempt for gambling. The group, however, was fond of golf, bicycling, tennis, and they enjoyed music and avant-garde art – of the kind seen at the Grosvenor Gallery.[24] The Souls were also avid readers and, in particular, enjoyed the contemporary novels of Edith Wharton and Henry James.

Lord Balfour Lady Wemyss

Edith Wharton made her first visit to Stanway in December 1909 for a weekend party arranged in her honour by Lord Hugo and Lady Mary Elcho. She was delighted by the conversation, that 'ranged brilliantly over literature, science, politics and art' in the 'eighteenth century drawing room with its Tudor ceilings and Queen Anne mirrors and log fires that warmed the part of the body that turned toward it'.[25] In the years following, Wharton often visited Stanway, and on one notable occasion fell off her bicycle in Broadway during an excursion. Wharton was much taken with Mary Elcho, who, in later years known as Mary Wemyss, would become the one English woman to whom she was most devoted (Plate 48).

In those golden Edwardian years – golden being a favourite word used by the Souls – visitors to Stanway, such as Johnston and Wharton, would enjoy a gentle programme that included walks in the garden, accompanied by Lady Elcho and her numerous Chow dogs (see Plate 48). After the purchase of a motor car, excursions went further afield into the Cotswold countryside with visits to the Guild of Handicrafts in Chipping Campden, established originally by C. R. Ashbee.[26] Then there were games of tennis, village cricket and croquet, along with household pastimes, word games and charades with the emphasis on hilarity rather than

erudition. At dinner, one of the 'great joys of Stanway was the talk' which the Elcho's youngest daughter described as exhilarating. Guests were expected to display quickness of thought, wit and verbal dexterity, and one wonders how the rather reserved, diffident Johnston responded to this challenge. But Lady Elcho was renowned for her skills at making all her guests shine: 'Nobody was allowed to feel nervous or inadequate for a moment. If they were, the hostess (and her children as they grew older) came to their rescue. Anyone left out of the conversation was thrown a lifeline across the table to help them re-enter.'[27]

Lawrence Johnston was never one of The Souls and only ever appeared on the fringes of this glittering society, but Lady Elcho remained a friend throughout his life, often visiting Hidcote and Serre de la Madone, his other garden in the south of France, until her death in 1937. Many others within the circle became his lifelong friends and among the closest in later life was Norah Lindsay, sister-in-law of Violet, the Duchess of Rutland, who epitomised the Souls' credo with her beauty and artistic talents. Nancy Lancaster,[28] though not a member of the Souls, was a close friend of many in the group and believed Johnston first met Norah Lindsay at Stanway in 1907.[29] Lancaster, too, later became a close friend of Johnston and often stayed at Hidcote.

By the time Johnston visited Stanway, the Souls had mellowed, and Lady Elcho and the other original members of the group, were making way for a new generation of young artists, aristocrats and politicians, many of whom were their sons and daughters, whose intent was to challenge the conventions of polite society. The 'Corrupt Coterie', as the succeeding group was known, flourished in the hectic years immediately before and during the First World War, and was led by Lady Diana Manners, the daughter of the Duke of Rutland. In the 1920s and '30s, Lady Diana became a regular visitor to Hidcote, after her marriage to Duff Cooper. Vita Sackville-West admired the Coterie's 'devil may care attitude' and expressed a similar desire to enjoy the present 'we may all be dead tomorrow, or there may be a war or an earthquake'.[30] Little did anyone realize how imminent that danger was or that the Great War would cut down many of the Coterie's number and, in so doing, greatly reduce its influence. By then, members of the American diaspora had also lost interest in the Cotswolds, and attention had been transferred to the glamour of the French Riviera, thus leaving that quiet, rural backwater to those with more horticultural interests. The First World War, too, finally brought an end to any lingering thoughts that Gertrude Winthrop may have had of moving from Hidcote Manor.

NOTES AND REFERENCES

1 Brown, J., *Eminent Gardeners.* Viking, London p. 48

2 **Francis ('Frank') Davis Millet** (1846–1912) was a noted journalist, intrepid traveller and talented artist. He was born in Massachusetts, and survived the Civil War on the Union side. He graduated from Harvard in 1869, became a journalist in Boston, and then studied art in Antwerp in 1871. He was a highly successful war correspondent for American and British newspapers, in particular during the Russo-Turkish War (1877–78), before returning to Paris to devote himself seriously to art studies. He served on the Fine Arts Jury at the 3rd Paris Exposition Universelle of 1878. He married Elizabeth ('Lily') Merrell in 1879 in Paris – Mark Twain was his best man – before returning to the States to paint and work for various Boston newspapers. *Harper's* magazine sent him back to Europe to write and illustrate articles, and he settled in England at Russell House, Broadway, in the Cotswolds around 1885, where he was host to a small (rather wild) colony of artists and writers. The Millets had four children, two of their sons being named Edwin and John Alfred Parsons. 'Lily' Millet joined the gardening circle and became an expert gardener in her own right, specializing in raising and cultivating carnations. The artistic colony gradually dispersed and, back in the US, Millet became involved in many committees at art schools and museums in New York and Boston, as well as travelling extensively. He was a war correspondent again in 1889, this time in the Philippines. From 1904 to 1911, he was Head of the American Academy in Rome. Tragically, he died in the *Titanic* disaster of April 1912. His body was recovered and buried in the Central Cemetery at East Bridgewater, Massachusetts.

Edwin Austin Abbey (1846–1911) was an illustrator and artist, born in Philadelphia. After studying at the Pennsylvania Academy of Fine Art, he became an illustrator for *Harper's Magazine* aged 19. He moved to England in 1878 where he befriended many expatriate American and British artists, notably Millet, Sargent, Parsons and the Pre-Raphaelite Brotherhood. In summer he lodged with Millet at Broadway. His success as an artist led to his becoming a Royal Academician in 1898, though he remained an American citizen, despite being offered a knighthood. His other commissions included murals for the Boston Library and Pennsylvania State Capitol, which were unfinished at the time of his death in London in August 1911.

John Singer Sargent (1856–1925) was a prolific artist and the most successful portrait painter of his era. His parents were from Philadelphia but travelled widely in Europe, basing themselves in Italy, where Sargent was born in Florence. Later they moved to France, where Sargent studied at the École des Beaux-Arts in Paris. He also studied in Switzerland, Rome and Florence. He visited America for the first time in 1876, to secure his American citizenship. A large proportion of his time was spent in Europe, where he was based in Paris, and then England, becoming famous for his portraits of the *haut monde*. He painted portraits of Edith Wharton's close friends, Egerton Leigh Winthrop in 1901 and Henry James in 1913, and the elderly Frederick Law Olmsted in 1895. His first great success at the Royal Academy came in 1887 with the 'Carnation, Lily, Lily, Rose', a scene of two young girls lighting lanterns in a stylised English garden. It was painted over two seasons in the garden of Russell House, Broadway, and was immediately purchased by the Tate Gallery. His output was prodigious, over 900 paintings and 2000 watercolours plus other sketches and drawings but, by the time of his death in England, he was dismissed as a relic of the Gilded Age, out of step with modern trends in art and the realism of post-World War One Europe.

3   **Alfred Parsons** (1847–1920) was born in Somerset, and in 1867 decided to devote his life to art. His first painting was hung at the Royal Academy in 1871 and he exhibited frequently at Burlington House, and at the Grosvenor Gallery, the home of the Aesthetic Movement. He became an illustrator for *Harper's Magazine*, and in 1894 published an illustrated article on his travels in Japan. A specialist in drawing naturalistic subjects, particularly flowers, Parsons was commissioned by William Robinson to illustrate his books, including the *Wild Garden*, after 1895. He also collaborated with Ellen Willmott, providing the etchings for her major work *The Genus Rosa*.

4   Mako, M., (2006) 'Painting With Nature in Broadway, Worcestershire', *Garden History*, **34** (1), 49.

5   There were several American illustrated literary, political and scientific magazines launched during the mid to late 19th century. Notable among the popular literary journals were *Harper's New Monthly Magazine* (1850), the *Century Magazine* (1881) and *Scribner's Magazine* (1887), all founded in New York. At first British writers were published, but increasingly American work took precedence, and writers such as Edith Wharton and Henry James contributed articles that appealed to the interests of the American diaspora. *Harper's* is still published, but the other literary journals ceased publication in the 1930s.

6   James, H. (1889) 'Our Artists in Europe', *Harper's New Monthly Magazine*, **179**(469), 50–66.

7   Farrer, J.M., *Mary Anderson*. Gutenberg eBook [eBook #14758].

8   de Navarro, M., *A Few More Memories*. Hutchinson, London, p. 132.

9   Andrew Prentice (1866–1941), was a Scottish architect who designed many Arts and Crafts houses in Gloucestershire and Worcestershire, noted for their exceptional refinement. He had been involved with Court Farm since 1900.

10 de Navarro, op. cit., p. 132.

11 Parsons, A., *Notes in Japan*, Harper, New York, p. 157.

12 Lucas, E., *Edwin Austin Abbey, Royal Academician*, Vol. 1. Methuen, London, p. 73.

13 Alfrey, N., 'On Garden Colour', in *The Art of the Garden*. Tate Publishing, London, p. 37.

14 The Aesthetic Movement (1870–1900) in Britain and America was a loosely defined movement in literature, fine art and decorative art, summed up by the slogan 'art for art's sake'. Its adherents believed the arts should provide refined sensual pleasure rather than be moralistic or sentimental. Symbols, such as the peacock and the colours green, yellow and blue – the 'greenery yallery, Grosvenor Gallery' satirised by W. S. Gilbert in the operetta *Patience* – were widely used. The movement came to an end after the trial of Oscar Wilde in 1895, but led the way into the Arts and Crafts period which followed (1900–25).

15 Brown, J., *Beatrix– the gardening life of Beatrix Jones Farrand*. Viking, London, p. 87.

16 Farrand, B., 'The Garden as a Picture', *Scribner's Magazine*, July 1907.

17 Clarke, E., *Hidcote*. Michael Joseph, London, p. 23.

18 Ibid.

19 James 'Monte' Waterbury and his brother Lawrence were part of the American polo team known as the 'Big Four' which successfully won the world championships at Hurlingham in 1909. Their success continued until 1914 when the team, captained by Monte Waterbury, was finally defeated at Westbury, New York.

20 Pearson suggests that Mrs Winthrop's desire to move from Hidcote may have been related to the sudden death of Johnston's younger brother Elliot early in 1912. Pearson, G., *Hidcote*, National Trust, p. 14.

21 Johnston was said to have asked a local man, William Pearce, to help with the garden in about 1907, but he may have had in mind help with just the vegetable garden.

22 Lee, H., *Edith Wharton*. Chatto & Windus, London, p. 233.

23 For an account about The Souls, see Abdy, S. and Gere, C. *The Souls*. Sidgwick and Jackson, London, p. 102.

24 The Grosvenor Gallery, founded in 1877 by Sir Coutts Lindsay and his wife Blanche, with the conductor, Charles Hallé, as one of the co-directors, was important to the Aesthetic Movement by providing a show place for artists whose works were unacceptable to the more classical and conservative Royal Academy, such as Burne Jones, Sargent, Watts and Whistler, all of whom received commissions from members of The Souls.

25 Lewis, R.W.B., *Edith Wharton: a biography*. Constable, London, p. 244.

26 The Guild of Handicraft was established in Chipping Campden by C. R. Ashbee in 1888, but closed in 1907. After 1908 the Guild was continued by George Hart and his son Henry.

27 Abdy & Gere, op. cit., p. 104.

28 Nancy Lancaster (1897–1994) was a wealthy American born in Virginia, niece of Lady Astor at Cliveden. In 1920 she married the bi-sexual journalist and investor Robert Tree and moved to England in 1927. They took a 10-year lease on Kelmarsh Hall, Northamptonshire, later moving to Ditchley Park, Oxfordshire, until their divorce in 1947. She was instrumental in developing the English Country House look, and was described by the British designer, David Hicks, as the most influential garden designer since Gertrude Jekyll.

29 Personal communication with Ethne Clarke, 21 September 2005.

30 Nicolson, J., *The Perfect Summer: dancing into shadow. England in 1911.* John Murray, London, p. 88.

CHAPTER SIX

EDITH WHARTON IN ENGLAND

While Johnston settled in at Hidcote, Edith Wharton was considering the possibility of moving to England, an interest that would continue until the outbreak of the First World War. Her passion for France, which would eventually become part of her very being, was still some way off. Even after staying at the Vanderbilts' apartment in the rue de Varenne, Paris, in 1906, Wharton was undecided as to where to make her future home. Henry James promoted the idea of an English life. As an Anglophile himself, he fancied the idea of Edith Wharton as a grand 'English' hostess, living, not surprisingly given his enthusiasm for the Cotswolds, in a splendid old house in Gloucestershire. For Wharton's part, she found the idea of living in England appealing. She had first visited England with her father, and though not as familiar with the country as she was with Italy, or increasingly with France, Wharton had been 'an enthusiast for English culture, literature, landscape, gardens, and houses since she was very young'.[1] In 1903 Edith wrote to Sara Norton, telling her that 'In England I like it *all* – institutions, traditions, mannerisms, conservatisms, everything but the womens' clothes, & then having to go to church every Sunday'.[2] Later she would tell her friend Elisina Tyler that 'the country and I were made for each other – but for the winter climate'.[3] Wharton found the grey overcast and damp days as disagreeable as the long winter cold of Lenox.

WHARTON AND THE ARISTOCRACY

After the publication of the *House of Mirth,* Wharton was feted by the aristocracy in England and could expect a welcome at any of their houses. In his biography of her, Percy Lubbock describes Wharton's imperious arrival at an English House Party, where she knew the people well:

> I can see her still, rustling forward with her quick step, hitching her scarf round her shoulders, advancing into the midst of the vast hall and the scattered company with a smile of embracing familiarity, with flying looks and side-glances of understanding, with an air of amused and confident anticipation.[4]

On those occasions, Wharton appeared to Lubbock – who was a good friend – 'simpler, easier, younger ... without a care on her mind among people who had none on theirs, without a strain on her resources among people who didn't tax their own'.[5] Wharton found herself among very influential women, similar to those in the New York society of her novels. Some were expatriate Americans she had known from her childhood days. Adèle Grant, the daughter of a wealthy New York stockbroker, was an old friend now married to the widowed Seventh Earl of Essex. After marrying in 1893, the couple had spent their honeymoon at Cassiobury House at Watford in Hertfordshire, once among the most celebrated houses and gardens in England (Plate 49). The gardens at Cassiobury were first laid out by Moses Cook (1660–1715), who presented the first pineapple grown in England to King Charles II. His partner in business, George London, laid out avenues there and, early in the eighteenth century, Charles Bridgeman also worked on the layout of the estate. At the end of that century, the Fifth Earl commissioned James Wyatt to remodel the house in the Romantic Gothic style, while Humphry Repton landscaped the park. Unfortunately, the Sixth Earl neglected the house over the next 50 years, and when his grandson inherited, it was in a poor state of repair. Many paintings and other works of art had to be sold to pay for repairs, but after Adèle's arrival parties and other entertainments resumed, with King Edward VII and Winston Churchill among the guests.

Plate 49 Adele Capell (*née* Grant) *c.* 1892, second wife of the 7th Earl of Essex, one of the so-called 'Lovely Five'.

When Edith Wharton first visited England, Adèle and her family were living at Bourdon House in Mayfair, in London – 'one of the last country houses to survive in that intensely urban quarter' – but at weekends there were large parties in the country at Cassiobury. In her autobiography, Wharton describes a Sunday, at the end of a brilliant London season, when 'my husband and I motored down there for lunch, we found scattered under the great cedars, the very flower and pinnacle of the London World'.[6] Among the guests were Lady Elcho, Henry James and John Singer Sargent. In the end, not even a wealthy American heiress could save Cassiobury, and when Lord Essex could no longer afford to maintain the house, the family moved permanently to London.[7]

The Astors at Cliveden, who had once been a part of Wharton's former New York world, were altogether more successful and celebrated. The house and estate had been bought in 1893 by William Waldorf Astor, heir to an immense American fortune. In 1882 he had been appointed US Minister in Rome, when he was only 34 years old, and from then on Astor reverted to his family's European roots and his life acquired, in his grandson's words 'a pattern of formalistic behavior which fell somewhere between that of a Roman emperor and his idea of a medieval baron'.[8] He collected ancient sculpture, along with medieval and Renaissance works of art, as well as associating with artists then working in Rome. On completion of his diplomatic duties, Astor bought Cliveden. Its imposing Italianate style, designed by Sir Charles Barry for the Second Duke of Sutherland in 1850, must have reminded him of the ancient and renaissance villas he had seen in Italy. The similarity of the garden front at Cliveden to the Villa Albani has often been noted.

When his son Waldorf married the Virginian heiress Nancy Langhorne in 1905, William Waldorf Astor gave them Cliveden and its collections as a wedding present. Nancy soon established herself as a celebrated hostess, and Cliveden entered its golden age, at the centre of political and literary society. Wharton first visited Cliveden in 1908 and returned four years later, with Henry James, who was a regular guest. On that occasion he became ill and was packed off back to his home in Rye, much to his personal relief since a stay at Cliveden was often a turbulent experience. But one can imagine that as her car swept past the Fountain of Love,[9] and Wharton saw the imposing north façade of Cliveden appear through the mists of a white morning in late November,[10] she would have felt every inch, the American duchess.

Nancy Astor was 17 years Wharton's junior, but they had much in common. Nancy was witty and saucy in conversation, though a devout churchgoer, yet almost prudish in her behaviour – a characteristic that appealed to older socialites like Wharton, though she in turn was not religious. But was there perhaps a tinge of envy in Wharton's feelings towards the chatelaine of this all-too-perfect Italianate villa? Stepping from the dining room on to the upper terrace, Wharton would have been reminded of The Mount, with its view over the garden and the surrounding landscape. At Cliveden, she would have caught a glimpse of the river Thames and Windsor Castle in the distance; and as she came down the steps to the lower terrace, Wharton would have seen

the balustrade from the Villa Borghese, so familiar from her childhood years in Rome (Plate 50). It was William Waldorf Astor's most inspired addition to the garden.[11]

Nevertheless, Wharton's experience of the upper echelons of English society was not entirely pleasurable. She admired the way in which it was socially acceptable for society women to pursue their own interests, as had not been the case in her own upper-class New York. Some women were patrons of the arts: her friend Gladys, the Marchioness of Ripon, whose sense of fun and quick enthusiasms always delighted Wharton,[12] was a great patron of opera and ballet, especially the Ballets Russes. At her home, Coombe Court in Surrey, Lady Ripon held celebrated dinner parties to which opera singers, artists and the literati were invited. Others, like the Duchess of Sutherland, were writers on a modest scale. Much later, Nancy Astor would become the first female MP, after the death of her husband. But though Wharton's own egotism, and snobbishness, meant that she enjoyed visiting the houses and gardens of the aristocracy, she objected to the sort of literary lionising which gave her entry to this society. Wharton found the people she met parochial and 'rather narrowly confined to their own topics';[13] she much preferred the intellectual freedom and stimuli she found in France.

Plate 51 Mary Jeune, later Lady St Helier.

CLOSE WOMEN FRIENDS

Wharton had just three particular British friends among all the upper-class women she had met. One was Lady Weymss (also known as Lady Elcho), whose house at Stanway was where she felt most comfortable and secure; another was Lady St Helier (Plate 51), also known as Lady Jeune, who at a first glance was the very opposite of the more reticent Wharton. During the last 30 years of the nineteenth century, Lady Jeune had been the leading society hostess of her day, prompting one American visitor to say that 'fortunate were those who, visiting London, took with them a letter of introduction to Lady Jeune'. As the daughter of an impoverished highland family, she had had an austere and simple upbringing, but achieved her position in society 'as much through her personality and natural gifts as through her aristocratic connections'.[14] When Lady Jeune's memoirs appeared in 1909, her publisher, Edward Arnold, said, of her parties and salons, that they were:

> ... the rendezvous of all that was best in society, the meeting place of men distinguished in literature, science, and art, famous generals and naval officers, legal luminaries and apostles of culture. It would probably be difficult to mention a single person of distinction, of either sex, who had not at some time or other been present at her receptions ... Her salons were the English counterpart of the brightest French salons.[15]

Plate 52 Arlington Manor, near Newbury.

Edith Wharton met Lady Jeune during one of her earlier visits to London, and in her autobiography observed that Mary Jeune could hardly have been more remote from her own tastes and interests. 'She was,' said Wharton, 'a born entertainer according to the London idea, which regarded, and perhaps, still regards the fighting through a straggling crowd of celebrities as the finest expression of social intercourse.'[16] Wharton had little interest in celebrities en masse, except for 'one or two of my own craft'. Nevertheless, Wharton and Lady Jeune became 'fast friends and my affections and admiration for her grew with the growth of our friendship'.

In 1905 Lady Jeune sold her country house, Arlington Manor near Newbury, Berkshire (Plate 52), and lived in London. Her parties became less frequent, and she took an increasingly jaundiced view of society, seeing it dominated by 'Mincing Lane millionaires', meaning newly arrived rich entrepreneurs. When her social life became less attractive, she turned to her other interests in politics and charitable work. Committed to helping the needy, Lady Jeune helped to organise the supply of thousands of hot meals for the needy in winter, and a holiday fund for children in summer – anticipating Wharton's own activities in the war, a few years later. In 1910 Lady Jeune became an Alderman on London County Council and took an almost proprietorial interest in the Garden City Movement, influenced by the New Zealand town planner Charles Compton Reade.[17] In 1928 London County Council began work on a vast garden city at Mitcham in Surrey, among the last remaining lavender fields, and named it the Lady St. Helier Estate.[18]

Wharton's other friend in England was very different. Mary Hunter was married to 'Charlie', the son of a wealthy coal entrepreneur with extensive mining interests in America, who was also a Tory MP. When Wharton first met her, she was 'beautiful, wealthy (as can be seen in Sargent's portrait – Plate 53), hospitable and boundlessly generous'.[19] The Hunters lived in a large house in Essex near Theydon Bois where Mary organised extravagant, and very haphazard parties, filling the house with artists, writers and musicians. Hill Hall, Theydon Mount, was an elegant late sixteenth century house, with a French-style inner courtyard and a splendid eighteenth century east front with giant columns and a grand pediment. The magazine *Country Life* noted that on the terrace were 'masses of lavender bushes against the house but no flowers' and 'great box bushes' in terracotta jars along the terrace (Plate 54).[20] A simple grass sward led the eye from a long stone terrace down to the lake. The broad swathe of grounds had been landscaped by Humphry Repton, with views towards the village church spire in one direction

Plate 53 Mary Hunter; a portrait by John Singer Sargent.

Plate 54 The south front of Hill Hall, Theydon Mount.

and the trees of Epping Forest in the other, with London in the far distance. But the exterior was of no interest to Mary Hunter who was not attracted to gardening; according to Wharton, she was 'congenitally incapable of interesting herself in horticulture'[21] and 'used to walk away if women talked of flower beds'.[22] Her only attempts at gardening was a 'made-to-order rose-garden' of which Percy Lubbock remarked 'it looked as if no-one had ever said a kind word to it'.[23] However her interior design was, according to Hermione Lee, spectacularly good. Edith Wharton would have responded positively to the dining-room with its panelled walls and ceilings taken from a Venetian house, the beautiful cupboards lifted from Italian sacristies and the fine Italian beds.[24]

When Ellen Willmott, the celebrated English gardener (Plate 55), visited Hill Hall, she was scathing about Mary's horticultural neglect, and is said to have remarked: 'Now ... Mary could have planted the beds with dressed crab and red cabbage, with large patches of cheese straws ...'[25] The mention of dressed crab alludes to the fact that Mary Hunter was prosecuted for hoarding food during the Great War, but continued to feed her guests with dressed crab throughout. Willmott

Plate 55 (left) Ellen Willmott.

Plate 56 (above) Warley Place, Essex.

was an influential gardener in England, who lived close by at Warley Place (Plate 56). She also owned gardens in France at Aix-les-Bains, and Boccanegra at Ventimiglia in Italy. Whereas Gertrude Jekyll, who was her great admirer, was a garden designer, Ellen Willmott was among the finest plantswomen of her day. Her garden at Warley extended to 55 acres (*c.* 22.25 hectares), and in its heyday, 104 gardeners were employed to tend the 100,000 species and varieties of plants grown there. Narcissi were a particular favourite, and she planted thousands of daffodils in the park, alongside wild species collected from all parts of Asia and Europe.[26] Willmott also had a passion for roses and, between 1910 and 1914, she wrote and published her master work, *The Genus Rosa*, illustrated superbly by Alfred Parsons.

Ellen Willmott lost most of her fortune in the First World War, and as she grew older she became increasingly eccentric and cantankerous. After her visit in 1923, Edith Wharton described, in a letter to Beatrix Farrand, the effect this had had on the garden at Warley. For Wharton, the visit turned out to be another occasion when she 'failed' to rise to the challenge of meeting a doyenne of English gardening:

I managed to see Miss Wilmot's [sic] garden (& the lady herself!) while I was at Hill. Mrs Hunter took me over with two or three people that Miss Wilmot knew (or knew about), so she paid not the slightest attention to *me*, & I was glad she didn't, as I felt half asleep, & I couldn't remember the name of a single plant! However, it all interested me *afterward* – you know how one sometimes wakes out of these trances, & finds that one has mopped up something with one's spongy brain? The little enclosed gardens must have been lovely when they were less jungly, but the wild garden that happens suddenly in the lawn in front of the house I thought appalling. The plants, of course, were most interesting, & all in glowing health – & considering she has reduced her staff almost to vanishing point it's a marvel to see such vigor of vegetation. I wish I could go back there some day with a clear brain, & a notebook.[27]

After Ellen Willmott died in 1934, many of the plants she had collected, or bred at Warley, were transferred to the garden of her sister Rose Berkeley, at Spetchley Park, Worcester; Rose was one of Lawrence Johnston's gardening friends.

In her biography of Edith Wharton, Hermione Lee notes how important Mary Hunter was to her life, and in her relationship with Henry James. James and Mary Hunter were close friends but, though he regarded her as stylish and gallant, he found her, like Wharton, to be an insistent hostess. This could lead to friction and, whenever Edith was planning a visit to England, the most delicate negotiations went on between the three of them. On one occasion, when a visit from Edith was pending, James wrote to Mary Hunter, begging her to 'stay' her 'hand a little as regard marked emphasis or pressure in urging her do so'. His reluctance, he explained, was because:

... if she [Edith Wharton] does come she will come wound up for an extensive *motor-tour* of these islands, in which she will look to me (very graciously and generously look) to accompany her. Now it happens that ... very much continuous and sustained and long drawn out motoring ... is the worst thing in the world for my health. If I could see her without that formidable question coming up it would be *admirable*! – but in fact it *always* comes up ... I haven't said Do, *do* come and we will tour over England, Scotland and Wales ... I think that what my little plea really amounts to is that you should most kindly not appear to throw me at all into the scales of persuasion. That is all that is asked of you by so precautionary and devoted old HENRY JAMES.[28]

HENRY JAMES

Edith Wharton had been friends with Henry James since 1904, when she and her husband first stayed at his home, Lamb House, Rye, in East Sussex. Afterwards James visited The Mount at Lenox on several occasions, and he had spent weeks travelling in France and Italy with Edith and Teddy. At first Wharton regarded James, 20 years her senior, as a mentor but after the publication of her novel *The House of Mirth*, their relationship became that of mutually respectful authors. In time, their friendship developed into one of deep affection as well as sharpness, bafflement, exasperation and, not least, contradiction. When in England, Wharton would divide her time between staying at Qu'Acre, Hill Hall and Lamb House. In her reminiscences she describes how a visit always began with an almost ritual performance, starting with:

> ... a large hug, and the two kisses executed in the middle of the hall rug. Then, arm in arm, through the oak-panelled morning room we wandered onto the thin worn turf of the garden, with its ancient mulberry tree, its unkempt flower borders, the gables of Watchbell Street peeping like village gossip over the creeper clad walls, and the scent of roses spiced with the strong smell of the sea. Up and down the lawn we strolled with many pauses, exchanging news, answering each others questions, delivering messages from other members of the group, inspecting the strawberries and the lettuces, in the tiny kitchen garden and the chrysanthemums in the greenhouse; till at length the parlour maid appeared with a tea tray and I was led up rickety outdoor steps to the garden-room, that stately unexpected appendage to the unadorned cube of the house.[29]

But James was not a natural host, even though he needed company. He lived a frugal life and went in terror of being thought rich, worldly or luxurious, often comparing his visitors' ideas of his supposed opulence and self-indulgence with his own hermit-like asceticism, all

Plate 57 Henry James, c.1905.

the time apologising for his poor food, whilst trembling that it might be thought too good. When Wharton looked back on her visits she wondered whether James 'did not find our visits more of a burden than a pleasure, and the hospitality he so conscientiously offered and we so carelessly enjoyed, did not give him more sleepless nights than happy days'. Wharton hoped not, 'for some of my richest hours were spent under his roof' (Plate 57).

Nowhere was the contradictory nature of Henry James more obvious than in his regard for the motor car. For while he spoke of his alarm at the arrival of the person Howard Sturgis termed 'The Firebird' he had, according to Wharton, a passion for motoring, and would take 'advantage to the last drop of petrol, the travelling capacity of the visitors car'.[30] When Wharton visited Lamb House they would both follow their customary behaviour of working before lunch, then starting out immediately afterwards on what James called 'great loops' of exploration. Wharton paints a delightful picture of those halcyon days:

James was as jubilant as a child. Everything pleased him – the easy locomotion, the basking softness of the landscape, the discovery of towns and villages hitherto beyond his range, the magic of ancient names quaint, crabbed or melodious. These he would murmur over and over to himself in a low chant, finally creating characters to fit them, and sometimes whole families with their domestic complications and matrimonial alliances. Except during his naps, nothing escaped him, & I suppose no one ever felt more imaginatively, or with deep poetic emotion, the beauty of sea and sky, the serenities of the landscape, the sober charm of villages, manor houses & humble churches, & all the implications of that much-storied corner of England.[31]

On one occasion when they visited Bodiam Castle and after a long silence, they looked at the water-lilies danced over by blue dragon-flies, James said 'summer afternoons – summer afternoons to me those are the most beautiful words in the English language'.

WHARTON'S INNER CIRCLE

Henry James was a part of what Edith Wharton called her Inner Circle, a small coterie of male friends of ambivalent sexuality. With them, Edith Wharton felt secure and that she could talk freely, laugh and joke, and be her natural self. She met Robert Norton and John Hugh-Smith on her first visit to the Elchos' house at Stanway, and they soon became part of Edith's circle of friends and confidants – 'Hugh-Smith at once, Norton more slowly – and remain within it for almost thirty years'.[32] Both men had been at Cambridge, which was a common factor among all Wharton's English male friends.[33] Norton was 40 years old and of such striking good looks that he was known as 'Beau Norts'. He had spent time in the civil service before pursuing a highly successful business career and, at the time he met Edith Wharton, was about to retire and devote himself to water-colour painting. Though he possessed considerable talent, Norton had little ambition, and his lifelong friend Gaillard Lapsley, another member of the Inner Circle, said that for him 'it was life he chiefly cultivated as a fine art: painting, reading, conversation, European travel, and such gentlemanly exercises as swimming and walking'. John Hugh-Smith was considerably younger, 'a small strongly built man with a powerfully etched face, a bullet head with a little moustache' who was very much the connoisseur, both in his educated taste of women and burgundy wine. He had been admitted to Trinity as a pensioner in 1899, where he formed a lifelong friendship with Percy Lubbock, another member of Wharton's Inner Circle. Hugh-Smith was about to begin a highly successful career in banking and industry, and in the years to come, he became Edith Wharton's closest confidant, party to her inner-most feelings.

Gaillard Lapsley, like Johnston, was born in 1871 into a New York family, and after studying at Harvard, held a few junior lecturing posts in the United States before coming to England and Trinity on a research scholarship. His particular interest was medieval constitutional history, which had been one of the subjects studied by Lawrence Johnston at Cambridge.[34] He took great delight in entertaining students in his panelled rooms at Neville's Court, and surprised his 'guests' at the end of the evening by offering them a cigar and a whisky and soda, affectations the students put down to his American ways. By the time he was elected a Fellow of Trinity College in 1904, Lapsley was already a member of Edith Wharton's Inner Circle. He had met Wharton in America before coming to England and, according to Lubbock, 'he seemed to know her differently from the rest of us – to know her as no-one could who only beheld her as an event, a meteor from overseas, spreading her train'.[35] He thought Lapsley 'even before he admired and applauded her' was 'fond of her'. His friend, Percy Lubbock, had just begun his appointment as librarian of the Samuel Pepys collection at Magdalen College, Cambridge.

HOWARD STURGIS

The lynchpin of Edith Wharton's Inner Circle was Howard Sturgis (1855–1920), and in the weeks following the visit to Stanway, Norton, Hugh-Smith, Lapsley and Lubbock all met Wharton again at Queen's Acre, known as 'Qu'acre', Sturgis's home near Reading. Sturgis was an American, born and educated in England at Eton and Cambridge. His father, another transplanted American, was a partner in Baring's Bank, who had died when Sturgis was young. So Sturgis grew up under the watchful domination of his mother, and became her devoted slave. They were frequently absent from Britain, and when at home kept to themselves. After his mother's death, he was, said Wharton, 'middle aged, lost and helpless as a child'. By way of recovery from his loss, he made his first visit to America to meet his Boston relations. During the visit he met Edith Wharton in Newport, soon after her marriage. In October 1905 Sturgis visited The Mount, with his old friend Henry James. Also present was the lawyer, Walter Berry, who had met Wharton in 1883 and become an immediate and close friend – so completing her Inner Circle. Gaillard Lapsley, who already knew Sturgis and James, was also at The Mount that weekend. Wharton once said of Lapsley that he was 'the sincerest Englishman I have ever known – with exception of Henry James – his stiff manner concealing a deeply affectionate nature'.

After the death of his mother, Sturgis moved to Queen's Acre (Plate 58) as a man of leisure, happy to pursue his interests in crocheting and embroidery. In her memoir, A Backward Glance, Wharton provides a vivid description of the house and its atmosphere:

Plate 58 Howard Sturgis (left) with a friend at 'Qu'ac near Reading.

A long low drawing room; white paneled walls hung with water-colors of varying merit; curtains and furniture of faded slippery chintz; French windows opening on a crazy wooden veranda, through which, on one side, one caught a glimpse of a weedy lawn and a shrubbery edged with an unsuccessful herbaceous border, on the other, of a not too successful rose garden, with a dancing faun poised above an incongruously 'arty' blue-tiled pool. Within, profound chintz armchairs drawn up about a hearth on which a fire always smoldered; a big table piled with popular novels and picture magazines; and near the table a lounge on which he lay outstretched, his legs covered by a thick shawl, his hands occupied with knitting-needles or embroidery silks, a sturdily built handsome man with brilliantly white wavy hair, a girlishly clear complexion, a black moustache, and tender mocking eyes under the bold arch of his black brows.

Such was Howard Sturgis, perfect host, matchless friend, drollest, kindest and strangest of men, as he appeared to the startled eyes of newcomers on their first introduction to Queen's Acre.[36]

Lawrence Johnston may have been among those newcomers to Queen's Acre, for many years later, at a lunch held to determine the future of Hidcote, the homosexual author James Pope-Hennessey described Johnston as 'one of those Howard Sturgis Americans'. Sturgis held court every Sunday for Cambridge alumni at Qu'acre,[37] and Johnston may already have been acquainted with some of the graduates who formed Wharton's Inner Circle, any one of whom could have introduced him to Sturgis. Though Johnston may only have hovered on the outer fringes of this close group of people – for as one of Wharton's friends observed, 'many are called but few are chosen' – he shared many of their values and ambitions. Others remarked that the group around Wharton was 'in truth a small circle of confrères surrounded by a larger concentric circle of peers who held the same convictions'.[38] The friends considered themselves selected and selective, and beleaguered; in Wharton's words from *The Custom of the Country*, they were the last of the 'aborigines, those vanishing denizens of a civilization doomed to rapid extinction by the material and political advance of philistine invaders from the mid west'. In reality, it would be the 'invaders' from Germany who would realize her worst fears. After the First World War, Wharton said her world and its civilisation had been destroyed for ever. Another concern of Wharton and her friends was a 'sense of place'. Most had chosen, by circumstance or design, to root themselves in another country – either England, France or Italy – and this made them acutely conscious of their need to establish their own identity. It is the meanings associated with, and generated by, a 'place' which help to determine an individual's personal and cultural identity. In time too, place and self slowly intertwine, and Wharton and those around her sought to understand the various meanings of 'place': as a sense of identity, a feeling of belonging, a connection to the past or a page in history, and yet, as Ellen Glasgow writes, they remained exiles on earth.[39] In time, the gardens at Hidcote would come to express those many meanings of place that sprang from the mind of their creator, Lawrence Johnston.

WHARTON AND THE INNER CIRCLE

It is right not to over-emphasize the importance of the Inner Circle, because the refuge Edith Wharton found within it grew from her own imagination. But in her memoirs, Wharton described the group as having an almost immediate sympathy between the various members, 'so that our common stock of allusions, cross references, pleasantries was always increasing, and new waves of interest in the same book or picture, or any sort of dramatic event in life or letters, would simultaneously flood through our minds'.[40] It was her friendships with these men which brought stability into her turbulent world. They did not threaten her position and left her core of 'self' undisturbed, allowing her to achieve what she most desired and could trust – the Platonic ideal of a marriage of minds, unmarred by fluctuations of passion. After the failure of her marriage and her ill-fated affair, Wharton had a deep mistrust of establishing a shared intimacy with people. To buttress her position, she surrounded herself with these men who were either sexless or homosexual, though any homoerotic desires among this upper-class Anglo-American, euphemistically older generation, were unvoiced or concealed.[41] They were, what her friend Nicky Mariano called, her 'male wives',[42] and among that group Wharton felt accepted for herself; she may even have sensed a secret heterosexual superiority.

Her platonic friendship with these men also explains her passion for gardens. She said in a letter to her friend Elisina Tyler, 'I like to love but not to [be] loved back'; and what was true for Edith was the same for her friend 'Johnnie' Johnston. In her novel *The Touchstone*, Edith Wharton neatly summarizes the meanings of the garden as a metaphor for the inner soul and its external physical expression: 'We live in our own souls as in an unmapped region, a few acres of which we have cleared for our habitation; while of the nature of those nearest us we know but the boundaries that march with ours.'[43]

While Wharton needed her circle, the 'male wives' viewed her with an affectionate scepticism, chauvinistically taking their superiority for granted, sometimes rebelling or grumbling about her orders and counter-orders, about going or not going for a picnic or a drive. None the less, they all felt most comfortable with a woman whom, as Bernard Berenson said, they saw as appealing, 'not in the first place and not at all for reasons of sex', no matter how far removed, 'but for the one deciding reason that ... certain society women are more receptive, more appreciative and consequently more stimulating'.[44] How true this was for Johnston. Throughout his life he was flattered by female admiration for his artistry, which they recognized more readily than did his men friends, who all tended to be 'plantsmen' or tennis players.

Many members of the circle around Edith Wharton, to which Lawrence Johnston can be added in later years, left virtually no diaries or memoirs, and the question has to be asked as to 'how much were their own identities' influenced by their friendships with Edith Wharton? Wharton had been 'self-educated in order to write', and in many ways a similar transformation was undertaken by the male members of the group. Their homoeroticism, or sexual indifference, set them apart and exiled them to the territory feminist critics assign to women writers: a kind of no man's land. This, claims Susan Goodman, might explain why the pattern of their artistic development seems female rather than male, in the sense that they all began their creative activities when they were nearer 40 years old than 20.[45] This can be seen in Norton's timeless, unpeopled landscape paintings, Lubbock's biographical writings and, not least, in Lawrence Johnston's creative work of art that is Hidcote, which he began as he approached his fortieth year. Of the circle of Wharton's English friends, it is Johnston who has left the most lasting legacy.

COOPERSALE

Wharton's own flirtation with England came to a climax in 1913 when Coopersale House, near to Epping in Essex, became available. It offered the potential for entertaining and gardening equal in scale to that at The Mount, and it would have given Wharton the opportunity to establish herself as one of the great hostesses and gardeners in England. That summer she drove to Essex with Percy Lubbock and Gaillard Lapsley to view the property. Lubbock had noticed a change in Edith since her divorce from Teddy Wharton in April, and 'thought it was natural then, if ever, the tie with Paris should be loosened and a new one made with England – at any rate England should give her a settled home in summer to replace The Mount'.[46]

The seventeenth century house, which looked across to Hill Hall, with distant views towards London, was a large, white-painted, three-storey L-shaped house, comparable in size to The Mount. It had 30 rooms with fine wooden doors, stone floors, wooden beams, a splendid wooden staircase and much stucco and panelling in the upstairs rooms.[47] Surrounding the house was a very large estate, and below the house was a lake added in the 1760s by the shadowy garden designer, Adam Holt, who had also carried out part of the work on the garden.[48] The house had been unoccupied since 1898 and the contents auctioned off. At the time of sale, the estate had been divided into lots. One lot was the house and 116 acres, which included a working farm, stables and outbuildings. The sale catalogue noted that 'the Pleasure Grounds and Gardens were inexpensive to maintain ... and include Shrubberies, Lawns, Shady Walks, exceptionally good walled-in Flower and Kitchen Garden with Round Pond, Potting and Tool Sheds, Vinery, Greenhouse, Forcing Pits, etc.'[49] A large amount of money was needed for restoration of the house since it had been neglected for 15 years but, in spite of this, Wharton offered £6000, which had to be raised by £500 to secure the property.

Wharton spent six months trying to decide whether to purchase Coopersale, which she was already beginning to call my Epping house. Henry James was keen on the idea and advised that it would be good for her work, providing 'a more *settled* current of production, especially flowing between big thick green English banks ...' In July, James wrote a long letter to Mary Hunter, lyrically describing the pleasure she would derive from having Edith as a neighbour:

> It's delightful to hear of Edith W's seeming really caught up by Coopersale. If she *is* really captured I shall envy you the near view (from your commanding position) of operations there – they will certainly be so interesting, so brilliant. You don't know her till you have seen her as builder and restorer, designer, decorator, gardener. I only say to my self a little but *after*? However I think the charm of the place itself answers a good deal of that question ... She will be to you anything but a banal or negative neighbour.[50]

To Percy Lubbock it also seemed 'a clear call but [Edith] wasn't sure'. Finally she decided to let it go. Perhaps it was the extent and cost of restoration that influenced her decision. The experience of Adèle, Lady Essex, at Cassiobury may have provided a salutary lesson, a reminder that not even wealthy Americans could always rescue crumbling English properties. (Then there was the difficulty of very high levels of income tax levied on foreign residents.) But perhaps Wharton had other doubts, in Lubbock's words, she was:

> ... attracted to the old house, but I now think that when it came to the point she was afraid – not of the house, for she would have loved to give the sweet and forlorn old place the care that was due, but in a manner afraid of England. Wouldn't it be safer to leave England as it was, holiday-ground for which she had no responsibilities – to leave well alone, where it was now so very well.[51]

Lubbock believed that if the war had not started the following year, she may 'have answered in favour of the house, after all', but the war to end all wars made her appreciate her love and commitment across the Channel. France would turn out to be her adopted home for the rest of her life. It is intriguing to think, that if Wharton had bought Coopersale she may eventually have become a part of Ellen Willmott's circle of friends, which would have brought her into earlier contact with Lawrence Johnston and Hidcote. But even if Johnston had known Wharton or her circle at that time, it is unlikely that he would have made much impression, or had little to contribute. Wharton's way was to place friends in what she called 'sets', to be indulged as appropriate and when necessary. The fortuitous time would come after the First World War, when Wharton had a garden of her own and the reputation of Hidcote was established.

NOTES AND REFERENCES

1 Lee, H., *Edith Wharton*. Chatto & Windus, London, p. 232.

2 Quoted in Lee, op. cit., p. 233.

3 Ibid.

4 Lubbock, P., *Portrait of Edith Wharton*. Jonathan Cape, London, p. 75.

5 Ibid.

6 Wharton, E., *A Backward Glance*. Constable. London, p. 221. Wharton much admired the work of Grinling Gibbons (1648 –1721), the Dutch woodcarver when she visited Cassiobury.

7 The house was reported to have been bought by Adèle's brother in 1908 but was demolished in 1927/8. The grand staircase, once thought to be the work of Grinling Gibbons but now attributed to Edmund Pearce, was transferred to the Metropolitan Museum of Art, New York. When the estate was sold, 190 acres (76 hectares) of flower gardens, parkland and woods were purchased by Watford Council, to create 'a people's park and pleasure ground'. Today it is the voices of Sunday footballers that can be heard beneath the tall cedars.

8 Quoted in *Cliveden*. National Trust, London, p. 39.

9 The Fountain of Love was the work of William Waldo Story, the son and pupil of the American sculptor and dilettante William Wetmore Story (1819–95) who settled in Rome in 1856. His home in the Palazzo Barberini became a centre for American expatriate cultural life, and Henry James was in regular attendance, as no doubt was William Waldorf Astor.

10 Lewis, R.W.B., *Edith Wharton: a biography*. Constable, London, p. 242.

11 William Waldorf Astor had privately bought the balustrade, from under the noses of the Italian authorities, when the villa was sold in 1892. The experts regarded it as neither a work of art nor an antiquity – though the statues, that stood on the carved pedestals were, and Astor had to replace them with other treasures. The balustrade was listed as Grade 2* by English Heritage in 1955.

12 Wharton, op. cit., p. 222.

13 Quoted in Lee, op. cit., p. 242.

14 Susan Marie Elizabeth Stewart-Mackenzie (1849–1931), was a member of the Seaforth family of Lewis and Brahan Castle (now demolished), and widow of Colonel Stanley and mother of his two young girls, one of whom, Dorothy Allhusen, became Edith Wharton's friend in the 1930s; from 1881 Mary was the wife of the judge, Francis Henry Jeune, Lord St Helier.

15 Quoted in Mary, Lady Jeune, *Kosmoid* no. 23 www. kosmoid.net/lives/jeune

16 Wharton, op. cit., p. 213.

17 Charles Compton Reade was secretary of the Town Planning Association and editor of its journal.

18 At Mitcham, London County Council followed the principles set out by Ebenezer Howard in *Garden Cities of Tomorrow* (1902). Existing trees, shrubs and natural features were preserved, and an eighth of the site was devoted to green spaces. As a young man Howard travelled in America and became acquainted with Walt Whitman and Ralph Waldo Emerson; whose circle included Frederick Law Olmsted. Howard also visited the 1893 World Columbian Exposition held in Chicago.

19 Wharton, op. cit., p. 297. Mary Smyth married Charles Hunter in 1875 and lived, first near Darlington, moving later to Hill Hall, Theydon Mount, which had been in the Smyth family since Tudor times. Her younger sister, Ethel Smyth, the feminist composer and suffragette, quipped in her memoir of 1940, *What Happened Next*, that Mary's 'sacred duty' was to spend every penny of her husband's money. In this she was successful; she built up an important art collection, which later had to be sold. After 'Charlie' died in 1916, Mary Hunter became a close friend, or even the mistress, of John Singer Sargent. She died in 1933.

20 'Hill Hall', *Country Life*, Vol. LXV, 12 May 1917, 476.

21 Wharton, op. cit., p. 299.

22 Quoted in Lee, op. cit., p. 238. Tilden, P., 'True Remembrance: memoirs of an architect', *Country Life*, 1954, 95. Tilden was the architect for Philip Sassoon at Trent Park and Port Lympne, both of which were visited by Edith Wharton and Lawrence Johnston.

23 Wharton, op. cit., p. 299.

24 Quoted in Lee, op. cit., p. 238.

25 Tilden, op. cit.

26 *Warley Place*, Essex Wildlife Trust, 2001, pp. 4–7.

27 Quoted in Lee, op. cit., pp. 238–9.

28 Quoted in Lee, op. cit., p. 240.

29 Wharton, op. cit., p. 245.

30 Wharton, op. cit., p. 248.

31 Ibid.

32 Lewis, op. cit., p. 244.

33 Venn, J. S., *Alumni Cantabrigienses, Part 11, Vol. IV*. Cambridge University Press, pp. 540 and 569; Norton was at King's College during Johnston's time at Trinity.

34 Lapsley was elected a Fellow of Trinity College in 1904 largely on the basis of his study *The County Palatinate of Durham* (1900).

35 Lubbock, op. cit., p. 73.

36 Wharton, op. cit., p. 225. Sturgis published three novels, all mildly autobiographical and homoerotic. His third, *Belchamber*, is considered his best, and was highly regarded by Edith Wharton. However, it was not well received by the public and, mortified by criticism from Henry James, Sturgis never wrote again.

37 Quoted in Goodman, S., *Edith Wharton's Inner Circle*. University of Texas Press, Austin, p. 51.

38 Ibid.

39 Quoted in Goodman, S., op. cit., p. 57. Born into an aristocratic Virginian family, Ellen Glasgow became a popular writer often compared with her contemporary, Edith Wharton.

40 Wharton, op. cit., p. 192.

41 Lee, op. cit., p. 245.

42 Elisabetta 'Nicky' Mariano (1887–1968) went to work for Mary and Bernard Berenson at I Tatti. She remained for 40 years becoming close friends with Berenson and many of his friends, including Edith Wharton.

43 Wharton, E., *The Touchstone*, www.page by page books.com, Ch. VII, p. 2.

44 Lee, op. cit., p. 408.

45 Goodman, op. cit., p. 80.

46 Lubbock, op.cit., p. 74.

47 Lee, op. cit., p. 152.

48 'Adam Holt (?1691–1750) Gardener : His Work at Coopersale House, Essex', *Garden History Journal*, Vol. 26, No. 2, Winter 1998, pp. 214–17.

49 Lee, op. cit., p. 253.

50 Ibid., p. 254.

51 Lubbock, op. cit., p. 74.

CHAPTER SEVEN

MAKING THE GARDEN AT HIDCOTE

Before Johnston and his mother could move to Hidcote, the old manor house, built in golden- buff freestone – a type of pure oolitic limestone – and roofed with stone shingles, had to be restored and enlarged. In those early years, Mrs Winthrop was undoubtedly the driving force at Hidcote: her initials GW can be seen on the hopper-heads of the gutters, proudly displaying her ownership of the house (Plate 59). The garden historian, Timothy Mowl, has suggested that 'the real garden genius' at that time could have been that 'resolute old lady', Mrs Winthrop,[1] but it is beyond the confines of the old garden that the true genius of her son, Lawrence Johnston, the garden-maker, would emerge.

THE HOUSE

The original house was soon to be linked to a new stone extension, built on the footprint of a pre-existing building. The architect for this work is unknown, though it is tempting to think it was Andrew Prentice, engaged on the recommendation of Mary (Anderson) de Navarro. The extension at Hidcote displays all the craft and sensitivity associated with Prentice's work, and the large stone-mullioned windows of Johnston's study in the new extension facing south towards the old garden, is similar to those seen at the Navarros' music room at Court Farm (Plate 43, p. 93). Mrs Winthrop was to live in the old manor itself, but the connecting door to her son's rooms in the extension could be locked on both sides, not dissimilar to the arrangement at Sturgis's 'Qu'Acre'. The entrance to the house was also altered. The original access led directly off the street, as was often the case with old manor houses, but this involved ascending two flights of steps. So it was replaced by a new entrance court created from the old farmyard.

Many choice plants, such as the New Zealand ribbon tree (*Plagianthus betulinus* – now *P. regius* – supposedly only hardy in the warmer south-west of England) were positioned around the walls of

Plate 59 Hidcote Manor; the hopper-heads of the drain pipes on the house extension display Mrs Winthrop's initials.

the courtyard. Later Johnston added plants he had collected, such as *Mahonia lomariifolia* from Yunnan. In one corner of the yard he converted an existing farm building into a Catholic chapel, though it was never consecrated, and he continued to worship at St. Catherine's Roman Catholic Church in Chipping Campden. In the windows of the chapel, Johnston inserted fragments of old stained glass, in particular one depicting the martyrdom of St. Sebastian, the patron saint of athletes and soldiers.

Helping with the work was Lieutenant (later Lieutenant-Colonel) Reginald ('Reggie') Cooper (see Plate 132, p.273). He became one of Johnston's closer, lifelong friends and may have encouraged Johnston in his catholicism. Cooper had been at Wellington College – the austere public school founded for the sons of army officers in 1859 as a memorial to the victor of the Battle of Waterloo – with Harold Nicolson, where the two also formed a close and lasting friendship. Nicolson described him as 'a beautiful and gentle boy'.[2] Many years later they would be part of what became known as the 'Foreign Office Circle', engaged in the restoration of derelict manor houses, always with impeccable taste, in the 'old-English' style. One of Cooper's first restorations was Cold Ashton Manor near Chipping Sodbury in the Cotswolds. Nicolson and his wife Vita Sackville-West were regular visitors, and she described Cold Ashton as 'the most perfect manor house in England'. Another of Cooper's friends, Christopher Hussey, said of Cold Ashton, 'everything has a natural and untouched appearance that only a most sympathetic restoration can give'. Its interiors were decorated with dark woodwork and tapestry wall-hangings and the Jacobean, Late Stuart and Georgian furnishings were 'as sensitive as the restoration' and 'neither give the impression of a collection or clutter up the rooms'.[3] The 'old-English' look was precisely what Gertrude and Lawrence wanted at first to achieve at Hidcote Manor.

It has been suggested that Johnston wanted his personal coat of arms to appear over the door, for pedigree was everything in the early years of the twentieth century, and he had many titled friends and fellow officers who might have been interested or impressed. It would have tallied, too, with his desire to become accepted as an English country gentleman. A London solicitor had been engaged earlier to investigate his pedigree on the spear side of the family. Mrs Winthrop believed that the family had significant Irish ancestry but, in July 1906, A. M. Burke wrote to

Plate 60 Johnston's clever use of perspective at the front of the house: by using urns on the other side of the road, the eye focuses on the view along the lime avenue, which narrows to a distant glimpse of the statue of Hercules.

inform Johnston that his searches had been in vain: 'Throughout the enquiry I have given particular attention to the question of armorial bearings but unfortunately none of the documents, wills, etc., relating to the family throws any light on this point.'[4] Burke did finally trace an Irish ancestor and provided a coat of arms, but the shield dating from when Mrs Winthrop purchased the property, was already in place above the new entrance.

The front of the house, where the small garden once opened almost directly on to the village street, provides a foretaste of Johnston's skill in visual deception. An elegant new wall screened the road and swept down from the corners,[5] to frame the view of a new lime avenue planted in the field opposite. In this way, the avenue leading to a statue of Hercules was drawn into the garden (Plate 60). This was one of several French motifs used by Johnston in the early years, and it is more than likely that he was familiar with the work of Le Nôtre, whose gardens at Versailles and Vaux-le-Vicomte are supreme examples of optical illusion. Likewise, when Johnston established a copse of beech trees to shelter the new kitchen garden, it was planted in a French quincunx pattern. It was bordered by an allée on the garden side where perhaps the intention was to create a formal entrance to the garden. It is possible that Johnston recalled those French gardens where formal allées open on to central vistas. In time, the imposing entrance would be discarded, but the idea of a central vista persisted.

THE GARDEN

Gertrude wanted the garden on the south side of the house to have the same traditional feel about it. It is hard to imagine Madam Winthrop putting pencil to paper, so perhaps Johnston was prevailed upon, as Jane Brown believes, to adopt the cottagey Arts and Crafts style, 'in Parsons' best nook tradition'.[6] Otherwise her architect could have been instructed to plan the gardens in the more 'fashionable' style seen at Court Farm. If Prentice was indeed the architect, this connection would explain why the hand of Alfred Parsons can be seen most clearly in the Old Garden at Hidcote. As mentioned before, he had designed the garden for Mary de Navarro but, unfortunately, most of his archive was destroyed in a fire, so there is no evidence to support the notion that he prepared any plans for Hidcote. Yet there may have been informal contact, for both Mrs Winthrop and Johnston were, like Edith Wharton, the sort of people 'prepared to seek expert advice but all the while remaining convinced of their own talents'.[7]

A motif of the Cotswold Arts and Crafts garden was a repetition of the architectural qualities of the manor house near the dwelling. At Hidcote the geometric beds contain, as Anna Pavord observed, all the signature features of such a garden: the 'old stone buildings enclosing small planted courtyards, clipped peacocks on top of bulging hedges, pleached limes, lilies, old roses, scent, romance'.[8] Topiary peacocks resting on their yew drums were a familiar motif used by Alfred Parsons, and peacocks themselves were regarded as symbols of beauty among followers of the Aesthetic Movement.[9] Another strong influence on the design of these old-fashioned gardens were the books, *Garden Craft Old and New* written by John Dando Sedding, and *The Formal Garden in England* by Reginald Blomfield. Both authors took inspiration from the formal gardens of the Italian Renaissance which, they believed, inspired the old English garden.[10]

Johnston used some of his favourite cottage flowers in the borders. In the Maple Garden these were mainly peonies, and in the White Garden[11] the borders were initially filled with phlox. These would have delighted Edith Wharton on her first visit to Hidcote. At the centre of the garden there was a circular lawn and a stone sundial. A similar sundial had featured in *Gardens for Small Country Houses* (1910) written by Gertrude Jekyll and Lawrence Weaver. For the amateur, this book, featuring gardens made by many of the key designers of the day,

Plate 61 The Phlox (now White) Garden at Hidcote, *c.* 1915; a Lumière Brothers Autochrome photograph taken by Archibald Renfrew.

including Lutyens, Mallows and Voysey, was considered the 'bible' of formal garden principles. On practical issues of garden design, it had a far greater impact than any other book of the period.[12] Johnston certainly used and borrowed details from it; besides the sundial, the timber gates at the end of the beech allée were identical to those at nearby Cleeve Prior Manor, which had been illustrated in the book's pages. The exuberance of planting in the phlox garden, and Johnston's 'keen eye for colour and colour effects',[13] was 'captured' on some of the early colour photographs, in this case taken by a local veterinary surgeon, Archibald Renfrew, in 1915, using the Lumière Brothers' Autochrome process (Plate 61). Roses and herbaceous flowers overflow the borders in a manner reminiscent of the illustrations Alfred Parsons made for Robinson's *Wild Garden*. Arthur Bateman, another Arts and Crafts architect associated with Broadway and the Cotswolds, said that Johnston 'had the best natural taste of anyone he knew ... and a wide knowledge of plants and good colour sense'.[14]

THE OLD GARDEN

Beyond the phlox garden (now the White Garden), Johnston replaced the old tennis court with two flower borders of unequal size, separated by a wide central grass path. Here he experimented with what he called his 'jungle planting', mixing shrubs, roses, herbaceous plants and alpines, with great skill and complexity. Already, at this early stage in his gardening career, Johnston had learned several principles for his planting, notably 'Plant only the best forms of any plant' and 'Plant thickly' in the knowledge that 'where the gardener doesn't put a plant nature will'.[15] The idea of a 'mixed border' had been suggested by William Robinson. In his book *Hardy Flowers* (1871), he stated that such planting requires 'many combinations of utmost beauty', in which the 'good association [is] emphasised' by contrasting one plant, in both flower and leaf, with another. Robinson proposed the use of hardy herbaceous plants, bulbs, alpines, the latest delphiniums, phlox and lilies along with shrubs and roses. The planting in the old garden resembled the borders at Russell House, Alfred Parsons' first garden, designed for the artist Frank Millet and his wife. In the garden he massed michaelmas daisies, chrysanthemums, phlox, godetias and pink knotweed.

When Avray Tipping visited Hidcote twenty years later, he found grey and pink were the predominant colours in the Old Garden, 'the first by persistent foliage, and the second by successional bloom'. The tulips in May, were followed later by *Eremurus robustus* and 'that best of sidalceas, 'Sussex Queen'', which Edith Wharton requested for her Paris garden. Then 'a long lasting groundwork of pink snapdragons, above which the feathers of *Tamarix aestivalis* arch over the boughs of *Rosa* 'Prince de Bulgarie', and twinkle the stars of single pink dahlias'.[16] Dahlias had not generally been used in mixed borders until Reginald Cory organised a trial at Dyffryn in 1913, to assess the garden merits of over 1000 varieties. Prior to that date dahlias were regarded only as exhibition blooms.[17]

At first Johnston may have had a greater interest in a new kitchen garden, established to the north of the farmyard, for such a garden was important to the economy of any Edwardian manor house. Even when he was in the Queen Alexandra Hospital, recovering from wounds sustained in the first Battle of Ypres during the Great War, Johnston was thinking more of a productive garden than an ornamental one. Records show that of the 80 or so books he borrowed from the RHS Lindley Library, only a few were about roses and alpines; the rest were about fruit, vegetables and subjects related to the kitchen garden. None was about garden design. From the outset Johnston was a keen plantsman and a skilled propagator with an 'eye' for superior plants – a talent he retained throughout his life. He made his debut at an

RHS London flower show as early as July 1911, receiving an Award of Merit for a Hidcote strain of *Primula pulverentula* which, according to *The Times*, 'added soft pink colours' derived from *Primula japonica*, to the more usual crimson flowers.[18] Given this early appearance at the show bench, it is odd that Johnston only submitted two further plants in his lifetime, both originating from his plant-collecting expeditions.[19]

INFLUENCES AND FRIENDS

In the early years at Hidcote, Johnston was not unaware of the changes taking place in American garden design, and it is the idea of structure that is particularly interesting, and where it sprang from. Edith Wharton had commented in her autobiography that soon after the publication of her *Italian Villas and Their Gardens*, 'it became a working manual for architectural students and landscape gardeners'.[20] At Court Farm, Mary de Navarro may well have introduced Johnston to Joseph Choate, the American Ambassador to the Court of St. James, who earlier had been critical of The Mount, and to the legendary banker J. Pierpont Morgan. Both were frequent visitors to the Cotswolds in the years after Johnston moved to Hidcote. They were widely-travelled 'connoisseurs of gardens', and too fastidious to accept the 'humble, rather bucolic traditions of the Arts and Crafts gardens'.[21] Rather, they preferred something more sophisticated than seventeenth century revivalist bowers, and found it in the Beaux-Arts-inspired gardens associated with American Renaissance architecture. William Mead, one of the foremost Renaissance Revival architects,[22] was another regular visitor to the Cotswolds. His sister Mary had married the artist Edwin Abbey and, after their marriage, they moved to Morgan Hall, Fairford, in Gloucestershire. They became part of a colony of artists and gardeners – their cricket festivals were particularly popular too.

Among the people Johnston met at this time was the former cricketer Captain Simpson-Haywood, a keen plant-collector, who was making his famous rock garden at Icomb Place, near Stow-on-the-Wold. Simpson-Haywood soon became a regular visitor to Hidcote. Also, Robert 'Bobbie' James, who was a friend of Mark Fenwick at Abbotswood, became one of Johnston's close friends and allies. Both men rejected the fussy details of a Parsons-inspired cottagey garden and shared instead, a taste for the stylish American-inspired, Beaux-Arts design. They were artists and intelligent perfectionists with an awareness of good taste, and they wanted the garden to have a semblance of order and structure. At the time Johnston began to extend his garden at Hidcote, James was laying out the garden at St. Nicholas, in Richmond, Yorkshire. There would be nothing cottagey around his Tudor manor house; instead he arranged large, elegant garden rooms and a hornbeam-hedged allée, 130 yards long (118m), with 18 feet (5m) wide double herbaceous borders.

In her account of *Eminent Gardeners*, Jane Brown suggests that Johnston and James may also have been influenced by the architect and landscape gardener Charles Platt, who may have been made known to them by his friend Alfred Parsons. Together with Beatrix Farrand, Platt was a leading designer of American East Coast country-house gardens, between the turn of the century and 1920. He was one of several artists – painters, sculptors, architects, and writers like Edith Wharton – who believed that a careful study of appropriate historic Italian models could provide the basis for a healthy reform of American gardens. But whereas Wharton thought Italian gardens should be a source of inspiration, with only selected Italianate features imported, Platt wanted to introduce the Italian garden in its entirety to the American landscape. After visiting Italy in 1894, he published *Italian Gardens*, with plans to guide would-be garden-makers. Platt was particularly interested in the long vista, as seen at the Villa Lante and the Villa Gamberaia. The concept of the vista connecting the house with the distant view, Brown suggests, was more suited to the American spirit with its wide-open spaces. Whereas an English garden-maker would seek to consolidate each patch of newly-won territory without gaining any sense of far-flung space, his American counterpart was the reverse, happy to achieve the vista first and fill the spaces in between at a later stage. To a certain extent, this is what Johnston would do at Hidcote.

THE NEW GARDEN

When Johnston stepped through the gate from the Old Garden, he was faced with rather nondescript grass fields and an arrangement of small enclosures. Here he was to create what Edward Hyams once described as the greatest, if not *the* greatest, of all twentieth century gardens.[23] Johnston, it seems, was ready to demonstrate that he was not only one of the more gifted artists in garden design in the history of English gardening, but also that he was a great plantsman and botanist. His achievement can be put in perspective, by a comparison with the recently-deceased, great gardener Christopher Lloyd (1921–2006). Both he and Johnston were great plantsmen and used plants in highly innovative and sophisticated ways, but Lloyd by his own admission, was not a designer. He inherited his father's garden much of which had been designed by Edwin Lutyens, whereas Johnston alone would conceive, design, plan and plant the garden at Hidcote. It has been said, rightly, that Johnston's garden is an amalgam of French, Italian, English and American influences. Such a plurality of motifs prompted Vita Sackville-West to observe, long after the garden was made, that 'the flawless originality of Hidcote's garden lay outside the restraints of precise genealogy when it comes to sorting the sources of influence on Hidcote's design and development.[24] But there was one obvious starting point, and this stems from Johnston's desire to become truly English for, as Jane Brown put it, Johnston had become 'one of those transatlantic cousins who can don tweeds and a Clydella shirt and look more English than any Englishman'.[25] In the first two decades of the twentieth century, there were two dominant approaches to garden-making. One was that championed by Thomas Mawson, set out in his book *The Art and Craft of Garden Making*. Though Johnston was as happy to take many ideas from its pages as he was from many other sources, he rejected Mawson's rather architectural approach. A glance at the book's pages shows it to emphasize formal structures, to focus on hard materials, with plants taking a secondary place. By contrast, Jekyll and Weaver set out a more organic, feminine approach in their book, *Gardens for Small Country Houses*, with plants shown overflowing the paths in almost every illustration. Above all, for Johnston and his friends, the Country House style was quintessentially English.

A study of plans in the latter book shows that there were five basic ingredients of any Country House garden: the kitchen garden and orchard, which Johnston had already established to the north of the house; the tennis lawn, which Mawson said should be close to the house; and the herbaceous border (Figs 7a & b). The fifth element, the pergola, was rejected by Johnston perhaps on grounds of cost. The book's plans show these elements laid out on a flat site, and had Hidcote shared a similar topography, it is likely that, however well designed, the garden would not have survived to the present day.

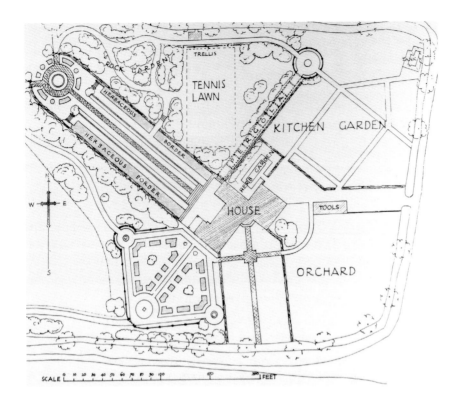

Figure 7a The layout of a typical Country House-style garden showing the basic elements of kitchen garden, orchard, tennis or croquet lawn, and herbaceous borders.

Figure 7b The arrangement of the basic country-house garden elements at Hidcote Manor, superimposed on the 1965 National Trust plan of the garden.

A=Kitchen Garden;
B=Orchard;
C=Tennis Lawn;
D=Herbaceous Borders.

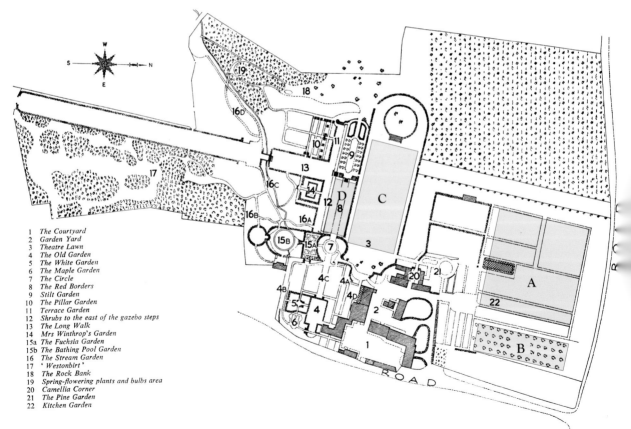

1   The Courtyard
2   Garden Yard
3   Theatre Lawn
4   The Old Garden
5   The White Garden
6   The Maple Garden
7   The Circle
8   The Red Borders
9   Stilt Garden
10 The Pillar Garden
11 Terrace Garden
12 Shrubs to the east of the gazebo steps
13 The Long Walk
14 Mrs Winthrop's Garden
15a The Fuchsia Garden
15b The Bathing Pool Garden
16 The Stream Garden
17 'Westonbirt'
18 The Rock Bank
19 Spring-flowering plants and bulbs area
20 Camellia Corner
21 The Pine Garden
22 Kitchen Garden

Almost all the gardens of the period have been lost, when fashions changed and rising costs saw them simplified or greatly altered – a fate that befell the gardens of Johnston's friends Bill Barrington, Bobbie James, Norah Lindsay and Ellen Willmott.[26] But at Hidcote Johnston was faced with a most exacting site, and it was his creative response to the challenging topography that made the garden both memorable and ultimately worth saving for posterity. To the west the land rose steadily to the escarpment, and to the south-west it dipped away, following the course of a sluggish stream, while the whole area was exposed to unfavourable weather. So the eventual garden was in many respects a response to pre-existing conditions, the topography, natural features and land use. As Graham Stuart Thomas said, the lie of the land was 'both a major obstacle and a heaven-sent opportunity to indulge every surprise'.[27]

Yet no plan was prepared for Hidcote. Avray Tipping, after his visit to the garden, mused on the absence of a Master Plan, offering the opinion that there must have been an overall plan 'in the mind's eye at least'. 'I suspect,' he continued, 'the scheme took a lot of worrying out and was of lengthy incubation.'[28] But although Tipping was right to say that much thought went into the design of Hidcote, the site conditions dictated that the rising ground beyond the gates of the old garden, was the only direction that could be fashioned into the formality of the herbaceous border; and the line of the stream, sloping gently downwards, dictated that this portion of the garden had to be treated informally. It was this fortunate 'coincidence' in the site conditions, and Johnston's creative genius, that ensured a happy 'marriage' of the formal and informal, in such a successful and influential manner.

One further reason why Johnston could not make a master plan, though his initial intention was to create an English country garden, was that, unlike Edith Wharton, he had neither an overall concept of the garden, nor any notion of how large it would become. Over later years he would change parts of the garden that did not seem right, and would constantly add new features that stemmed from his fertile imagination or which he had seen in other gardens, often merely to accommodate new plants. Therefore, the garden grew incrementally, which was hardly surprising, since Johnston was dependent on his mother's annual allowance, and Mrs Winthrop certainly considered her son to be a spendthrift. So the garden was an unending series of projects, the completion of one leading on to the next. Armed with just string, canes and a sketch, Johnston would set out his ideas on the ground, with the help of friends like Mark Fenwick, George Lees-Milne, Clarence Elliot, Bobbie James and others,[29] adjusting the plan as he went along. After visiting the completed garden with Johnston, Thomas wrote that, 'the whole thing was a challenge and he enjoyed the challenge as much as the assembly of plants'.[30]

The piecemeal approach to its design makes Hidcote unlike any Arts and Crafts garden, which would have been conceived and planned in its entirety by a garden designer on the drawing board. The Arts and Crafts architect, Ernest Barnsley, was doing just that at nearby Sapperton – 30 miles from Hidcote Bartrim – as he completed his first plans for Rodmarton Manor in 1909 for Claud and Margaret Biddulph.[31] This is one of the foremost examples of an Arts and Crafts house and garden in the country. Barnsley designed the gardens as an integral part of the overall scheme with the south-facing spaces divided by walls or hedges into a series of outdoor rooms, each with its own character. The resulting architectural rigidity was only partially overcome by the excellence of the planting, whereas at Hidcote the natural exuberance of the plants eventually overwhelmed the garden's structure.[32]

THE MAIN VISTA

Nowhere is Johnston's skill more apparent than in the main vista. It is the defining feature of Hidcote which undoubtedly helped to ensure the garden's survival. There is no way of knowing how or when the idea for it evolved: perhaps from Johnston's travels in France or Italy, or gleaned from Edith Wharton's *Italian Villas and Their Gardens*. It is possible that the idea was suggested by Alfred Parsons – the notion of infinity being an essential concept within the Aesthetic Movement of which Parsons was part – or perhaps Johnston even subscribed to those aesthetic ideals. At Court Farm, Parsons had earlier placed the wide herbaceous borders so that they led the eye to a distant view of Broadway Tower, an eighteenth century folly once occupied by William Morris; or it may be that Johnston had his own sudden moment of inspiration as he walked his dogs over the fields. Whatever its source, Johnston appreciated that the Cedar Terrace he had created earlier, perhaps for this very reason, was aligned with the gates of the old garden and that, by extending this linear axis to the western skyline,

Plate 62 The main vista
and red borders at Hidcote,
looking towards the house.

Plate 63 The main vista at
Hidcote seen from the red
borders, with the twin gazebos
backed by the Stilt Garden
and the Gates of Heaven,
hooded over by evergreen
oaks brought from France.

he would create the main vista of the garden (Plates 62 & 63). As luck would have it, at the end of this vista, in the very centre, was the church spire of Pebworth, glowing golden at sunrise and sunset on fine summer days, not unlike the Duomo of Florence which was well known to him.

Johnston began to create this vista by instructing his gardeners to undertake the major excavation necessary to level the sloping ground (Plate 64). Once complete, Johnston and his friends laid out a grass rondel, a feature often used by Charles Platt. This was to be the centre point from which the herbaceous borders of the main vista and the Fuchsia and Pool gardens radiated.[33] These borders were arranged on either side of a lawn, and terminated in a grass bank, with a large beech tree beyond and a tall farm hedge. Johnston could not proceed further until the area, known as the Theatre Lawn, had been levelled.

The two herbaceous borders were planted more conventionally than they are today. In their planting Johnston did not use the colour spectrum devised by Gertrude Jekyll, which was then at the height of its popularity. It is tempting to believe Johnston followed the guidance given by Thomas Mawson:

> Flowers in the border should be considered not alone for their colour in the arrangement, but for their tone or relative amount of white or dark into which their colours resolve themselves.

Plate 64 Lawrence Johnston and his gardeners in the Old Garden at Hidcote. The stone-mullioned window of the new extension can be seen on the left.

This is more important, or more so, than their colour. White, light yellow, pale pink or pale blues that are light in tone, are as needful as the bright reds, brilliant blues and vivid orange hues; in all cases the graduations or contrasts must be arranged and massed according to both tone and colour. They should offer to the eye one clear picture, or a series of pictures, one at a time and should purposefully express distinct intentions ... Massing ought to be the rule and expanses of one species of flower, because each flower possesses its own unique harmonious range of colour; this favours boldness in the arrangement of the herbaceous border ... Judging from the standpoint of harmonious colour schemes, generally speaking the prearranged border does not impress, rather it serves to point to the moral of Ruskin's axiom that 'nothing great is ever effected by management'. This must not be construed to mean that it is to be haphazard and no prearrangement. Cottage gardens are our exemplars, their glory being that they rely chiefly upon a few well placed plants which have grown into their place for a generation or more and the place has grown to them ... It is just this sense of easy nonchalance which is lacking in the strained hybrid arrangements of harmoniously arranged borders.[34]

In the *Art of Planting*, Graham Stuart Thomas describes Johnston's approach as recalled by Walter Bennett, one of the long-serving gardeners at Hidcote: 'there would be a fair sized planting of A with a similar planting of B adjoining it, each composed of several plants for major effect. But here and there he would put an odd plant or two of A overlapping B and vice versa. And like as not an isolated A or B would be popped in some distance away to reinforce this supposition.'[35] As Thomas observed, this was not only very effective, but it was a real art to achieve, requiring a painterly eye.

THE FUCHSIA AND POOL GARDENS

These gardens were offset at right angles, in what had been an enclosure of small fields running parallel to the wall of the Old Garden. The hedges of these fields determined the size of the gardens, and Johnston used the device of circles to create the optical illusion of larger spaces. Because the brick wall of the Old Garden was not quite at right angles to the main vista, the gardens had to be placed off centre. This meant

that they touched the boundary on one side and left wide borders on the other. Johnston used abundant planting to disguise this anomaly; in the Fuchsia Garden a tapestry hedge of various colours and textures – green and variegated hollies, box, green and copper beeches – was used to compensate for the absence of a flower border. In the *Art and Craft of Garden Making*, Mawson considered that such planting made a most delightful combination in winter: 'the fox red leaves' of the clipped beech are 'a perfect contrast with the rich green of the holly'.[36] At the end of the Fuchsia Garden, five stone steps led down, through an arched hedge flanked by two topiary birds, into a sunken pool garden. In Mawson's opinion, nothing was as emblematic of domestic felicity as 'a yew arch surmounted by a pair of clipped doves over a white painted gate'.[37] In this first phase, the pool was a small sunken half-moon, and beyond, the land sloped upwards with a fan-shaped arrangement of wedge-shaped panel beds, reminiscent of a Mawson design (Plate 65 l & r).

The Fuchsia and Pool gardens are the most enclosed and secluded places in the overall plan. Mawson had believed that 'there [was] a certain seductive mystery' to be 'gained by partially concealing and judiciously screening some parts from the immediate view'. Indeed, many small openings, and narrow paths linking small gardens, entice visitors on, revealing perfectly proportioned 'rooms', each one displaying beautifully composed garden pictures.[38] However, the garden at Hidcote was not designed with many visitors in mind; it was 'not meant to have any people in it any more than the beholder

Plate 65 (left) A view of the Fuchsia Garden and the original Pool Garden adorned by topiary birds at Hidcote, 1907–14; (right) the Fuchsia Garden today – the original pool has been replaced by the Bathing Pool, and the topiary birds have grown to a monumental size.

of a landscape painting is meant to get inside it'.[39] Rather the garden was an articulation of space, establishing its creator's sense of place, and as such it was 'something to contemplate but not intrude upon; something to be moved by, as by any other work of art, because it has been accomplished'.[40]

MRS WINTHROP'S GARDEN

The herbaceous border is retained by a shallow retaining wall; below it is what is known today as the Winter Border, flanked by a wide gravel path. This formed the 'spine' from which smaller gardens could be counterbalanced, and eventually the Long Walk as well. The first small garden is known affectionately as 'Mrs Winthrop's Garden'. It was open to the south and was like a sunken Mediterranean garden, recalling 'the Riviera where Gertrude had spent so many years'.[41] In summer, feather cushions in her favourite colours of blue and yellow, were scattered on the wide, low brick steps, though one can hardly imagine the demure 'Madam' Winthrop lounging in such a fashion. Agapanthus, alchemilla and mounds of *Hypericum* 'Hidcote' reinforced the blue and yellow theme (Plate 66).

Close inspection of Mrs Winthrop's Garden reveals Johnston's almost naive approach to construction: his design contrasted with the practice in 'Arts and Crafts gardens', where the 'architect' paid

Plate 66 Mrs Winthrop's Garden today with its blue and yellow theme.

meticulous attention to the layout and construction of every hard-landscape detail, making them a feature in themselves. Johnston designed for 'effect'. He used the cheapest and most utilitarian materials to hand. In Mrs Winthrop's Garden, the four corner beds are outlined with mere concrete blocks arranged around a brick circle; and throughout the garden, Johnston displayed either his lack of interest in hard materials or, more likely, he had to make do with whatever he could because of a shortage of funds. He worked quickly using recycled materials because they were available and cheap, though his artistic eye ensured that they had aesthetic merit. Staddle stones form the path in the Old Garden; tiles on edge and second-hand bricks are used for the steps and path in the Pool Garden, as well as in Mrs Winthrop's; and when Johnston turned his attention to the Stream Garden, cobble stones were gathered from the surrounding farmland to make the paths. Like many amateurs, Johnston did not attempt to link the various projects together, so cobbles placed horizontally in one path meet others placed vertically, or they give way to hoggin (Plate 67). The same expediency applied to the numerous plant-houses and shelters erected throughout the garden. Johnston's primary aim was to create places for plants, with each project featuring a different assemblage and colour arrangement. Planting was used to mask any deficiencies in construction, especially where there was a change of level, and done so skillfully that one is unaware of retaining walls, terraces, slopes or other devices used, while the garden progresses down the slope to the stream.

With Mrs Winthrop's Garden in place, Johnston could not resist the temptation to link it to the Pool Garden. Narrow, meandering paths, just wide enough for himself, were laid across the stream and, as Anna Pavord commented, 'his instinct' as a gardener 'would have been to dress the foreground with a little planting', so beginning the Upper Stream Garden. The stream running north-east to south-west in a shallow valley, away from the line of the Cedar terrace, formed a triangular wedge of land. It was originally undistinguished, but Johnston and his gardeners sculpted its banks to make it a major

Plate 67 The Stream Garden at Hidcote: paths joining in different patterns.

feature of the garden (Plate 68). This Johnston 'dealt with on strictly Robinsonian lines, making a wild and woodland garden by the planting of a discreetly chosen collection of exotics, some of them rare'.[42] In making this part of the garden, Johnston would have taken inspiration from Mark Fenwick's stream garden at Abbotswood.

TRAVELS TO EGYPT AND ITALY

Flushed with the success of these early projects, Johnston decided it was time to travel, encouraged perhaps by Edith Wharton's book, *Italian Villas and their Gardens*. In 1913 he was granted leave of absence from the Northumberland Hussars for two months, from 5th February to 5th April, with permission to travel abroad, specifically to 'Egypt and the Courts of Italy'.[43] His request to travel may have been prompted by a 'weak lung' which seems to have been an hereditary problem. Cairo with its dry desert air had become a favoured place for those with respiratory problems. Travel

Plate 68 The Stream Garden in spring at Hidcote as it is today.

to Egypt had been pioneered by Thomas Cook in the 1870s, and it had become a very popular destination for English and American visitors. 'The Nile,' one traveller, James Clarke, wrote, 'is now being visited by crowds almost equal in number to those of the multitude who flock to the Riviera. It has become a fashionable resort.' Egypt and its antiquities had also become a favoured topic of conversation among guests at Saturday to Monday house-parties.

There is no record of the extent of Johnston's trip to Egypt, but like many wealthy tourists, he may have taken a cruise on the Nile, to see the sights of ancient Egypt. A private sailing boat, a *dahabiyya*, could be hired in Cairo, complete with cook and crew, aboard which tourists would slowly sail down the Nile to Aswan. Frequent stops would be made to explore ruins and meet local dignitaries; the more artistic travellers like Johnston would take time to record the local scenes in water-colours. At night they would sit on deck, under an awning, transferring their impressions to morocco-bound diaries. In 1913 Karnak was the centre of archaeological excitement. If Johnston visited the newly excavated temple, he would have approached through a 'stilt garden' of citrus trees, their outlines crisp from a January clipping.[44] On arrival at Aswan, tourists made their way from the bustling quayside to the Old Cataract Hotel, built for well-to-do visitors by Thomas Cook in 1899. Located on a bluff, it overlooked the home of Lord Kitchener, Johnston's Commander in Chief during the South African War. Kitchener was an enthusiastic gardener, who collected plants throughout the world for his Nile-side garden, especially those from Australia and South Africa. Johnston could have made a short *felucca* crossing to visit Elephantine Island and the garden.

From Egypt Johnston travelled to Italy. There he visited Arthur Acton and his garden at 'La Pietra', among the grandest and most famous villas and gardens in Florence. It had been built originally for the Sassetti family in the 1460s, but Acton's wealthy American wife, Hortense Mitchell, bought the property in 1907.[45] For more than the next 20 years the Actons re-created a sixteenth century Tuscan garden, designed as a series of outdoor rooms surrounding the villa. The terraces, parterres and fountains were linked by hedged walks, which created vistas inside and outside the garden. The Villa La Pietra was the centre for lavish entertainment for Florentines and the wealthy Anglo-American residents in the villas surrounding the city, and the Actons would have provided Johnston with an entry to this glittering society.

Among the visitors to La Pietra were Wharton's friend Bernard Berenson and his wife Mary, who lived at the Villa 'I Tatti'. In 1909 the English architect Cecil Pinsent was commissioned to design and supervise the planting and construction of the garden. With help from another of Wharton's close friends, the writer-scholar Geoffrey Scott, Pinsent re-created an early Renaissance, green garden. The lower garden was an outdoor room, completely enclosed by hedges, and the steep slope above was terraced to form a series of parterres enclosed by immaculately clipped box hedges. Pinsent also redesigned the Villa Medici, at Fiesole, for a neighbour and friend of the Berensons, Lady Sybil Cutting, who bought the garden in 1911, after the death of her husband Bayard Cutting, a former Secretary to the American Embassy in London and friend of Edith Wharton. On the lower terrace Pinsent created a simple arrangement of lawns, parterres and pots of lemon trees, arranged around a circular fountain. The focus and highlight of the garden was a distant view of Brunelleschi's

Duomo Santa Maria de Fiore, its dome glinting, like others, golden in the Tuscan sunlight.

Johnston would most certainly have visited the Villa Gamberaia in Settignano, which Edith Wharton described as 'probably the most perfect example of producing a great effect on a small scale' (see Plate 22, p. 51). It had been purchased in 1896 by Princess Jeanne Ghyka who, according to Berenson, was a narcissistic Romanian lady who lived mysteriously, in love with herself perhaps and certainly with her growing creation, the garden of the Gamberaia. Together with her American companion Miss Blood, she transformed the parterre to the south of the villa into a spectacular water garden. Remnants of old flower beds were replaced with four rectangular pools framed by box and colourful borders of irises, lilies, tree roses, and oleanders. The water garden culminated in a pool of water lilies and aquatic plants, enclosed by a cypress arcade, a 'green theatre'. Alongside the house was the 'bowling green', a pre-existing feature, some 246 yards (225 m) long. Years afterwards when Berenson visited the Villa Gamberaia, he found it neglected and 'yet,' he wrote, 'the place retains its charm, its power to inspire longing and dreams, sweet dreams. Its beauty so uncared for is still great enough to absorb one almost completely, the terraces, the ponds, the great apse of cut cypresses, the bowling green as you look at it from the grotto toward the south, is like a great boat sailing through space, the view over the quiet landscape of the Chianti hills and further over domes and towers to the snow-capped Apennines and the Arno glimmering in the plain'.[46]

THE THEATRE LAWN

When Johnston returned from Italy, he was ready to create his own 'green garden', the Theatre Lawn. This bold, unadorned feature is at odds with the rest of the garden, but its simplicity greatly adds to the unique character of Hidcote. It is what Tim Richardson called in his account of Hidcote, 'the subversion of expectations'.[47] More specifically, it is an example of what the Danish garden architect Erik Erstad-Jørgensen, a contemporary of Johnston, called the 'architectonic style of garden'. In an article, written in the early 1920s, Erstad-Jørgensen referred to a drawing in Blomfield's *The Formal Garden in England* that showed a carp pond surrounded by yew hedges. This, he noted, showed how simply and unaffectedly English gardeners could use hedges to attain atmosphere. 'Gardens of this kind', he said 'are not imitations

THE FISHPOND : WREST : BEDFORDSHIRE

Plate 69 The carp pond, an engraving taken from Reginald Blomfield's *The Formal Garden in England*. Erik-Erstad Jørgensen, a Danish contemporary of Johnston, described this as an example of the 'architectonic style' of garden.

of nature but clearly bear the mark of human will and work, and what gives them character are the straight lines and even planes' (Plate 69).[48] The Theatre Lawn has precisely the same character and atmosphere.

Nevertheless, Johnston saw this part of the garden as the ideal location for tennis, croquet and entertaining, all essential activities at any country house. Mawson had said that 'recreational grounds essential to a modern garden, the tennis and croquet lawns and formal archery or open air badminton court and their level lawns, together with steps, walls and clipped hedges, form the architectural setting of the house'.[49] Inigo Thomas, who illustrated *The Formal Garden in England*, laid out a lawn of similar dimensions at Barrow Court, near Bristol, between 1892 and '96.[50] Johnston may have been familiar with this feature, at least from glancing through the pages of *Country Life*, or at Court Farm where he would have noticed that Parsons had undertaken major earth-moving to level the ground for the requisite tennis and croquet lawn. About Hidcote, Avray Tipping observed that in order to 'get the lawn level for games, much soil must have been removed from its higher end'. Johnston realized he could retain the beech trees behind the house, and level the lawn to a point at which it would be 'at grade' with the top of the bank, above the herbaceous borders. The excavated soil could be 'used to create a plateau',[51] retained by a 10-foot retaining wall on the lower side. The 200-year-old beech trees at the far end of the

Theatre Lawn, which have since fallen, were encircled by a low wall, so making the 'stage' on which Mary de Navarro would present her annual plays. The result was a simple, spacious and peaceful space (Plate 70). One wonders whether Johnston's appreciation of topography, and a masterful eye in the manipulation of levels, stemmed from his experiences as a cavalry officer, accustomed to an instant assessment of the terrain.

Plate 70 The Theatre Lawn at Hidcote.

THE REST OF THE GARDEN

Before the work of excavation at Hidcote could be completed, Britain and Europe were plunged into the carnage of the First World War in 1914, and Johnston was recalled to his regiment at Newcastle. Sometime in the years that followed, Johnston returned to complete the Main Vista. The bank terminating the herbaceous border was replaced by a retaining wall and a flight of steps, shaded by the giant beech tree. On either side were lead vases cast in London. Two hip-roofed gazebos were built as an integral part of the wall. Johnston was away for much of this time, but Timothy Mowl has suggested that Gertrude Winthrop may have played some part in their construction, though there is no evidence of her involvement. Anna Pavord believes Johnston may have seen similar structures at Compton's End, the Hampshire garden of the Arts and Crafts architect Herbert Kitchen.[52] But gazebos and pavilions of this type featured prominently in *Gardens for Small Country Houses*, which suggested that 'their success depends as much on their skilful placing as upon their form and materials'.[53] At Hidcote, the placing, form and materials were indeed exemplary, ensuring the gazebos' place as the iconic feature of the garden. Johnston painted the walls and roof of the gazebo on the north side, and used tiles on the working surface, where the butler prepared refreshments (Plate 71). On the other, south, side, the gazebo doors framed the view over the fields; in time Johnston would lay out another long allée to the skyline – the Long Walk – but for the moment the lawn only extended as far as the stream (Plate 72).

Beyond the steps, Johnston planted the Stilt Garden, a *pallisade à l'Italienne*; two rectangles of pleached hornbeams, designed to enclose *boules* courts. With maturity, the Stilt Garden would create a remarkable foreshortening effect, creating an optical illusion, whereby the main vista in 'its level first section looks its length. And beyond, the rise of the ground brings everything near to you, so that you wonder why the high end-gates look so faint and spidery'[54] . The Gates of Heaven, supported on brick pillars, surmounted by two Watteau-inspired cherubs, frame the sky, making it an integral part of the garden. One wonders whether Johnston, who had an interest in Renaissance churches, had in mind the ceiling of the Sistine Chapel

Plate 71 Inside the North Gazebo at Hidcote, with its tiled surface, where refreshments were prepared for Johnston and his guests on the adjoining Tennis Lawn.

Plate 72 The Long Walk at Hidcote seen from the South Gazebo; in the first phase of making the garden, it extende only as far as the stream in th middle distance.

Plate 73 A view of the Vale of Evesham with Bredon Hill in the distance seen from the level viewing platform beyond the 'Gates of Heaven'.

for, as one French writer expressed it, there is an 'irrepressible desire to go upwards towards the sky' (see Plate 63, p.139).

Beyond the gates, Johnston levelled the ground to form a viewing platform, bounded by a ha-ha, overlooking the prospect of the Vale of Evesham and Bredon Hill beyond (Plate 73). By removing hedgerows in the foreground, Johnston created a Reptonian landscape of the kind seen at Chesters. On either side, evergreen oaks, imported from France, framed the view and 'bolster[ed] the falling contours'[55] (see Plate 63). The whole panorama exudes the very essence of 'Englishness' that Johnston craved, 'no less than the vale of the Avon leading into that stretch of land in which lies the heart of Shakespeare's poetry'.[56] This firmly contradicts Timothy Mowl's recent dismissal of the view as no more than 'broad tracts of featureless countryside'.[57] Wendy Hitchmough, in her book on *Arts and Crafts Gardens*, makes the point that at Hidcote 'the stone steps, a pair of brick pavilions symmetrically disposed, and a fine wrought-iron gate framing a view of the distant landscape are classically arranged in a composition, [and] owe nothing to cottage (or even English) traditions'.[58] Johnston completed these projects after returning from a war in which he barely escaped with his life; had he died then, Hidcote would have been no more than a mere footnote in garden history.

Notes and References

1   Mowl, T., *Historic Gardens of Gloucestershire*. Tempus, Stroud, p. 147.
     Clarke, E., *Hidcote – the Making of a Garden*. Revised edition. Norton,
     London, p. 33.

2   Quoted in Lees-Milne, J., *Harold Nicolson 1886–1929*. Chatto and Windus,
     London, p. 10. In the first letter he wrote to his parents from Wellington
     College (19 March 1901), a deeply depressed Nicolson said Cooper was
     the only boy he could get on with.

3   Hussey, C., 'Cold Ashton Manor', *Country Life*, Vol. 18, No. 464, 25
     November 1908, 738–42.

4   The letter was sent to Johnston at Little Shelford which suggests his mother
     may have remained in the village, though there is no evidence for this.

5   Johnston would have seen a similar curving wall in Alfred Parsons' own
     garden at Luggers Hall, and in Lutyens' work at Abbotswood, for Mark
     Fenwick.

6   Brown, J., *Eminent Gardeners*. Viking, London, p. 50.

7   Clarke, E., *Hidcote – the Making of a Garden*. 1st edition. Michael Joseph,
     London, p. 25.

8   Pavord, A., *Hidcote Manor Gardens*. The National Trust, London, p. 10.

9   Mako, M., 'Painting with Nature in Broadway, Worcestershire', *Garden
     History*, Vol. 34, No. 1, 57. Oscar Wilde championed the use of Peacocks
     as a symbol of beauty.

10   After studying old gardens, Sedding said he had become 'an advocate of
     old types of design which I am persuaded are more consonant with the
     traditions of English life, and more suitable to an English homestead'.

11   The phlox were still there in 1929 when Avray Tipping visited Hidcote,
     but sometime later they became infected by eelworm and were replaced
     by a white garden; perhaps at the suggestion of Edith Wharton, who had
     made a similar garden at The Mount.

12   Tankard, J., *Gardens of the Arts and Crafts Movement*. Abrams, New York,
     p. 94.

13   Fretwell, K., 'The Real Major Johnston Revealed', *Country Life*, Vol. 194
     (10), 9 March 2000, 118–21.

14   Quoted in an unpublished report on Hidcote Manor Gardens for the
     National Trust by K. Fretwell, 2000.

15   Whitsey, F., 'A Passion for Planting', *Daily Telegraph*, 21 July 2007. This was
     among the many dictums of Mark Fenwick, who said that it was important
     to 'always have the best of any plant: go for a good rent payer, something
     that will give you a long flowering season – it won't cost any more'. And
     when asked how you can tell the best, he would reply: 'That is for you to
     decide; you must use your judgment and you will become more discerning.'

(From: Arnold, C., *Happy as Kings*. Wilton 65, Bishop Wilton, York, pp. 83–4.) This quest for excellence was something Johnston also pursued.

16 Tipping, H. A., 'Early Summer at Hidcote Manor, Gloucestershire. The seat of Mr Lawrence Johnston', *Country Life*, Vol. 67, No. 1727, 22 February 1930, 292. It is worth noting that Henry Avray Tipping (1855–1933) was born at Ville d'Avray near Paris, and used his second name instead of Henry.

17 The trial was organized for the National Dahlia Society and the Royal Horticultural Society.

18 *The Times*, 4 July 1911.

19 Pearson, G., *Hidcote*, The National Trust, p. 35. In July 1925 Johnston received an award of merit for *Pistorinia intermedia*, an annual he introduced from Morocco; and in October 1929, for *Gordonia axillaris*.

20 Wharton, E., *A Backward Glance*. Constable, London, p. 139.

21 Brown, op. cit., p. 55.

22 William Mead was a partner in the firm of McKim, Mead and White, the leading practice in American Revivalist architecture.

23 Hyams, E., *The English Garden*. Thames and Hudson, London, p. 155.

24 Sackville-West, V., 'Hidcote Manor', *J. Royal Horticultural Society*. Vol. 74, No. 11, November 1949.

25 Brown, op. cit., p. 52.

26 There are no Jekyll gardens in the ownership of the National Trust.

27 Thomas, G. S., *Gardens of the National Trust*. Weidenfeld & Nicolson, London, p. 154.

28 Tipping, op. cit., p. 286.

29 James Lees-Milne said that his father, who lived close by at Wickhamford, was always at Hidcote in the early days.

30 Thomas, op. cit., p. 25.

31 Greensted, M., 'Rodmarton Manor, the English Arts and Crafts Movement at its best', *Antiques Magazine*, June 2001.

32 *Gardens for Small Country Houses* was reissued in 1999, but it was given the more marketable title of *Arts and Crafts Gardens*. This term was unknown in 1910 and its application to the Country House garden is both confusing and obscures a lost garden style.

33 The various parts of the garden, such as the Fuchsia and Pool gardens, were named by The National Trust after they acquired the garden.

34 Mawson, T., *The Art and Craft of Garden Making*. Batsford, London, pp. 121–2.

35 Thomas, G. S., *The Art of Planting*. J.M. Dent & Sons in association with The National Trust, London, p. 19.

36 Mawson, op. cit., p. 275.

37 Ibid., p. 277.

38 Ibid., p. 154.

39 Hyams, op. cit., p. 153.

40 The absence of any garden records makes exact dating and the order in which Johnston made the garden impossible to determine.

41 Clarke, *Hidcote*, 1st edition. Michael Joseph, London, p. 49.

42 Hyams, op. cit., p. 152.

43 After moving to Hidcote, Johnston had to attend only the summer camps of the Northumberland Hussars, making occasional visits to Gosforth, but as a serving officer he had to obtain permission to leave the country.

44 The stilt garden reflected the influence of the French-born Director of Egyptian Antiquities, Gaston Maspero.

45 The Sassetti family were managers of the Medici bank. Hortense was the daughter of William H. Mitchell, President of the First National Trust Bank, Alton, Illinois. Arthur Acton, a painter, collaborated with the architect Stanford White in purchasing works of art for wealthy clients in America who were creating their own Italianate villas and gardens.

46 Berenson, B., *Sunset and twilight – the last diaries, 1947–1958*. Harcourt, Brace & World, New York. pp. 54-5.

47 Richardson, T., *English Gardens in the Twentieth Century*. Aurum, London, p. 117.

48 Stephensen, L. S., *Garden Design in Denmark – G. N. Brandt and the Early Decades of the Twentieth Century*. Packard, Chichester, pp. 34-5.

49 Mawson, op. cit., p. 127.

50 'Barrow Court', *Country Life*, Vol. 11, No. 263, 18 January 1902, 80-5. Barrow Court was the home of Sir Martin Gibbs, High Sheriff of Somerset. The tennis lawn was very similar in shape and dimensions to the Theatre Lawn at Hidcote: enclosed at one end by a semi-circular balustrade with two central pillars and ornamental gates framing a view of the distant Quantock Hills.

51 Tipping, op. cit., p. 293.

52 Pavord, op. cit., p. 10.

53 Jekyll, G. and Weaver, L., *Gardens for Small Country Houses*. Country Life, London, p. 207.

54 Tipping, op. cit., p. 292.

55 Thomas, op. cit., p. 41.

56 Hadfield, M., *Gardening in Britain*. Hutchinson, London, p. 428.

57 Mowl, op. cit., p. 148.

58 Hitchmough, W., *Arts and Crafts Gardens*. Pavilion, London, p. 136.

CHAPTER EIGHT

THE FIRST WORLD WAR

The making of the gardens at Hidcote was interrupted by the dramatic events of the First World War. During the previous year, 1913, there had been no suspicion of the catastrophe that was to occur in Europe; if there were any war clouds over Britain, they related more to unrest in Ireland than to Germany. In May, following his return from Egypt and Italy, Lawrence Johnston attended a cavalry officers' course, and was promoted to the rank of Major the following month. Osbert Sitwell, who was attending a training course at Aldershot during this time, recalled being told by the instructors that war was inevitable and that it would be a cavalry war: 'At last the horse would come into its own ... We ought to thank our stars ... for the fact that the Boer war had been recently vouchsafed as a model dress rehearsal for this approaching conflict. In many ways Europe resembled the Great Veldt and the people of Europe resembled those of the Veldt'.[1] It was after his promotion that Johnston joined Boodle's, the second oldest gentleman's club in London, popular with military men who frequented the club during their visits to Town. It had a reputation for being stodgy, refined and completely English.[2] He was probably accepted as a member too, because he was well connected in army circles and more recently had attended the summer camp of the Northumberland Hussars, held in the grounds of Blagdon Hall, the home of Lieutenant-Colonel the Viscount Ridley. Morale would have been high among officers and men, for as Sitwell observed, 'never had Europe been so prosperous and gay'. In June, King George V celebrated his 'official' fiftieth birthday, an event marked by the hugely popular Trooping of the Colour in London, and by parades throughout the country, in which the Northumberland Hussars took part dressed in their fine uniforms. The summer was long and hot that year, the herbaceous borders at Hidcote would have been at their peak in August, and the evening air, filled with the scent of phlox.

The following year, while the Northumberland Hussars held their camp as usual, Edith Wharton was making extensive plans for the summer: first a quick dash to Barcelona and the Balearic Islands, for the most part by car, and then to England. She had rented a house to be closer to Henry James in Rye, and intended to realize her 'life long dream of a summer in England'.[3] By late June 1914, there was still no hint of the impending disaster that was to follow the assassination of the Archduke Ferdinand and his wife Sophie in Sarajevo. On that fateful day, Edith Wharton was taking tea with Jacques Blanche at his house in Auteuil, a town between the River Seine and the Bois de Boulogne, watching as groups gathered at tea-tables while others walked up and down the flower-bordered turf. 'Broad bands of blue forget-me-nots edged the shrubberies, old-fashioned *corbeilles* of yellow and bronze wallflowers dotted the lawn, the climbing roses were budding on the pillars of the porch.'[4] News of the assassination was met with a momentary shiver among the company, but no one believed that these events in a minor Balkan province were serious. Yet the word 'mobilisation' gradually entered the minds of politicians throughout Europe for, when Wharton arrived back in Paris at the end of July, she found the city gripped by rumours of war. The following day the unbelievable happened: Germany declared war on Russia, and mobilisation of the French army indeed began.

The Reality of War

Edith Wharton's response to what she would later describe in 1915, as 'a calamity unheard of in human annals', was to throw herself into the war effort on behalf of the French. In early August 1914 she helped set up a work-room for women and children left destitute by the departure of their menfolk to the army, but even by the end of the month, there was still an air of unwillingness to accept the enormity of the unfolding situation. On 4th August, Germany declared war on Belgium and promptly invaded the country. Britain had agreed to protect Belgian neutrality, and so Prime Minister Asquith had no option but to declare war on Germany. Major Johnston thus was instructed to return to barracks in Newcastle upon Tyne, leaving behind his gardeners at Hidcote who continued the task of levelling the ground for tennis (later the 'Theatre Lawn').

At the end of August, meanwhile, Edith Wharton and her entourage departed, as planned, for her holiday in England; she continued to think of England as 'a great rich garden' protected from world events.[5] She took up residence at Stocks in the Chilterns, on the borders of Hertfordshire and Buckinghamshire, in a house she knew well, owned by her friend, the novelist Mrs Humphrey Ward and her husband. The Wards were anxious to let the property, because it had become too expensive to maintain: Mrs Ward actually charged Edith extra money for the garden vegetables. Henry James thought Stocks ideal for her; the house is 'much modernized & bathroomed some years back – not, doubtless, on the American scale, but very workably & conveniently. And it's civilized and big-treed & gardened & library'd & pictured & garaged in a very sympathetic way ... I kind of see you *at rest there* under fine old English umbrage'.[6]

Wharton had been looking forward to spending the summer in England and was anticipating having her friends about her. But it was not to be, for, as she wrote, 'there was something oppressive and unnatural about the serene loveliness of the old gardens, the cedars spreading wide branches over the deserted lawns, the borders glowing with unheeded flowers'.[7] News of the war slowly filtered through, and Wharton soon came to feel alien and terribly alone in this quiet rural backwater of picturesque villages. There were no telephones in the house, and the London papers came late and irregularly. Wharton believed that the war would be contained in Belgium, and was shocked to hear of the German advance and the possible siege of Paris. She quickly realized the enormity of her mistake in going to England, and writing to a friend in Paris, she admitted that 'until this moment I never knew how much I love France and my French friends'. After much difficulty Wharton finally managed to return to Paris in October and at once threw herself unstintingly into work, supporting both those in need and the campaign to involve the United States in the military struggle.

MOBILISATION

In Newcastle during the early days of August 1914, there was a sense of excitement and uncertainty. In his diary, a young Methodist minister, James Mackay, provided a graphic account of the scenes and mood.[8]

> **Saturday Aug. 1st.** Great excitement prevails all over the country. News has come that Russia is mobilising and Germany has presented an ultimatum. People are alarmed everywhere. People are buying large quantities of foodstuffs especially flour.
>
> Grave fears are held for our own country. People are talking in hushed whispers everywhere. Great anxiety prevails.
>
> **Sunday Aug. 2nd.** Coming home from Sunday School I bought a war edition (my first Sunday newspaper). The situation is very

acute. A special cabinet meeting has been held. The feeling in the country is electric. We wait with great anxiety the statement of Mr Asquith on Monday.

Monday Aug. 3rd. At 9-30 a.m. left Central Station for Stocksfield with 45 Mission members. The weather was splendid but the great dark war cloud hung over us. We could not dispel our anxiety try as we would. Despite this, a very enjoyable outing.

At every railway station on the way up a military guard is stationed. The whole community seems alive with uniformed men. Several trainloads of soldiers passed us on their way to the city.

News has come to hand that the naval Reserve have orders to mobilise. War between France and Germany has been declared. Things look very black. Germany's high-handed action makes our interference almost inevitable.

Tuesday Aug. 4th. The great news of the early morning is that Britain has presented an ultimatum to Germany. The Army and the Territorials received mobilisation orders.

11.00 p.m. Went down into the city. Crowds had gathered at the Central Station and in front of the 'Chronicle' offices, waiting for the declaration of war to be made known

One of the Army's first tasks was to acquire horses, which were required in large numbers, not only for the cavalry but to move the guns – at this time they were the main 'motor' of the army. Eventually some two million horses would be slaughtered on the Allied side alone during the conflict. A soldier in the London Territorial Army described how requisitioning worked:

Small parties were sent out, under a man with some technical knowledge, to requisition horses for the Transport Section. They could stop any likely-looking horse encountered, and remove it from the cart or van it had been drawing. The person in charge was given a receipt and a requisition order. The horses were brought back to Charterhouse Square, where they were inspected by a Vet, and, if suitable, were retained, the owners being paid compensation by the Government. Any not accepted were returned to the owners. The horses retained were exercised daily by being led round and round the Parade Ground – formerly the school playground.[9]

That something similar was happening in Newcastle is evident from The Reverend Mackay's diary, whose entry for August 5th reads:

> Great excitement and sorrow prevails in the city. All the volunteers have been called out as well as the reservists. Soldiers have been leaving the city in great numbers all day.
>
> Went down town to see if I could see any soldiers ... 800 soldiers have been quartered in Tilleys Rooms, Market Street. Armstrong College has been turned into a hospital. At St. Thomas's Church an unusual scene presents itself. The floor of the church is littered with straw and about 50 or 60 Territorials are gathered there. Horses by the score are feeding in the church yards.
>
> At the barracks in the evening great crowds have gathered. Soldiers are leaving every hour.[10]

The Northumberland Hussars had taken over the racecourse at Gosforth, where they remained until September when the regiment moved to Lyndhurst in the New Forest in Hampshire. Major Johnston was the officer in charge of transport. In August the British Expeditionary Force of 110,000 officers and men had crossed the channel with 'the declared aim of helping our allies, the French'. However, the British Government, in particular the First Sea Lord Winston Churchill, had promised also to assist the Belgians. Such assistance proved futile when the German Army swept across Belgium and into France, and in late September the Government took fright and decided to send more troops to save Antwerp. This led to the creation of a new 7th Division, formed between 31st August and 4th October, and it included the Northumberland Hussars among its ranks.

At Lyndhurst the forest was looking at its best with the bracken turned golden-brown. In any other circumstances, a forest camp in the warm sun of early autumn would have been a delight. But experienced officers, such as Johnston, wrote of the difficulties of a new Division struggling to be born: difficulties of army procedures, of organising men and horses. One officer wrote home: 'we are hard at it and I fancy we shall be much older men if not in years at least in experience before we get things shipshape'. At 42, Johnston was already older than many of the other men around him. Soon after the Hussars' arrival at Lyndhurst, the territorial troops were inspected, on 6th September, by the Division's Commander, General Capper.

A month later, on 4th October, the officers and men of the 7th Division left for Southampton in a 12-mile convoy, their final destination unknown. Knowledgeable observers said it was among the finest Divisions to have left Britain. Yet even experienced veterans of the Boer Wars, who had bravely led cavalry charges in South Africa, could not anticipate what they were about to experience on the Western Front in northern France and Belgium. General Capper decided to sail for Zeebrugge in the first troop ship, the *Minneapolis*. The Northumberland Hussars, as the Division's cavalry, were to embark with him. Capper's plan was to be in Belgium before the main body of troops arrived. The *Minneapolis* left at noon on 5th October and, after threading its way through enemy minefields, arrived at Zeebrugge the following day, though none of the men, and few officers, knew their destination. Men and horses were crowded on to every available space at the end of the harbour mole, but by three o'clock they had all left by train for Bruges. The trains were

Plate 74 The Northumberland Hussars on the Zillebeke Road, moving up to Ypres, October 1914. Major Johnston was in charge of motor transport.

decorated with flowers and the men were cheered all along the route. But when seeing the British and Belgian flags flying at half-mast, it was feared that Antwerp had already fallen. Though the city survived a few more days, it was already too late to save it.

The 7th Division and the 3rd Cavalry Division were redirected to Ypres, with instructions to prevent the Germans advancing to the coast at Calais at all costs. 'And thus,' said E. J. Kennedy, Chaplain Major to The Expeditionary Force, 'the small force of under thirty thousand men pressed on to the heroic task of holding up the main body of the enemy; not less than two hundred and forty thousand men.'[11] It was assumed that if the German thrust could be halted before it reached the sea, the war could won, but that failure to do so would cede victory to the enemy. Faced by the Germans' overwhelming superiority, the 7th Division had to fight a rearguard action all the way from Ghent to Ypres, where they were to make their stand (Plate 74). They reached Ypres on 14th October, 'as peaceful and welcoming as Lyndhurst after a long march through the New Forest'. It was an old-fashioned sleepy place with a tree-shaded canal which seemed very remote from the war, as E. J. Kennedy recalled in his memoirs: 'the first view of Ypres was glorious. As we marched through the great square in front of the Cloth Hall, I was struck with the mediaeval aspect of the place. The gabled houses carried one's imagination into the long ago; whilst the glorious Cloth Hall of the eleventh century, backed up by the equally fine cathedral of similar age, presented a picture not easily to be forgotten. Alas! When I next saw it, the place was a heap of crumbling ruins.'[12]

THE FIRST BATTLE OF YPRES

On 19th October the first battle of Ypres began. Although the Northumberland Hussars was a cavalry regiment, and one of the few yeomanry regiments to remain horsed throughout the war, their role was already changing. A contemporary account on the first day of the battle recalled that it was no longer possible to push cavalry patrols beyond the line of the infantry who were dug in and needed an unrestricted line of fire. The cavalry had gradually developed 'from a fluid line of mounted men occasionally dismounting to use their rifles' to a 'rigid line of men occasionally using their horses to move from one part of the battle field to another'.[13] This was scrappy warfare and the 7th Division attempted to hold some five and a half miles

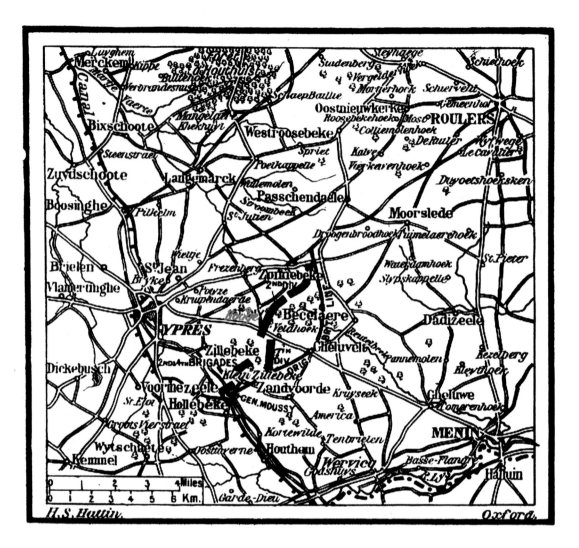

of frontage. In these early months of the war, before the stalemate of trench warfare ensued, both armies were still very mobile. When the German army pushed forward, allied soldiers were forced to find whatever cover they could, attempting to dig scrapes in the ground but, with trenching tools in very short supply and efforts to find agricultural implements in nearby farms and villages unsuccessful, this proved largely fruitless. The desperate plight of the officers and men was described in the official account of the war: 'Here they hung on like grim death, with almost every man in the trenches holding a line which was of necessity a great deal too long – a thin, exhausted line against which the prime of the German first line troops were hurling themselves with fury. The odds against them were about eight to one,

Map 4 A map of the first Battle of Ypres; Major Johnston was wounded at Hooge, which is east of the city.

and when the enemy found the range of a trench, the shells dropped into it from one end to the other with the most terrible effect.'[14]

At first the Northumberland Hussars were held in reserve. The Regiment's new role was to act as a general reserve for the sorely tried infantry, and as a contemporary account related, 'fling ourselves into any gap that appeared dangerous'. On the evening of Thursday, 22nd October, the weather changed, and an Indian summer day gave way to a black, rainy night. The Regiment had retired out of range of shellfire, and was hoping for a good night's rest, but hardly had the men 'laid down the horse lines and set about the preparation of a meal, when orders came to turn out on the instant'.[15] Confusion reigned, and in a sea of mud, with saddles and blankets sodden and everyone seeking his mount in the inky darkness, Major Johnston and his men were ordered to move to Hooge Château (Map 4). The cavalrymen had to lead their horses along the road in the blackness with the greatest caution to avoid being shot by their own, nervous sentries who would fire at anything that moved.

From early next morning the Regiment came under heavy bombardment from 'Black Marias', shells that came over in clusters of four 'with a villainous roar and clouds of yellow smoke', which made it unpleasant for officers and men to run with heavy equipment across a turnip field to assist the infantry. In the evening the Regiment withdrew to Hooge Château. Very early the following day the chaplain, Edward Kennedy, related how he was held up by the Northumberland Hussars, as they 'came by in splendid order on their way to entering the action'. The Germans were advancing on two sides, shelling hard and inflicting many casualties. During the misty dawn, General Capper, Commanding Officer of the 7th Division, was forced to use his only reserve, the Northumberland Hussars, and in so doing the Regiment became the first Territorial Force to see serious action. Under increasing pressure the infantry,

> ...had been forced to give ground, and it was just at the moment when the gap was ominously widening that the regiment, waiting in reserve, was called to assist. There was a hurried rush across the miry fields, and through a wood filled with dead and wounded, to the trenches, where the remnants of several regiments were collected. Here we remained several hours under very heavy rifle and shell fire, unable to retaliate

very effectively, owing to the poorness of the field of fire. But these gallant riflemen stuck to it, their crisp fire orders never seeming to falter. Then came the crowning incident of the day. A line of Scots Guards suddenly rose to the order of 'Come on, the Scots Guards' echoed by Major Sidney's 'Come on, Northumberland Hussars, and together Guards and Hussars charged against a swaying mass of grey figures and finally drove them over the hill. Our casualties, considering the severity of the fighting, were relatively light, but among the wounded were Major Johnston and Lieutenant Laing'.[16]

The following day, while severe, desperate fighting continued, Lieutenant Clayton was wounded by machine-gun fire, hit by a bullet in the side of the head. He was among the Regiment's 300 casualties, which included the death of its commanding officer. In the Official History of the first Battle of Ypres, General Sir James Edmunds said that 'though this was the first action of any Territorial unit, the regiment (Northumberland Hussars) had carried out the task assigned to it in a thoroughly effective manner; the Hussars defiantly checked the German advance'.[17]

Major Johnston had been hit by shrapnel, which had entered the right side of his chest, ironically piercing his weaker lung. At this point fact and fiction tend to blur; it has been said that Johnston was taken for dead and only saved by the fact that the officer in charge of the burial party, Colonel Henry Sidney, not only recognized Johnston but saw him move. Whether or not this was true, Johnston was sent back to England a week later on 31st October aboard the *St Patrick*. The doctors' assessment of his wound at the King Edward VII Hospital for Officers decided that, although it was 'severe' it was 'not permanent', and the Medical Board estimated he would be 'incapacitated for military duty for 10 weeks'. Johnston had come perilously close to death, and though his first experience of this war was over, he could proudly number himself among the 'old contemptibles', those officers and men who had seen service by 22nd November.[18]

Back at Broadway, Mary de Navarro watched the Belgian refugees arrive: 'poor frightened people – some without hats, some in overalls, children carrying shabby dolls, women with kitchen utensils, just as they had rushed from their homes'.[19] Grim days followed when the English wounded returned from the front. At Lamb House, Henry James, despite his ill-health, had given his studio over to Belgian refugees. In

Plate 75 Mary Anderson as 'America' in the pageant held at the Queen's Hall, London, after the United States entered the war.

Paris, Wharton was ashamed and angry at the American position of neutrality, especially after the sinking of the *Lusitania* in May 1915. Her friend Theodore Roosevelt wrote in agreement, and described Woodrow Wilson as 'the worst President we have had since Buchanan'[20] – whose consort had been Harriet, Elliott Johnston's sister-in-law. Henry James's response was to take out British nationality, and though Edith Wharton was upset by this reaction, she even considered adopting French nationality. With typical pragmatism, however, she pleaded a lack of time, and said that it was more important to make oneself useful. Wharton wrote impassioned poems, essays and novels imploring her country to join what she regarded as a fight for civilization. These were published in America, and in one of her most effective propagandist war poems, 'The Great Blue Tent' (1915), she invoked the flag of America which is urged, by the 'winds of war', to turn itself once again into the tattered 'shot-riddled' flag of freedom it once was in the War of Independence.[21] Later, after the American entry into the war in 1918, Mary de Navarro returned to the stage, to great acclaim, in a celebratory pageant arranged and presented by the opera singer Clara Butt at the Queen's Hall, London. Known of course as Mary Anderson, she appeared as 'America'; after Butt had wailed about America not joining the Allies, Mary emerged through a forest of allied flags as the personification of the Statue of Liberty, uttering the rousing line 'Hold! Into your firmament I cast my stars' (Plate 75).[22]

THE CONTINUING STRUGGLE

With the Germans' advance on Paris and their race to the sea halted in the first Battle of Ypres, the mood in France changed radically. There was a realization that the war was going to be a long hard struggle. Unlike the many American expatriates who returned home, Edith Wharton's love of her adopted country saw her work tirelessly to help defeat this affront to France. Her war work took many forms, but its common theme was that if someone was in distress, she would respond. Wharton helped 'the great army of refugees' who flooded into the city from northern France and Belgium and organized four hospitals to take care of tubercular patients. She established 'Children of Flanders' rescue committees to take care of 1000 young people, and campaigned to raise funds for all these activities. When the war settled into the stalemate of trench warfare, Wharton travelled to the war zone in her car, 'laden to the roof' with whatever medicines, bandages, cigarettes and chocolates could be packed in. The French High Command was conscious of the propaganda value to be derived from these visits by such a prominent author, who was also an outspoken champion of America's entry into the war (Plates 76 & 77). Wharton wrote a report after each trip, which became a series of articles in *Scribner's Magazine*, and when published as *Fighting France* it became a best-seller. In 1916 the French Government recognized and honoured her work with the award of the Légion d'Honneur. Later the French military called on her to inspect the regions evacuated by the German army, at the time when Major Johnston was acting as a liaison officer with the French Army.

Johnston made a gradual recovery from his wound, and on 24th June 1915 the Medical Board in Bristol declared him fit for General Service. He did not return to frontline duties for another twelve months, and his whereabouts during this time are not known. In April, the War Office had split the regiment, keeping its Headquarters and A squadron with the 7th Division in England. Johnston could have

Plate 76 Edith Wharton with Walter Berry, meeting French troops at the front.

Plate 77 Edith Wharton visiting the ruins of a village in her new car, which would have been stuffed with cigarettes, chocolate and other luxuries.

been involved with reorganization and further recruitment. In May the following year, all units were reformed in France. On 10th June 1916 Johnston returned sporting the red tabs of a staff officer. His friend Savile Clayton, who had been wounded at Ypres at the same time as Johnston, waited a year and half before he too returned to the artillery horse lines in France (Plate 78). Johnston joined the HQ staff as Second in Command of the Regiment which, soon after his arrival, received orders to move to billets on the River Somme. That evening the officers arranged a boxing tournament for the men (see Plate 36, p.75), and the Commanding Officer took a final parade before the start of the Somme offensive the following day. The officers' engagement in fox hunting on farmland behind the trenches had, by this stage of the war, been prohibited on account of crop damage and the ill-will it engendered among the local population.

By September part of the Regiment was at La Serre, a shallow ridge, improving trenches in an area where some of the heaviest fighting took place. For most of February 1917, Johnston was temporary Commanding Officer of the Northumberland Hussars, till the previous Commanding Officer was replaced. In August he returned to the 1st Army School at Aldershot, and in October attended the Senior

Officers' Course, where he was being prepared for further promotion; but ill-health interrupted his remaining war years. In December, the Director of the Army School wrote to inform the War Office that in his opinion, Johnston was 'unfit to return overseas'. However, in March 1918 he returned as a Staff Officer, firstly with liaison duties at the Headquarters of the British Mission to the French Army, and subsequently in July at the Reinforcement Camp, Cavalry Corps. In August Johnston left the unit on sick leave and returned to England, staying at Boodle's. He may have had a recurrence of respiratory problems caused by the earlier wounding or brought on by gas, but he was to take no further part in the war. On 2nd January 1919 he requested permission to proceed to the south of France to stay at one of Lady Derby's houses; many officers were travelling south to convalesce in one of the houses and gardens owned by English expatriates on the Côte d'Azur.

Plate 78 Horses belonging to the officers of the Northumberland Hussars in the ruins of a cottage at Etri Cour, during October 1917; many of the horses would die due to exposure in the primitive conditions.

THE FINAL YEARS OF THE WAR

In November 1915 Edith Wharton was also taking breaks from her exhausting war work, visiting the south of France and in particular the town of Hyères, near Toulon. There, in an atmosphere of sunshine and flowers, she was able to relax and continue to write; 'it is heavenly here, and I marvel at the thought that I used to be bored on the Riviera! It is delicious just to dawdle in the sun, and smell the eucalyptus and pines, and arrange bushels of flowers bought for 50 centimes under a yellow awning in a market smelling of tunny fish and olives'.[23] Yet, despite these interludes, Wharton felt 'drained' when the war ended. By then, many of her old friends had died, including Henry James and Egerton Winthrop, and several of the younger men she had known were casualties of the war. She had grown tired of Paris and decided it was time to leave the city and open a new chapter in her life.

In the spring of 1918 she discovered the village of Saint-Brice-sous-Forêt, north of Paris, which had been in the direct line of the Germans' last desperate push, and under the trajectory of 'Big Bertha' shelling of the city. Not surprisingly Edith Wharton was able to buy cheaply an eighteenth century house in the village, the 'Pavillon Colombe', with its remnants of a beautiful old garden (Plate 79). Wharton had driven out to the suburb with her friend Elisina Tyler,

Plate 79 The street façade of the Pavillon Colombe at St-Brice-sous-Forêt, which Edith Wharton bought during the last days of the war.

and as she recalled in her memoirs, 'the orchards were just bursting into bloom and we seemed to pass through a rosy snow storm to reach what was soon to be my own door'.[24] Despite the derelict state of the house, Wharton immediately fell in love with the Pavillon Colombe, where 'at last I was to have a garden again – and a big old kitchen garden as well, planted with ancient pear and apple trees, espaliered and in cordon and an old pool full of fat old gold fish'.[25] Once the armistice had been signed, Wharton began converting this long-deserted estate into a gathering place for her Inner Circle and for the happy few who would shortly include Lawrence Johnston. Upon settling into the house she recalled that 'peace and order came back into my life', with the 'leisure to enjoy the two pursuits that never palled, writing and gardening'. Edith Wharton was now ready to devote herself to her friends and her gardens, and for the remaining years of her life she was able to live in her new home at Saint-Brice from late spring to autumn, and then travel south to spend the winter

Plate 80 The Château Ste-Claire at Hyères in the south of France.

in Hyères, where she bought the Château Sainte-Claire (Plate 80). So 'when winter comes, and rain and mud possess the Seine Valley for six months, I fly south to another garden, as stony and soilless as my northern territory is moist and deep with loam'.[26]

By now Wharton had acquired a thorough knowledge of gardens and plants, and indeed, even from 1903, her letters reveal an increasingly detailed horticultural knowledge especially of flowers; with the acquisition of these new gardens her enthusiasm knew no limits. She studied catalogues, visited nurseries and, something shared with Johnston, was a constant searching for rare and improved plants. As Judith Fryer noted from her letters, 'one might deduce that Wharton attended more to deliberate choosing and placing of flowers than to the choosing and shaping of words and images in her books'.[27] In the years to come Wharton, with her two gardens, would become known and respected by her friends as a 'super-gardener'. She would be greatly assisted by Major Lawrence Johnston, whom she first mentioned in a diary entry for 12th March 1923 after a lunch at which the renowned literary and political hostess, Lady Sibyl Colefax, was also present.[28]

By the 1920s the gardening and social reputation of Hidcote, and its creator, had been established in society circles, enhanced by a royal seal of approval when The Prince of Wales visited the garden in 1919 – a visit that Lady Colefax may well have arranged. It is highly likely that Wharton had met, or at least was aware of, Johnston before the lunchtime meeting in 1923, perhaps through Egerton Winthrop, but their friendship was now set to blossom. Johnston was once described by James Lees-Milne as a 'Henry James character, a sort of passionless pilgrim, very nice, very correct, afraid of committing himself to an opinion on anything save gardening'. But for Wharton, after the intellectual excitement of her middle years and the recent traumas of the war, this late flowering of a friendship with 'Johnnie' Johnston was precisely what she was seeking: he was a 'guru' who was undemanding, but who shared her passion for gardening, gardens and the plants that filled them.

NOTES AND REFERENCES

[1] Sitwell, O., *Left Hand Right Hand, Vol. 3, Great Morning*. Macmillan, London, pp. 124–5.

[2] Johnston's membership was probably proposed by Mark Fenwick, a member of the club.

3 Wharton, E., *A Backward Glance*. Constable, London, p. 337. When she was married their visits to Europe had been in autumn and winter, to avoid clashing with Teddy Wharton's sailing, golf and other sporting interests.

4 Ibid., p. 336.

5 Lee, H., *Edith Wharton*. Chatto and Windus, London, p. 463.

6 Ibid., pp. 462–3.

7 Wharton, op. cit., p. 343.

8 Quoted in Brown, M., *1914*. Pan, London, pp. 17–8.

9 Ibid., pp. 50–1.

10 Ibid., p. 52.

11 Kennedy, E. J., *With the Immortal Seventh Division*. Hodder and Stoughton, London, p. 34.

12 Ibid., p. 40.

13 Edmunds, J, E., *Military Operations France and Belgium – 1914*, Vol. 2. Macmillan, London, p. 197.

14 Ibid.

15 Pearce, H., History of the Northumberland Yeomanry. pp. 83–4.

16 Ibid., pp. 85–6.

17 Edmunds, op. cit., p. 197.

18 These were the original regular soldiers or reservists who derived their nick-name from the famous 'Order of the Day' given by Kaiser Wilhelm II at his headquarters in Aix-la-Chapelle on 19 August, 1914: 'It is my Royal and Imperial Command that you concentrate your energies, for the immediate present upon one single purpose, and that is that you address all your skill and all the valour of my soldiers to exterminate first the treacherous English; [and] walk over General French's contemptible little Army.'

19 de Navarro, M., *A Few More Memories*. Hutchinson, London, p. 132.

20 Quoted in Lee, op. cit., p. 455.

21 Wharton, op. cit., p. 456.

22 de Navarro, op. cit., p. 160.

23 Lewis, R. W. B., *The Letters of Edith Wharton*. Scribner, New York, pp. 361–2.

24 Wharton, op. cit., pp. 362–3.

25 Ibid., p. 363.

26 Ibid.

27 Fryer, J., *Felicitous Space – the Imaginative Structures of Edith Wharton and Willa Cather*. University of North Carolina Press, Chapel Hill, p. 172.

28 Wharton, E., Diary, 1920–37. Lilly Library, Indiana University, Bloomington. The diary does not say where the meeting took place, but it was likely to have been at Ste-Claire, when the hyacinths – one of Wharton's favourite flowers at Hyères – were in full bloom.

CHAPTER NINE

HIDCOTE AND FRIENDS

Johnston may not have stayed long in the south of France, for in March 1919 he was, in the military term of the period, 'disembodied',[1] but it was not to be the immediate end of his military career. Though the Northumberland Hussars were disbanded after the war, the Regiment was reformed in 1920 with Major Johnston as Second in Command. However, he finally left the army two years later, on 1st November 1922, with a distinguished military career behind him and the right to use the title of Major for the rest of his life. His friend George Saville Clayton had retired from the Regiment the previous autumn, but died suddenly in December at the Midland Hotel in Manchester. Johnston was now 51 and, like many retired military men before and since, set about his private life with renewed energy, both in the garden and within his circle of friends.

Among his group of influential friends were other wealthy amateur gardeners with time to indulge their passion for gardening – people such as E. A. Bowles at Myddleton House, Enfield, The Hon. Robert James

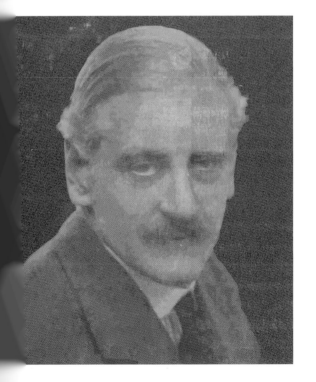

Plate 81 The Hon. Robert ('Bobbie') James (left): a photograph taken from his obituary in the Gardener's Chronicle, 1961; (right) Friends discussing plants at St. Nicholas, Richmond: Bobbie James (in hat), Norah Lindsay and Lawrence Johnston.

at St. Nicholas, Richmond in North Yorkshire (Plate 81),[2] Reginald Cory at Dyffryn House, near Cardiff, and Ellen Willmott at Warley Place, Essex and her sister Ruth Berkeley at Spetchley Park, Worcester. Lady Serena James, recalled how the friends would arrive at St. Nicholas bearing boxes of plants, bags of seeds and countless cuttings, and there would be endless conversation about plants, plant collecting and recent developments in their gardens. The visits would be reciprocated, and the friends would arrive at the respective houses, similarly laden with plants and with much to discuss. Mary de Navarro also found Johnston to be 'a generous gardener', who gave her 'many precious plants'. It was through her visits to Hidcote, 'where I saw for the first time many tiny flowers' intense radiance and was enchanted by their loveliness',[3] that Navarro became an enthusiastic and knowledgeable gardener. Encouraged by Johnston, she became close friends with Clarence Elliot,[4] a leading expert on alpine plants, who became a regular guest at Court Farm. Elliot even constructed what he called a small 'alp' in the garden, planted with his own finds from the Alps, Pyrenees and South America.

Plate 82 Gertrude Winthrop in old age.

Gertrude Winthrop was by now suffering from the onset of senile dementia, which was to cloud her final years (Plate 82). In May 1921, she took a last voyage to New York on the RMS *Lapland*. When his mother's health and influence declined, Johnston turned more and more to his closest female friends: those society women Berenson described as 'more receptive, more appreciative and consequently more stimulating'. His name begins to appear more frequently in the letters of Norah Lindsay, and in the diaries and letters of Edith Wharton. In October 1924 Wharton wrote to Berenson, describing Johnston 'as her new and very nice gardening friend'.[5]

NORAH LINDSAY

Among Johnston's closest friends was Norah Lindsay, née Bourke, who came from Ireland; her father was a younger son of the 5th Earl of Mayo. In 1895, she had married Captain Henry

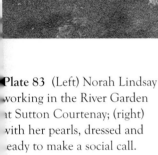

Plate 83 (Left) Norah Lindsay working in the River Garden at Sutton Courtenay; (right) with her pearls, dressed and ready to make a social call.

('Harry') Lindsay, and the couple lived in London, and at the Manor House, Sutton Courtenay in Oxfordshire. The latter was a wedding present from Harry's cousin Lord Wantage; it was located four miles south of Abingdon close to the River Thames. The Souls often met there 'with the purpose of playing lawn tennis, the piano and the fool and other instruments of gaiety'. In his diaries the American-born socialite, 'Chips' Channon, noted that the Lindsays entertained 'many a budding genius from Oxford', and 'moulded the youth of England', as they 'bathed in the backwaters of the Thames or read poetry in the rose garden'.[6] Lady Diana Cooper, leader of the so-called 'Corrupt Coterie', remembered the garden as 'the place of all others for romance and gathering rosebuds and making hay and jumping over the moon ... Flowers literally overflowed everything and drifted off into a wilderness'.[7] It is not known whether Johnston was invited to these parties, or what he would have made of them, but he certainly met Norah Lindsay in 1907, when he first visited the Manor House.

The Lindsays' marriage was unconventional, and with Harry spending most of his time in London, Norah was free to socialize and garden at Sutton Courtenay (Plate 83). This she did with great success. In 1904 Lindsay was invited to write her own description of Sutton Courtenay for *Country Life*. In the article, she confessed to having an admiration for Italian gardens: 'Indeed there is more than a memory

Plate 84 Sutton Courtenay; looking towards the house through the Long Garden with its exuberent planting and Italianate topiary.

of Italy in my garden ... I would have been a much lesser gardener had I not worshipped at the crumbling shrines of the ancient gods of Florence and Rome. There I learnt the magic of black sentinel cypresses, translated in our northern clime to Irish yew and juniper'.[8] 'Sentinel pillars' and other topiary forms were scattered throughout the Long Garden at Sutton Courtenay, creating the formality against which luxuriant informal planting could be matched – though her sister complained that the planting was 'untidy and weedy' (Plate 84). Lindsay's friendship with Johnston, and exposure to his more conservative approach and innate sense of good taste, would temper her inclination to overdo things, whilst he would adopt the spontaneity of her planting and theories on colour.

In 1920 the Lindsays separated, and though Norah was allowed to stay on at Sutton Courtenay, it was without financial support. Not surprisingly this situation, as Duff Cooper said in his diaries, caused her great distress.[9] The house was often rented out in order to raise funds, while Norah was obliged to stay with friends, including prolonged stays at Hidcote. In 1924 her friend Nancy Lancaster suggested that Norah should charge for the 'design services' she had been providing free at the many places where she stayed. Allyson Hayward, in her biography of Norah Lindsay, suggests it was while staying with another friend, Lady Horner at Mells Manor, when she realized that her 'services' in the garden were worthy of payment.[10] So at the age of 51, Lindsay became a garden consultant out of economic necessity but, even though she had many clients, her financial circumstances remained precarious. Among her clients were Lady Astor at Cliveden, and Philip Sassoon at Port Lympne who became one of her closer friends. These were both places where Norah and 'Johnny' (the shortened nick-name used by Lindsay) Johnston stayed. Nancy Astor was Lindsay's most difficult client; she was strongly opinionated and staunchly anti-Catholic, so her acquaintance with Johnston was less than fulsome.

Throughout these difficult times Norah never charged Johnston for her advice; on the contrary, he provided her with a 'home' at Hidcote, and paid for their trips to the south of France, where they visited Edith Wharton, or to Venice. They also toured gardens and nurseries in England and Ireland, often accompanied by Colonel 'Reggie' Cooper. On more than one occasion they travelled to weekend parties at Mount Stewart, the home of the Londonderry family, who were socially acquainted with Nora's own family, the Bourkes. Recalling these visits years later, the Marchioness of Londonderry's daughter remarked that it was expected that Norah and Johnny would always travel together. In the 1920s it was more difficult for a lady to arrive alone than it was to arrive with a gentleman, witness the difficulties of Lily Bart in Wharton's book, the *House of Mirth*. At Mount Stewart, Lady Londonderry had been creating extensive formal gardens since 1922, including an Italian garden with features derived from the Palazzo Farnese, Caprarola, and the Villa Gamberaia.

By 1926 Norah's friendship with Johnston had deepened and, following a stay in June, she wrote to tell her sister that, at Hidcote 'all is beauty, peace and spoiling. Delicious dinner last night out in one of the glasshouses full of lilies and scents and everything quiet and restful and no bother at all.'[11] She mentioned sleeping in a room hung with huge canvases, painted by Johnston. These gave a birds-eye view of the gardens; the paint so thick that they were like tapestry moquettes (Plate 85). In the following spring, Norah, and her children Nancy and Peter, spent weeks at a time at Hidcote, and in her very uncertain world, Johnston was providing the security and attention she lacked; 'he is,' she wrote to a friend, 'such a cosy companionable creature and has my three passions in Excelsis – gardening, travelling, and reading out loud'. At times she called him affectionately, her 'funny old man' or a 'good little man', even a 'favourite uncle', which, she said, 'is why I like him'. Her letters provide an invaluable insight into the life of this very private man; 'we have,' she wrote after one visit to Hidcote with her daughter Nancy, 'spent an extremely enjoyable and cosy uneventful week here, leading the most comfortable existence with dear Johnny. Every morning he goes off to plough at 8.00 am' – evidence that Johnston did not entirely give up his farming interests – then 'Nancy and I go for a long ramble over the little hills and copses of this enchanting Cotswold country. We lunch at one and sometimes go for an expedition afterwards or merely a walk.'[12] Johnston would let Norah use his car whenever she wanted, and sometimes Lindsay made expeditions to other gardens; on one occasion she drove to Bodnant to see 'the Aberconways' beautiful place in Wales', returning with the car packed with treasured plants. Sometimes Lindsay would walk over to Kiftsgate to practice on Heather Muir's piano, 'as I dreadfully miss that when I am here', and in the evenings there would be visits from various neighbours, 'chiefly the Muirs who are first class [bridge] players'[13] (Plate 86).

Lindsay's praise of Johnston the gardener, and of the garden at Hidcote, was also unstinting. Shortly before her death in 1948, she said that his 'sense of scale, design, and texture combined with horticultural knowledge was of the highest order, exquisite taste and unusual colour sense, have all worked together to produce a garden unrivalled in England'.[14]

Plate 85 A study of flowers painted by Lawrence Johnston for Heather Muir at Kiftsgate.

Plate 86 Heather Muir created the garden at Kiftsgate after 1920, inspired and helped by Lawrence Johnston.

THE HON. BILL BARRINGTON AND THE MÉNAGE À TROIS

One of the places Norah and Johnny visited regularly was Nether Lypiatt Manor near Stroud, the home of Mrs Violet Gordon Woodhouse. At first Violet was not so well-disposed towards the quiet, self-effacing Johnston, and after one visit she was reported to have said that she would only tolerate Johnston for the pleasure of Norah's company.[15] Eventually she must have mellowed, for she often stayed at Hidcote. Violet Gordon Woodhouse was the most celebrated harpsichord and clavichord player of her time, and very much a part of what Hermione Lee described as the second model of

Plate 87 Violet Woodhouse and her *ménage à trois*. The Hon. Bill Barrington is at the top of the photograph in the hat.

English society – artists, writers and musicians. The Sitwells, George Bernard Shaw and Frederick Delius were frequent visitors to her London house, even Picasso on one occasion, and she would revel in their brilliant conversation and, in return, entertain her guests with a recital. What was extraordinary about Violet Woodhouse was that she shared her life and her house with, at first, four very different men including her husband; one of the 'companions' was the dashing young cavalry officer, the Hon. 'Bill' Barrington, whom Johnston had met as a young man at Trinity College, Cambridge (Plate 87).

Johnston had discussed the development of the Hidcote garden with Barrington from its outset, though their conversations were far from one-sided. Barrington had been encouraged to take up gardening and garden design by Woodhouse, when the *ménage à cinq* moved to Southover Manor, Lewes, in 1901. Her hope was that gardening would alleviate the possibility of boredom when Barrington was no longer engaged with the part-time militia – and so it proved. As a water-colour artist and architectural historian, Barrington was already fascinated by 'the interplay of water, trees, plants and open spaces, of light and shade, of different heights and colours',[16] and, like Johnston, he took to gardening with a lifelong enthusiasm. He read gardening books and subscribed to such journals as the *Garden*, the magazine run by William Robinson, and was soon exchanging ideas and visits with the 'father of the naturalist school of garden designers'. In 1908 the *ménage* moved to Armscote House, near Stratford-upon-Avon, which provided Barrington with a farm and the potential of another garden. Almost immediately, he renewed his acquaintance with Johnston who was by then at Hidcote Bartrim, some four miles away. Both men were just beginning to lay out their gardens and, after his experiments at Southover, Barrington was keen to share his own well-developed ideas on colour, tone, balance and design with Johnston. Their verbal exchanges were to influence the gardens at Armscote, Hidcote and later at Nether Lypiatt. Barrington believed that a garden should give the impression of having been there for ever. Its relationship to the surrounding fields, hills and buildings would have a naturalness born of scrupulous attention to detail, whilst the paths, terraces and low walls could enjoy the same consideration as borders, with lavender falling over edges and rock plants, thyme, snapdragons, hollyhocks, lupins, pinks and valerian growing out of rocks and crevices. Orchards and avenues, far from being independent of the main garden, should flow out of it, with casually mown paths and spring and autumn flowers under-planted in the long grass.

The final move to Nether Lypiatt was made in 1923, and Barrington immediately followed up the ideas he had discussed previously with Johnston. These involved the use of hedges to divide the garden into four compartments, each with a medlar or mulberry tree in the centre. Yew seedlings from Hidcote were laid out in parallel lines, 33 yards (30 metres) long, and below them were overflowing herbaceous borders. Tapestry hedges similar to those at Hidcote, planted with box, ash, yew, beech, holly and hornbeam, separated the flower garden from the kitchen garden. At the south end, a high hedge traversing the garden was 'pierced by a yew tunnel beyond which the central axis was prolonged by an avenue of limes through the orchard'.[17] Nothing remains of the garden now, only its spirit, as evoked by Osbert Sitwell as a 'vanished sun of another age … glows upon the gardens. With its high yew hedges and stone walls, with its exquisite dark-toned flowers, for example bergamot, moss roses, columbines in various shades of night and flowing water, among the shrubs a honey-scented ceanothus, the spicy blossoms of which are the colour of Violet's hair, and another hung with small red lanterns – it provides endless pleasure for the hostess and the guests'.[18] Woodhouse had taken to dyeing her hair blue, almost a vivid violet-mauve, much to the consternation of more than one visitor.

In his autobiography, Sitwell mentions the visits of Norah Lindsay to Nether Lypiatt, but makes no mention of Johnston. Lindsay was readily incorporated into life there, for she was witty, entertaining and also musical, playing the piano well; and much to the delight of Bill Barrington, she took a keen interest in food. Like Violet, she had her own wayward, even eccentric dress sense, and according to Diana Cooper, often wore tinsel and leopard skin with baroque pearls and emeralds – though her biographer Allyson Hayward doubts whether these were real, given her impecunious state. Not surprisingly Woodhouse regarded Johnston as too reticent for her taste, although she recognized his professionalism, which was a considerable compliment, given her own striving to achieve musical perfection. Just as she accepted Johnston for the pleasure of Norah's company, so she was prepared to include him in her life for Bill's sake. Barrington and her husband Gordon were both totally ruled by Violet, and if she disapproved of anyone it was pointless, even for Bill, to issue invitations. However, the three gardeners would spend hours sitting in one of the lower rooms of

Plate 88 Ethel Sands in her London house at The Vale, Chelsea, in 1922.

ate 89 Nan Hudson in 08 at Newington.

the manor – 'masculine rooms, comfortable studies and smoking rooms' into which 'strayed baskets of apples and pears, shallow wicker trays of walnuts, even occasional vegetables, a turnip or carrot, roots of flowers, a piece of bass, so that by the contents of the room, even coming out of a trance in a vacuum, you could judge of the season by these traces of the earth's fruits.'[19] There they would discuss gardens, exchanging ideas about design, colour arrangements and plants. Both Barrington and Johnston were influenced by Norah's way of letting flowers overflow and spill into each other: up walls, into water and round trees and shrubs, until they eventually drifted off into wilderness.

Barrington made drawings of the lower rooms, perhaps to recall those happy times. He shared his love of painting with Johnston, who had made a studio at the end of the tender plant house when he first moved to Hidcote. Eventually this had to give way to plants and the easel was transferred to the study, where he painted a still-life of flowers and two large canvases depicting the red borders in all their summer glory, remembered by Norah Lindsay. Sadly, these paintings have been lost. Johnston also painted the ceiling and frieze in one of the larger rooms at Kiftsgate for Heather Muir, assisted by her three daughters, who rubbed the paint with boot polish for three days to achieve the desired 'antique' appearance.[20] He also created murals in the domes of the gazebos at Hidcote; perhaps he was inspired by his artist friends, among them Rex Whistler who painted the celebrated murals and *trompe l'oeil* at Port Lympne for Philip Sassoon.

Whistler was Norah's long-time friend whom she mentioned in a letter to her sister, describing a visit he made to Sutton Courtenay, on a cold day in February 1933. Her neighbour, Margot Asquith, was holding an auction of her surplus belongings, and as a result, 'We had such an extraordinary incursion of people here on Sunday to see Margot's things that I have only just recovered from the joyful surprise of unexpectedly receiving to lunch Ethel Sands (Plate 88), Nan Hudson (Plate 89), Reggie Cooper (see Plate 133, p.273), Lee Ashton, George Churchill ... Rex Whistler and his brother (Lawrence), Francis Stoner and Johnny brought six and masses of food and wine'.[21] Twelve unexpected guests were squeezed on to bedroom chairs around the hall table 'with our elbows inlaid into our neighbours' ribs' to enjoy a simple meal of mutton broth, baked potatoes and apple tart. Norah's consternation was understandable, for a visit to the artist Ethel Sands and her companion Nan Hudson, Johnston's cousin, at Newington Manor near Oxford, was always a highly organized affair with the most excellent food playing an important part. Nevertheless it was an occasion of great hilarity and after lunch, when most of the guests had left, Norah enjoyed a 'tame meal' with 'Johnny', Rex Whistler and his brother and Francis Stoner, who lingered afterwards to see the garden, which was 'a mass of aconites, hepaticas and a few nice tall hellebores'.[22]

At Court Farm, one of Mary de Navarro's visitors was E. F. Benson, author of the Mapp and Lucia novels.[23] The epicene 'Frank' Benson had been infatuated with Mary, in a non-sexual way, since his time at Cambridge where he had kept a photograph of her beside his bed. In his novel *Queen Lucia*, Benson poked fun at life in Broadway, which became the fictitious village of Riseholme. In the book, Olga Bracely, the opera singer, may have been Mary Navarro, and it is tempting to see a touch of the manner and appearance of Lawrence Johnston in the character of Georgie Pillson. Pillson is believed to have been based mostly on Howard Sturgis, a close friend of Benson's brother Arthur, but it was undoubtedly a composite portrayal. Georgie or Mr Georgie, never just plain Pillson, like Lawrence, appears first wearing a straw hat, but his face is described as pink and round, with blue eyes, a short nose, very red lips and a firm little brown moustache clipped very short. His character was not obtrusively masculine and the important ingredients in his nature were feminine: 'in common with the rest of Riseholme, he had strong artistic tastes, and in addition to playing the piano, made charming water-colour sketches', which he framed at his own expense and gave to friends – all characteristics of Lawrence Johnston. Georgie, in a similar way to Johnston's relationship with Norah Lindsay, was devoted to Lucia in a totally asexual way: 'there never had been, or ever would be, the smallest approach to a flirtation between them'.[24]

A RETURN TO HIDCOTE

After the war, Johnston found much of his earlier work on the garden had been neglected in his absence, and his first task was to put this in order. A particularly pressing problem was the damage caused

Plate 90 Lawrence Johnston with his head gardener Frank Adams.

by summer droughts on the heavy Cotswold clay. The problem was resolved by the installation of an extensive system of irrigation pipes throughout the garden, fed by a reservoir sited on the hill above Hidcote Bartrim. Another response to the climate was the construction of an all-weather tennis court. Such courts, made with a blended mixture of brick, which enabled them to dry out more quickly than grass, had been developed by En-Tout-Cas in 1909, but they did not become popular until after their introduction by the Lawn Tennis Association in the 1920s. The court was located in a corner of the kitchen garden and enclosed by hedges; on one side this was cut into a sequence of 'windows', allowing the circulation of air to assist drying in wet weather. Reginald Cory used a similar hedge at Dyffryn to allow glimpses of the Theatre Garden. It is not certain when the all-weather court was constructed at Hidcote, but Johnston continued to play lawn tennis on grass.[25] When Avray Tipping visited Hidcote in 1930, he mentioned tennis courts on what is now called the Theatre Lawn (see Plate 70, p.149).

With Hidcote growing in size and stature, Johnston appreciated that his own considerable skills as a designer and plantsman needed to be matched by a person who could implement his ideas – a right-hand man who could be relied upon 'to do what was necessary without being told'.[26] Johnston had the ability to surround himself with people, both friends and staff, who could complement his own strengths, or compensate for his deficiencies. This was particularly true when he appointed his first and only head gardener Frank Adams in 1922 (Plate 90). Adams was 32 years old, the son of a butler, and having been a royal gardener at Windsor Castle, possessed the sort of credentials Johnston was looking for, in every respect. He not only matched Johnston's growing knowledge of plants but had the practical skills to implement, or reject his ideas. Johnston was constantly thinking of new projects, often inspired by features he had seen in other gardens, both in England and abroad, and when he was at Hidcote the two men would spend Sunday in the study working out the next idea for the garden. Johnston had a great deal of faith in Adams' acumen, and if his head gardener said a scheme was not feasible, or perhaps too expensive, he was inclined to respect his opinion: so much so that the housekeeper, Miss Marsden, who managed Johnston's financial affairs after his mother's death, often enlisted Frank Adams' help in curbing their master's wilder excesses in the garden. When Johnston departed for the south of France in late autumn, Adams was left to put into operation all the plans they had made during the summer.

One of their first tasks was to refine the Pool Garden. By 1927 or '28, Johnston had seen the old raised pool in Edith Wharton's garden at the Pavillon Colombe, and the way in which the water reflected the sky and clouds. This may have inspired him to replace the pond at Hidcote with a circular raised pool, which almost completely filled its space.

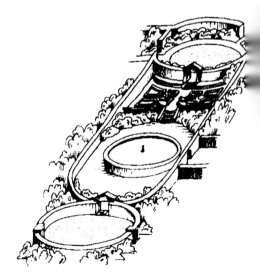

Figure 9a Graham Stuart Thomas's sketch of the three rondels at Hidcote.

The pool was surrounded by a yew hedge, and in time the raised water would reflect a fine architectural 'green' archway. In the centre of the pool a cherub and dolphin fountain recalls a similar fountain at the Pavillon Colombe. Shallow steps lead up to a small circular green lawn enclosed by a hedge of yew and box, with a painted iron seat, a *giardino segreto*. The simple, classical arrangement of the pool garden completed the vista of the three circular gardens leading from the rondel. Looking back, 'tiers of hedges rise parallel to one another, terminating finally in the yew hedge of the Theatre Lawn.[27] It is as effective as any 'green garden' seen in Italy, and in the opinion of the National Trust's first gardens adviser, Graham Stuart Thomas, it was 'one of Lawrence Johnston's crowning achievements'[28] (Fig. 9a).

The pool doubled as a swimming pool. On most summer mornings the Muir daughters, accompanied by their governess, would walk over from Kiftsgate for a dip in the pool. The water was made all the more inviting by the addition of Mediterranean-blue dye. The adjacent thatched 'Italian House', reminiscent of the Garden House that Parsons had designed for the Millets at Russell House, was used as a changing-room. The interior was decorated with a fresco,[29] which has since been obliterated by the weather, two decorative 'icon' tiles and a delightfully carved bas-relief, using the same stylized figure Johnston portrayed on his linocut bookplate. On summer evenings, guests would gather in the Italian House for cocktails and alfresco meals, seated on Johnston's collection of Regency garden furniture.

A CHANGING EMPHASIS

During the 1920s Johnston became more of a plantsman than a designer. Timothy Mowl has written that, in the early years of the Hidcote garden before Johnston returned from the war, there must have been a general Arts and Crafts feel to the garden enclosures, but 'once the hedges became overwhelmed by flower colour that mood diminished'.[30] Now the 'plants' had moved centre stage and Johnston's skill was in overlaying the architectural framework with an exuberance of 'jungle' planting. Graham Stuart Thomas, who saw the planting in its heyday during the 1930s said; 'There would be one plant climbing over another, a group of disparate shrubs united by a continuous under-planting of some lowly flower; there would seldom be a single clump of any herbaceous plant or bulb, rather it would be grouped here and there creating the effect of its having sown itself; the colours were mostly blended to separate schemes with occasionally a deliberate clash. Seldom is one plant given one whole piece of ground; it shares it with others. All this hangs together because of the firm design, which is so much enhanced by the vertical lines of dark evergreen hollies and holm oaks'.[31] This exuberance of planting over the architecture distinguished Hidcote from pure Arts and Crafts gardens, such as Snowshill, Rodmarton and especially the gardens of Thomas Mawson where the 'hard landscape' was always in evidence. In these gardens the design and fashioning of those elements, whether paving, walls, pergolas and so on, were important features of the garden, to which the planting remained subservient (Plates 91 & 92).

Plate 91 Hidcote Manor: the main vista, c.1929, with the optical illusion described by Avray Tipping – 'the level first section looks its length, and beyond, the rise of the ground brings everything near to you, so you wonder why the end-gates look so faint and spidery'.

Plate 92 The herbaceous borders at Hidcote, c.1929. Thomas Mawson, in his book *The Art and Craft of Garden Making*, said that many terrace schemes fail due to a lack of decisive and marked terminations, allowing the end of the terrace to fade away. He recommended that a circular seat could be a solution to this problem. Johnston followed this advice, but adopted Gertrude Jekyll's suggestion that such seats should be made of English oak and allowed to weather to a silvery patina.

In the 1920s and '30s Johnston, with the help of his new head gardener Adams, was constantly adding specialist features to the garden, one of the first being the Alpine Terrace. An enclosed alley known as the Terrace, which had more than a passing resemblance to Charles Platt's sketch of the 'Hedge Walk' in the Quirinal garden,[32] was made alongside the high retaining wall, below the Stilt Garden. A raised alpine bed, which ran beside the wall, was protected in winter by a wood and glass frame. Here Johnston could trial many of the alpines and succulents he collected, along with others obtained from his friend and fellow collector Clarence ('Joe') Elliot.[33] Seeing the terrace 30 or so years later, Vita Sackville-West described how a dwarf mauve campanula had been allowed, after the Hidcote principle, to seed itself in brilliant patches along the terrace, where normally it did not belong.[36]

Plate 93 The Pillar Garden at Hidcote, c. 1960s, underplanted with peonies.

The adjoining Pillar Garden, one of Johnston's more Italianate gardens, was made early in the 1920s, filling in the rectangular space beside the hedge of the Long Walk. There has been speculation about the inspiration behind the 22 identical columnar yews on their square bases. Similar designs are illustrated in Mawson's *The Art and Craft of Garden Making*, and more prosaically, it has been suggested that Johnston merely found a job-lot of clipped yews in a Belgian nursery.[35] Nevertheless, the Pillar Garden is more likely the outcome of Johnston's close friendship with Norah Lindsay. The trees are reminiscent of the mounded yew and box at Sutton Courtenay, and pillars, very similar to those at Hidcote, were a 'signature' feature of many gardens designed by Lindsay, notably at Blickling Hall in Norfolk. In Johnston's Pillar Garden, the slope is skilfully manipulated into a series of shallow terraces, on which he planted peonies, another of his favourite flowers; blowsy tree peonies on the top level with borders of double pink herbaceous hybrids further down, spilling out over the path (Plate 93).

Beyond the Pillar Garden, the natural incline of the land sloped towards the stream and this Johnston and his head gardener transformed into the Rock Bank.[36] Mawson had written that features such as rock gardens should be concealed and not be visible from the house, where any 'natural dingle or depression which could be screened from the more important features of the grounds would form a fitting place for them'. This is exactly the location of the rock bank at Hidcote, though its position is more likely to have been another example of Johnston's pragmatic problem-solving. So far as design went, Mawson had said; 'Rock gardens above all else should aim to reproduce some particular phase of nature. In the Alps (whence the idea came) the wealth of floral display is inset amongst high rocks and large boulders interspersed with low shrubs snugly shouldered with spruces and mountain pines, with snow-capped mountains behind, and it is the background and foreground which imparts sentiments to the flowers. Minus this or other picturesque and suitable settings, an alpine garden is lame.'[37] Mawson's remarks may have been an influence, but by now, Johnston had extensive experience of plant-collecting in the Alpes Maritimes in France with Wharton, Bowles and others, and appreciated the distribution of alpine flora and the terrain in which they grew.

In the 1930s interest in plant geography was expanding and the 'father' of plant ecology in Britain, Arthur Tansley, overlapped with both Johnston and Cory at Trinity College, Cambridge. In 1911 he published a paper on the types of British vegetation, which led to his seminal work on plant succession in which he explored the relationship between soil, water, light and the development of vegetation. In the area below the Rock Bank at Hidcote, known today as the Spring Slope, Johnston sought to replicate a similar seral succession. It began with the stream side then led to the semi-openness of an alpine meadow, with a rich variety of taller herbaceous vegetation, and culminated in a rock scree and alpine bank. Two small pools, creating specialist habitats for plants found in the outflow of glacial meltwater, completed the sequence. Much of this innovative ecological planting was simplified by Graham Stuart Thomas after the National Trust's acquisition of the garden, ostensibly on account of maintenance costs. Today, it is being restored as part of current restoration plans, though in modified form due to the shade cast by maturing trees.

Beyond the Rock Bank and the Pillar Garden, Johnston extended the Lower Stream Garden to meet the field boundary line. The path leads through trees and shrubs before finally opening to another, if less dramatic, view over the fields and hills.[38] In approximately 1919, Johnston had extended the garden into the area known as the Wilderness, which was planted with trees and shrubs for spring flowers or autumn colour. Alongside, the Long Walk was extended to the skyline.[39] Johnston once again played with the perspective by gradually narrowing its width by a metre, to accentuate its length, as well as reducing its overall height as it progressed.[40] At the far end the gates have a resemblance to the Johnston Gate at Harvard Yard, Cambridge, Massachusetts, designed from 1889 to '90 by the Renaissance Revival architect, Charles Follen McKim.[41] The view through the Hidcote gates towards the Malvern Hills lacks the dramatic impact of the other vista beyond the Gates of Heaven.

In the l920s and 1930s Johnston adopted what Lindsay called his 'collector's style of gardening' with large numbers of a particular species all lined up together. The Lower Stream Garden became festooned with small circular plant labels each with a raised number, made in cast aluminium, most probably from the Royal Label Factory, Stratford-upon-Avon. Unfortunately the plant books recording the numbers, and the plants to which they referred, disappeared when the head gardener left in 1957. Norah Lindsay disagreed strongly with what she called a 'tricked up' garden, and although they would make changes together, 'if she went away for an extended time, she'd come back to his tricked up ways again!'[42] Johnston was influenced in this style of planting by the garden at Nymans, which he first visited in May 1919, with Mark Fenwick, shortly before he left the army.[43] The Sussex garden was laid out originally by Ludwig Messel, with a vast collection of trees and shrubs. His son, Leonard ('Lennie') Messel and his wife Maud, were more fascinated by the number of species, and different varieties, within one genus. At first they concentrated on a few plant families, though rhododendrons were Lennie's greatest love, and he was always eager to buy new species and hybrids. Later the collection extended to magnolias, camellias and hydrangeas. After his initial visit, Johnston called in frequently and became a close friend of the Messels, but he could never confine himself to a single or even a few genera, so Hidcote became packed with many 'collections'. As Sackville-West said later, 'it was as a botanist and plant hunter that Major Johnston would wish to be thought of',[44] but even though he became a passionate collector, he never lost sight of the aesthetic value of plants and their arrangement.

WESTONBIRT

During his final years at Hidcote, Johnston's passion was for collecting trees and shrubs, though the way he used them would show his skill in combining the botanical with the aesthetic. His inspiration came from the celebrated arboretum at Westonbirt, which had been started nearly a century before by Robert Holford – though the estate was originally laid out by his father George at the beginning of the nineteenth century in the 'picturesque style'. George Holford followed the principles set out by the landscape gardener and painter, William Sawrey Gilpin. In *Practical Hints upon Landscape Gardening* (1832), Gilpin emphasized variety of form in trees and shrubs and favoured grassy glades between 'promontory' beds of shrubs, rather than insipid sweeps. Robert continued to follow the key principles of the 'Picturesque' – variety, connection and intricacy – when he began the arboretum in the 1850s. In turn this was continued by his son George Lindsay Holford[45] when he inherited the estate in 1892, though by this time there was an ever-increasing influx of new trees and shrubs to accommodate. In an article about Westonbirt, William Goldring wrote:

> The outline of the vista is not monotonous; here the shrubbery projects, there it recedes; at one point some favourite tree is made to stand out boldly, as if to emphasize the projection; at another point one may see a group of shrubs which like all the sunshine they can get ... nowhere can be seen harsh or monotonous lines: the skyline is always broken by columnar trees. The groundline around the shrubberies is never continuous. The shrubs are always planted to spread out and fall on the turf, and in order to break the outline, here and there a spreading bush ... is planted out boldly away from the main mass.[46]

Johnston was so overwhelmed by the aesthetic appeal of Westonbirt during a visit sometime in 1926 that he returned with his head gardener, Adams, to show him the 'picturesque' effect he wanted to recreate at Hidcote. He planned a new area beyond the Wilderness, to be known as 'Westonbirt', in acknowledgement of the older arboretum (Plate 94 l & r). Lord Morley,[47] who had inherited the estate, generously gave Johnston many trees and shrubs. These initial plantings were seen later by Tipping, though by the 1930s Johnston was already reciprocating, by sending trees and shrubs back to Westonbirt, raised from the many new plants he was growing from seed. By then Johnston had an international reputation as a collector, and was constantly receiving plants and seeds from all over the world. The Frameyard, near the tennis court, was the centre of this enterprise, where 'hundreds of pots of sown seeds, each with an asbestos cover to exclude light and retain moisture, [were] sunk in beds of sand retained by railway sleepers'.[48]

In the 'Westonbirt' Garden the glades and vistas were unlike any other part of Hidcote. Groups of trees, and individual specimens selected for their autumn colour, were positioned so the beauty of their bark or foliage could be more easily appreciated. Russell Page contrasted Johnston's mature style of planting with the pictorial effects of the earlier conventional manor house garden; 'Major Johnston freed himself from his frame and learned to handle plantings and compositions in a bold and unexpected way. For instance, on the outskirts of the garden lay a piece of undulating grass-land with a quiet view over stone-walled fields merging into the distant blue hills. Here

Plate 94 (left & right) In his later years Lawrence Johnston was inspired in his planting by the 'picturesque' principles he saw at Westonbirt. Since Johnston's time, the planting had become overgrown and the vistas were no longer visible. Recent restoration aims to restore the special character of Westonbirt at Hidcote today (left) – the ancient 'ridge and furrow' pattern in the turf is clearly visible in the foreground – compared with part of the current Holford Ride at Westonbirt Arboretum (right).

he planted the higher parts of the ground with large groups of many kinds of berberis, red in autumn with their translucent berries and colouring foliage, which stressed the undulations of the whole site. But what lifted this scheme on to a higher plane were tufts and groups of yuccas, Y. flaccida, Y. filimentosa and Y. gloriosa. Exotically Mexican, their sharp foliage and creamy candelabra spikes of flowers defied the expected and made a new kind of world, an apt setting for a flock of rosy pink flamingos unbelievably wading in the shallow pond which was the centre of this garden'.[49]

The influence of this planting can be seen in many gardens made by Page, especially his late work for the PepsiCo headquarters in Purchase, New York. This follows the same 'picturesque principles' that inspired Johnston; a sinuous path of amber gravel threads through the landscape, past massed groupings of trees dividing the lawn into smaller gardens, each containing a sculpture – 'I use the trees as sculptures and the sculptures as flowers, and then take it from there. It's a cross current thing'.[50] At Purchase, New York, Art Price's 'Birds of Welcome' greet visitors at the entrance to the sculpture garden, just as the flamingoes and other exotic birds once greeted visitors to the Westonbirt Garden.

At Hidcote the birds did not survive long after Johnston's departure, and in the intervening years the subtlety of the 'picturesque' planting was also lost. The careful management required to maintain the effect was absent; background evergreens were allowed to dominate and hydrangeas were extensively planted throughout. As a result, little remains of the bold, unexpected groupings and massing of plants admired by Page, though some of the original, picturesque quality can still be discerned. It is hoped that current restoration work will reinstate the uniqueness of this part of the garden.

Russell Page was one of the few 'outside' people to see Hidcote in its prime, which he described in a radio broadcast of 1934.[51] Though from the late 1920s until the outbreak of the Second World War in 1939, the garden was opened to the public for a few days each summer, in support of the Queens Institute of District Nursing.[52] After Vita Sackville-West saw the mature garden in 1949, she praised the originality of Johnston's approach to planting, in particular the way in which he mixed trees, flowering shrubs and roses with herbaceous plants, in a single composition. In the intervening years this style of planting has become familiar, but in the 1930s it was new, evoking a comment by one observer, that 'this man is planting his garden as no one else has ever planted a garden'.[53] Before Johnston began gardening, other gardeners such as Gertrude Jekyll, had devoted different parts of the garden to displays for separate times of the year – spring borders, summer borders and the like. At Hidcote every part of the garden had its own plants, colour scheme or feeling intermingled so that floral colour was produced at different times of the year. As Graham Stuart Thomas explained it:

> Some areas of Hidcote are given to isolated shrubs, with a through-planting, or ground-cover, of some plant which would make a great display either in contrast or sympathy with the shrubs, to subside into respectable greenery for the rest of the year. This is because one of the great arts in planting for effect during the whole year, or at least for its growing months, is to choose plenty of plants whose foliage presents a good appearance the whole time, and especially after the flowers have faded.[54]

Vita Sackville-West's single regret was that, on the occasion of her visit, Johnston was away from Hidcote, and the many questions she had wanted to ask went unanswered; she was not alone in her regrets, for sadly Johnston never wrote about his garden or gave an interview.

Notes and References

1. This curious word for 'discharged' or 'retired' appeared on Johnston's military records. After the Second World War, a different word 'demobilised' was used in this context, which was known colloquially as 'demobbed'.

2. The Hon. Robert ('Bobbie') James was the younger son of the 2nd Lord Northbourne of Betteshanger House and estate in Kent. Robert's brother Walter, later the 3rd Lord Northbourne, was an artist member of the Etruscan School in the 1860s, which included Italian and British painters – among them George Howard, 9th Earl of Carlisle, and Lord Leighton – who were devoted to the Italian countryside and in reviving the traditions of landscape painting of Claude Lorrain and Nicolas Poussin. Robert also painted, and the brothers used to visit the Cotswolds together. They exhibited at the Grosvenor and New Galleries in London. Lady Serena James, Robert's wife born in 1901, was the only child of the 10th Earl of Scarborough. After Serena's marriage, her mother who was

known for her rudeness, was horrified that St. Nicholas was not a great country seat, and exclaimed, 'she's going to live in a little cottage by the road'. The James's were distinguished gardeners; the robust and beautiful white rambler rose 'Bobbie James' was named after St. Nicholas's owner. After Bobbie James died in 1960, Lady Serena kept the garden going till her death in 1999. A useful review is Hepworth, V. & Kernan, C., 'The Hon. Robert James and St. Nicholas'. *Yorkshire Gardens Trust Newsletter*, No. 9, Autumn 2000/Winter 2001, 8–10.

3 de Navarro, M., *A Few More Memories*. Hutchinson, London, p. 186.

4 Ibid., p. 257.

5 Quoted in Lee, H., *Edith Wharton*. Chatto and Windus, London, p. 529.

6 James, R. J., ed., *Chips: The Diaries of Sir Henry Channon*. Orion, London, p. 68. 'Chips' Channon became a naturalized British subject, and was a Conservative Member of Parliament from 1935 to 1958.

7 Cooper, D., *The Rainbow Comes and Goes*. Century, Idaho, pp. 66-7.

8 Lindsay, N., 'The Manor House, Sutton Courtenay, Berkshire – 1 The Gardens', *Country Life*, Vol. 66, 1904, 152–3.

9 Norwich, J. J., ed., *Duff Cooper Diaries, 1915–51*. Weidenfeld & Nicolson, London, p. 125.

10 Hayward, A., *Norah Lindsay – the Life and Art of a Garden Designer*. Frances Lincoln, London, p. 78.

11 Quoted in Hayward, op. cit., p. 112.

12 Lindsay, N., letter to her sister Madeline, December 1931; quoted in Hayward, op. cit., p. 112.

13 Ibid., p. 213.

14 Lindsay, N., *House and Garden*, Vol. 3, April 1948, 46-51.

15 Quoted in Fretwell, K., Hidcote. Unpublished report for the National Trust, 2000.

16 Douglas-Home, J., *Violet – the Life and Loves of Violet Woodhouse*. Harvill, London, p. 66.

17 Hussey, C., 'Nether Lypiatt Manor', *Country Life*, May 1934.

18 Quoted in Douglas-Home, op. cit., p. 237.

19 Ibid.

20 Whitsey, F., *The Garden at Hidcote*. Frances Lincoln, London, p. 27.

21 Lindsay, N., letter to her sister Madeline, February 1933; quoted in Hayward, op. cit., p. 188.

22 Ibid.

23 E. F. Benson was living at Lamb House, Rye, where he wrote six 'Mapp and Lucia' novels, the town becoming 'Tilling'. After Henry James's death the house was briefly rented by Robert Norton, where he was visited by Edith Wharton. Benson, a friend of James, took the lease in 1919 and after 1925, lived there all year round.

24 Benson, E. F., *Queen Lucia*. Black Swan, London, p. 33.

25 On the Riviera circuit the courts were all made of clay, so perhaps Johnston considered himself at a disadvantage playing only on grass. The all-weather surface certainly would have been appreciated by his guests from the south of France.

26 Clarke, E., *Hidcote*. Michael Joseph, London, p. 38.

27 Thomas, G. S., *Cuttings from My Garden Notebooks*. John Murray, London, p. 288.

28 Pavord, A., *Hidcote Manor Gardens*. The National Trust. London, p. 54.

29 The mural was not as elaborate as those painted that year for Nan Hudson and her companion Ethel Sands by Vanessa Bell and Duncan Grant in the loggia at the Château d'Auppegard.

30 Mowl, T., *Historic Gardens of Gloucestershire*. Tempus, Stroud, p. 14.

31 Thomas, G. S., *Gardens of the National Trust*. Weidenfeld & Nicolson, London, p. 23.

32 Morgan, K. N., *Charles Platt the artist as architect*. MIT Press, Cambridge, Massachusetts.

33 Joe Elliot was a friend of Lawrence Johnston who lived at Moreton in Marsh; he established the Six Hills Nursery specializing in alpine plants at Stevenage in 1907.

36 Sackville-West, V., 'Hidcote Manor'. *J. Royal Horticultural Society*, Vol. 74, No. 11, November 1949, 476–481.

35 Whitsey, op. cit., p. 111.

36 In making his rock bank Johnston was influenced by his friends who had created similar features. At St. Nicholas, Bobbie James asked Ellen Willmott to create a rock garden, and at Abbotswood, Mark Fenwick had earlier asked the Pulham brothers to make an extensive alpine rock garden, in the character of the Swiss alps, as a setting for his house (see Plate 40, p.80).

37 Mawson, T. H., *The Art and Craft of Garden Making*. Batsford, London.

38 Charles Platt had suggested that trees and shrubs could be used in this way to screen out the countryside and control the view.

39 In 1930, Avray Tipping noted that the Long Walk, 'is bent, the fall of the first half being balanced by the equal rise of the second half'. An accompanying photograph shows a mature hornbeam hedge running down to the stream, and beyond a much younger hedge extending to the gates at the far end of the walk.

40 The hedge today (2009) is too high to be authentic, and should be lowered by nearly half a metre.

41 Brown, J., *Eminent Gardeners*. Viking, London, p. 55.

42 Personal communication with Allyson Hayward, 12 November 2007.

43 Nicholson, S., *Nymans*. Sutton, Stroud, in association with National Trust, p. 75.

44 Sackville-West, V., *Hidcote Manor Garden*. Booklet published by Country Life for the National Trust, London, p. 10.

45 George Lindsay Holford was well known in horticultural circles and was a council member of the RHS and founder member the Garden Society; the one surviving visitor's book (1892–1912) includes the names of other members, including Reginald Cory and E. A. Bowles. It is likely that Johnston also visited sometime after, perhaps with Norah Lindsay.

46 Goldring, W., 'Westonbirt', *The Garden*, February 1886; quoted on the Forestry Commission website under Westonbirt → The History of Westonbirt's Landscape.

47 Lord Morley was a nephew of George Holford.

48 Whitsey, op. cit., p. 23.

49 Page, R., *Education of a Gardener*. Harvill, London, p. 201.

50 Schinz, M. and van Zuylen, G., *The Gardens of Russell Page*. Stewart, Tabori & Chang, New York, p. 248. A reprinted edition was published by Frances Lincoln, London, in 2008.

51 Page, R., 'Hidcote Manor Microcosm'. *The Listener*, 22 August, 321–3.

52 When Hidcote opened its gates to the public on 12 August 1933, the gardens at Etal Manor and Chesters were also open. Both the new owners of these properties had served with Johnston in the Northumberland Hussars.

53 Sackville-West, V., *J. Royal Horticultural* Society, op. cit., 478.

54 Thomas, G. S., *The Art of Planting*. The National Trust, London, p. 19.

CHAPTER TEN

EDITH WHARTON AND HER FRENCH GARDENS

In the early 1920s, when Lawrence Johnston was about to leave the army, Edith Wharton was enthusiastically involved with overseeing the restoration work at the Pavillon Colombe near Paris with her architect Charles Knight, and in supervising the clearing and planting of the gardens at Sainte-Claire at Hyères, near Toulon in the south.

THE PAVILLON COLOMBE AT SAINT-BRICE

The 'Pavilion' had been designed in 1769 by the architect François-Joseph Bélanger as a country retreat for the mistress of the Prince de Guémené – Marie-Catherine Ruggeri, an actress at the Comédie-Italienne – affectionately known as 'Colombe', the Dove. It was exactly what Edith Wharton wished to re-create, as a place where she could write, receive guests and entertain her Inner Circle of friends. Later, with the work having been completed, a visitor said that when you stepped into the courtyard behind the austere walls fronting the village street, you stepped back 200 years. Wharton had restored the house perfectly in every detail; on the ground floor there was a sequence of interconnecting rooms, each with French windows opening on to the terrace (Plate 95):

Plate 95 Pavillon Colombe; the rear view of the house with windows opening on to the terrace.

Through the window my eyes rested among the green trees whose trunks were shot by the late sun-rays. Stone jars with pink climbing geraniums stood out against the vivid fat grass of a wet summer, and the smell of box rose pungently from the formal clipped hedges. Beyond the garden came the sound of the outer world, voices, autos, the church bell, but so faint that it scarcely touched the consciousness. The garden itself held such a deep tranquility that one dwelt among its most secret leaves against the quiet sky of evening.[1]

When Wharton arrived at Colombe, she found that the garden had been abandoned since 1914 and 'even before that had not had what Anglo-Saxons would consider real care'.[2] She began developing the garden in 1920 and was not short of expert advice. She discussed her garden notes and plans with her niece Beatrix Farrand, who by then was established as one of America's leading landscape gardeners and engaged on one of her more prestigious commissions, for Mildred Bliss at Dumbarton Oaks, Washington DC – regarded today as among America's finest gardens. Wharton constantly wrote to Beatrix about her garden: 'it's so much tidier, and more nearly finished than last year ... Oh, if only you and I could talk across the fence'.[3] Johnnie Johnston was also on hand to offer advice, plan and design parts of

Plate 96 The terrace at the Pavillon Colombe, where Edith Wharton and her guests would take lunch.

the garden, and in 1923 Wharton instructed her London bookseller to send a copy of Jekyll and Weaver's *Gardens for Small Country Houses*, which would become a source of inspiration.

She also found an old picture showing the sort of *jardin à la française* which the terrace windows once faced. Edith Wharton wanted to restore the garden to its original layout and splendour, but as was the case with so many gardens of the period, it had long been adapted into a *jardin anglais* – though 'the grove of trees beyond and the oblong basin and fountain beneath their shade were still untouched'.[4] The *jardin à la française* was heir to Italianate gardens and introduced in France in the mid-sixteenth century. Gardens in this style began with the view seen from the principal rooms of the house, which looked out over the terrace which, in turn, dominated the garden (Plate 96). From the terrace, the layout of the garden could be observed like a *tableau* presented for inspection. A central path, leading from the terrace, provided the 'axis of perspective', with lines of trees, parterres, and water basins formally placed on either side. The whole *jardin à la française* was divided into a series of rooms, arranged on the route of a predetermined walk. Nature was allowed to re-establish itself, further away, in the form of forests and meadows. By comparison, the *jardin anglais*,[5] which replaced the French garden in popularity during the eighteenth century, was irregular in layout with extensive lawns and tortuous paths, designed to be more naturalistic (Fig. 10a) – also the style used to great effect by Olmsted in Central Park, New York (see Fig. 1a – The Ramble).

Eventually the seven-acre (nearly three hectares) garden at Colombe would consist of several different areas, something visitors would describe as a series of rooms in the English style, arranged in stages leading away from the house (see the aerial view in Fig. 15a, page 319). Three shallow steps, flanked by urns, led down to a wide gravel terrace extending along the whole of the garden side of the house, bordered by a row of orange trees in green wooden planters. On the right, when looking from the house, was a lower lawn bordered by a yew hedge. Below the terrace and a long bed of lavender was the formal garden with box-edged squares of lawn, which became Wharton's *parterre français*; 'My first task was to level the bumpy lawn dotted with coleus and canna beds and extending from the house to the little grove; to cut down straggling "ornamental trees" and root up laurel and hydrangea borders. Having retraced the main lines of the old garden, set the

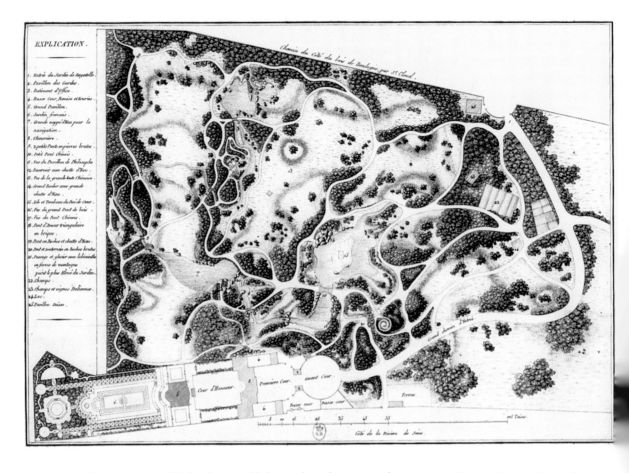

fountain playing, re-established the old boundary between the grove and kitchen-garden by means of a clipped box hedge and gateway, I was able to turn my attention to the planting'.[6]

A path bordered by box hedges led from the house into the wood which she called her grove, where there was a large, old reflective stone pool and the ground covered with ivy, Solomon's seal, and with primroses in spring and cyclamen in autumn (Plate 97). Wharton enriched this palette with periwinkle, St John's wort, lily of the valley and autumn crocus. In the centre of the pool was a fountain in the form of a cherub on the back of a dolphin, blowing his own trumpet. The path continued through an iron gateway into a potager planted with a mixture of flowers, fruit and vegetables. The potager was divided by an arcade of pleached limes running down to the southern boundary wall. Along the wall was a wide border of evergreen shrubs, rhododendrons, flowering quince and magnolias planted by a previous owner, which in spring were 'still a glory of yellow and

Figure 10a A plan of the garden of the Bagatelle, Paris, an example of the naturalistic jardin anglais, which contrasts with the formal area around the house.

Plate 97 The pool at the Pavillon Colombe which had enormous old goldfish still living in it.

Figure 10b Henri Trésol's plan for the garden at the Pavillon Colombe.

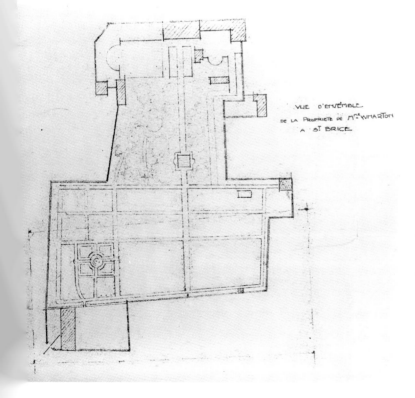

VUE D'ENSEMBLE DE LA PROPRIETE DE M.e WHARTON A St BRICE

white and salmon pink'. The whole garden was surrounded by an old wall, ten feet high, covered in the shady parts by ivy and elsewhere by clematis, roses, wisteria and trumpet vines, creating the effect of a *hortus conclusus*. In the fruit garden the walls supported espaliered pears, apples, peaches and nectarines, and grapes; and in front of the rhododendron border, a small orchard, cut in two by pleached limes, was planted with apple, pear, plum, cherry, quince and peach trees. When Henri Trésol made new plans for the garden in 1924, this area included a new rose garden and the blue garden that Edith designed with Johnnie Johnston (Fig. 10b).[7] Johnston was familiar with the formal blue garden at Abbotswood planned earlier for Mark Fenwick by Edwin Lutyens along lines advocated by Reginald Blomfield (Plate 98). The garden at Colombe was

Plate 98 The Blue Garden at Abbotswood, designed for Mark Fenwick by Edwin Lutyens.

Plate 99 The Blue Garden at the Pavillon Colombe, designed with the help of Lawrence Johnston.

cruciform in design, with the lawns enclosed by a low box hedge and the planted areas consisting entirely of blue flowers, including blue hibiscus (Plate 99).

In contrast to the largely 'green' areas near the house, the walled garden was a blaze of colour; the vegetable plots were bordered by cordon apple trees, in places with fruit trees trained into pyramids. In front was an edge of low box hedging, and between there was a wide border of brightly coloured, mostly annual flowers. Wharton had a passion for repeating groups of strong, vivid colours, and was extremely knowledgeable about how to contrive the effects she desired.[8] In her early plans and the extensive notes and plant lists prepared for her head gardener, she spelled out clearly what was required, both in detail and for broad effect. She wanted groupings of 'oranges, yellows, and pale yellows' for the great border in the central allée, with 'orange calendulas, heliopsis, yellow calceolarias, and yellow snap dragons, and behind those very floriferous yellow dahlias that have always been planted in the border of dahlias'. These were to be followed by groups of blues, violets and mauve; for example, anchusa, delphiniums, mauve dwarf asters, heliotrope, violet petunias, violet china asters, *Verbena canadensis* and *V. rigida*, ageratum and blue delphiniums. Further on, she wanted white and pink colours: pink and white penstemons, similarly coloured snap dragons, white browallia; then large groups of truly blue anchusa, delphinium, lobelia, bachelor buttons (*Centaurea cyanus*) and blue browallia. These were to be followed by yellow daisies, heliopsis and, in front, Cape marigolds, Siberian wallflowers, straw-coloured and orange nasturtiums, orange Californian poppies and dwarf yellow calceolarias. In her note to the head gardener, she stressed that it was essential for groups of yellow to be distinct from groups of rose (or pink) colours by plantings of blues or violet, and some tufts of perennial plants with silver foliage would be good to separate the groups.[9] The colour of the planting was intensified by a rich background of blue and purple cabbages, silver-green leeks, crimson beets and emerald lettuce.

Wharton had an especial fondness for roses, and often used them as a metaphor to describe the showy society of New York or the ephemeral beauty of a heroine, such as Lily Bart in *The House of Mirth*, the book whose working title was originally 'The Year of the Rose'. Her earlier experiences with Morton Fullerton point to her awareness of the

'language of flowers', and when, in *The Age of Innocence*, Newland Archer sent a bouquet of yellow roses to Ellen Olenska, the flowers symbolized jealousy, infidelity, even a decrease of love. She wrote enthusiastically about her new rose garden (Plate 100) to Daisy Chanler in 1929:

> My new rose garden is promising and I find this soil so decidedly made for rose growing that I mean to plant hundreds more this autumn, and root up nearly all the old varieties. The new ones are so much more worthwhile and one can now get varieties of every kind to which mildew is unknown.[11]

Russell Page, who saw the gardens at Colombe when Wharton was there, regarded the design as an Hidcote-type plan of a connecting series of garden compartments in which 'one narrow path traversing half a dozen openings through a hedge or wall will lead into as many gardens, each retaining a domestic scale'. He described how the garden was a sequence of sun and shade, open spaces and high hedges, with grass plots and woodland, flower gardens, avenues, and grassy orchards; 'each section of this long garden is seen from the house as a succession of narrow glimpses of sunshine and shade, the full shape and treatment of each part only being evident as you pass in turn through them'.[12] It is possible that Page over-emphasized Johnston's initial influence on the garden. He may even have misunderstood the nature of a *jardin à la française*, but what is obvious from this description is the accord between the two gardeners, and it explains why Wharton became such 'a frequent, delighted and often envious visitor to Hidcote'.[13]

HYÈRES: SAINTE-CLAIRE

In the south of France, Edith Wharton, exhausted after her exertions in the First World War, had discovered the old Château Sainte-Claire in Hyères at the end of the war. She had been taking a four-month sojourn at the town's Hôtel du Parc accompanied by Robert Norton, who had been recently released from the British Admiralty. Hyères is the most southerly town of the Var, 18 kilometres east of Toulon, with a very favourable climate of hot dry air through the winter, sheltered from the mistral and the cold, though not to the total exclusion of bitter frosts which could have disastrous effects. The mostly mild climate of Hyères had attracted the first wave of British visitors to the south of France in the nineteenth century. Robert Louis Stevenson, for example, stayed in a cottage within the grounds of Ste-Claire. But as attention switched to the seaside, Hyères located three miles from the coast, saw its popularity decline, so that by the turn of the century it had become a quiet, almost forgotten corner of the Côte d'Azur.

Wharton found the unfashionable character of Hyères to her liking: a perfect writer's refuge and a complement to St-Brice. Yet there was more to Hyères than the favourable climate, for it satisfied Wharton's need for association with a sense of place, something that became important to her after meeting Charles Norton, Professor of Fine Arts at Harvard, many years before. Perhaps taking a more literary or artistic approach, Wharton remained a lifelong devotee of Norton's vision of a present whose meaning, richness and reality was rooted in the past: 'it was he who opened my eyes to everything worthwhile'.[14] It had shaped her earlier response to Italy and its gardens, and now it seemed to her that no part of the Mediterranean mainland, with such blessings of climate, fertility and scenery, had played so continuous a role in European history as at Hyères. It was the true Provence, existing as it had been lived in for 2000 years, taking no heed of the artificial life of the cosmopolitan 'Riviera' – a name she disliked intensely. She spoke of the emotions aroused in her by 'the physical beauty of color and form and light, and of the more subtle atmosphere of association evoked by every town and hamlet, every mountain chain and river, almost every stone of that favored land'. For Wharton, so envious of the French and their heritage 'of people who have a real *patrie*', Hyères was a perfect idyll. Here she was to spend some of the happiest years of her life; it was 'good to

grow old – as well as to die – in beauty; and the beauty of this little place is inexhaustible'.[15] (Plate 101)

Plate 101 Château Sainte-Claire at Hyères; a 19th century print of the castle.

Hyères helped to restore Wharton's sanity after the destruction and personal loss of the war, and in her friend Robert Norton's uncomplicated manner, making 'neither effort nor demand', she found the perfect companion. They 'talked long and happily as they pursued their discoveries, day after day, in those early months of leisure and liberation'. Together they explored the sun-drenched countryside of Provence:

> He sat with her in the car, till even the patient car refused the task she set it; she walked with him – she was always a light-footed walker on an unknown trail. They scrambled, they lost their way, they were possibly benighted – nothing mattered in such a cause; with Norton she could even allow the countryside its own freedom, as she did, and follow its moods. Or on a fine spring evening, on a hillside overlooking a lonely bay while he sat and drew, she could watch and wait nearby as the scene shaped itself into a poem, an impression piece in words which matched his painting'.[16]

Plate 102 A view of Ste-Claire from the old town of Hyères, taken in 2007.

Plate 103 A view from the terrace of Ste-Claire over the red roofs of the old town of Hyères, with the Romanesque church just below the house (2007).

On one of their rambles around the old town of Hyères, they came across a ruined fort, overlooking the town, and Wharton immediately determined to have it on a long lease. The property they found was the convent, 'Sainte-Claire du Vieux Château', which at first she leased and later purchased in 1927. It reflected the duality of Edith Wharton's life: the brilliant, successful façade hiding the need for an austere solitude. This duality was apparent in all her houses: at The Mount in Lenox, at Colombe in St-Brice and here at Hyères. Wharton would have been well aware that the convent's former occupants were even more symbolic of her life: 'the 'Clarisses', the poor Claires who dedicated their lives to God in remembrance of Ste Claire, the companion of St Francis of Assisi, who herself preached poverty and abnegation'.[17] Throughout her life Wharton mostly denied herself the personal physical contact she often desired, and no doubt she believed that the Côte d'Azur would satisfy both a moral and physical distance from any possible temptation, as well as provide her with the time in which to write. At Hyères, Wharton was able to complete one of her most successful novels, *The Age of Innocence*, in just seven months, between September 1919 and March 1920. Though her intention had been to revive her declining popularity, for it was seven years since she had published a major novel about old New York, Wharton actually needed a best-seller to fund her new houses and their gardens.

The house at Ste-Claire was in the old part of town, high above the new town, and built in the ruins of a château (Plates 102 & 103). The old fortress towers, walks and convent buildings had been restored, but no one had lived in the house for almost 50 years, and it could only be approached on foot. Charles Knight, the architect already involved at Colombe, was engaged to take on the restoration project. Wharton wanted to renovate the existing buildings and add a winding access road for visitors. Once this work was started, she could turn her attention fully to the garden, which she had begun to do in 1919, a year before actually moving in. Ste-Claire offered her the chance to create a garden that was different to all her other ones. Her biographer and member of her Inner Circle, Percy Lubbock, believed that the garden was 'the nursery of her own young charges that were always on her mind':

> ... and those of Ste-Claire were a wilder brood ... than the orderly bevies of the pavilion [Colombe]. They gave her more trouble from the beginning, and they might for that reason be closer to her heart. She was not as playful or indulgent as some, but she planned untiringly for the young things' higher good. The tangled wilderness, that at first lacked even soil for their nourishment, was soon blossoming in a score of nooks, sheltered clefts, friendly little enclosures, enhancing as by accident its negligent charms'.[18]

THE GARDEN AT STE-CLAIRE

Around the house were 25 acres (c. 10 hectares) of 'luxuriant tangle, thorny, flowering always aromatic' vegetation, typical of the maquis, with ilex, carob trees, wild olives and century plants (Agave americana) with their tall candelabra spikes of flower. Within this natural setting Wharton set about creating six acres of terraced gardens, within a very short space of time (Plate 104). A great deal of money was spent on building terraces, importing soil, constructing pergolas and paths, many of which were tiled, and of course, on the planting. In her introduction to Alice Martineau's book, Gardening in Sunny Lands, Wharton wrote of the excitement experienced by a gardener used to the cold conditions of the north, when moving south to garden:

> The first months are a long honeymoon. Dazzled by the possibilities of growing what previously could be cultivated under glass or coaxed through an existence of semi-invalidism in the uncertainty of the 'sheltered corner', he looks around him in wonder at other people's gardens. He discovers still newer treasures in catalogues of local nurserymen, he summons them in consultation, he wanders through their nurseries; and every visit and every consultation results in a cargo of fascinating novelties.[19]

Plate 104 Ste-Claire in 2007: the unkempt garden with one of the terraces of the original garden overgrown with acanthus, fennel, and the local scrub vegetation which Edith Wharton saw before she started to make the garden.

In addition to her forays to local nurseries, she sent long lists of requests to Vilmorin in Paris and to Telkamp, the Dutch tulip and iris grower, ordering bulbs in their thousands for both St-Brice and Ste-Claire. The blue and pink hyacinths that lined her tiled paths and which, according to Percy Lubbock, had to bud and bloom in harmony, were possibly bought from specialist growers in nearby Toulon. A few years before Henri de Vilmorin introduced his book, *Flowers of the Riviera* (1893), by saying that 'Wintering on the Riviera had become such a common feature of modern life, so many ... resort annually to the sun-warm shores of Hyères, Cannes, Nice or Mentone – that most educated Englishmen of our days are familiar with the climate, sights and produce of maritime Provence'. Vilmorin recommended planting acacia, eucalyptus and *Narcissus minor*, which could be found wild on the hills bordering the coast (and can still be found today on the Île de Gros, offshore from Hyères, one of Wharton's favourite places to visit) and *Tulipiana clusiana*, which he said 'could be plucked from the fields'; also roses, which were 'everywhere on the Riviera; they grow in hedges, hang from trees, cover the front and sides of houses, overtop fences and line railway tracks'.[20] The most popular types were *R.* 'Indica major' and Banksian roses which flowered in spring, but the rose-grower M. Nabormand, *rosiériste* of Golfe-Juan, who visited Ste-Claire in 1920 when the terraces were under construction, left 'in raptures at the opportunity for growing camellias and gardenias and all the roses that ever were'. Like all good gardeners, Wharton was keen to learn about new plants and visit inspirational gardens, and in March 1922, in a letter to her niece Beatrix Farrand, she described a trip she had made to a group of 'the best gardens on the Riviera'.[21]

The gardens were at Cap Ferrat and included the Italianate 'Villa Sylvie', inspired by the Villa Medici at Fiesole, and the 'Villa Rosemarie', both designed by the English architect and garden designer Harold Peto. The Villa Sylvie was built in 1902 for Ralph Wormeley Curtis, a member of a wealthy Boston family, and his wife Lisa. The Curtises were part of the group of American expatriates which included Isabella Stewart Gardner, Henry James, Vernon Lee, John Singer Sargent and Edith Wharton. After her visit, Wharton wrote that 'I never saw anything in England even remotely approaching them as pure *flower gardening*. Such colors ... harmonies, and such sheets of radiant color ... Such Botticellian effects of narcissus, tulip & crocuses (all miraculously in bloom at once) took my breath away & made me feel ready to shake you for not being with me, you idiot.'[22] But as with The Mount, Wharton had her own ideas about planning and creating her garden at Hyères. She wanted a 'dramatic, various and surprising garden which would provide continuing interest, beauty and color' all through the months she spent in the south of France, usually from November to April.[23] She was particularly ambitious and experimental in the range of plants she wanted to use, and her encyclopaedic mind was filled with the names of plants from South Africa, Australia and California, plants recognized today as 'Mediterranean'. A writer for *Country Life* observed that 'Mrs Wharton is not satisfied with growing routine plants or shrubs ... every few yards are plants rarely seen on the Riviera ... rather one gets the feeling everywhere that plants are grown for a genuine appreciation of their own individual value, and not for their massed effect, as is usual on the Riviera'.[24]

To grow such a range and diversity of plants, Wharton's first challenge – as it was for other gardeners along the coast – was 'to provide the denuded rocky surface with soil'. Robert Norton observed, 'into this she threw herself intrepidly and within a year, the old house had come alive'.[25] The work involved constructing terraces up the hillside, to be watered by a system of underground pipes, and linked by a series of paths. Drainage was also necessary, since there could be heavy and damaging rain-storms in the autumn. Substantial retaining walls were needed to create level areas for planting and lawns, and in places dynamite was used to create holes in which to plant trees. Existing old trees were retained to give age to the garden and at the edges to provide a natural background – 'their rather flat tones and natural grey make an adequate foil for good plants'.[26] Alice Martineau, who visited the garden in late February and early March in 1923 and 1924, described the layout of Ste-Claire as a 'series of gardens, sheltered and sunlit ... tucked away on terraces under the old walls and towers in grey stone. In some of these gardens are freesias and narcissus, in others roses; on the terrace are mandarins, and in a shady corner grow camellias, azaleas, and arums'.[27]

The sense of colour was almost overwhelming; the terraces were opulent, theatrical and intense. But as was the case with all her gardens, Wharton never lost sight of the overall design, and was equally interested in the relationship between house, garden and landscape. Images of the garden 'give glimpses of ... neat terraces of lawns, pergolas or pavilions, bordered by packed drifts of coloured flowers on the slopes; exotic and native plants setting each other off; and at every point interconnections made the gardens, the view, and the castle ruins'.[28] It is for this reason that when the house was sold after her death, the gardens were described as among the finest in France.

Wharton received practical help at Ste-Claire from Johnnie Johnston, as she had done at St-Brice. In October 1924 she told Minnie Jones that 'the angelic Lawrence Johnston came from Menton to spend two days with me and helped me incalculably in all my planting plans.[29] Johnston's own terraced garden at La Serre de la Madone enthralled and influenced her, for like Ste-Claire it was constructed on a steep hillside and required terracing and irrigation. Plants were soon arriving at both her French gardens from Hidcote and Serre. In her notebook she recorded plants sent from Hidcote, which included leptospermums, *Linum arboreum* and the Bush Monkey flower *Diplaeus*, all destined for Hyères. The list for St-Brice was more extensive: *Sidalcea* 'Sussex Queen', *Salvia bethellii*, *S. vergata* [sic], *Penstemon* 'Newbury Gem', and *Dahlia* 'Delice' were among the herbaceous plants along with *Hydrangea thunbergii*, viticella clematis varieties 'Kermesina' and 'Rubra Grandiflora' and *Tropaeolum speciosum*.[30] *Country Life* found it difficult

Plate 105 The terrace at
Ste-Claire with its two plane
(Platanus) trees.

to describe the six-acre garden at Ste-Claire, 'as it contains so much
and is so intimate but one point presents itself: Mrs Wharton's garden
is fashioned more than most Riviera gardens after the conception of a
garden in the British Isles'.[31]

Visitors to Ste-Claire had first to climb a steep winding road from the
town, bordered with blue iris and overhung by prickly pear (*Opuntia*)
and Judas trees (*Cercis*), before entering a courtyard which led to a broad
terrace in front of the house. Here Wharton and her friends would gather
to 'take coffee after luncheon' and admire a commanding view over
the town, with its churches, red roofs and in the distance, salt marshes
and the sea. On the terrace two plane (*Platanus*) trees were 'kept low
as is the fashion in France' (Plate 105), and in the centre a great Judas
tree was flanked by a wide border of veronicas (h*ebes*) in shades ranging
from deep purple to pale pink, and opposite a group of blue echiums.
The side of the house was covered by purple *Hardenbergia* and on a wall
beyond were the orange flowers of *Buddleja madagascarensis* (Plate 106).
Above were bushes of *Viburnum suspensum* with creamy-white scented
flowers in February and March.

To the east of the house, the gardens followed the irregular contours
of the hillside and were planted with fine specimens of shrubs and

Plate 106 The delightful winter-flowering shrub, *Buddleja madagascarensis*, close to the house in 2007, which was first planted by Edith Wharton.

small trees, including more Judas trees and a double crimson-flowered cherry (Fig. 10c). By a huge carob tree (*Ceratonia siliqua*) was a swathe of blue violets backed by an ivy-clad tower – although Wharton used massed colour effects, they were never allowed to overwhelm the natural beauty. Above was a little lawn bordered by cypress which Wharton trained into arches on metal frames, and at the far end, a pergola seat was smothered with white anemone roses (Plate 107). A few steps led down from the lawn to a terrace planted with mandarin orange trees and carpeted with yellow freesias. This small lawn acted as a central point for the terraces in the east garden, lying below the rocky hillside, which led up to the towers. On one terrace there was a formal rose garden, on another an orangery, and a third had a mixed planting of cherry trees, daffodils and spring flowers. Planting was not confined to the main terraces; any patch of level ground was ablaze with red flax, vinidiums, irises, and rocks were covered with blue felicia and the small pale pink and white daisy, erigeron. North of the hillside a rough track led to the round tower (Plate 108) through the old olives and woods where the floor was carpeted with wild anemones, orchids, violets and periwinkle.

To the west of the house, in a sheltered area favoured with plenty of sun, a rock garden was blasted from the hillside to create an

1 Araucaria heterophylla (syn. A. excelsa)
2 Brugmansia arborea (syn. Datura)
3 Iochroma
4 Dracaena draco
5 Arbutus unedo
6 Trachycarpus fortunei
8 Cedrus deodara
9 Erythrina christagalli
0 Acca sellowiana (syn. Feijoa)
1 Myoporum
2 Acacia cultriformis
3 Acacia dealbata

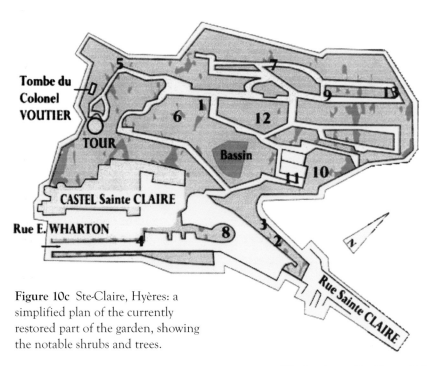

Figure 10c Ste-Claire, Hyères: a simplified plan of the currently restored part of the garden, showing the notable shrubs and trees.

The Garden at Ste-Claire 213

Property of Mrs. Royall Tyler

Sainte-Claire-le-Château, Hyères, France.
Gardens

Plate 107 Ste-Claire: the terrace with cyprus trees trained into arches, and a pergola seat surrounded by anemone roses.

Plate 108 The walk to the tower at Ste-Claire

Plate 109 Part of the restored garden at Ste. Claire planted with cactus and succulents..

environment for all the subtropical plants that thrived on the Riviera. Here Wharton grew rare plants from Morocco and the Canary Islands along with many cacti and succulents, and in its prime the collection was said to be more complete than that of the Prince of Monaco's celebrated garden at Monte Carlo (Plate 109). Beyond this group among the rocks and grey agaves were drifts of orange and red chasmanthe (*Antholyza*) which merged into bushes of wild mastic (*Pistachia*). Vivid orange *Lampranthus aureus* carpeted the ground under the lilac-flowered statice. Just north of the rock garden was a tall pergola, its pillars rising from a bed of tulips and blue violas. On the west side of the house, as well as the east, small paths were cut out of the rock and here Wharton planted and naturalized many species of echium in large masses; blue *Echium fastuosum* near copper-coloured cupheas, and on the steeper sides of the path, the white and blue biennial *Echium decaisnei* and behind, among the rocks, were many brilliant scarlet aloes.

Wharton was highly regarded not just as a plantswoman but for her skill in grouping unusual and different plants for their aesthetic effect. Like Johnston, she packed her borders with drifts of many flowering plants, on the slopes and elsewhere, spilling over the paths. Wharton was totally involved with her garden and its plants, emotionally and intellectually, though she did not dig or weed, and had a team of gardeners who carried out her wishes. She walked continually in her garden and interviewed the head gardener several times a day. According to her friend Daisy Chanler, Wharton 'loved her flowers as other women love their children and was tireless in her care of them'.[32] Her love of plants and extensive knowledge of them, allied to her descriptive skills, made her few essays on gardening among the most evocative of garden writings: for example, in *Spring in a French Riviera Garden*, when she described that moment of transition from winter to spring, the most exciting moment of the year for garden-lovers in the region:

> The roses are over, and have been cut back for April blooming; Narcissus Paper-White and Iris Tingitana have shed their last petals, Bouganvillea Sanderiana has rolled up its magenta tapestries, and the flowerful Bignonia Capensis is only a sheet of brightly varnished foliage. But as one mounts from terrace to terrace what a hurrying of flower-feet is in the air! The tireless Laurustinus leads the way, already thrusting its snowy corymbs among last year's blue-black berries; the Photinias are crowning their stately growth with burnished terminal shoots and broad

flat flower clusters; the single-flowered Kerria Japonica is breaking into golden bloom, and the single yellow Banksia that climbs through it is already showing a few flowers.

Here clumps of Eremurus are thrusting up between the faded flowers of the Diplopappus; in another corner, tucked away in warm clefts along the path, the species crocuses Tomasinianus and Sieberi are folding up their last blooms; but purple cups of Imperati and the great vain glorious chalices of Enchantress still burn in the sunshine, and the vivid golden stars of Crocus Susianus nestle low in their striped leaves. Nearby the tulip Kaufmanniana spreads its first water-lily petals, the tiny Humilis has already put up a frail flower of pinkish mauve, Sylvestris is hung with dangling buds, and the plump flowers of Tulipa Greigii are forcing apart its thick snake-petalled leaves. Further on, in another sunny nook, the species Irises are weaving their enchantment; here Sind-pers has already unfurled its ethereally lovely flowers, there the exquisite lilac-blue of Reticulata Cantab lies like a fragment of sky on the brown earth. The yellow remontant Pumila, Souvenir du Lieutenant Siret, which bloomed all through the summer and autumn, is again thick with bursting blossoms, the outspread blue and purple stars of Histriodes major still linger, and Bucharica and Sind-reichii are unfolding their fluted sheaves, and the Hispanicas thrusting up their grassy filaments.

But the tale of April in a Riviera garden is too long to tell: as well try to crowd a symphony into a 'half-hour of music'. When the peaches and cherries are in bloom, and all the late tulips, narcissi, ranunculus [sic] anemones and irises come rushing up, mingling with the roses, lilacs and peonies to swell the mighty chorus, one can only fall back on the closing lines of Schiller's Hymn to Joy, to which Beethoven gave the wings of immortality.[33]

Wharton's delight in her garden's response to spring sunshine is abundantly obvious in this extract but nature could also be extremely cruel. Daisy Chanler recalled one winter when an unusually hard frost killed 'many fine old trees, and plants that had taken many seasons to collect ... Edith was as Rachel weeping for her children, and would not be consoled'.[34] Wharton experienced such vagaries in the winter weather almost from the outset of her time at Ste-Claire; at Christmas-time in 1920, she wrote about a cold mistral followed by two nights of severe frost, and how all the gardens from Marseilles to Menton were wiped out. 'My terraces were just beginning to be full of bursting sprouting things, and it was sickening to see the black crapy rags which, a few hours before were heliotropes, 'anthemises', tradescantia, plumbago, arums, geraniums – all the stock in trade of a Riviera garden'.[35] But ever optimistic, as all gardeners have to be, she noted that 'normal weather has come back, and my bulbs are all sprouting, and this prodigal nature will repair things in a year – except that some trees may be lost'.[36] That this paradise had its hidden dangers was something any gardener new to the Riviera had to learn, where 'slight differences of soil, or the degree of shelter available, seem to count more than in more equable climes'.[37]

Like all gardeners, Wharton was always complaining about the vagaries of the weather and was in the habit of remarking in her diary that it was the worst February or the worst August, the coldest winter or hottest summer in 20 years or in history. Nothing, however, prepared her for the severe frosts of February 1929 when the temperature dropped below freezing and stayed there, while winds raged around the Château. Edith could only watch as she celebrated her 67th birthday in a blinding snowstorm, and by mid-February she acknowledged that her lovingly planned gardens had been all but wiped out. She expressed the depth of her feelings in a letter to Gaillard Lapsley; 'Oh Gaillard, that my old fibres should have been so closely interwoven with all these roots and tendrils'.[38] So personally did she experience this loss that she suffered a nervous collapse, and in March caught a severe chill from which she nearly died. Robert Norton was so concerned that he sent for Elisina Tyler, who came down from Aligny and gradually nursed her back to health. She was ordered to take a complete rest and by the end of July was able to travel to England and spend time at Hidcote, amid Johnnie's 'tormentingly perfect garden'.[39] She started to re-create her own garden upon her return, and in early October found a new head gardener, Joseph, the ablest of all her Riviera gardeners. Her first head gardener, Bérard, had to be replaced, as 'I was throwing away a great deal of money quite uselessly'. The problem was that poor Bérard was good at building stone walls for the terraces, but 'he kills flowers much more successfully and effectively than do their enemies, such as caterpillars and green fly'.[40] With the new gardener in place, Wharton started to visit nurseries again, consulting horticulturists and an expert on rock gardens. The crisis passed and by Christmas her guests were amazed to find the terraces at Ste-Claire restored and once more in bloom, though Edith herself never quite regained her full energy and spirit.

A DAY WITH EDITH WHARTON

Edith Wharton would follow the same daily routine at both her houses, and 'If ever by any unthinkable contretemps', wrote Robert Norton, 'some cogwheel in the elaborate machinery were blocked the resulting confusion would be held a disaster of the first magnitude! But it was the machinery and its oiling which enabled her to get through so much'.[41] Norton became her most regular companion at Ste-Claire, and in a letter to John Hugh-Smith she described their days together: 'I work all morning, and he goes off sketching. [Plate 110] About 12 we meet, and start off with a lunch basket for the sea shore or the hills. After lunch we walk for 2 hours or more, then we come back deliciously air and sun drunk, and after dinner we talk books – not peace or war!'[42] Guests would start the day with breakfast in their rooms; at Colombe in the summer a tray would arrive 'crowned with peaches, apricots, and a dish of strawberries and cream'.[43] Eventually the guests would come

Plate 110 Hyères; Robert Norton sketching – he was a key member of Edith Wharton's 'Inner Circle' and a friend of Lawrence Johnston.

downstairs and spend the morning in the garden or, at Ste-Claire, they might receive notes on walks, or perhaps visit Charles de Noailles at St. Bernard, while their hostess spent the morning in her bedroom at work on her writing or correspondence until midday. Then, with writing over for the day, she would come into the garden, elegantly dressed, with gloves and a straw hat. She might pause to talk to a guest on the terrace before taking up her basket and clippers and bustle out into the garden with tiny dogs at her heels. There were always dead roses to cut or a shrub to prune, perhaps one that had put out a shoot in the wrong direction – in the garden, as in the drawing room, things had to behave. As Lubbock observed in his biography of Wharton, 'she would have no shirking or sulking, and it was a stupid little plant that ever dreamed of dodging her eye'. There would be a 'happy conference with the head gardener over new plans or head shaking over a rare plant which had ungratefully failed to respond to special feeding'.[44]

Lubbock paints a vivid picture of Edith Wharton, the châtelaine of Colombe, as the consummate author and gardener:

> And when she now stood on the good soil of her garden, with her broad-leafed hat and her basket on her arm, calling and waving to the window where Grosse [her long-serving servant] looked out and smiled down on her; or when she whisked round and made off to her business among the flowers, with her pair of toy-dogs pottering and scuffing at her heels; or when, her basket filled, she stepped out, young as ever in the straightness and lightness of her attack for a further survey of the garden's diligence – with that neat right-and-left twitch of her elbows as she stepped, and that elegant manner of moving and placing her feet (said another observant friend) that always reminded me of the exquisite nicety with which a small donkey picks its way and places its feet on a stony path: in short wherever you first caught sight of her, active and occupied, in this picture of her creation, this design of order and beauty she had conjured from her brain, she seemed to be settling down to peace in the world with the happiest assurance that everything around her, all for which *she* need answer, was right and for her, a field sufficient and convenient for good work through the years ... there, to be sure, is a writer of books propitiously installed: and how satisfying to think of a writer in the midst of it all, enjoying it all – and then forgetting it all, alone with her book, at the centre of the design.[45]

Once the garden had been tended at Colombe, it was time to feed the enormous old goldfish, said to have been put in the pond by one of the kings of France; 'Edith taking crumbs from an embroidered bag, would bend over the pond calling to them'. A lavish lunch would follow, served on the terrace if weather permitted. Even on a warm summer's day a typical menu at Colombe might include lobster *à l'américaine*, followed by a tender roast chicken with peas, fillets of sole and a very creamy and delicious strawberry dish. After lunch Edith and her guests would take an obligatory walk in the garden; then at Colombe there could be a visit to a gallery in Paris, or at Ste-Claire a drive to a picturesque spot in the motor car, often taking a picnic.

Wharton was particularly fond of picnics, which always followed the same pattern. In his biography of her, Lubbock provides an insight into what these were like:

> Tastes may differ concerning a day in the country, how it should be designed for pleasure: but on one point there could be no disagreeing when Edith led. Everyone must prefer, in sunshine and fair weather, a meal in the aromatic open among myrtle and lentisk, to sitting at a table under a ceiling; they must indeed. Some may say her passion for a picnic was excessive; but she didn't stay to argue. In good time the picnic was packed into the car, with all the right equipment, complete in every detail.[46]

The car had been adapted to take the 'right equipment', with a receptacle for maps and guide-books, a book box, a net to hold sticks, umbrellas, and capes and rugs of different thicknesses. After the drive to the destination, came first the selection of the right spot for the picnic, chosen by Wharton with, said Norton, 'the care and deliberation of a Roman general selecting the site of a fortified camp' (Plate 111):

> The tree, the mound, the gentle slope that provides a back for Edith, facing aright, with its due sun and shade. That found and Edith settled, the strapped hampers, which Edith liked to think of as strapped bales, were set by her side, the rugs spread, the guests star-scattered in their places ... Nobody at this point is to help her; she unpacks, distributes, apportions all'.[47]

A typical lunch of eggs, cheese, olives, chicken, ham, salads, chocolate, oranges and coffee, with the portions efficiently dealt out by the

Plate 111 Edith Wharton, seen here with Robert Norton (second right) and Gaillard Lapsley (far right), was often joined by Lawrence Johnston and Norah Lindsay on picnics in the countryside around Hyères.

hostess, was followed by a long walk until tea-time. Wharton was known to walk long distances even in later life and demanded perseverance and action from her guests. In the evening they would all dress for dinner and enjoy another lavish meal with wine, though she did not drink alcohol, followed by fine cognac. Afterwards they would retire to the library, where they sometimes took books from the shelves and read aloud, her particular favourites being Hardy's *Return of the Native* and Austen's *Sense and Sensibility*. Wharton also loved conversation on subjects that mattered to her – music, art and architecture, literature, natural beauty and civilized human contact – and as an accomplished host she would match the subject to her guests' interests. But Lubbock also makes it clear that laughter too, was never far away: 'I am unable to imagine a company of people, be they who they may, grouped around Edith, without hearing the ring of her laughter soon resounding over the talk; she couldn't silence it in any tongue'.[48] Some guests found the daily regime disconcerting, and yet the men of the Inner Circle tended to share Wharton's own need for routine. What she could not tolerate was pretence and foolish people who tried to bluff her; on one occasion in London, a young Somerset Maugham tried to outsmart her and he was never allowed to become a friend.

Johnston became friends with Robert Norton at Ste-Claire, not surprisingly, for they had much in common through watercolour painting, music and books, and they may also have known of each other from their days at Cambridge. Throughout the 1920s and '30s when Johnston stayed with Wharton in France, whether at Colombe or Ste-Claire, there would be much laughter and talk of gardens, plants, new varieties and regular visits to nurseries and gardens, hunting for novelties and plants suited to their gardens. There were always news and reminiscences of mutual gardening friends, for Edith loved gossip the details of which Lapsley believed she used in her writing. In late October, Wharton would leave Colombe and move into a hotel while the servants closed up the 'pavilion' for the winter and opened the house at Hyères. In the spring the procedure was reversed, with the difference that she would often visit friends before arriving, sometimes visiting Johnnie at Hidcote.

It is a pity, as Hermione Lee points out, that Wharton never wrote a novel about a gardener, because gardening and writing novels share common qualities: 'a disciplined structure and imaginative freedom, a reworking of traditions into a new idea and a ruthless elimination of dull, incongruous or surplus materials all come to mind – not to mention patience, stamina and attentiveness'.[49] It is also to be regretted that Wharton did not publish more as a garden writer for, as we have seen, in the little she did write, she revealed a detailed knowledge of plants and provided, as would be expected, a lyrical description of her garden. Yet there was perhaps a more fundamental reason why neither Wharton nor Johnston left an account of their garden. It was not so much that their gardens were works of art in themselves and need not be written about, as Lee suggests, but because each garden was its maker's own private world into which he or she alone could escape from the exigencies of daily life. Wharton expressed this feeling on returning to Ste-Claire after an extended absence: 'Back again after eight months away. Oh the joy of being alone – alone; of walking about in the garden of my soul!'[50] To have written about it would have admitted other, unknown people, and broken the spell of an intimate, private world. Edith's friend Daisy Chanler expressed it very well: her garden was 'somehow an image of her spirit, of her innermost self. It shows her love of beauty, imagination, her varied knowledge and masterly attention to detail; like her, it is somewhat inaccessible. Her garden is a symbol of the real Edith'.[51]

NOTES AND REFERENCES

1. Vivienne de Watteville, quoted in Dwight, E., *Edith Wharton – an extraordinary life*. Abrams, New York, p. 212.

2. The description of the garden at Pavillon Colombe is from an unfinished account by Wharton, 'Gardening in France', in Bratton, D., ed., *Yrs. Ever Affly.* University of Michigan Press, Ann Arbor.

3. Quoted in Dwight, op. cit., p. 223.

4. Ibid., p. 217.

5. The *Jardin Anglais* was fashionable from 1775 to 1815. After the end of the Seven Years War in 1763, French noblemen visited England to see the English landscape garden, and the style soon began to appear in French gardens, replacing the *jardin à la française*, as designed by Le Nôtre. Among the first and most extensive examples was one at the Bagatelle in the Bois de Boulogne, west of Paris (1777–84) partly designed in the natural English style for the Comte d'Artois, brother of Louis XVI, who later became Charles X, by the Scottish garden designer Thomas Blaikie, nick-named the 'Capability Brown of France'. The formal garden spaces close to the château were linked by underground tunnels to the surrounding park, which in turn included a lake bordered by rocks, a winding river and cascades. Though Blaikie was scornful of the French fashion for the *jardin anglo-chinois* at the Bagatelle, the garden contained picturesque scenes with Chinese *fabriques* designed by Bélanger, the architect of the house. Royal patronage and the influence of gardens, such as the Bagatelle, saw the *jardin anglais* replace many formal gardens in France, as well as in the Netherlands and the German States.

6. Dwight, op. cit., pp. 219-20.

7. Ibid., p. 216.

8. Lee, H., *Edith Wharton*. Chatto and Windus, London, p. 528.

9. These notes are translated from the French and quoted in Dwight, op. cit., p. 219.

10. *Beatrix Farrand Society News*, Summer 2007.

11. Craig, T., *A House Full of Rooms: Architecture, Interiors, Gardens*. Monacelli, New York, p. 170.

12. Page, R., *Education of a Gardener*. Harvill, London, pp. 131-2.

13. Lee, op. cit., p. 530.

14. See p. 30 & ref. 33, Chapter 2.

15. Quoted in Dwight, op. cit., p. 235.

16. Lubbock, P., *Portrait of Edith Wharton*. Cape, London, p. 166.

17. Collas, P. and Villedary, E., *Edith Wharton's French Riviera*. Flammarion, Paris, p. 65.

18. Lubbock, op. cit., p. 109.

19 Introduction in Martineau, A., *Gardening in Sunny Lands*. Cobden-Sanderson, London, 1924.

20 Vilmorin, H. de, *Flowers of the French Riviera*. Spottiswoode, London, p. 1.

21 Lee, op. cit., p. 554.

22 Letter to Beatrix Farrand, 16 March 1922..

23 Lee, op. cit., p. 554.

24 'A Riviera Garden: Sainte-Claire-le-Château, Hyères'. *Country Life*, Vol. 64, No.1659, 3 November 1928, 610-3.

25 Dwight, op. cit., p. 139

26 Ibid.

27 Martineau, op. cit., pp. 243-7.

28 Lee, op. cit., pp. 554-7.

29 Ibid., p. 555.

30 Edith Wharton's notebook, Lilly Library, Indiana University, Bloomington.

31 *Country Life*, November 1928 , op. cit., 613.

32 Goodman, S., *Edith Wharton's Women – Friends and Rivals*. University Press of New England, Lebanon, New Hampshire, p. 132. Daisy Chanler said that Wharton did not like children, an opinion shared by others. Lubbock maintained that she was terrified of children but others commented on her kindness, and that Edith's gift was in treating children as adults – Lee, op. cit., pp. 701-3.

33 Wharton, E., 'Spring in a French Riviera Garden'. Wharton Archives, Beineke Rare Books and Manuscripts Library, Yale University, New Haven, Connecticut. Some of the plant names Wharton mentions have either been updated or they are incomplete. Dwight, op. cit., provides a more accurate list, compiled by Nicolas H. Ekstrom: *Bougainvillaea sanderiana* syn. *Bougainvillaea glabra* 'Sanderiana'; *Bignonia capensis* syn. *Tecomaria capensis*; Laurustinus syn. *Viburnum tinus*; *Banksia* syn. *Rosa banksiae*; *Diplopappus* syn. *Aster* sp.; Tomasinianus syn. *Crocus tommasinianus*; Enchantress syn. *Crocus vernus* 'Enchantress'; *Crocus susianus* syn. *Crocus angustifolius*; Sind-Perss syn. *Iris* 'Sindpur'; Reticulata Cantab, syn. *Iris histrioides* 'Major'; Hispanicas syn. *Iris xiphium*.

34 Goodman, op. cit., p. 132.

35 Lewis, R. W. B., *The Letters of Edith Wharton*. Scribner, New York, pp. 436-7.

36 Ibid., p. 437.

37 Ibid.

38 Lewis, R. W. B., *Edith Wharton – A Biography*. Scribner, New York, p. 487.

39 Ibid., p. 489.

40 Lee, op. cit., p. 555.

[41] Norton had a very close and special relationship with Edith Wharton. Aristocratic friends believed that she was in love with him (Lee, op. cit., p. 250). After her death, Norton began to write a memoir of her, but handed his notes to Percy Lubbock when he was designated the official biographer.

[42] Dwight, op. cit., p. 251.

[43] Lee, op. cit., p. 535.

[44] Lubbock, op. cit., p. 169.

[45] Lubbock, op. cit., pp. 131–2.

[46] Ibid., p. 167.

[47] Ibid.

[48] Ibid., p. 168.

[49] Ibid., p. 132.

[50] Lee. op. cit., p. 559.

[51] Ibid., p. 560.

THE GARDENS

① La Mortola
② Serre de la Madone
③ Villa Noailles[2]
④ Ste. Claire
⑤ St. Bernard (Villa Noailles[1])

Map 5 The Côte d'Azur (Riviera) in the south of France showing the location of some of the gardens of Edith Wharton and Lawrence Johnston and their friends.

CHAPTER ELEVEN

JOHNSTON AND THE FRENCH RIVIERA

Lawrence Johnston was spending much of his time at Hidcote in the early 1920s, but he was also looking for a suitable property in the south of France. His mother was by now suffering from senile dementia, and had taken to wandering aimlessly around the garden at Hidcote talking to herself, and would soon be confined to a wheelchair. Johnston's own health was also a concern; he had contracted malaria at some point, probably in South Africa, and was subject to recurring bouts of the disease. Others have thought, too, that he may have been gassed during the Great War in addition to receiving the shrapnel wound in his chest, and probably had only one lung. He was now aged in his fifties, and so these problems of health, together with childhood memories of the south of France and time spent convalescing at one of Lady Derby's properties after the war, may have encouraged him to look for a property near the Mediterranean. Undoubtedly, an important consideration was his desire to extend the gardening season, thus freeing him to create a garden he had dreamed about.

MENTON

In 1924 Johnston and his mother stayed in Menton, which is situated on the Mediterranean coast between Monte Carlo and the Italian border, at a place called 'Mer et Monts' accompanied by her butler Alfredo Rebuffo and his valet 'Pop' Brown. The area around Menton had been recognized as a health resort and a suitable place for invalids. A Manchester doctor, John Henry Bennet, suggested as early as 1859 that Menton, with its ideal winter climate – a favourable microclimate, sheltered from cold winds by the surrounding mountains, and the proximity of the sea – provided patients suffering from tuberculosis with the exact conditions necessary for a full recovery. This may have been why Johnston's mother and stepfather had spent their winters in the region. Bennet himself was tubercular, and had come to the area expecting to die. Yet not only did he survive, but he went on to create a celebrated garden. His gardening experiences resemble closely those of Edith and Johnnie sixty years later. 'I purchased a few terraces, some naked rocks, and an old ruined tower, on the mountainside, near

Mentone, some 300 feet above the sea, with a south-westerly aspect and sheltered from all northerly winds. Here ... I set to work and ... we think we have done wonders in the course of a few years only.'[1] That work involved the familiar tasks of importing soil to supplement the scarce amounts of top soil, digging reservoirs and diverting a watercourse, but Bennet's real innovation was in his choice of plant material. He had begun with species well known on the Riviera, only to discover that plants from the southern hemisphere, in particular those from Australia and South Africa, thrived in the garden and came through the winter unscathed: chorizemas, kennedias, ixias, sparaxis, pelagoniums and many succulents and cacti. Bennet was among the first English residents to make a serious collection of these plants, and his writing did much to popularize the Riviera as a place for winter residence and gardening.

Bennet's garden was situated to the east of the town, in the fashionable area of the Baie de Garavan, but Johnston had to buy land on the other, north-west side of Menton in the Val de Gorbio. It is likely, as Alice Martineau suggested, that all the available seafront properties had long since been acquired by other British and American visitors. But Johnston may have been impressed by the picturesque charms of the valley. Augustus Hare, artist and garden connoisseur, claimed in 1887 that it presented a series of pictures in its 'little chapels, old chestnuts overhanging them, and ruined oil mills and broken bridges'.[2] Johnston, like Edith Wharton, was anxious to avoid the 'glamour of the international set', and preferred the rustic quality of the valley. It is possible, too, that his mother was being treated at the Sanatorium de Gorbio. The favourable microclimate of the Val de Gorbio had earlier attracted Lady Forres, who had established a house and garden at the Villa Mont Agel. The garden was described by Alice Martineau, a friend of William Robinson, in her book *Gardening in Sunny Lands*, published the same year as Johnston's arrival in Menton. The Agel garden, wrote Martineau, is unique and situated in an old lemon grove; 'A wisteria-covered pergola leads from the house into the garden which consists of consecutive terraces, with flowers everywhere beneath them. Other narrow terraces are planted each in a different style ... The cultivated part of the garden is cleverly merged into the maquis, and on one side of the hills a bank in full sun has been completely smothered in Lavendula dentata'.[3] Louisa Jones notes that Lady Forres had already experienced the more naturalistic Robinson–

Jekyll style, and perhaps was even aware of Hidcote which was becoming influential among gardeners.[4]

SERRE DE LA MADONE

Johnston was delighted when he first saw a farm close to the Villa Mont Agel, at a place known as Les Moulins. It was one of several small farms on the lower hillside, each with vineyards and terraces of olive, almond and citrus trees, with the upper slopes covered in Mediterranean maquis of pine, holm oaks, cistus, juniper and myrtle. On 24th January 1924, Johnston bought his first piece of land from a M. Fortuné Ambroise Giloan, an artist and curator of the municipal museum in Menton. Further purchases followed in 1928, 1930, 1934, and even as late as 1939 when he finally acquired the top of the hill to give him an unencumbered view of the sea. By then the property extended to approximately ten hectares, and Johnston renamed the whole estate 'Serre de la Madone'.[5] The old farm and its surrounding land were on the slopes of a very protected, west-facing hillside, and the soil was untypical of the region, being 'deep, very sandy neither acidic nor alkaline'.[6] It was ideally suited to the growth of trees, shrubs and almost any kind of flora. When each parcel of land was acquired, Johnston developed and expanded an elaborate system of collecting and distributing spring water, so essential for the survival of plants during the hot, dry summer months. Earlier, Bennet had concluded that the reason why horticulture was so utterly neglected in the south of Europe, was because 'mere ordinary gardening ... is attended with considerable expense, owing to the necessity of summer and even winter irrigation, if any degree of excellence ... is to be obtained.[7]

Soon after the first purchase, Johnston set about converting the farmhouse into a gentleman's residence, adding two wings on either side. Norah Lindsay described in a letter to her son Peter, how she would go up to the garden from Menton, with Johnny [sic] and Reggie Cooper, to meet the architect or builder or someone who was working on the house (Plates 112 & 113). 'The house,' she said, stands 'behind his garden terraces so there is quite a climb to get to it;' the road had yet to be built, and it was, she said 'tiny, but going to be in time, quite lovely'. In that November of 1924, the sun shone and, she continued, 'the lemon trees were all in bloom and smelt quite delicious', and just behind the villa 'the wild hill is covered in

Plate 112 Serre de la Madone: the dining room in the house extension with views over the mountains to the village of Gorbio, c.1930.

Plate 113 Serre de la Madone: the comfortable living room in the extension, with its art nouveau fireplace, opening on to the garden, c.1930.

pine, olive, arbutus, rosemary, myrtles with the loveliest walks along the top where you look down upon Italy and Bordigherra ... the sweet scents are intoxicating as one goes along in the hot sunshine with leaping locusts and bright golden butterflies flitting about and the sandy floor red with fallen arbutus berries.'[8]

In the following year, on Sunday, 1st March 1925, Edith Wharton and Johnnie Johnston had lunch at Serre and made an afternoon visit to Lady Forres at Villa Mont Agel. Johnston who was always influenced by, and took ideas from, gardens he liked, must have admired the gardens of his neighbour and in particular the use of terraces. Though, as Will Ingwersen,[9] who later worked at Serre as a young gardener in 1934, observed: 'Lawrence Johnston was a man of great imagination and the design of the garden on its many terraces was entirely his.'[10] That said, the layout of Serre is reminiscent of Italian Renaissance gardens. There was no plan of the garden, which was also the case with Hidcote, but as Ethne Clarke in her account of Hidcote pointed out, in attempting to understand any garden it is worth considering what was or may have been the main entrance (Plate 114). Clarke cites the example of the Villa d'Este where today visitors enter the garden from the house at the top of the slope, whereas originally the entrance was at the foot (Fig. 11a). Previously, when entering the garden, and while they made their way past the terraces via the central stairway, visitors would have been impressed by the grandeur of the site rising majestically up the hillside to the villa, and would have had time to reflect on the importance of Cardinal Ippolito d'Este. But it is at Serre de la Madone, rather than at Hidcote, where

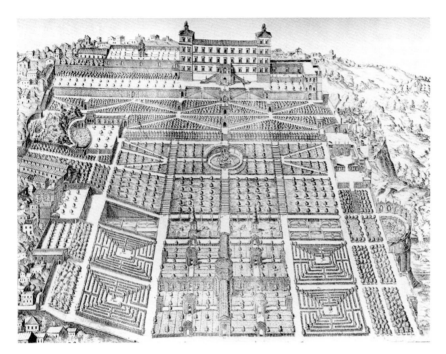

Figure 11a Plan of the Villa d'Este gardens *c.* 1575.

the similarity with d'Este and other Italian gardens is more noticeable. At Serre the garden is entered a third of the way up the slope; after leaving the oval courtyard and passing through a heated greenhouse that Johnston called the Winter Garden, visitors arrive at the major cross axis provided by a series of fishponds and a central staircase. Just as at the Villa d'Este, from here they gain their first clear view

Plate 115 Serre de la Madone: the main axis looking towards the house, flanked by new extensions on either side of the old farmhouse.

of the villa, five terraces above (Plate 115). One doubts very much that Lawrence Johnston saw himself as a latter-day cardinal but he was happy, nevertheless, to take inspiration from Ligorio's design.

In contrast with this formal entrance, visitors on foot – then as now – approached the garden from the Gorbio road at the bottom of the garden, from where an informal path winds up numerous steps, taking a rather indeterminate route into the garden (Fig. 11b). On the right of the path are four columns around a circular pool – remnants of the cool greenhouse – and to the left are the shallow terraces of the rockery where Johnston once grew many of the alpines he had collected in the region. Shade from the massive podocarps planted by Johnston, and Washington palms planted before he arrived, has transformed the site, and the alpines have given way to hellebores and sarcococcas. The path brings the visitor to a basin at the foot of the more formal flight of steps, guarded on either side by a terracotta sphinx (Plate 116). To the left is a small parterre in which four rectangles of dwarf box, each containing a spreading pollarded plane tree, surround a small circular pool and a fountain overhung by daturas (brugmansia). The parterres were once filled with double-flowered periwinkles and thousands of red and white tulips (*Tulipa clusiana*) perhaps collected in the surrounding hills. On the right, the

Figure 11b Plan of the modern gardens of Serre de la Madone.

1   The Cool Greenhouse
2   The 'Rond-Point'
3   The centre of the composition - the fish ponds with the central stairway
4   The Villa
5   Casa Rocca – originally servants' quarters
6   The Moorish garden
7   The Belvedere
8   The Fountain of the Daturas
9   The Garden of the Planes
10 The Angel's Staircase
11 The Rock Garden

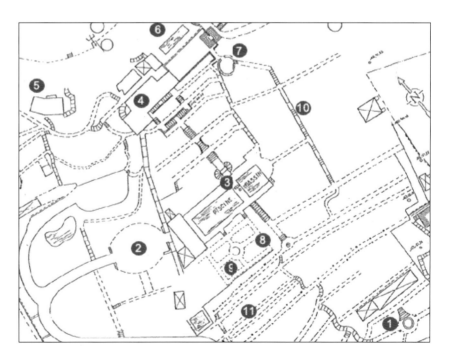

terraces have been taken over by drifts of orange *Chasmanthe bicolor*, a close relation of crocosmia.

From the plane trees, steps lead to the fishponds at the centre of the garden and the water garden where Johnston would take his early morning swim; 'a vast pool at the foot of the whole hillside ... this is the heart of the design. The sky of Provence, beautifully calm, is reflected in the three compartments of the pool, its azure magically decked with red, then with yellow lotus. Opposite, Venus emerges from the waves to welcome you.'[11] This statue of Venus was known as 'Mrs Winthrop' even in Johnston's day, but unfortunately the original figure was sold after his death (Plate 117).

The central axis at Serre de la Madone provides the strong unifying theme of the garden, and again just as in the garden at the Villa d'Este, it begins with a rondel filled with box. It is accompanied by a sequence of spring-fed fountains and pools; some of the staircases had fountains set into the sides. The illusion of the Italian Renaissance was strengthened by statues placed at the end of the terraces. Following the example of many Renaissance gardens, the central axis divides below the house, with elegant stone steps leading up to a narrow terrace in front of the house. At the sides of the garden Johnston retained the old dry-stone terrace walls – 'restanques'[12] – so as to contrast with the new walls of the central formal gardens. Parts of the original olive groves at the edge were also kept so that the garden would merge into the surrounding landscape. As Alice Martineau advised: 'where the indigenous maquis is already established, the planting should be carefully merged into it by means of [such] shrubs of semi-wild character as arbutus, laurustinus, the many cistuses, lavender, broom and so on, instead of cutting it off by some hard dividing line of hedge or fence.'[13] Both Johnston and Wharton followed this advice, with formal designs merging gradually into the wilder landscape.

To the left of the villa was Johnston's collection of rare camellias. These were particularly difficult to grow and required summer irrigation. Bennet describes how he had to mix chestnut leaf-mould in place of peat, which was unobtainable in the region, mixed with sand and charcoal.[14] This was reminiscent of the work Johnston undertook in the Stream Garden at Hidcote in preparation for rhododendrons. Located among the camellias was the 'Casa Rocca' to house the guests' servants. On the other side was a Moorish garden with a pavilion

Plate 116 One of the terracotta sphinxes at the start of the main axis.

Plate 117 (left) The fishponds on the central axis, with the statue of Venus scurrilously known as 'Mrs Winthrop', where Johnston would start his day with an early-morning swim, c. 1930.

Plate 118 (right) The blue-tiled loggia at Serre, which Norah Lindsay admired, c. 1930.

housing an orchid collection; Spanish tiles were set in the surrounding walls which enclosed a rectangular pool once filled with water lilies. Norah Lindsay regarded this as one of Johnston's *chefs d'œuvre* at Serre (Plate 118); 'sitting in the Moorish loggia with its amber cushions and blue tiles watching the vast dragon-flies hawking around the vast tropical water lilies all radiant with the powerful early sun against the dark shadow of the hillside gives me the greatest happiness.'[15] From here the steep 'Angel's staircase', harking back to a statue that once stood at its summit, led to a small circular building with its wisteria-covered trellis which Johnston called the 'Belvedere'. It was once part of a vast aviary covering one and a half hectares in which there were parrots, hornbills, cranes, peacocks, ibis and golden pheasants. From the Belvedere there were magnificent views over the water garden to the hills beyond. On the upper levels the terraces led off to secret glades filled with flowering trees, an arboretum planted with many rare trees and shrubs, though it is inaccessible now due to landslides. By the 1930s, Johnston was recognized internationally as a distinguished plantsman, and large quantities of rare trees and shrubs found their way into Serre from all parts of the world.

The planting effects at Hidcote that Vita Sackville-West had called 'jungle-like', though never 'a jungle allowed to deteriorate into mere jungle', became even more profuse and exuberant in the favoured climate at Serre. Johnston seems deliberately to have combined the botanical value and the artistic merit of his planting palette in order to create dramatic effects, in ways that anticipated the work of the Brazilian landscape architect, Roberto Burle Marx (1909-94), a decade or so later: 'large swathes of the same species but in different varieties; the use of graphic individuals as contrasting accents or smaller groupings in the midst of large waves of plants; a preference for strikingly architectural and often exotic foliage; and above all a magic blending of disparate elements that raises the viewer into another dimension.'[16] So Chinese tree peonies emerged from carpets of Algerian iris, surrounded by rare bulbs from South Africa and Mexico; carpets of blue agapanthus set alight by the orange bird of paradise plant (*Strelitzia reginae*); and huge red dragon heads and giant foliage of the Mexican *Beschornia yuccoides* were used for dramatic effect. On the broad terraces the pink flowers of the mass-planted *Amaryllis belladonna* contrasted in autumn with carpets of blue leadwort (*Plumbago capensis*). At the margins the existing wild maquis contrasted with an avenue of callistemons and Mexican succulents, and Californian ceanothus grew out of Mediterranean wildflowers and bulbs. Russell Page noted that to orchestrate such unusual harmonies needed a master's eye, though not everyone was so enamoured with the planting or the garden. Norah Lindsay expressed a concern about its design or rather the lack of it:

> ... he has put far too many vast pottery jars, and mounted the biggest of all on a sort of bracket of stalactites!! This in the middle of a tiny, tiny iris garden, so that this monster jar looks terribly 'close-up' and out of place. I find Evelyn Waugh agrees entirely with me in the longing for more space and design and vista. He has these vast pots everywhere but with no vista to them. The central staircase is lovely and if I were he, I would continue it and cut down to the road. Of course in six to seven years he'll have the most marvellous collection of rare things, but such a jungle – already lots of shrubs are dying from being so close. However, he loves it all so passionately and hates the faintest criticism, and Kitty Lambton said it's very touching the way when he makes a new thing he says to her, 'This is just what Norah will love', whereas I think the garden has been spoilt by his trelliage [sic] and tricks'.[17]

When Johnston first went to Serre he wanted his head gardener at Hidcote, Frank Adams, to move south with him, but Mrs Adams was not keen on the move. Instead a young gardener named Frensham, who had been trained by Johnston's friend Robert James at St. Nicholas, Richmond, and was already working at Hidcote, was appointed and moved with his family to Serre. The fact that Frensham had received sound horticultural training, but relatively little in designing gardens, may have appealed to Johnston who took control of such matters himself. In his account of *The English Garden Abroad*, Charles Quest-Ritson pointed out that English garden-owners abroad expected to work in the garden themselves, and Johnston, who by now was more English than many born in the country, seems to have been no exception. This 'perennial idiosyncrasy' was not a matter of being unable to find staff – Johnston had twelve full-time gardeners at Serre – but stemmed from a belief that the French and Italians could not understand the British national passion for gardening. It was after all a way of expressing one's British identity and this made hands-on gardening acceptable among gentlemanly garden-owners. 'Take me as you find me' may have been a sentiment coined to express a relaxation of the social reserve when abroad, a safeguard which for some, and that almost certainly included Johnston, had to be constantly maintained at home. As Fred Whitsey observed, 'even had he wished to work in the garden [Hidcote] the canons of propriety that ruled in a private garden in those days would have forbidden it'.[18]

Johnston was content to direct his staff and oversee the jobs in hand, like a good army officer, ensuring that they were well done – though this may be a matter of how the nature of 'work' is defined. Some regarded him as a 'stiff little man', 'formal, proper' and a 'demanding employer, who although prepared to listen to the opinions of others, would expect things to be done the way he wanted them carried out, and would readily show his displeasure if they were not'.[19] There was nothing unusual in this attitude, which was echoed by meticulous owners and head gardeners alike, and Johnston shared these characteristics with many of his gardening friends. E. A. Bowles never saw eye to eye with his head gardener in all of the 40 years he was at Myddleton House.[20] Perhaps one reason why Johnston enjoyed Serre so much was simply because he was able to relax the social formality. Nevertheless the English trait of getting one's hands dirty amazed, and sometimes appalled, the continental well-to-do.

The Marquis Ernest de Ganay, a noted French horticulturist, visited Johnston and said that 'he comes to greet you in his corduroys straight from his terraces, with dirt on his hands like any gardener'. In February 1933, Norah Lindsay described how she spent a few days working in the garden with Johnny:

> Came down bright and early as usual and consecrated the day by working in the garden. Johnny had an enormous conglomeration of pots waiting to go in. So I spent the day with him finding places for about thirty buddleias, new mimosas, etc. It's quite dry, with sandy, grassy terraces behind the house, which are already planted with minute seedling shrubs you do not notice unless you plop a plant on the top of it ... Johnny worked hard planting, carrying up pots – as everything is up hill – and then lugging huge cans of water too![21]

The daughter of Alfredo Rebuffo, Mrs Winthrop's butler, also said that what Johnston liked best was to be in his garden:

> ... early in the morning, dressed in his tweed jacket with leather elbows and tweed golf pants, with a cap on his head he could be found advising Mr Frenchum [sic] how to arrange the plants in his garden. Pushing the wheelbarrow himself and followed by his seven dachshunds, his two Pyrenean sheep dogs, and his bull-mastiff, Bob, he went up and down, all over his domain'.[22]

Dogs were a part of his life, as they were for Edith Wharton; her favourites were always Pekingese and she would judge her visitors by their attitudes towards these animals. Johnston initially kept spaniels and retrievers, but later surrounded himself with dachshunds (see Plate 149, p. 302). When Norah Lindsay arrived in September 1935, she wrote to her sister Madeline that Johnny was, 'looking better than I've ever seen him in his blue jersey, linen trousers', had 'three satin dachshunds who rushed at me as if they had never seen me before and clung to me and followed everywhere. This quite upset Johnny and Fredo who are insanely jealous and say it's the first time the dogs have taken to anyone'.[23] Rebuffo had been hired by Johnston as his butler after his mother's death, but became head gardener, close friend and finally his medical attendant in the 1950s when he, like his mother, succumbed to dementia.

Johnston would often travel down to Menton in September, and return to Hidcote in March or April in time to see the flowering of the spring bulbs. At first he drove to Menton in his Lancia, often with Norah Lindsay and Reggie Cooper, with the chauffeur following in the Bentley with the dogs, but by the 1930s he was travelling by train, Pullman class, from Calais via Paris to the Riviera. The proud boast of the famous Blue train, the *Côte d'Azur Rapide* which had come into daily service in 1929, was to reach 'Paris in only thirteen and a half hours'. Film stars and celebrities of all kinds, including Edith Wharton, joined the wealthy British in surroundings of luxury, eating superb food and drinking fine wines on their train journeys north and south. An unavoidable part of such travel was tipping at all stages of the journey, and Johnston kept a meticulous record in his notebook of what he called bribes, a penny here, a shilling there. The Riviera 'season' had always ended on 21st April, and everyone returned home by the end of the month. At first the British mistrusted the summer air, but by the mid-1920s Riviera summers were very much in vogue. The exodus north, however, remained important for gardeners, as Gertrude Jekyll wryly noted: 'Those who care for their gardens, do not as a rule come out much before Christmas, and leave at the latest by the middle of May.' And for those keen on roses such as Edith and Johnnie, it meant that 'any rose that does not flower freely during the late autumn or early spring is of little importance, however beautiful it may be'.[24]

When Johnston was away from Serre, the house was in the care of a live-in married couple, but when he was in residence he employed a head butler, a chauffeur who took care of the two custom-built vehicles, a first-rate pastry cook and three kitchen assistants. Johnston entertained a great deal, as he did at Hidcote, and 'many crowned heads were invited to his table'. On those occasions it has been said that he was a 'witty, urbane, slightly eccentric gentleman, who delighted in showing important visitors round the different levels of his garden, his many dachshunds at his heels'.[25] But as Madame Bottin further observed, he often found the 'occasions tedious and quite frequently claimed sick leave'.[26] Mrs Norah Warre, one of Johnston's closer friends in the south of France and a keen gardener, agreed that he could be diffident and hard to get to know, but once 'the reserve had been breached he was an extremely generous friend'.[27] Her 10-acre garden at Roquebrune near Cap-Martin, was without any really designed structure, but was a collection of as many interesting and rare plants as it was possible to cram into the available space. Some of these rarities had come from Johnston, who often gave her plants he had collected, in the hope that they would grow in the very different aspect and soil to that at Serre, and so be in reserve if his own failed.

LA MORTOLA

Edith Wharton became a frequent visitor to Johnnie Johnston at Serre, and the two would visit nurseries and gardens throughout the region, including 'La Mortola', situated a few miles from Menton across the border in Italy. In March 1925 they took tea with the Hanburys, the owners of La Mortola. The estate had been bought by Thomas Hanbury in 1867. He had been impressed by the beauty of its location and particular climate, and decided to turn the existing farmland into a place for botanical experimentation and the acclimatisation of exotic non-European plants. Under his direction and later that of his widow, La Mortola developed into being among the finest English gardens on the Riviera, which also contained one of the foremost private collections of plants in the world. The Hanburys were Quakers and it was their intention to use their wealth 'to display God's handiwork and demonstrate the usefulness to man of many members of the plant kingdom'.[28]

By 1920 the garden had passed to Cecil Hanbury and his wife Dorothy, who treated La Mortola as her personal fiefdom, and in so doing, made herself unpopular with locals and the gardening fraternity alike. This was not helped by her thoroughly unpleasant manner, especially as she disparaged 'all botanists, horticulturists, garden designers, and possessors of expert knowledge, unless they were related to her by marriage'.[29] Dorothy upset friends of La Mortola by declaring that 'most gardens have too many plants', adding 'I am going to say that there can be too many labels and specimens visible'.[30] What she thought of Serre de la Madone is not recorded, but an exception was made for Edith Wharton, perhaps due to her celebrity and, more significantly, because she was an authority on Italian gardens. Dorothy was passionate about Italian gardens and had already created an Italianate formal garden in England. Now she was redesigning a part of the garden at La Mortola, to give it an Italian overlay. Until this time La Mortola had been essentially

Plate 119 La Mortola, the home of Dorothy Hanbury.

a botanical garden, but Dorothy thought that it should have a greater structure. So she was adding long vistas, pools, fountains, flights of steps and balustrading, urns, columns and a magnificent cupola complete with statues among the cypress; near the house she made three small Italian gardens planted with box, lavender and aromatic herbs. More botanically-minded visitors might have been offended, but these alterations gave the garden a more logical structure and solved the problems of levels, perspective and direction that had been left unresolved by Sir Thomas Hanbury. The changes added greatly to the overall aesthetic enjoyment of La Mortola, and one suspects that Edith and Johnnie, with their admiration for Italian gardens, would have approved (Plate 119).

Dorothy was also a great admirer of Benito Mussolini and took pride in being the first English woman to be given the right to wear the *distintivo* – the badge of the fascists – and was further disliked because of it. In the 1920s, many British conservatives and retired military men warmly welcomed Il Duce, conveniently overlooking his other misdemeanours, because he was considered to be a bulwark against communism. At the time Edith Wharton was resolutely anti-unions and anti-socialist, and had numerous French friends with right-wing sympathies, some of whom were members of the extreme organisation, *Action Française*.[31] As Wharton's biographer Hermione Lee makes clear, it would be dangerous to over-dramatize these right-wing links for, at the time of visiting La Mortola, she was merely expressing an admiration for Mussolini's efficiency.

FRIENDS AND NEIGHBOURS

Playing tennis continued to be an important part of Johnston's life, and when in the south of France he would play regularly with Edith Wharton. He was also a member of the tennis club in Menton, though

Maybud Campbell, who was to become one of the town's distinguished gardeners, recalled that until Johnston was pointed out to her at the tennis club, she had no idea he even had a garden. This was a further example of Johnston's reserved nature. He would not have introduced himself, especially as he was considerably older than her, but he would have known her father, the local doctor to the English winter visitors in Menton, who had assembled a collection of citrus species and varieties. Maybud Campbell was to become an expert on the natural flora of the Alpes Maritimes, where Johnston made frequent plant-collecting excursions.[32] He had visited the *arrière pays*, as it was known, on one occasion with Edith Wharton (she was aged 69 at the time). A year before Johnston's death, in 1957, Maybud Campbell bought the Casa Rossa (now called Val Rahmeh) in Menton. The house and garden had previously been owned by Sir Percy Radcliffe, who had acquired the site in 1905 when he was Governor of Malta. After his retirement, he built the Mediterranean-style house in 1926 and laid out an art-deco garden, adding many exotic plants alongside the more fashionable mimosa, eucalyptus, palms and succulents. After Radcliffe's death, Johnston took a lease on the house for a season, just before the outbreak of war in 1939, and prepared an inventory of the plants in the garden. This was used later by Maybud Campbell after her arrival at Casa Rossa, and in the course of the next few years she added many subtropical and tropical plants, including an extensive collection of daturas.[33]

Another of Johnston's friends, and a frequent tennis partner, was the Vicomte Charles de Noailles at Hyères whom he had known for many years (see Plate 144, p.295). His mother was English and he had been educated partly in England. During the war he stayed for a while with Norah Lindsay at Sutton Courtenay where he could have met Johnston.[34] De Noailles was part of the avant-garde *milieu* in Paris when he met and married Marie-Laure Bischoffsheim in 1923 – curiously in the same year that she had had a brief 'fling' with the artist and writer Jean Cocteau. After her marriage she was known as the Vicomtesse du Bizarre and, though later events transpired to reveal that Charles de Noailles was homosexual, the ill-matched couple produced two daughters. In 1925, impressed by 'The Art Deco' exposition in Paris, Charles de Noailles invited the architect Robert Mallet-Steven to design a summer house, the Villa St. Bernard, at Hyères on the hillside next to Edith Wharton's Ste-Claire. The modernist house

Plate 120 Charles de Noailles' Villa St-Bernard on the hillside near Edith Wharton's Ste-Claire at Hyères.

Plate 121 The triangular cubist garden designed by Gabriel Guevrekian in 1927.

was built of concrete, prismatic in form and was deliberately alien to its locale (Plate 120), brooding close to the skyline above the old town of Hyères.[35] The garden was even more controversial having been designed by Gabriel Guevrekian in 1927. This was a triangular cubist garden (Plate 121), comprised largely of inert ceramics, concrete and crushed glass, rather than living materials.[36] It differed markedly from the garden tradition favoured by Edith and Johnnie who sought to harmonize formality and naturalism. One can imagine that neither house nor garden at St-Bernard appealed to their taste but, despite these differences, Charles de Noailles became one of Wharton's new friends. She met him first in Paris when he was 'a trim sturdy young man in his late twenties with a handsome face and black moustache who shared her passion for gardens'.[37] He regarded her as a great gardener – very serious technically

– an opinion supported by the books in her library, which included a well-marked copy of Hugo De Vries's book on plant-breeding experiments, published in 1907 (Appendix 1). When at Hyères, Wharton would often walk along the ridge to visit or take dinner with Noailles (Plate 122), especially when Johnnie and Norah were staying with her.

It has been suggested that Marie-Laure de Noailles, additionally known as the surrealist muse, was a stronger supporter of the avant-garde than her husband. Norah Lindsay, a frequent guest at Ste-Claire, was in no doubt that he had 'a very queer notorious wife who was always doing wild things and rushing about with disreputable men or turning herself into a bolshie and interrupting meetings which is her latest display of exhibitionism'.[38] After the furore that followed the making of Luis Buñuel's film 'The Golden Age', which was funded by the de Noailles and filmed at the villa, Charles became disenchanted with the avant-garde and spent his time bringing up his daughters and gardening. He was laying out a Mediterranean garden below the house, in a style very similar to Wharton's garden at Ste-Claire, and in time he became acknowledged as one of France's great horticulturists. In 1947 de Noailles started a new garden at Grasse in the Alpes Maritimes very much in the Anglo-Saxon tradition, starting with formality near the house and merging into the natural landscape. Though the garden is on a steep slope similar to the one at Serre de la Madone, it has more than a hint of Hidcote; with garden rooms linked together by water, twin gazebos on the lawn terrace and steps leading down to a peony terrace – the plants collected so enthusiastically by Johnston.

FINANCIAL RESTRAINTS

Meanwhile, the acquisition of Serre de la Madone had put an additional strain on Johnston's finances. He once claimed to have 'no money' and told Frank Adams in the 1920s, that his mother would only allow him £600 a month,[39] which was far too little to run both Hidcote and Serre de la Madone. Now with his mother's ailing health, he became increasingly concerned about his financial future. In a manner reminiscent of Lucretia Jones, Mrs Winthrop had arranged her will so that her son would not have access to her substantial capital, and would receive only the income from her estate, which was in excess of $1,500,000.[40] Johnston was worried that his income would be at the mercy of American trustees, relatives barely known to him, just as it had been for Edith Wharton with such unsatisfactory consequences. While he was considering his position, Edith Wharton made a return visit to Hidcote early in the spring of 1925, to see Johnston's 'incomparable garden'. She had made her first visit in September the previous year, and afterwards they had gone to the RHS Autumn Show in Holland Park, London. Unfortunately his mother's serious illness intervened and, as she told Daisy Chanler afterwards, their planned motor-trip to York and Durham, no doubt intending to visit Johnston's friends, Captain Edward Compton at Newby Hall, near Ripon, and the Hon. Robert James at St Nicholas, Richmond, had to be cancelled.

Johnston decided he had no option but to apply to the English Courts of Protection and have his mother declared incompetent because of her senility, which 'led her to believe she is being persecuted by her maid'.[41] A General Order of August 1925 made Johnston responsible for Gertrude's English property, allowing resources to pay for her 'journey to and winter residence in France' and permitted him 'the use and occupation free' of Hidcote Manor. In March the following year, Johnston applied successfully to the American Supreme Court to have his mother's property administered by the Bank of New York and Trust Company. Gertrude Winthrop was to die at Serre in December that year when Hidcote Manor passed into Johnston's sole ownership, along with a 'life interest in the entire residuary estate, which upon his death is to pass to his issue'.[42] At the time of her death, his mother was receiving an income from her estate of $600,000.[43] Her brother James and his daughter both received annuities. Johnston was said to have been incensed 'that his cousin Katherine should take part of what he considered to be rightfully entirely his own'.[44] He made arrangements for his mother to be buried at Mickleton churchyard in Gloucestershire (see Plate 154, p.310), a short distance away from the other graves. He told Norah Lindsay that he had 'ordered a Pall of violet silk entirely covered with violets with a cross of palm fronds in the middle and you wouldn't see any coffin'.[45]

After his mother's death, Johnston relied on his secretary Miss Marsden to administer his financial affairs while he continued to pursue his ambitious plans for Hidcote and Serre, on an even greater scale than before. Three years later came the New York Stock Market crash of 1929, leading to an economic depression which was to last throughout the following decade. This had a devastating effect on expatriates like Wharton and Johnston who were dependent on American investments and properties for their income. Wharton told Beatrix Farrand in 1931 that 'my income has been so much reduced in the last few years that, when I don't publish a novel, I have very little superfluous cash'.[46] She was forced to consider reducing the garden staff at Ste-Claire and Colombe. Although he was not American, Charles de Noailles was said also to have lost millions, but was thought to have possessed millions more in far-flung real estate elsewhere. For Wharton the stress caused by these financial worries came at a time when her health and energies were already failing. In the months following the destruction of her garden in January 1929 as the result of a massive storm, Wharton's health collapsed. She had influenza and a high fever, followed by what was described by a friend as '*une crise cardiaque*'.[47] The use of digitalis to treat her suggested an irregular heartbeat which would make her liable to have a stroke. In the spring of 1931, she did indeed suffer her first stroke while staying at Hyères. Afterwards the doctors said she had made a full recovery, but her life in future years was taken at an easier pace.[48]

Johnston, who was totally dependent on income from his mother's estate, must have been similarly affected by the 1929 crash. His financial situation was further exacerbated when, in 1934, the French Government introduced new laws which taxed properties and incomes, as well as assets held abroad by permanent residents such as Edith Wharton. Hidcote had already become a financial burden for Johnston, and when he arrived back from Menton in December 1935, he told Norah Lindsay that he was turning Hidcote into a company so he could stay in England as long as he liked. She told her sister, 'this will save him £2,000 a year. So he is hoping to get back in June which will be delicious as I mind losing Hidcote and Johnny in summer more than anything.'[49] A month later, when Norah was staying at Serre, Johnston told her that he was so overdrawn that he had abandoned all his schemes at Serre de la Madone and 'was going to have to rent Hidcote and just stay quietly and receive his friends and stop buying'.[50] In fact Norah did not see him that summer, and it was October, when she returned to Sutton Courtenay after an absence of two months, before she saw Johnny, 'small and brown', sitting in the garden on his way back from Menton. Writing to her sister afterwards, Norah said, we had 'a long crack as I hadn't seen him since February'.[51] He told her that he was not opening his garden and only staying for three weeks to see his lawyers before returning to Menton. After lunch he said he must go as he was desparate to see Hidcote after an absence of nearly a year. While the decade progressed, life became more difficult for Edith and Johnnie, though neither became bankrupt nor forced to sell their houses, and despite their reduced financial circumstances, they did not curtail their travelling.

NOTES AND REFERENCES

[1] Bennet, J. H., *Winter and Spring on the Shores of the Mediterranean*. Churchill & Sons., London, pp. 99–100.

[2] Quoted in Jones, L., *Serre de la Madone*. Dexia Editions, Paris, p. 22.

[3] Martineau, A., *Gardening in Sunny Lands*. Cobden-Sanderson, London, p. 172.

[4] Jones, op. cit., p. 18.

[5] According to Louisa Jones, in southern France *Serre* refers to mountains or small hills; in this instance, to a long ridge relating to the Madone mountain close by, and not, as the French Government Tourist Office says, 'gardens of the Madonna's greenhouse'.

[6] Arnaud Maurières and Eric Ossart, garden designers, in a report commissioned by M. Yarmola, Chief Architect for Monuments Historiques, 1992; quoted in Jones, op, cit., p. 25.

[7] Bennet, op. cit., p. 100.

[8] Quoted in Hayward, A., *Norah Lindsay – the life and art of a garden designer*. Frances Lincoln, London, p. 113.

[9] Will Ingwersen (1916–1990) was a specialist in alpine and rock gardening and accompanied Johnston on plant-collecting trips to the Alpes Maritimes and Morocco. After his time at Serre de la Madone he continued at the Birch Farm nursery started by his father Walter, on land gifted by William Robinson.

[10] Jones, op. cit., p. 25.

[11] Ganay, E., de., quoted in Jones, op. cit., p. 27. The Great Pool was built during Ingwersen's time – quoted in Jones, op. cit., p. 25.

[12] *Restanque* is a Provençal term applied originally to dry-stone walls built into the beds of intermittent streams to collect alluvial material. More generally the term is applied to dry-stone retaining walls built on steep hillsides to support terraces.

[13] Quoted in Jones, op. cit., p. 38.

[14] Bennet, op. cit., p. 114.

[15] Hayward, op. cit., p. 95.

[16] Page, R., *Education of a Gardener*. Harvill, London, p. 201, quoted in Jones, op. cit., p. 41.

[17] Hayward, op. cit., p. 195.

[18] Whitsey, F. *The Garden at Hidcote*. Frances Lincoln, London, p. 19. Unfortunately Charlie Frensham committed suicide shortly after going to Serre. Johnston then appointed Henry Lloyd as head gardener. Lloyd was important in laying out the garden, and after he died in service, Johnston placed a memorial tablet on one of the stone clematis pillars in the garden.

[19] Clarke, E., *Hidcote*. Michael Joseph, London, p. 26.

[20] Hewitt, B. *The Crocus King – E. A. Bowles of Myddleton House.* Touchwood Books, London, p. 36. Bowles visited Johnston at Serre de la Madone in March 1928.

[21] Hayward, op. cit., pp. 114-6.

[22] Jones, op. cit., p. 23.

[23] Hayward, op. cit., p. 190.

[24] Quoted in *The Guardian*, 13 September 2003.

[25] Collas, P. and Villedary, E., *Edith Wharton's French Riviera.* Flammarion, Paris, p. 91.

[26] Quoted in Jones, op. cit., p. 23. Madame Bottin was the daughter of Alfredo Rebuffo.

[27] Clarke, op. cit., p. 90. When Norah Warre arrived on the Riviera with her husband 'Ginger' in 1902, her garden at Roquebrune was no more than a steep, rough hillside with a few pine and olive trees. For over 75 years Mrs Warre worked at transforming this unpromising terrain into a natural woodland setting by clearing rocks, terracing sometimes with walls as much as 12 feet high, and the importation of tons of top soil to supplement the meagre limey, heavy clay.

[28] Moore, M., *La Mortola.* Cadogan, London, pp. 118-9.

[29] Quest-Ritson, C., *The English Gardener Abroad.* Viking, London, p. 70.

[30] Ibid.

[31] *Action Française* was a fascistic, violently nationalistic movement founded in 1898.

[32] Maybud Campbell was an extraordinary women who had been an opera singer and a 'doughty' botanist working at the British Museum. Each year she travelled to the south of France in summer and made collections of the local flora.

[33] Increasing debts forced Maybud Campbell to sell the property in 1967; it is now known as the Val Rahmeh Botanical Garden, named after the wife of Sir Percy Radcliffe.

[34] According to Ethne Clarke, Johnston asked Charles de Noailles when he was then 18, to take a gift of rhododendron seed to Guillaume Mallet at his house, 'Le Bois des Moutiers' near Dieppe in Normandy. This would have been in 1910 when Johnston had only just started to develop Hidcote and his interest in rhododendrons was many years in the future.

[35] Treib, M., ed., *Modern Landscape Architecture.* MIT Press, London, pp. 38-9.

[36] Guevrekian designed a 'Garden of Water and Light' at the Exposition Internationale des Arts Decoratifs et Industriels Modernes of 1925 – or Art Deco as it became known – and the notoriety it achieved prompted Charles de Noailles to commission a second garden for his villa at Hyères.

[37] Lewis, R.W.B. *Edith Wharton: a biography.* Constable, London, p. 448.

38 Letter to her sister Madeline, February 1937; quoted in Hayward, op. cit., p. 219.

39 In excess of £25,000, using the Retail Price Index of the Economic History Association.

40 In excess of £18 million today, using the Consumer Price Index, Economic History Association.

41 *New York Times*, 14 March 1926.

42 *New York Times*, 29 January 1927.

43 In excess of £7 million per annum, using the Consumer Price Index, Economic History Association.

44 Clarke, E., *Hidcote – the Making of a Garden*. Revised edition. Norton, London, p. 76.

45 Quoted in Hayward, op. cit., p. 112.

46 Lee, H., *Edith Wharton*. Chatto and Windus, London, p. 683.

47 Ibid., p. 681.

48 Ibid., p. 683.

49 Quoted in Hayward, op. cit., p. 264.

50 Ibid., p. 199.

51 Ibid., pp. 212–3.

CHAPTER TWELVE

PLANTS AND PLANT COLLECTING

In 1920 E. A. ('Gussie') Bowles and other leading horticulturists formed the Garden Society, an elite all-male dining-club whose members were not only wealthy and passionate gardeners but keenly interested in the 'cultivation, increase and exchange of plants, and especially plants of more recent introduction'.[1] Membership was limited to 50 garden-owners, all Fellows of the Royal Horticultural Society, who met at least twice a year to discuss plants and exchange gardening knowledge, usually on the first night of the RHS spring meeting – now the Chelsea Flower Show – and the night of the first RHS autumn meeting in November. On these occasions members were encouraged to bring some flower or plant of horticultural or botanical interest, and give a short account of it after dinner. In 1921 Johnston's friend and neighbour at Abbotswood, Mark Fenwick, had been elected to the Society and subsequently wrote to Lionel de Rothschild at Exbury asking whether he would support the nomination of Lawrence Johnston, 'who is a very keen and good gardener'.[2] A year later, in May, Johnston was invited to join, and thereafter regularly attended its meetings. Election to the Garden Society secured Johnston's place within the senior echelons of the horticultural world and brought him into further contact with the likes of his friends Reginald Cory of Dyffryn and Sir George Holford of Westonbirt; also with H. D. McClaren, later Lord Aberconway of Bodnant, Frederick Stern of Highdown, and William Wright Smith, Regius Keeper at the Royal Botanic Garden, Edinburgh. From 1923 onwards Johnston received plants from the Royal Botanic Garden (known as the 'Botanics'), and since he was a keen plant-collector, he returned the favours, for the exchange of plants and information was in the spirit of the Society's Latin motto, *Petimus Damusque Vicissum* ('Turn by turn we ask and give'). Towards the end of his life Johnston said he was more interested in plants than the design of the garden, and many features at Hidcote and Serre de la Madone were added merely to accommodate plants gathered on his plant-collecting expeditions. Several plant shelters were erected at both gardens to house the very special and delicate species (see Plate 166, p. 323).

One of his earlier trips was to Lauteret near Grenoble in the Alpes Maritimes in 1922 with Bowles and his friends Susan Garnett-Botfield and Richard Trotter, who also became a member of the Garden Society. Johnston continued to visit the region for several years, visiting the coastal Alps with Edith Wharton and the inland higher Alps with Mark Fenwick and also Will Ingwersen. In his engagement diary for April 1929, Johnston mentions walking north of Nice in the Vésubie valley, which runs north-east from the River Var into the heart of the Alpes Maritimes. Reginald Farrer, the pioneer of modern rock gardens, described the solitude of the valley in his book *Among the Hills*. It was, he said, 'a miracle that this delightful place so rarely sees an English visitor'.[3] In April the fields and slopes would have been rich in spring flowers: anemones and pulsatillas, drifts of crocus and fritillaries, orchids and spring gentians. But all that Johnston records is the terse comment, '20 miles very long'.

Earlier in 1923 Johnston was part of a syndicate which sponsored an expedition headed by the German plant hunter, W. T. Goethe, to collect plants and seeds native to the Andes, from which he later received material from Edinburgh. After his mother died in 1926, Johnston was at last able to pursue his interest in plant-collecting outside Europe, though it is uncertain how many trips he made or backed. It is possible that he sponsored an expedition to Mexico, since a garden of succulents at Serre was called 'Mexican'. In 1926 he was a sponsor of Frank Kingdon-Ward's expedition to the northern frontiers of Burma, to collect mainly rhododendron seed, along with meconopsis and primulas.

SOUTH AFRICA

His first recorded expedition was to South Africa in September 1927, when he returned to that country with Collingwood 'Cherry' Ingram, who led the trip, and his old friend Reginald Cory. By now Cory had become a generous horticultural benefactor; in turn he funded George Taylor, a recent Edinburgh graduate who was later to become Director of the Royal Botanic Gardens, Kew, so that he could join the expedition. The purpose of the enterprise was to collect plants for their own gardens as well as for Kew and the Botanics. Ingram mentions in his memoirs, *A Garden of Memories*, the richness of the Cape flora and how it had been diminished by collecting and the introduction of alien weeds. These so-called 'khaki weeds' were the result of seeds embedded in the fodder brought from England and elsewhere to feed the horses during the Boer Wars.

At Cape Town Johnston arranged for two vehicles, a Jeep and a Buick, to be ready (Plate 123). Much has been made of Johnston taking along his valet and his chauffeur, something he did on all his trips, for that was normal for a gentleman of leisure. (Edith Wharton always travelled with her cook, a maid, the chauffeur and even her dogs.) The South African venture was to last three months and, after starting with the Cape flora and a visit to Kirstenbosch Botanical Garden, they travelled along what is now known as the 'Garden Route' to Knysna, and then north to the Drakensberg Mountains. George Taylor later recalled that for Cory the expedition was more of a 'social affair', and that Johnston did not scour the countryside as keenly as Ingram or he did.[4] Nevertheless, there was intense rivalry; on one occasion Ingram spied a solitary gladiolus on his side of a gully, and was concerned that his friends, quartering the ground on the far side, would spot the plant first and be able to reach it more easily. The arrangement was that a member of the group could keep a single plant; otherwise material would be divided between the four with the surplus sent to the botanic gardens. On that occasion, Ingram walked nonchalantly away and sat on a rock until his friends had passed; then he was able to collect the plant.

Plate 123 South Africa; of the seated figures, Lawrence Johnston is to the left of George Taylor.

Johnston's interest at this time was still for plant material that could be grown in such temperate English gardens as Hidcote, and this would explain why, in Taylor's opinion, his fellow plant-collector did not appear to be very knowledgeable – in the field at least. Yet Johnston's experiences in South Africa encouraged him to be more interested in plants that could be grown in his Mediterranean garden. His enthusiasm for finding new plants was illustrated by an incident on the way to the Transkei. Collingwood Ingram recounts how he:

> ... was driving the Buick with Johnnie sitting by my side and Reggie Cory on a seat behind. Suddenly in an excited voice Johnnie shouted, 'Stop, stop! We've just passed a plant of superlative beauty: a plant we must, at all costs, collect'. I steered the car to the side of the road, stopped it and got out; the three of us then hurried back to where Johnnie had seen his wonderful plant.
>
> Sure enough, high up on a precipitous roadside slope and partly hidden by the vegetation was what certainly appeared to be a large crimson-coloured bloom of some unknown liliaceous species. Although the climb was exceedingly steep, and as there were plenty of trees and shrubs to give me secure foot and handholds, I had no real difficulty in reaching my objective. I cannot recollect now whether I was more amused or more disappointed when, at the end of that climb, I discovered that the mysterious plant of 'superlative beauty' was not a plant at all but a piece of red paper which had seemingly been carried to that lofty ledge by an upward gust of wind'.[5]

Ingram attributed this mistake to proof of the strange tricks imagination can play on a person, but it will be a familiar experience to anyone who has plant-spotted from a moving vehicle. The plants Johnston brought home were given to his head gardener Frank Adams to propagate, and in 1929 he sent a selection to the Royal Botanic Garden in Edinburgh. One intriguing entry in Johnston's notebooks suggests that the party may not always have travelled together; in South Africa he notes that he must write to Ingram, and then records seeing a wonderful pea bush in the Viljoen Pass and that Nan had asked a local guide to obtain seeds. Could this have been a reference to his cousin Nan Hudson, who was a keen gardener, for later after the whole party had been on the Garden Route, Johnston mentions receiving two letters from N?

Early the following year, Johnston was back in Africa and travelled to Kenya to climb Mount Kilimanjaro, in the most amenable month of the year. He motored from Nairobi to Murangi and on 14th February started out on the easiest of the trails, reaching the stone-built Bismarck Hut at 8700 feet (2700 metres). The following day he went to the top of the forest and collected impatiens, violet and senecio seeds. On 17th February, in a very rare descriptive passage in his engagement diary, he notes that he walked to Peter's Hut and 'in the gully found Hypericum yellow' – there has been speculation that this may have been the famous 'Hidcote' variety, though this has been much disputed. At night he returned to the Bismarck Hut, and having ascended and descended 3200 feet (1020 metres), it is hardly surprising that his entry was a terse 'very tired'. On the 21st he returned to Peter's Hut at 12,500 feet (3780 metres), which is located in the semi-alpine zone where the vegetation consists of mainly heathers, *Erica arborea*, and scrub plants. Johnston found seeds and bulbs of gladiolus, tritonia and orchis. Again he records arriving very tired, adding that the boys nearly burnt the hut down by making too big a fire. This must have been galling for Johnston, who had paid for the mountain huts to be restored for use before his expedition.[6] On 23rd February, Johnston returned to Murangi and ten days later travelled to Blantyre by motor.

After his return to England, Johnston wrote his one and only article, 'Some Flowering Plants of Kilimanjaro', published in October 1929 in *New Flora and Silva*, in which he described finding plants of the endemic giant groundsel:

> After all, I realised that in all that waste of dry grass and scrub and even tropical forest, where lush green leaves prevent the growth of many flowering plants, Kilimanjaro has its little flower gardens, hidden in rocky dells, sheltered from the wind and watered by streams from the melting snows. The King of these little valleys is Senecio Johnstonii [Plate 124] ... as picturesque a plant as so essentially an ugly one can be. It looks like a huge artichoke of pale green leaves on a woody stem, sometimes as much as 15 feet high, and often branched into several heads. The old leaves, dry and brown, hang down and cling to the stem, making a thick mantle from which the brilliant green leaves arise. This colour tells tremendously against the neutral background of the rocks and grass. It often grows on a high boulder or a mound with great effect, as if conscious of its

kingly status. The plant was not in flower but I secured a good supply of seed, and I hope that, at least in some places, it will prove hardy in England'.[7]

CHINA, RHODODENDRONS AND GEORGE FORREST

From the 1920s onwards, members of the Garden Society were intensely interested in rhododendrons from south-east Asia and associated plants, such as primulas, lilies and the blue poppy, meconopsis. The British horticultural elite was besotted by rhododendrons, the nearest it ever came to emulating the Dutch tulipomania of the seventeenth century. Some members of the Garden Society, for example Gerald Loder at Wakehurst Place, were able to replicate an entire Yunnan landscape in their gardens.

Plate 124 *Senecio johnstonii*, the endemic giant groundsel, on the slopes of Mount Kilimanjaro.

Those with smaller gardens and on less favourable sites, had to make arrangements to accommodate these acid-loving plants. At St. Nicholas, Robert James made a rock garden, with the help of Ellen Willmott, which was entered through a collection of rhododendrons, grown in pockets of imported soil. At Hidcote, where the soil was strongly alkaline, Johnston employed teams of men to excavate tons of unwanted soil in three areas of the Stream Garden and in the narrow north-facing border, under the cottage wall, in the Old Garden. In the Lower Stream Garden low dry-stone walls were used throughout to enclose 'pockets' of acidic soil, created by mixing huge quantities of decayed sawdust from local sawmills with clinker from Chipping Campden railway sidings, and lime-free loam.

Enthusiasm for rhododendrons and other Asiatic plants had been stimulated by collectors, most notably George Forrest. He had started searching for new plants in China during 1904, in north-west Yunnan, but it was not until his third expedition that rhododendrons featured prominently in his collections. That journey had been sponsored by J. C. Williams of Caerhays Castle in Cornwall, who planned to enrich his garden with the new species introduced from China. Twenty years later, by the time Forrest had received the Victoria Medal of Honour from the Royal Horticultural Society in 1921, as well as the highest horticultural honour in America awarded by the Massachusetts Horticultural Society, he had collected over 25,000 plant specimens and discovered over 1000 plants new to science, including many rhododendrons.[8] Forrest was a dedicated, even obsessive plant-collector, who was single-minded in his desire to satisfy the requests of his sponsors. He was described, however, as difficult to deal with. He would not suffer fools gladly and became highly suspicious of other people's motives. His temper would flair up if he felt affronted, let down or not trusted; and like most plant-collectors, he was a loner, happy with his own company, and perhaps only truly content when he was by himself in the mountains.

By 1929 George Forrest was aged 57, still fit and able to walk 30 miles a day and keen to undertake one last trip to China. In April 1929 Johnston wrote to the Regius Keeper of the Edinburgh Botanic Garden, William Wright Smith, expressing an interest in sponsoring such an expedition, and in turn Wright Smith wrote to Forrest that 'he is evidently keen and quite willing to make the journey here if he can advance arrangements for the trip'.[9] It is likely that Johnston did meet Forrest in May,[10] but arrangements did not proceed smoothly. In August, Wright Smith indicated to Forrest that much depended on J. C. Williams and [Lionel] Rothschild,[11] 'especially the inclination of Williams', adding that 'I think you should let Major Johnston have a line from you'.[12] At the end of the month, Forrest wrote to Wright Smith saying that 'after all that had transpired and giving the matter consideration from every angle, I have decided to have nothing further to do with [the] present proposal and I am writing to Mr Johnston informing him of my decision'.[13] After Johnston's second visit to Edinburgh, in September, Forrest evidently changed his mind.

In October, Johnston met Williams in London (see Chapter 13). Then in November members of the Garden Society, including Wright Smith and Rothschild, discussed with Johnston and other keen gardeners, the possibility of sponsoring Forrest's final trip to Yunnan. Forrest had estimated that £4000[14] would be needed, and Wright Smith hoped to find eight people willing to contribute a £500 share. In the event only four were willing to subscribe that amount. These included the Royal Horticultural Society at Wisley, Lionel de Rothschild of Exbury and Lawrence Johnston. Nevertheless, news of Forrest's last expedition soon spread, and by December letters offering smaller subscriptions were being sent to Johnston. One of Forrest's initial concerns was having the expedition funded by so many small contributions, and the complications that might arise when satisfying so many 'masters'. Eventually there were 39 subscribers, including Johnston's friends Robert James and Reginald Cory. The full list reads like a who's who of rhododendron collectors, and included the Marchioness of Londonderry of Mount Stewart, Lt Col. Horlick of Achamore, Isle of Ghiga, H. D. McLaren of Bodnant, G. Loder of Wakehurst Place and Col. S. Clarke of Borde Hill. Why Johnston with his small garden – if compared with Bodnant or Wakehurst Place – and with its limited space for rhododendrons, should have been prepared to take an eighth share in the expedition, especially as he claimed to be so short of money, is unclear. It may have been an attempt to confirm his place among the top ranks of horticulturists, but it was more likely that it was his craving for adventure and the opportunity to visit Yunnan that provided the real incentive. He had considered going there alone the year before, but rejected the idea in favour of accompanying the famous George Forrest on his final expedition the following year (Plate 125). For an obsessive plant-

Plate 125 George Forrest during his last plant-collecting expedition.

collector like Johnston, Yunnan province in south-west China must have reached legendary status as a botanical paradise, the 'home' of so many recently-introduced plants, and a place that had to be visited.

It is equally difficult to imagine why Forrest would want to ally himself with Johnston: he had never taken anyone with him from Britain before; perhaps on this occasion he was swayed by Johnston's help in enrolling subscribers and his £500 share in the expedition. The two men were roughly of the same age, though very different in temperament. Forrest was advised against taking Johnston as a travelling companion by Cherry Ingram and the others on the South African expedition, but he did not fully understand their reasons – until it was too late. It was very clear from the outset that the two men approached the expedition very differently. For Forrest it was his last chance to visit places he had known for more than 20 years and 'hoover up' any remaining desirable plants; in the process he could satisfy the expectations of his many sponsors. So he set about organizing the expedition with a single-minded purpose. For Johnston, the journey was always going to be a combination of work and pleasure, and his approach to the trip was similar to that of Reggie Cory during the earlier expedition to South Africa.

In September 1930, Wright Smith informed Johnston's friend Bobbie James that 'Major Johnston and Forrest are rapidly completing arrangements and I think everything is well in hand for the expedition'.[15] The two men sailed for Rangoon in November 1930, but on arrival frictions soon emerged. Forrest expected Johnston to share in the practical preparations for the venture: in securing passports and permits, calling on the various officials, booking berths and buying tickets. But Johnston had other plans, so that Forrest wrote in a desperate letter to William Wright Smith on 26 February 1931, 'had I raked GB with a small tooth-comb I couldn't have found a worse companion than Johnston, and I cannot say how often during the three months I have cursed myself for being so foolish in consenting to him accompanying me! I have indeed

Map 6 Lawrence Johnston used the old south-western silk road to rejoin George Forrest at Tengyueh in Yunnan, China. The town is surrounded by geothermal hotspots, and the hot springs where Johnston recovered from his near-fatal excursion are to the south of the town.

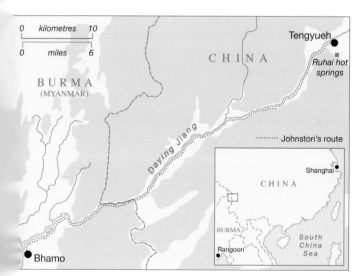

paid for my folly.'[16] In Bhamo, Johnston spent his time socializing with the British Deputy Commissioner and his wife, leaving Forrest 'to engage the chairs, coolies and mule transport'. Forrest expressed his frustration in his letters: 'there was much he could have done to lighten my labours but he was busy gadding around ... and every day riding in the morning, tea and tennis in the afternoon and bridge at the club in the evening'.[17] This summarizes the lifestyle Johnston had enjoyed for many years, and obviously Forrest was not going to change his sponsor's ways. When challenged, Johnston informed him that 'making up lists of stores and purchasing them bored him to destruction almost and besides it was too hot to attend to such matters'. Out of frustration and anger Forrest challenged Johnston, asking him 'if he thought he was a Cook's courier arranging a tour for him and if he thought I was paid to attend to him'.[18] Johnston's response was not recorded, though the answer, even if not spoken, would probably have been 'yes' to both questions. Certainly Johnston never apologized and there can be no doubt that, even though he recognized Forrest's reputation as a pre-eminent plant-collector, he would have regarded their relationship as the same as that between an officer and a non-commissioned officer.

This was, of course, the age of gentleman plant-hunters and, whereas Forrest personified the 'Baden-Powell' spirit of adventure, others, like Joseph Rock who was in the region at the same time, were more concerned with appearance and comfort. Rock was an Austrian who had taken American citizenship whom Forrest, needless to say, regarded as a serious rival but a 'most unreliable person'. Photographs of Rock, taken in some of the most rugged country, rarely show him without a coat and tie, and when out collecting, his baggage train would stretch half a mile or more accompanied by his many servants and mercenaries, including a chef trained in Austrian cuisine. Rock liked to eat seated at an elegant table set with white linen and a gold dinner service.

When Forrest prepared to leave for Tengyueh, he was informed that Johnston had fallen seriously ill: 'apparently he had caught a severe chill through exhausting himself playing tennis and then sitting cooling off instead of changing'. The British Divisional Surgeon reported that Johnston was in a very bad state internally, with 'chronic congestion of the liver, lungs exceedingly weak and heart and kidneys bad', and 'it would be extremely dangerous for him to attempt a journey into

Yunnan'.[19] Johnston decided he would not go on, so with a sense of relief Forrest left him behind and set out for his beloved mountains on 4th January 1931. Unfortunately for him, a day after his arrival at Tengyueh, Forrest was laid low with a 'sharp attack of ptomaine poisoning' (salmonella), and in his letter to Wright Smith he wrote, 'to add to my discomfort I was told that Johnston, ignoring medical advice, had left Bhamo on 14th January'.[20]

Travel in Yunnan can be extremely arduous, even today, but 80 years ago there were few roads, and travellers were in constant danger from warring tribes. But Johnston undertook a nine-day trek in subtropical conditions, along the old trade route, through the mountains and gorges of the River Daying Jiang and its tributary, to rejoin Forrest at Tengyueh in western Yunnan on 22nd January. Although carried in a sedan chair, a mode of travel used by Forrest and by another Cotswold-born plant collector, Ernest ('Chinese') Wilson, the journey placed a great strain on Johnston, who was more used to the luxury of a chauffeur-driven car. As a result, his condition deteriorated further. Forrest noted that it was only the attention he received from a doctor in the Indian Civil Service, present to serve the Consul and High Commissioner, that saved his life: 'else I fear poor Johnston would have gone under for good. Apparently there is Bright's disease in the family, a fact he did not divulge to me at Bhamo'.[21] The doctor reported that under no circumstances should he proceed further because his organs and kidneys were in such a critical condition that in the event of another attack he might die suddenly. Johnston at last realized the seriousness of his condition and 'decided to give up and return home and arranged to leave Rangoon in mid April'.[22] Forrest, though keen to proceed to Lichiang, would not leave until he was certain that Johnston had left. He feared that Johnston would change his mind and wrote to Wright Smith: 'he changes his mind more frequently than his socks, I give no guarantee what he shall eventually do. The only point I am quite positive about is that he shall not travel with me.'[23]

When Johnston decided that he could go no further, he 'coolly asked Forrest for his share of the stores'. These had been sealed already for the overland journey to Lichiang, and Forrest knew that breaking them open would invite thieves to steal from them. He could not contemplate repacking and resealing the packing-cases, which was so essential in the damp climate. He offered to pay Johnston for his share of the supplies but was refused, which Forrest regarded as 'an attempt to give me further trouble'.[24] He angrily informed Wright Smith that 'Johnston was not a man, not even a bachelor, but a right good old spinster spoilt by being born a male. A person more utterly selfish I have yet to meet, and I'm not the only one here who thinks so.'[25] In his reply on 11th March, Wright Smith ignored Forrest's outburst and wrote that he had received two short letters from Major Johnston expressing disappointment, 'but writing, I thought, in very good spirits and with a commendable spirit of resignation. He talks of looking in at Paradeniya on the way back and I certainly think he should do so.'[26] (Paradeniya Botanic Garden near Kandy in Ceylon [now Sri Lanka] was founded in the fourteenth century, and has always had a notable collection of orchids.)

Plate 126 *Jasminum polyanthemum* growing in a Yunnan hedgerow; though introduced earlier, Johnston grew this plant in the shelter at Hidcote, and helped to increase its popularity.

Forrest's fears about Johnston's unpredictability were justified. After the decision not to accompany Forrest to the Upper Shweli valley – where previously Forrest had collected many fine rhododendrons and other plant species – Johnston decided to undertake a trip to Yung Chang Fu on his own and against the doctor's advice. Once again the trek proved too much for him, and on his return journey, two or three days' travel from base, he sent a runner ahead with a plea for the doctor's assistance. 'The upper portions of his body, shoulders and neck swelled up so that the neck almost disappeared. His face swelled so he couldn't see and eventually he fainted. It must have been a very close call.'[27] The doctor arrived just in time, but Johnston later told Forrest that 'he thought he was going to die'. Upon his return to Tengyueh, Johnston was covered in eczema and urticaria from head to his midriff, but after a few days he departed for the local hot sulphur springs, where he had frequent and prolonged baths. A few days later, the doctor reported a great improvement. On his way to the Ruhai Springs he discovered *Iris wattii* growing near an irrigation canal which he dug up and later grew successfully at Menton. Ironically, in view of future events, Forrest observed that 'he was the most obstinate person and if he doesn't get away from here next week he may stay here for keeps'.[28]

Plate 127 (left) *Mahonia siamensis* flowering at Serre de la Madone.

Plate 128 (right) *Hypericum forrestii*, a widely-distributed plant in Yunnan, China.

Forrest had waited to see Johnston off on his journey home 'before I proceed on mine'. Johnston did finally leave in mid-April and returned to Menton by way of Ceylon at the beginning of June. Wright Smith wrote to Forrest on 16th June to say that 'Major Johnston is somewhere in France but I have no word of him yet'.[29] Later, Will Ingwersen tried to draw his experiences in Yunnan out of Johnston, but 'he was evasive and would recount nothing of them'.[30]

Johnston's adventures were over but he had 'tasted the thrill of plant hunting in China'.[31] He introduced to Hidcote the climber *Jasminum polyanthemum* (Plate 126), and the superb *Mahonia siamensis* (Plate 127) which, though not totally hardy in Britain, grows and flowers magnificently in Johnston's southern garden at Serre de la Madone. Forrest had related that Johnston 'nearly went dotty' when he saw a particularly fine specimen of *Camellia speciosa* in flower.[32] Another shrub Johnston must have seen flowering in many places beneath the canopy of deciduous trees would have been *Hypericum forrestii* (Plate128); with its large yellow flowers and prominent stamens it bears a close resemblance to the ubiquitous *Hypericum* 'Hidcote'.

Forrest continued his expedition, collecting specimens of primula, nomocharis and lilium in even greater abundance than before, altogether some 400 to 500 species. Consignments of seed kept coming from Yunnan, much to the delight of the sponsors. Forrest wrote, 'if all goes well I shall have made a rather glorious and satisfactory finish to all my past years of labour',[33] but sadly within days of writing those words he was dead from a massive heart attack on 6th January 1932.

Johnston received a substantial amount of the seed collected by Forrest, since he was a major shareholder in the expedition. It was at about this time that he gave seeds to Guillaume Mallet at 'Le Bois des Moutiers' in Normandy. Mallet's interest in English gardens had started at the age of ten when, in 1870, he was sent to England to escape the Franco-Prussian War. He greatly enjoyed the public gardens on the Isle of Wight and, as Lane Fox noted, 'he filed these in his mind besides memories of his own family's fine French gardens and their plants'.[34] Later, after he bought the Moutiers estate in 1897, Mallet and his wife Marie Adelaïde, engaged the young Edwin Lutyens to design the house and formal garden. This took the form of seven enclosures, including a double herbaceous border leading up to the house, and a long pergola. Gertrude Jekyll provided planting plans and, though some of her proposals were implemented, Mallet undertook much of the planting himself (Plate 129). He also planned

Plate 129 'Le Bois des Moutiers', the former home of Guillaume Mallet at Varengeville-sur-Mer in Normandy.

the adjoining parkland, with its collection of rare trees and shrubs, including Himalayan rhododendrons, along with azaleas, camellias, magnolias and herbaceous plants, in accord with the ideas he found in William Robinson's book, *The Wild Garden*.

Another of the books Mallet studied extensively was Mrs Van Rensselaer's *Art Outdoors* – the book which earlier had influenced Beatrix Farrand – which prompted his lifelong fascination with the landscape and garden as a work of art. In many respects, Le Bois des Moutiers shares much in common with Hidcote, for both Mallet and Johnston intermingled with aesthetic societies on their doorsteps. In Mallet's case it was one centred on Dieppe and the Normandy coast, where the painter Walter Sickert held court. So whilst Mallet and Johnston each created an 'English garden', their gardens were influenced nevertheless by other sources, notably from France, Italy and America.

Johnston's cousin Nan Hudson, and her companion Ethel Sands, were a part of the Dieppe circle. Living near Dieppe too was the artist Jacques-Émile Blanche, who had a house and studio in Offranville; he had become friends with Nan and Ethel when they visited Dieppe soon after they first came to Paris. Blanche was among Edith Wharton's oldest French friends, and she was a frequent visitor to Offranville, with its 'garden bursting with flowers' and 'a beautiful orchard behind'. Many years later, when Blanche was unwell and considering whether to sell the house, Wharton advised against it, for 'too many good memories are attached to it'.[35] It is most likely that Johnston and Wharton visited Le Bois des Moutiers, Auppegard and Offranville on their excursions from the Pavillon Colombe.

Johnston continued to sponsor plant-collecting expeditions: in 1932 he and five other subscribers paid £25 each to sponsor an expedition to Formosa, led by the Japanese collector Kan Yashiroda, receiving a share of the seeds and plants sent to Kew. When Norah Lindsay visited Hidcote in November that year, she found that for once Johnny had organized 'quite a party, as he had Mark Fenwick and old Charles James and Captain Kingdon-Ward who is delightful to meet like all explorers'.[36] Kingdon-Ward, who received the Victoria Medal of Honour from the RHS that year, had recently returned from an expedition to the harshness of northern Burma with Lord Cranborne. Around the table they no doubt talked about his new discoveries, including a particularly outstanding slipper orchid, the rainbow orchid *Paphiopedalum wardii* (*Cyprepedium wardianum*),[37] and the carmine cherry, *Prunus cerasoides rubra*, whose ruby-red blossoms Kingdon-Ward described as 'a frozen fountain of precious stones'. A year later, Johnston revisited the Maritime Alps and the Atlas mountains in Morocco with Will Ingwersen, who was working at Serre, and the Swiss Alps. In 1938 Johnston, now aged 69, was planning his own trip to Burma with Charles de Noailles, but the onset of war and the invasion of Italian soldiers brought Johnston's plant-collecting to an end.

Notes and References

1   Quoted in Pearson, G., *Hidcote: The Garden and Lawrence Johnston*. Anova Books for The National Trust, London, p. 32.
2   Ibid. An informative photograph exists of members of the Garden Society at their dinner of 3rd November 1925, which was broadcast unattributed in the film about Lawrence Johnston and the making of the garden at Hidcote by BBC 4 on 8th June 2011. It can be seen in a Garden Society Annual Report kept in the reference section of the RHS Lindley Library in London. Permission to reproduce the picture in this book was declined by the copyright holder, the Garden Society, because 'the Society has always been and remains a private dining society'.
3   Farrer, R., *Among the Hills*. Headley Brothers, London, pp. 172–200.
4   Clarke, E., *Hidcote*. Joseph, London, p. 81.
5   Ingram, C. (1970) *A Garden of Memories*. F. and G. Witherby, London.
6   Fretwell, L., 'The Real Major Johnston Revealed'. *Country Life*, 194 (10) 9, March 2000.
7   Johnson [sic], Lawrence, 'Some Flowering Plants of Kilimanjaro', *The New Flora and Fauna*, No. 5, Vol. 11, October 1929.
8   McLean, B., *George Forrest plant hunter*. Antique Collectors Club, Woodbridge, p. 175.
9   W. Wright Smith to G. Forrest, 11 April 1929. Forrest Archive, Royal Botanic Garden, Edinburgh.
10 Pearson, op. cit., p. 33.
11 Lionel de Rothschild owned a celebrated rhododendron garden at Exbury, on the edge of the New Forest near Beaulieu in Hampshire. He was a major sponsor of plant-collecting expeditions.
12 W. Wright Smith to G. Forrest, 15 August 1929. Forrest Archive, Royal Botanic Garden, Edinburgh.
13 G. Forrest to W. Wright Smith, 31 August 1929. Forrest Archive, Royal Botanic Garden, Edinburgh.

14. Approximately £120,000 (National Archive March 2009).

15. W. Wright Smith to R. James, 2 September 1929. Forrest Archive, Royal Botanic garden, Edinburgh.

16. G. Forrest to W. Wright Smith, 26 February 1931. Forrest Archive, Royal Botanic Garden, Edinburgh.

17. Ibid.

18. Ibid.

19. Ibid.

20. Ibid.

21. Ibid. Bright's disease is an acute disease of the kidneys, first identified by Richard Bright in 1827, now known a nephritis. There was at first no successful treatment for the condition, but warm baths, laxatives and diuretics were recommended. Dietary modifications were also suggested.

22. Ibid.

23. Ibid.

24. Ibid.

25. Ibid.

26. W. Wright Smith to G. Forrest, 11 March 1931. Forrest Archive, Royal Botanic Garden, Edinburgh.

27. G. Forrest to W. Wright Smith, 31 March 1931. Forrest Archive, Royal Botanic Garden, Edinburgh.

28. Ibid.

29. W. Wright Smith to G. Forrest, 16 June 1931. On 3 June, Wright Smith had written that he had no news of Johnston's safe arrival in France, but presumed it must have been around the start of June. Forrest Archive, Royal Botanic Garden, Edinburgh.

30. Whitsey, F., *The Gardens at Hidcote*. Frances Lincoln, London, p. 25.

31. McLean, op. cit., p. 190.

32. Probably *Camellia saluenensis*, introduced by Forrest.

33. Quoted in McLean, op. cit., p. 203.

34. Lane-Fox, R., 'English style à la Française'. *Financial Times*, 28 July, 2007.

35. Lee, H., *Edith Wharton*. Chatto and Windus, London, p. 703.

36. Hayward, A., *Norah Lindsay – the life and art of a garden designer*. Frances Lincoln, London, p. 186.

37. *Paphiopedilum wardii* was reported to have become extinct in the latest study of wild orchids in Burma (Myanmar). *J. Royal Horticultural Society*, Vol. 133, No. 6, 2008, 363.

CHAPTER THIRTEEN

The Diary Years 1929–1932

In the 1920s and '30s Johnston (Plate 130) enjoyed being part of the high society merry-go-round, though his name rarely appeared among the lists of guests at marriages, funerals, garden parties, formal dinners and other social events, as recorded by *The Times* of London. Although Johnston may be described as possessing a retiring disposition, he was certainly no recluse as has been suggested. On the contrary, he was constantly travelling widely visiting friends and gardens in Britain and France. Even at Hidcote, as Frank Adams's daughter recalled, the garden was always full of people. This aspect of Johnston's life has always remained obscure until the emergence of an engagement diary for the years 1929 to 1932. This document has made it possible to gain a revealing glimpse into Johnston's life among the private world of upper-class and horticultural society in the years between the wars.[1] His was a peripatetic life style, made possible by the motor car and a chauffeur, as the following selected entries make clear.

Plate 130   A studio photograph of Lawrence Johnston taken in the 1930s, probably in the south of France.

DIARY ENTRIES FOR 1929

Upon returning from Kenya, Johnston went to see Mrs Royall (Elisina) Tyler, on the Quai Bourbon in Paris on **14th April**, in order to enquire about Edith Wharton's health. Wharton was by then recovering from debilitating illness, though it would be the end of the month before she could recommence her diary with the words, 'Crawling back to life after two months of illness'. When her health declined, Wharton became increasingly dependent on Elisina.[2] In the next month, Johnston returned to Hidcote, and on **10th May** spent the weekend at Bodnant with Henry McLaren, a fellow member of The Garden Society. McLaren had been entrusted with the detailed care and development of Bodnant gardens by his mother, Lady Laura Aberconway, after he had come down from Oxford in 1901. Like Johnston, he possessed the rare talents of being a knowledgeable plantsman and a brilliant designer, and so with the encouragement of his mother, McLaren laid out the notable series of Italianate terraces that stepped down from the house towards the River Hiraethlyn. McLaren also sponsored plant-collecting expeditions by George Forrest and Frank Kingdon-Ward, whose recent introductions of primulas would have been of particular interest to Johnston. New rhododendrons and magnolias, collected by Ernest Wilson, had also been purchased from the Veitch nurseries. Johnston's diary entry for 10th May also includes the first mention of what might be described as 'medical problems' – referring on this occasion to tablets for seasickness and sciatica. As we have seen, Johnston did not enjoy the best of health, and the engagement diaries include frequent appointments with doctors and hospitals in London, Manchester, Paris and the south of France.

On **3rd June**, Reggie Cory and Cherry Ingram were at Hidcote, keen no doubt to discuss the outcome of their South African expedition. Ingram had collected more than 100 species of gladioli during the trip, and was raising them at his home, The Grange, at Benenden in Kent. They were often joined by their mutual friend Simpson-Hayward, whose rock garden at nearby Icomb Place was said to be the finest in the country. Five days later, **8th June**, Johnston travelled to Sonning on the River Thames in Berkshire to visit his friends Lord and Lady Forres, from Mont Agel, Menton, who were spending the summer at 'The Deanery'.[3] Designed for Edward Hudson in 1903, The Deanery was the result of one of the early collaborations between Lutyens and Jekyll, and had become recognized as an important landmark in early twentieth century house and garden design (Plate 131). The successful interpenetration between house and garden prompted Christopher Hussey to say that The Deanery finally settled 'the controversy', created by Reginald Blomfield and William Robinson, 'between formal and natural design. Miss Jekyll's naturalistic planting wedded Lutyens' geometry in a balanced union of both principles.'[4] Hudson used his magazine *Country Life* to promote what he called the 'Country House and Garden' style, thereby reaching a wide and

Plate 131 Gertrude Jekyll beside the terrace bridge at Deanery Garden, Sonning.

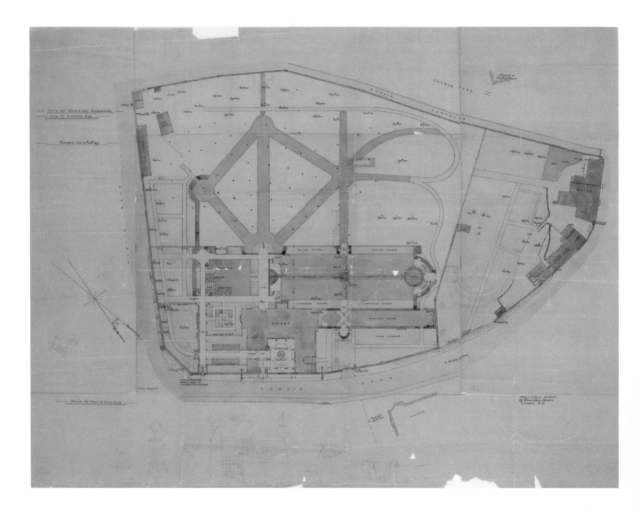

Figure 13a Plan of the Deanery, Sonning, designed by Edwin Lutyens. A massive oak door opens from the street into a covered passage alongside an open court with a small central pool. Straight ahead is the front door to the house, opening on to a passage leading through the house to the garden door and out to the main terrace. From here the asymmetrical axis leads to a generous flight of steps where formality gives way to rough-mown grass rides through an old orchard. To the left of the front door a vaulted arch of brick and chalk connects the little entrance court to the main garden, opening first on to the herb garden and a transverse view of the pergola. Beneath the pergola, a path leads forward between the little rose garden and the spring garden with magnolias set against the wall, to emerge between broad pillars of yew on the upper terrace. From here the main path leads via the circular steps to the meadow thickly planted with bulbs. In the angle of the great oriel window squared steps lead down to the lower lawn. The long central iris rill, broken midway by a square fountain-pool, ends in a circular lily-pond backed by winding steps leading to a view-point at the boundary wall. At the other end, a vaulted archway over a circular pool – a favourite Lutyens device – carries the balustraded causeway of the main axis.

discerning audience (Fig. 13a). Johnston and perhaps his mother were among those who were influenced, especially at the time of his early thoughts about laying out the garden at Hidcote.

Bryan and Jeannie Bellew made one of their many visits to Hidcote in June. Sir Bryan was heir to the baronetcy of Barmeath in County Louth, Ireland, and married to Jeannie Jameson, of the Irish whiskey family. After their marriage they came to live at Malcolm House, near Moreton-in-Marsh, Gloucestershire, before returning to Castle Barmeath. Both were keen tennis players, and Jeannie was also a passionate gardener with a particular interest in violas; at Malcolm House, she bred the viola that carries her name, 'Jeannie Bellew'. While the Bellews were staying at Hidcote, Mrs McCalmont of Adelstrop House, near Stow-on-the-Wold, came to lunch. The author, Jane Austen, had often stayed at Adelstrop, when the house was a rectory occupied by her uncle, the Reverend Thomas Leigh. The house and its surrounding parkland designed by

Plate 132 Lady Sybil Colefax with Cecil Beaton.

Humphry Repton, is thought to be the inspiration for Austen's novel *Mansfield Park* (1811).

On **15th June**, Johnston travelled to Lytchett Heath in Dorset, the home of Lady Cecil who, when writing under the name of Alicia Amherst, was the author of A *History of Gardening in England*. Her book had been among the first books Johnston borrowed from the RHS's Lindley Library, and another copy was also on Edith Wharton's library shelves. Lady Amherst's other guest was Lady Sibyl Colefax (Plate 132), a leading hostess and a great 'salonnière', who once said, 'I do not trouble to know everybody, but I have succeeded in knowing everybody I cared to know'.[5] Lady Colefax was a frequent visitor at Hidcote and enthusiastic about the garden, ensuring that it was high on the list of places to be visited by fashionable society. Later, in the final years of Johnston's time at Hidcote, she did much to secure the garden's survival under the auspices of The National Trust (see Chapter 14).

In October 1929, Lady Colefax lost her personal fortune in the Wall Street crash, and like Norah Lindsay, was obliged to earn her own living. She became a highly successful interior designer; later her company was known as Colefax and Fowler, synonymous with stylish furnishings and designs, and still trading today. Colefax was greatly influenced by the philosophy of The Souls, who advocated simplicity in design. In particular, she admired its expression at 'The Clouds', the childhood home of Lady Wemyss, which had been designed for Percy and Madeline Wyndham by Philip Webb in 1886. There the interiors were essentially plain, with unstained oak panelling and white walls. Even the curtains in the drawing-rooms were made of plain white fabric; but it was the William Morris carpets which gave the rooms a rich colour. Johnston records in his diary a certain May Norris's suggestion that he should decorate his rooms at Menton in a similar fashion – with walls the colour of light stone or parchment, whitish curtains and 'Cherviette' white chairs with a dark tiled floor and dark bookcase.

From Dorset Johnston travelled to Dyffryn, returning two days later with Mark Fenwick. Perhaps it was the Dahlia Garden that Cory had added to the West Gardens that excited Johnston's curiosity on this occasion. In championing dahlias as ornamental plants, Cory preferred the more tasteful, single varieties, but only a few of the many grown at Dyffryn in those years now remain in cultivation. One is the still popular 'Bishop of Llandaff', raised by a Cardiff nurseryman, William Treseder, in the 1920s, which was planted extensively in the borders at Dyffryn, and can still be seen.[6] Johnston planted it in the famous red borders at Hidcote.

After his return to Hidcote from Wales, Johnston's cousin Nan Hudson came to stay, and was joined by Norah Lindsay and Christopher Hussey. Hudson's enthusiasm for gardening had intensified after she acquired the almost derelict Château d'Auppegard near Dieppe, in the autumn of 1920. She devoted much time to restoring both the garden and the house, even neglecting her painting, and only left Auppegard during those brief periods 'when nothing required planting, transplanting, pruning or similar nurture'.[7] Christopher Hussey was aged 28 when he began to establish his reputation as a leading authority on domestic architecture and gardens. English garden history was largely an unexplored subject when he published *The Picturesque: Studies in a Point of View* (1927). Whereas Amherst had been largely interested in 'gardening history', Hussey was concerned with the history of ideas, and in particular the aesthetic intentions that underlay the Picturesque Movement, and those of its largely forgotten protagonists, Richard Payne Knight and Uvedale Price. Hussey had spent his childhood at Scotney Castle, Kent, among one of the most picturesque places in England, but did not realize that it was a designed landscape until he was in his early twenties, since it had merged seamlessly into the English countryside. Scotney was largely the work of his grandfather, Edward, and the artist William Sawrey Gilpin.

On **18th June**, Johnston made one of his regular visits to 'Reggie's' at Cothay Manor, accompanied by Mark Fenwick on this occasion. Reggie Cooper (Plate 133) had bought the fifteenth-century manor in 1925, and lived there until

Plate 133 Reginald Cooper.

1936 (Plate 134). 'The Manor,' wrote Hussey, is 'concealed among the deep lanes that wind from Wellington towards the Devon border. The countryside is one of rich, red earth ... The banks of the narrow road in spring are beds of wild flowers.'[8] Cooper created his Hidcote-inspired garden around the house (Plate 135), with 'rooms' arranged either side of a long yew walk, enclosed by hedges, each with its own individual character.

Four days later the artist Ethel Sands, Nan Hudson's companion, was at Hidcote. Mark Fenwick and Reggie Cory arrived on the following day; in the diary Johnston wrote 'a *Yucca whipplei* for Reggie'. Nan Hudson returned two days later, most likely to collect plants for her garden. It is to be regretted that neither Hudson nor her companion, who both painted interiors and gardens, set up their easels at Hidcote. On the 29th Lady Bearsted came to tea, and two days later Johnston returned the visit, taking lunch at 'Sunrising', near Banbury. Sunrising had been inherited by the 2nd Lord Bearsted from his father, founder of the Shell Transport & Trading Company, as part of the Upton House estate. Lord Bearsted was improving the house and gardens at the time of Johnston's visit; the seventeenth century house was being substantially remodelled by the architect and garden designer Percy Morley-Horder, who had trained with George Devey, the architect who did much to inspire the Arts and Crafts

Plate 135 Cothay Manor; one of the garden rooms in the Hidcote style laid out by Reginald Cooper.

revival. Morley-Horder had restored Nether Lypiatt Manor some years before, and Violet Woodhouse and her husband were so impressed by an article in *Country Life* about the house that they bought it the same year. The gardens at Upton and Sunrising were largely laid out by Morley-Horder under the direction of Lady Bearsted, but in June 1930 the garden designer Kitty Lloyd-Jones prepared further detailed designs for the gardens. She was among the first women to gain a qualification in horticulture and, like Norah Lindsay, Lloyd-Jones prepared her proposals while staying at clients' houses, returning later to supervise the garden staff.[9]

A cold winter and early spring had made 1929 a difficult gardening year: snowdrops and aconites had not flowered until March, whilst daffodils did not bloom until the 1st of May. In July the weather finally changed for the better, and a glorious summer continued until early November, with what *The Times* described 'as a truly wonderful display by hardy trees, shrubs and plants'. On **5th July**, Mrs Roper, a notable gardener from Forde Abbey in Dorset arrived, and on the following day was joined by her son and gardener. Forde Abbey on the Dorset and Somerset border had been a Cistercian monastery. Early in the eighteenth century a cascade and ponds were created there by Monsieur Beaumont, who later worked at Levens Hall in Cumbria. The house and grounds declined in the following century until new owners took over and added a kitchen garden, shrubberies and flower beds. But it was the arrival of the Ropers that made Forde Abbey one of the country's important gardens, by adding herbaceous borders, a bog garden, a very large rock garden and an arboretum. Meanwhile Johnston was travelling to Compton Wynyates in Warwickshire. The fine Tudor mansion was the home of the 6th Marquess of Northampton whose father had replaced the earlier Victorian parterres with an elaborate topiary garden, believing that the parterres were too expensive to maintain and that topiary would be in keeping with the architecture of the house. After lunch Johnston motored to Suffolk for the weekend, driving up the 200-year-old lime avenue to Broke Hall, the home of Lady Saumarez. This once vast estate, on the banks of the River Orwell, had been planned by Humphry Repton in 1794, and the famous Red Book for it was open for inspection.

On **19th July** Johnston went north to visit half-timbered houses in Cheshire and Lancashire with Bill Barrington and perhaps Reggie Cooper, who was particularly interested in Tudor houses. The houses

Plate 136 Little Moreton Hall, Cheshire.

had mostly been featured in *Country Life* during the preceding months: Smithills, near Bolton, Moreton Old Hall (Plate 136), Bramhall Old Hall, near Stockport, Speke Hall in Liverpool and Ordsall Old Hall, the oldest building in Salford. When he returned, Johnston was visited by the rock garden specialist E. B. ('Bertram') Anderson, a founder member of the Alpine Garden Society. During an earlier visit, Johnston had given him the unusual climbing hydrangea, *Decumaria barbara*, which Anderson was growing on the wall of his house at Hemyock, in Devon. In his memoirs, *Seven Gardens or Sixty Years of Gardening*, Bertram recalled noting its pleasant scent at Hidcote, though 'Lawrence Johnston said he could not detect this because the foul pipe I carried about obscured it! Needless to say he was a non-smoker.'[10] Johnston was generous in giving plants to his friends, and on this occasion Anderson came away with *Antholyza watsonioides*, *Clematis scottii x coccinea*, *Mertensia thibetica* and *Cautleya robusta*, the Chinese butterfly ginger, which was the only one to survive in Bertram's garden. The following day George Simpson-Hayward, another good friend of Bertram Anderson, came for lunch and in the afternoon there was a visit by the Bellews and Heather Muir from Kiftsgate Court.

On **7th August** Johnston made one of his regular visits to Abbotswood. Arthritis was increasingly confining Mark Fenwick to a wheelchair, though he remained an enthusiastic gardener and a regular exhibitor at the RHS shows in London, arriving formally attired in morning suit and top hat. When Fenwick created an alpine meadow below the house many years before, he was helped by the schoolboy Russell Page. Impressed by his enthusiasm and eagerness to learn, Fenwick took Page to various gardens in the Cotswolds. Hidcote in particular made a great impression on the young gardener so that in *The Education of a Gardener*, written 40 years later, Page said Hidcote was the best modern garden he knew and the one which most influenced his work. Particularly impressive was Johnston's ability to combine plants in a visual way. 'I remember,' he said, 'a double border of old-fashioned roses combined with equally old fashioned *Peonia officinalis*. The path between was edged with *Campanula portenschlagiana* and mustard green *Alchemilla*, which used to be called Lady's Mantle.'[11]

On **12th August** Johnston was visited by the secretive artist Aubrey Waterfield whose work was much admired by Kenneth Clark and others fortunate enough to see it. The artist had bought the 'Fortezza della Brunella' in the 'wind-grieved Apennine' in 1916, and thereafter Waterfield and his family had immersed themselves in the rural of life of Tuscany. Waterfield also studied Italian gardens, and illustrated the guide books written by his wife Lina. On **4th September** Avray Tipping, the Arts and Crafts designer and writer, visited Hidcote. His article in *Country Life* the following year would be the first published account of Hidcote.

On **10th September**, Johnston travelled to Cornwall and visited P. D. Williams at Lanarth. He probably visited Hemyock on the way to see what Bertram Anderson modestly described as his 'fairly interesting garden'. On the **14th** Hidcote was visited by Lady Horner, one of the more influential of The Souls. Her house, Mells Manor in Somerset, had been renovated by Edwin Lutyens in 1900, and though it is assumed that Gertrude Jekyll prepared planting plans for the garden, the main planting was undertaken later by Norah Lindsay. Lady Horner described her close friend as 'an artist and the garden is her paintbox'.[12]

Following Johnston's trip to the West Country, Mr & Mrs Blathwayt came to Hidcote for the weekend of the **28th**, no doubt bearing gifts of many plants. Mrs Blathwayt was a dedicated plantswoman with a famous garden at West Porlock House, on the west Somerset coast. She was an avid plant-collector and had made several expeditions to alpine regions on the Continent, with her head gardener Edward Percival, and knew the Vésubie valley near Nice well. Mrs Blathwayt was at the centre of a nexus of dedicated gardeners on Porlock Bay, all well known to Lawrence Johnston. One of the more celebrated was Norman Haddon who, not unlike Johnston, was extremely shy and retiring, leaving few details of his garden at 'Underway'. His Accessions Ledger records the regular receipt of rare and interesting plants from Lawrence Johnston and Hidcote during the late 1920s and early '30s. Many of the plants he received had a borderline resistance to frost: species such as the epiphyte *Rhodostachys (Fascicularia) bicolor*, *Azara serrata* and the evergreen *Philadelphus mexicanus*. On the Monday Johnston was off to Scotland and the Royal Botanic Garden, Edinburgh. Having determined to make a plant-collecting trip to China, Johnston was meeting the Regius Keeper, William Wright Smith and George Forrest, to discuss plans for the collector's final expedition to Yunnan (Chapter 12).

On **10th October 1929**, Johnston went to the Savoy Theatre in London with Reggie Cooper to see the play *Journey's End* written by R. C. Sherriff. A reason for their visit may have been the actor Melville Cooper, who had been a serving officer in the Seaforth Highlanders and who had been wounded and taken prisoner during the war. He played the part of 2nd Lieutenant Trotter who, in the hours before the impending advance, talked about his garden as an escape from reality; in the agonising minutes before two officers go over the top, they passed the time by talking about the New Forest and the glorious summer at Lyndhurst. It must have been a poignant experience for the two theatre-goers who had lived through the reality of war only ten years before.

During the following morning Johnston met J. C. Williams of Caerhays to discuss Forrest's impending expedition to Yunnan. Williams and his cousin, P. D. Williams of Lanarth, had founded the Rhododendron Society in 1916. Membership initially had been confined to owners of distinguished Cornish 'rhododendron gardens', but the Society had slowly expanded, by invitation, to owners of other great southern gardens, such as Sir Edmund Loder's 'Leonardslee' and his brother's Wakehurst Place, and Leonard de Rothschild's Exbury. By the time of the meeting, membership had been extended to the curators of Botanic Gardens, and to collectors like George Forrest, as well as to Johnston's friends, the Hon. Henry McLaren at Bodnant and Sir George Holford at Westonbirt. As we have seen, Johnston sought financial support from members of this elite society to help to finance Forrest's final expedition to Yunnan.

On **1st November**, Jeannie Bellew and Mrs Wills from Misarden Park arrived at Hidcote in the afternoon. Misarden, a seventeenth-century manor house, with spectacular views over the golden valley near Cirencester, had been bought by Captain Wills in 1915. The east wing was rebuilt by Lutyens in 1920, after it had been destroyed by fire. At the side of the house, where the formal gardens had been in existence since the seventeenth century, the architect simply added to the topiary.

On **7th December** Johnston travelled to Trent Park, the Hertfordshire home of Sir Philip Sassoon, for the weekend (Plate 137). Sassoon was a politician, art collector and a lavish host, who entertained all the most important people in society, either at his London home in Park Lane, at Trent Park at Christmas-time, or in summer at Port

Lympne, the house he built in Kent. It was at Lympne that the novelist Mrs Alice Dudeney met Edith Wharton in 1924 and was clearly not impressed; 'I thought her detestable.' On her return home she read *Ethan Frome* and commented, 'Wonderful! What a pity she's such a hateful person'. For Johnston, however, Philip Sassoon was another of his epicene 'bachelor' friends, in whose company he could relax, talk about gardens and play tennis.

Philip Sassoon was only aged 23 when his father died in 1912, after which he became one of wealthiest men in England. When elected to his father's parliamentary seat at Hythe, he also became the youngest Member of Parliament. At the time of Johnston's visit, Sassoon was Under Secretary for Air in the Conservative Government and had just returned from an epic flight to India. But despite his inheritance and political success, Sassoon remained an 'outsider' in British Society, and from his earliest days sought to compensate by becoming, in Robert Boothby's words, the 'greatest host and the greatest gardener'.[13] He set about renovating Trent Park, and from the wide terrace, constructed on the north front, Sassoon and his guests could view a menagerie of cranes, white and black swans, exotic breeds of ducks and geese, ibis, spoonbills, and even king penguins. They could catch a glimpse of deer with their antlers gilded to catch the sun. Among the many sports facilities in the extensive grounds was a swimming pool and orangerie designed by Reggie Cooper, flanked by borders planted by Norah Lindsay (Plate 138). Everything about Sassoon and his garden was cast in the mould of the Arabian Nights. A weekend at Trent, said Robert Boothby, was an unforgettable experience: 'the beautifully proportioned red brick house, the blue bathing pool surrounded by such a profusion of lilies that the scent at night became almost overpowering, the flamingoes and the ducks, the banks of exquisite flowers in the drawing room, the red carnation and cocktails on one's drawing room-table before dinner, were each and all perfect of their kind'.[14]

Plate 137 Philip Sassoon, *c.* 1929.

Plate 138 Trent Park, Hertfordshire. The beautifully proportioned red brick house, and the blue bathing pool was designed by Reginald Cooper; the herbaceous borders were the work of Norah Lindsay, *c.* 1929.

On the following Monday, Johnston had lunch with Sassoon's sister Sybil, the Marchioness of Cholmondeley, at her home in Knightsbridge. Johnston must have had a particular friendship with Sybil, for earlier in 1929 her young daughter Alvin had stayed at Hidcote. Sybil was more restrained than her brother, and did not give parties or enjoy dances, preferring dinner parties when she could meet 'figures in politics, cultural life and sport who had accomplishments of their own and not merely prominent because of birth or wealth'.[15] Johnston would have been included in at least one of those categories. Sybil also provides another clue as to the circle of friends in which she and Johnston mixed. Neither the Marchioness nor her husband chose to mix with the gentry; it was, she said, 'frequently the country grand, in contrast to what one might call the 'national' upper class, who were the least welcoming to those they regarded as outsiders'. The notable exceptions to her rule were The Prince of Wales and his brother the Duke of York, who were entertained regularly by the Sassoons. Many members of the landed aristocracy, however, regarded the royal family as outsiders.

There are few noteworthy entries in 1930. Johnston left for the Far East in the latter part of that year to go plant-collecting with George Forrest (Chapter 13).

Diary Entries 1932

The engagement diary recommenced after Johnston's return from Burma and China in 1932. On **1st March** at Serre de la Madone he was visited by Evelyn Sands, the sister-in-law of Ethel, Nan Hudson's companion. Evelyn was a wealthy American who had been Johnston's near neighbour at Ebrington Hall, Gloucestershire, after her marriage to Ethel Sands' brother Alan. In the 1920s the Alan Sands had moved to the Château Bastide de l'Abadie near Cannes, and she often accompanied Nan Hudson on her painting tours of France. Evelyn was a passionate medievalist and dressed in eccentric Gothic clothes, and even decorated the château walls with hundreds of tiny flowers and animals on a deep blue background, to resemble the Palais des Papes at Avignon. On the **14th**, Johnston travelled to Italy visiting places familiar to Aubrey and Lina Waterfield – Pisa, Lucca, Sienna, Viterbo, Perugia and finally Florence. They had written guides to Perugia, the artistic centre of Italy. Lina was a well-known figure in the Anglo-American community of Florence, and so many doors were opened to them. In his diary Johnston specifically mentions visits to the Baglioni Chapel in the Church of Sta. Maria Maggiore in Spello, near Perugia, to see the altarpiece of the Renaissance painter, Pinturiccio. Then they proceeded to Spoleto to see the apse of the Cathedral painted by Filippo Lippi, the artist zealously patronised by the Medici family.

On **9th April** Johnston dined with General Sir John Du Cane, the former Governor of Malta, and his wife Ethel at their house in Garavan, Menton. In the early years of the twentieth century Sir John's sisters, Ella and Florence, had travelled extensively in the Far East, painting and taking copious notes about gardens and plants. Their book, *The Flowers and Gardens of Japan*, added to the growing interest in that country and Japanese gardens. Their mother, the Dowager Lady Du Cane, had been a dedicated plantswoman with a painterly eye, and at 'Mountains', the family's dower house near Maldon, Essex,[16] she created a garden full of many rare and unusual plants, with picturesque views as well. After their mother's death, the sisters assumed responsibility for the garden. The Du Canes became regular visitors and tennis partners, in both Menton and at Hidcote. On the evening of Johnston's dinner with the Du Canes, Sir Louis Mallet arrived to stay at Serre de la Madone. He was a diplomat and close friend and confidant of Philip Sassoon, and was the leading figure in

Plate 139 Nelson Cottage, Cheltenham, the home of Johnston's friend, Ruth Peppercorn.

the Foreign Office Circle interested in renovating old manor houses. Before the war he had restored a fourteenth-century yeoman's house, Wardes at Oatham in Kent, complemented by a small formal garden, in the knot garden tradition. Mallet was also a close friend of Edward, Prince of Wales, and it is perhaps more than a coincidence that on **16th April** there is a single entry in the diary, HRH. The Prince of Wales was an active gardener at Fort Belvedere, his Sunningdale residence, where Norah Lindsay was involved with the garden. On **6th May,** Edith Wharton was an overnight guest; Johnston had written in his diary, in large heavy letters, 'Edith comes to stay'.

Soon after Johnston's return to Hidcote in **June**, his good friends Kenneth and Lilah Shennan came to lunch. The Shennans had moved to Shipton Oliffe Manor, near Cheltenham, after their marriage on St. Valentine's Day, 1929. The old manor house at Shipton Oliffe had been repaired by Norman Jewson, the Arts and Crafts architect, who between the wars, was known as 'the gentleman's architect'. Shennan was said to be a gardener of 'faultless taste',[17] though he said he owed a great deal to Hidcote and to Major Johnston. On **1st July**, Johnston visited the Midlands; in the party was a Miss Ruth Peppercorn who had recently moved to Cheltenham. Peppercorn came from a long-established Bedfordshire family; her father was a farmer and land agent at Eaton Socon. At the time, Miss Peppercorn had a flat in a Regency villa overlooking Pittville Park, close to the celebrated Pump Room. Later she moved to the nearby Nelson Cottage, described by *Country Life* as a small Regency cottage of delightful proportions and taste, 'formed by a personality in sympathy with the house' (Plate 139).[18] The small front garden had more than a hint of Johnston's involvement, with two circular box-edged beds on either side of the flagged path, each filled with peonies, martagon lilies, carnations and mulleins; a white clematis draped over the slender regency iron arches beside the front door, to 'ramble on the tracery of the veranda'. Inside Peppercorn had painstakingly restored the house, prompting Christopher Hussey to write that 'everything is in keeping with its period and character'.[19] The one exception was a modern painting, hanging above the Regency fireplace, at the far end of the living room. In the *Country Life* illustration this would seem to be a watercolour of a large flower, perhaps *Magnolia delavayi*, a slightly tender species from Yunnan and western China, which continues to grow in the sheltered north-east corner of the courtyard at Hidcote (Plate 140). The guess is that it was painted by Lawrence Johnston. Ruth Peppercorn became another of Johnston's close female friends, and years later Norah Lindsay's daughter Nancy regarded her as a rival for his attention, and possibly for the inheritance of Hidcote itself.[20]

Plate 140 A watercolour painting of a magnolia hangs over the Regency fireplace at Nelson Cottage, Cheltenham.

On **5th July** there was the first of several entries referring to the 'Lily meeting'. Following the introductions from south-east Asia, lilies had become very popular garden plants, and the RHS was anxious to avoid the establishment of another breakaway society devoted to the species. A standing committee, under the chairmanship of Frederick Stern was set up in 1932, and Johnston, who had visited Stern's garden in an old quarry at Highdown, near Worthing in Sussex, a few years before, was co-opted on to the committee. He served for a year, by which time the RHS Lily Group had been formed with the intention of encouraging the cultivation of lilies, fritillaries and nomocharis. It was Johnston's only incursion into inner workings of the Royal Horticultural Society.

In **September** Johnston journeyed through Normandy and on to Menton. On the **15th** he was joined at Serre de la Madone by Reggie Cooper. In **October** he travelled north and arrived at St-Brice on the **17th** to stay with Edith Wharton. After seeing Ruth Peppercorn in Paris on the **22nd** he left for Hidcote. After his return to England, there is a rare mention of Johnston in the society pages of *The Times*. His diary entry for **5th November** is just 'Owl's wedding'. It refers to the wedding of Lieutenant General Sir Percy Pollexfen de Blaquiere Radcliffe, General Officer Commanding, Scottish Command. After the wedding, Major Johnston lunched with Major Fenwick and his wife.

This is the last entry in the diary, except for an inevitable reference to a doctor, and the mention of Lactofermer for his troublesome stomach and a treatment for roundworms.

NOTES AND REFERENCES

[1] Pearson, G., Jones, G. and Beeston, M., Lawrence Johnston Notebook 1925-1928; Diaries 1929-1932. Transcripts and Indexes of Places, People and Plants. Unpublished.

[2] Lee, H., *Edith Wharton*. Chatto and Windus, London, p. 681. Elisina's second marriage was to Royall Tyler, an American diplomat and specialist in Spanish and Byzantine art; they lived in style with a Paris apartment on the Quai Bourbon and the Château d'Aufigny in Burgundy on the Côte d'Or.

[3] The house had been made available by Edward Hudson, who was about to put the property on the market.

[4] Bisgrove, R., *The Gardens of Gertrude Jekyll*. Frances Lincoln, London, p. 16.

[5] *The Times*, 26 September 1950.

[6] Torode, S., *Dyffryn – an Edwardian Garden*. Glamorgan Record Office Publication, p. 33.

[7] Baron, W., *Miss Ethel Sands and Her Circle*. Peter Owen, London, p. 87.

[8] Hussey, C., 'Cothay Manor'. *Country Life*, Vol. 66, 29 October 1929.

[9] Berger, R., 'Kitty Lloyd Jones: Lady Gardener and Nurserywoman'. *Garden History*. Vol. 25, No.1, Summer 1997, 107–116.

[10] Anderson, E. B., *Seven Gardens or Sixty Years of Gardening*. Michael Joseph, London, p. 38.

[11] Page, R., *Education of a Gardener*. Harvill, London, p. 19.

[12] Hayward, A., *Norah Lindsay – the life and art of a garden designer*. Frances Lincoln, London, p. 105.

[13] Boothby, R. , *I Fight to Live*; quoted in Stansky, P., *Sassoon: The Worlds of Philip and Sybil*. Yale University Press, London, pp. 49–50. Boothby was MP for East Aberdeenshire, 1924–58. Sassoon's family was Jewish, originally from the Middle East, but moved to India in the nineteenth century where its members made a considerable fortune from the opium trade. In the second half of the century, Sassoon's grandfather came to live in England.

[14] Stansky, op. cit., p. 171.

[15] Ibid., p. 182.

[16] Bradley-Hole, K., *Lost Gardens of England*. Aurum, London, p. 119.

[17] Pavord, A., *Hidcote Manor Garden*. National Trust, London, p. 28.

[18] Hussey, C., 'Nelson Cottage, Cheltenham'. *Country Life*, Vol.100, 2589, 30 August, 394–7.

[19] Ibid.

[20] Clarke, E., *Hidcote – the Making of a Garden*. Revised edition, 2009. Norton, London. p. 127.

CHAPTER FOURTEEN

THE FINAL CHAPTER

Edith Wharton withdrew further from society when she entered her seventieth year, and was content with seeing just a few loyal friends. She continued to write until the end of her life, but it seemed that another part of her only wanted to be shut away and to cultivate her gardens. As Hermione Lee observes, 'her gardens became almost symbolic of her retreat from the modern',[1] in all its manifestations; and as she grew older, many of her friends were aware that Edith was becoming increasingly erratic, eccentric and demanding. It was perhaps loneliness and a sense of isolation that prompted her sometime in the 1930s to list most of the close friends left to her. Among the 40 or so names were the remaining members of her Inner Circle: Lapsley, Hugh-Smith and Norton, also Ogden Codman who had lived for many years near Paris, and Lawrence Johnston. Also on the list were Beatrix Farrand and her husband, though Beatrix's successful career meant that Wharton rarely saw her niece. Other English friends included Kenneth Clark,[2] who had started his career in the art world with Bernard Berenson, and Lady Aberconway of Bodnant, who had created a large Italianate garden at the Château de la Garoupe on the Cap d'Antibes. To keep these friends bound into her network, Wharton frequently sent letters from wherever she was staying, keeping them informed of the happenings, health and incidents in the lives of her friends, as well as her own. A letter to Clark's wife Jane, written in London, told her that she must 'not fail to run over to Hidcote before August 1. It is a sight not to be missed'.[3] Edith also wrote to Gaillard Lapsley from Ste-Claire in a similar vein: 'the garden is in a state of exuberance. I had a three day visit from LJ last week and now have to depend for social sustenance on dear Philomène'.[4] But this outward display of sociability masked even more the inner reserve she had experienced since childhood, which she concealed from even her closest friends. Few could penetrate Wharton's adopted outward self-assurance, but increasingly when sadness or fatigue overcame her, she would slip quietly away and seek solace in her garden.

In these later years her friendship with Johnnie Johnston strengthened, for with him there was no intellectual pretence; they were just two old friends and gardeners talking together. They spent many hours planning Edith's two gardens, evolving designs that allied the twin concepts of serenity and a pleasant sense of surprise – motifs that Johnston had employed successfully at Hidcote, and which formed the inspiration of Edith's life and writing. There might have been another strand to their friendship; Johnston was a devout Catholic and in these later years, Wharton's own spiritual feelings deepened. She had never been a religious person but now she was increasingly drawn to the rituals of the Roman Catholic Church, and many of her friends sensed that she was thinking of converting. However, her attraction to Catholicism was as much aesthetic as it was devotional, 'delighting in the spectacle of prayer'.[5] Thus, the Pavillon Colombe at St-Brice was opened every year on 15th August with the procession of 'Les Enfants de la Marie' (Plate 141). Wharton supported the Curé there and the local church, and at Ste-Claire she befriended the nuns nearby, though this may have been prompted by her love of gossip.

Plate 141 The Feast of the Assumption at the Pavillon Colombe.

By now Wharton's gardens were admired as much as her books, by those who saw them or heard about them. Fanny Butcher, literary editor of the *Chicago Tribune*, said in an article 'In a Sunny French Garden', written after a visit to the Pavillon Colombe in 1931, that 'Mrs Wharton loved her gardens, as well she might have, and walking with her in them was like meeting her very special friends'. She wrote that Wharton was proudest of her blue garden – the one she had laid out with the assistance of Johnnie Johnston – 'in which only blue flowers grew – pansies, delphiniums and a plant from Italy, Nepeta mussinii'.[6] But the vagaries of winter continued to pose problems, and in February 1934 Wharton told Berenson that the garden at Hyères had escaped the onset of particularly bad weather, but that poor 'Johnston's garden had been ravaged the day after he and R and Mrs Lindsay got there. He evidently had the tail of the Corsican blizzard'.[7] It is assumed that the 'R' refers to Reggie Cooper who was a regular travelling companion. This group of three must have made a rather jolly, if somewhat unusual, travelling party; James Lees-Milne later described Cooper as a 'funny old thing, as round as humpty-dumpty' complete 'with eye glass'.[8] His shape was testimony to his enjoyment of good food and wine.

CORRESPONDENCE WITH BEATRIX FARRAND

Of all the people on her list of friends, the one she most longed to see was her niece Beatrix Farrand, but distance made their meetings infrequent. Letters became a substitute for what Wharton called 'garden talks': 'We've been too long without seeing each other & you've been too long without seeing the other side of the world. And oh! the garden talks we are going to have!'[9] Edith constantly expressed regret and sadness at being apart from Beatrix in her letters, and soon after moving to St-Brice and Hyères, she tried to persuade her niece to come and see her new gardens. In March 1920, she sent a fulsome description of the country around Hyères:

> Here at present the country is gushing with roses ... which after one outburst in Dec., and then flowering all winter, have now cast aside all restraint, and are smothering walls, house-fronts & balconies in white, crimson and golden breakers of bloom – it is getting to be *agony* not to talk of all this ... with you face to face; & whatever Max decides for the future, I do hope you & he will dash away for a few weeks before 1920 is over & come & embrace ... the chrysanthemums.[10]

It was to no avail, and in October she wrote from Pavillon Colombe: 'I want awfully to see you after all these years, & I'm already talking gardens – talking with you in spirit. Oh! what orgies we'll have on my 23 terraces.'[11]

Over the years, the letters reveal that though they rarely met, their friendship transcended that of aunt and niece: they were close friends, garden enthusiasts and very knowledgeable gardeners. Wharton regarded Farrand as a kindred spirit, a professional equal, a woman with strong opinions and drive (Plate 142); both had succeeded in fields largely dominated and determined by men. On occasions Wharton briefly showed her envy of Farrand's talent, but in their correspondence they were also able to express their innermost thoughts: in Wharton's final years 'talk of the garden became a means to talk of other, more dangerous things: old age and encroaching death'.[12] 'Their creative, collaborative practice,'[13] meant that they raised the garden difficulties they were experiencing and exchanged ideas and suggestions for improvements. Each woman enjoyed teasing the other about her garden, in which there was always an element of friendly competition.

Both gardeners' contagious excitement can be seen in their letters.[14] They would send bulbs back and forth, offer advice and consolation and, most significantly, recognize each other's influence and presence in their gardens. In a letter dated 7 February 1931 from Ste-Claire, Edith acknowledged the gift of some 'wonderful irises' (Plate 143): 'I have just been out with the gardener placing the treasures in our very best soil, and can hardly wait to see them bloom ... It is delightful to think that my enjoyment of them will be associated with you.'[15]

There is also a sense of the maternal running through the correspondence, for both women had no children, and Wharton frequently anthropomorphized her flowers, emphasizing what Lapsley and Tyler had written about her when referring to her plants as her children. After Beatrix had made one of her rare visits to Ste-Claire, when the irises failed to impress, Edith wrote:

Plate 142 Beatrix Farrand in later life.

Plate 143 Irises still growing at Ste-Claire in 2007.

Every day for the last week I have longed for you, for your beautiful irises are in their glory. You will remember that when you were here you were disappointed that they had not made a more vigorous growth, and I was depressed because I felt that I must in some ways hurt their feelings, and that they were going to be sulky about it. But their only grievance was the cold wet weather, and as soon as the sun came back they burst into vigorous growth, and for the last few days they have been a glorious spectacle.[16]

When the irises continued to thrive, Beatrix wrote:

Are you in the market for more American iris? There are some good ones, especially of the yellows and coppers which have appeared in the last few years. And as your Ste-Claire iris children seem to be thriving may they not have a few newcomers added to them in whatever colors would fit into the rest of the family? It amuses me to hear that Fulva has flowered well with you as she is usually a persnickety lady.[17]

They continued to exchange letters almost to the time of Edith's death. Perhaps the ultimate manifestation of their correspondence was the impact it had on Wharton's fictional portraits of gardeners. Although her female characters are rarely writers, they are sometimes gardeners who, in the spirit of Beatrix Farrand, maintain a commitment to the principles of design and a love of the garden.[18]

LOUIS BROMFIELD AND THE PRESBYTÈRE SAINT-ÉTIENNE

Meeting new people was no longer easy for Wharton, but on 10th June 1931 Johnnie and Edith made a visit whose outcome would greatly enrich the final years of her life. They lunched with Louis and Mary Bromfield at their 'pretty house', the 'Presbytère Saint-Étienne' in Senlis, 40 or so kilometres north of St-Brice.[19] By 1932 their relationship had matured into a deep friendship; the attachment between them was described by Bromfield as a close bond, 'as close in many senses as I have ever known and was rooted in the soil'. Bromfield had never known anyone who loved the earth more than Edith Wharton, and it was this shared love of the land that bridged the disparities between them – she was 30 years his senior and though both American, they came from totally different worlds. In 1931,

Bromfield signed a long-term lease for the Presbytère Saint-Étienne which at the time was derelict, and both house and garden were in need of restoration. In October or November of 1931 Louis Bromfield wrote, informing 'Mrs Wharton' that planting, manuring and pruning were all done and there was nothing left to do. Even 'the new garden on the other side of the brook 'la Nonette' is finished ... we planted two hundred roses, dwarf and climbing, and countless perennials and early flowering annuals. Really next year the place should be a jungle'.[20] In April the following year a letter was sent to 'Dear Edith'; their friendship had also blossomed, describing the 'garden as a miracle ... but of course the real fireworks will come at the end of next month'.[21] Bromfield had learnt much from Edith Wharton, and received advice from Johnston about his style of jungle planting within a formal setting. Bromfield visited Hidcote in the spring of 1933 but Lawrence Johnston was away, which was something, Edith Wharton told Bromfield in a letter, 'Johnnie' would have regretted.[22] Russell Page said of Bromfield's wonderful garden that it was the only garden in France, 'where the hybrid musk roses ... Penelope and Pax and others ... were allowed to grow into large loosely trimmed bushes hanging over the river, loveliest with their clusters of cream and white and rose pink flowers just as the light began to fade'. The garden also had an impact on the local inhabitants; 'so striking with its colour contrasts that it soon became the favourite destination of the local bourgeoisie in their strolls about town. Its fame spread over the countryside, and farm families would flock from miles around Senlis in their black Sunday clothes to gaze in awe at the calla lilies, hollyhocks, pink and white carnations, black-eyed Susans, and roses of every hue that crowded the bank of the narrow brook.'[23]

EDITH WHARTON'S LAST YEARS

Despite slowing the pace of her life, Wharton continued to travel and pursue a busy schedule; during her time in England, which she visited every year from 1931 to 1936, she moved from one grand house to another, with an undiminished appetite for new explorations. In July 1933 she enjoyed a long rest at Hidcote; afterwards writing to Berenson from Stanway on 10th July: 'I was dog tired, body and mind. I was very glad of a long rest at LJ's in the green peace of a garden very different to the one at Menton, but equally perfect. My trip was interrupted by a five day trip to Wales with Gaillard Lapsley then back to Johnnie's for

twenty-four hours, then to Mrs Allhusen and then a pleasant weekend
with Lady Weymss.'[24] Her travel plans were always complicated, and
she expected friends to fall in with her itinerary, and be more than a
little tolerant of her late arrivals. Whilst at Hidcote she had written
to Dorothy Allhusen to tell her that:

> ... I am so glad it will suit you to have me on Thursday. I rashly
> said I wd. turn up for tea, but I forgot my host had asked my
> old friends from Oxford, the Wm. Bucklers, to lunch here that
> day, and as my chauffeur says the run is about 85 miles, and I
> may not be able to get away till 3.30 or after, I may turn up a
> little late for dinner – I hope not.[25]

Wharton frequently arrived late for meals but remained unruffled;
at 'Batemans' she was late for lunch with Rudyard Kipling and his wife
and, finding that they had eaten nearly all there was in the house, 'she
stayed for tea (to get more food)'.[26] On another occasion she arrived
at her beloved Stanway to find 'we were to dine in 15 minutes ... so
I participated in tweeds, surrounded by lovely visions in cloth of gold
& rosy chiffon'.[27]

In May 1935 Edith Wharton (Plate 144) was distressed to receive a
letter at Ste-Claire from Johnston's butler informing her that Johnnie
had been taken ill with bronchial pneumonia on the day of his arrival

at Sir Philip Sassoon's house and was seriously ill.[28] A telegram was sent at once, to which Johnston replied 'Distinctly better'. In a letter to Kenneth Clark, Edith expressed the hope that 'he was out of the woods but he has so little powers of resistance that I am still anxious'.[29] Lawrence Johnston did recover, and in December 1935 Edith was writing to Bromfield asking if he knew of a new Spanish rose called *Apeles Mastres*; Lawrence Johnston had told her it was the most beautiful rose in the world.[30] Previously, Johnston's medical problems had continued after his return from Burma and China, and in 1932 Edith Wharton recommended that he should visit Dr Valmyre, her own medical specialist in Hyères. After several consultations by Johnston, Wharton recorded that he was progressing satisfactorily, and in February four years later, she told Gaillard Lapsley that Johnnie had visited Ste-Claire twice to consult Dr Valmyre, 'who has done him a power of good and persuaded him to eat normally'. In the same letter she said that Norah Lindsay had been for a few days and that the Nicolsons were to come in two days' time. Another visitor in April was Lady Wemyss, who was now suffering from senile dementia, and in another letter to Lapsley, Edith noted that 'she is much frailer than last year, she is going on to Johnnie's'. Johnston continued to respond to Valmyre's treatment and she informed Lapsley that 'I have just had a jolly telephone from J. to whom I expect to pay a visit after easter'.[31] During her visit to England that year Wharton visited Glyndebourne, where the gardens had been designed by her niece. That summer proved to be the last when Edith, Johnnie and Lewis Bromfield could meet, for by now Wharton was becoming increasingly frail. In the spring she was ill with 'three successive attacks of flu' and was recovering from a mild stroke. At the end of August whilst Wharton was having lunch with the Bromfields, Louis happened to mention a dahlia breeder and grower who lived a little way from Senlis, and in spite of her frailty, she insisted on paying a visit. Bromfield described the grower as 'a strange wild character ... with bright blue eyes and fierce moustache, a communist, not in a doctrinaire way but in a primitive, fundamental fashion'.

Bromfield related how on arrival, much to his amazement, there was an immediate rapport between the two of them:

> When he saw how this woman who appeared to be an old lady,
> loved and understood all plants and between the two of them –

Edith Wharton, friend of Henry James, who dined in the most beautiful homes in the world and this half-wild communist peasant – something wonderful and beautiful happened. For a time they became brother and sister. They talked of flowers, of soil, of fertilisers, of climates, and she ordered from him dahlia after dahlia she never lived to see in flower. And at last we went away burdened with a great bouquet he had cut and given us; there were so many flowers – and dahlias have gigantic but amazingly fragile blooms – that they more than filled both our cars. She was weary when at last, later in the afternoon, she finished tea and set out for St. Brice, but I had never seen her happier. [32]

Plate 145 The genial Vicomte Charles de Noailles in later life.

This was the last time Bromfield saw her. She went to Hyères as usual in September, travelling first to Italy to visit the Berensons at I Tatti, and then on to Serre to stay with Johnston. There must have been other excursions for the three friends earlier in the year, since in December 1936, eight months before her death, Wharton wrote to Bromfield, requesting the address of a nurseryman near Mortfontaine, 'where we all went last summer when Lawrence Johnston was staying with me'. It seems that Johnnie had ordered a very big and splendid magnolia to be delivered *mis en bac* in the spring and neither he nor Edith could remember the address of the nursery. And 'Johnnie wants to be sure that the "mis en bac" has been done'.[33]

Wharton was in excellent form at Christmas, which was spent as usual at Ste-Claire. Charles de Noailles came to dine (Plate 145), and Norton and Lapsley dared to hope that she would return to her former self. Sadly this was not to be as her health deteriorated, exacerbated by the personal loss of her oldest friends and companions, as she wrote to William Tyler in May 1937; 'I had a planned visit to Lawrence Johnston for a few days, then on to the Veneto but I went kaput soon after wiring you – partly because I lost two old friends, Kinky (her Pekingese dog) and dear Lady Wemyss, who had been with me here so lately. A friend of thirty years. I felt so utterly alone and lonely'.[34] Upon her return to Paris, she was staying with Ogden Codman at the Château de Grégy, south of Paris, when she suffered another stroke, and on 3rd June Wharton had to return to the Pavillon Colombe by ambulance. Beatrix Farrand arrived on 21st June but Elisina Tyler, who had taken control of the sickroom, did not want her there, and thought that her visit might make Edith anxious.[35] By July (Plate 146) she had recovered enough to move to a chaise longue placed near a window in her bedroom; finally she was carried downstairs and taken out into the garden in a wheelchair. Visitors who saw her said that she examined her roses carefully and seriously as she always did, but as the author Mme Sainte-Reine Tuillandier wrote: 'we followed three paces behind so that she may not exert herself to talk. Silently she held out a rose to me. I took it and kept it, knowing it to be the last goodbye; a wave of the hand, and I left her. Ten days later she was gone.'[36]

Edith Wharton died on Wednesday, 11th August 1937 and after lying in state for two days she was lowered, somewhat ignominiously, from her bedroom window to the courtyard of the Pavillon, where a guard of honour of local firemen and French veterans of the First World War stood to attention. They also followed the coffin later to the Protestant Cimetière des Gonards in Versailles where it was carried by the pallbearers she had asked for, six of the twenty-five old friends who assembled around her grave to sing 'O Paradise, O Paradise'. A tearful Johnnie Johnston had travelled up to the funeral with Robert Norton, and as he stood at the graveside he knew he had lost one of the most important, and strongest, women in his life. Perhaps, too, he appreciated that the ties that held the friends of Edith Wharton together were now broken: it was to be the last gathering of the Inner Circle. Wharton's grave in the American part of the cemetery summed up her life: she would remain forever part of French soil but in life, and especially in her novels, she was always an American (Plate 147).

Plate 146 Pavillon Colombe: the last photograph of Edith Wharton taken c. July 1937.

Plate 147 Edith Wharton's grave in the Cimetière des Gonards, Versailles.

THE SECOND WORLD WAR

The death of Edith Wharton marked the beginning of the decline of the world Johnston had known. Once again the threat of war was hanging over Europe; the Versailles Peace Treaty of 1919 had been torn up and, in desperation, France and Britain sought to appease Hitler with the Munich Agreement, signed a month after the funeral. War was averted for the time being, but further tragedy struck Johnston at the end of the following summer when his head gardener, Frank Adams, died at the early age of 49 (see Plate 90, p.183). Johnston had always maintained that he would never hire another head gardener, and true to his word, he took over the task himself and looked to Albert Hawkins, who had been responsible for the kitchen garden, as his overseer. As is often the case, a 'vegetable' man is very different from those with a flair for the 'ornamentals', and the staff at Hidcote, though intensely loyal to Johnston, found it difficult to take orders from Hawkins. Inevitably standards began to decline, though imperceptibly at first. In that year, 1938, Robert Norton, his closest friend within Wharton's Inner Circle, also died.

In September 1939 the halcyon days of the inter-war years were brought to a sudden and decisive end with the onset of the Second World War. Following the invasion of Poland, Britain and France declared war on Germany, but at first nothing further happened while the potential combatants tried to find a way of avoiding total war. In the 'Phoney War' that followed, many people were lulled into a false sense of complacency, believing that the Germans would not dare to attack the much-vaunted Maginot Line, which ran through France from the north all the way down to Menton. Johnston may have shared this optimism, or perhaps, after his experiences in the First World War, he thought the south of France would not be affected by hostilities. Norah Lindsay said he seemed to have been quite oblivious to 'any European happenings and his little plans go on quite simply in spite of Mussolini trying to upset the whole world'.[37] Norah Lindsay was a part of the set of people revolving around Cliveden, the home of the 2nd Viscount Astor, who believed war with Germany could and should be avoided.[38] Whatever Johnston's views and state of mind were, he headed south as usual in the autumn of 1939 and stayed on into the summer of the following year.

On 10th May 1940, the 'Phoney War' came to a swift and terrible end with Germany's invasion of France and the Low Countries. On seeing the success of the German Army's blitzkrieg, the Italian leader, Mussolini, saw an opportunity for territorial gain and mobilized the Italian army for an attack against France along its southern border. Norah Lindsay wrote to her sister that, after listening to all the talk of war, she was beaten down by events and had only a huge well of pity for her French friends:

> ... the de Ganays and Noailles – and all the people in the south – Johnny who is at Evelyn Sands with all his menagerie. It's cruel to think Italy will get all that coast – lovely Serre de la Madone where so many happy months of my life have been spent – and my poor Johnny whose whole life interest is in that place. I got an absolutely wretched letter from him written June 6 just before Italy came in, and he was utterly sick at leaving his

matchless garden ... I fear unless he's already tried for a ship at Bordeaux he'll not get away'.[39]

Johnston and the other foreign residents, however, did make their escape. While the Italian troops prepared to invade, a hurried evacuation caravan was organized to take British civilians away from Menton. Leaving behind his chauffeur, Fred Daniels, and his dogs, Johnston was eventually evacuated from Marseilles in an overloaded collier, and endured a long and arduous journey, without food and fraught with danger, back to England. After the trauma of this event Johnston's health became a matter of serious concern for his friends, and many were of the opinion that he never fully recovered from the ordeal. Mussolini's army only reached as far as Menton before a ceasefire came into effect on 25th June, but the military occupation of Serre de la Madone, first by the Italians and later the Germans, 'deeply ravaged Johnston's property', both the house and the garden.

Norah Lindsay had been equally traumatized by the loss of her beloved house and garden at Sutton Courtenay, which had been requisitioned for use as a school. After paying a last visit, when she was 'appalled to see the decay of my adored garden', she wrote to tell her sister that 'I was glad to leave – I felt like a ghost as if already dead and my poor sad soul allowed back for one glimpse. Every stone, every path, every twig, held memories of my days working there and Nancy wandering around with Peter. It was the old adored Sutton, yet not mine'.[40] Norah Lindsay was by now totally dependent on her friends for places to stay, and Hidcote became the bedrock of her life, where she could enjoy simple meals with Johnny, occasional outings in the car and 'reading to each other every night and talking endlessly about gardens and life before the war'.[41]

In April and May of 1941 Johnston experienced a series of catastrophes when his financial situation deteriorated further. The current lessees at Hidcote had given their notice and he was 'preparing to move into the gardener's cottage or else shutting up Hidcote, save his bedroom, or else selling or letting it'.[42] He had kept his money in France to escape taxation and now it was being taxed there. Norah Lindsay wrote to her sister, 'He's in an awful panic and doesn't know what to do. I think he could easily save on his garden which costs him £500 a year, as he still keeps heated greenhouses and the big plant house where he sits. But it's his only delight'.[43] Johnston had reached a low ebb, and presented a sad, lonely

Plate 148 Mark Fenwick (front row, far right) and RHS Chelsea Show Committee members, 1930, with his shooting stick, already showing signs of the arthritis which later crippled him. Other members, many of whom were friends of Lawrence Johnston, are: front row (l to r), W. Cuthbertson, E. A. Bowles, C. T. Musgrave, Gerald Loder, R. D. Trotter, C. G. A. Nix; back row (l to r) A. Simmonds, R. Cory, G. Monro, E. A. Bunyard, J. B. Stevenson, L. Sutton, H. D. McLaren, D. Hall, W. R. Oldham.

figure, especially when the Theatre Lawn was dug up as part of the 'Dig for Victory' campaign. In 1942 a troop of American soldiers was billeted at Hidcote, but when Norah arrived in August she found Johnny looking well and madly working in his garden, which was as lovely as ever; 'five people cutting hedges and growing vegetables to sell. The grass is mown and war is non-existent!'[44] Johnston no doubt was able to enjoy visits to his London Club, Boodle's, where unrationed venison, hare, rabbit, salmon, woodcock and grouse, were regularly supplied by its hunting and shooting members.[45]

When Johnston eventually returned to Serre he found most of the furnishings in the house had been destroyed and the garden badly damaged.[46] One stone bench had an inscription, 'W (Viva) IL DUCE' that had been carved by a bored soldier.[47] By this time Johnston was beginning to experience the onset of dementia, just as his mother had suffered earlier, with long bouts of total amnesia and periods of profound confusion. After the war it seemed as though Johnston was, as Ethne Clarke observed, 'fulfilling his desired destiny of becoming a dotty English bachelor of military bearing, living out his years in a crumbly stone manor attended by a devoted retinue of lifelong retainers, and absorbed totally in the continued cultivation of the garden, his sole creation'.[48] In those years he could be seen driving through the village in his old car, taking tenants on shopping trips to nearby Chipping Campden, and having left his menagerie behind in France, he gathered around him a pack of seven dachshunds which followed him everywhere, causing him to continually shout at them for some misdemeanour.

Johnston's friend Mark Fenwick was also in failing health (Plate 148). After his London home was bombed, he moved permanently to Abbotswood. By now he was crippled with arthritis and confined to a wheelchair. In time he lost interest in the garden, and though his head gardener tried to keep it going, it suffered from the lack of its creator's supervision. Fenwick died in January 1945. His daughter

Constantia could not distinguish in her mind the huddle of friends and neighbours gathered at the funeral, but she could recall 'Lawrence Johnston of Hidcote (little Johnnie to us all) looking so old and frail and pinched with cold'.[49]

NANCY LINDSAY

The death of Edith Wharton had been a bitter blow for Johnston and perhaps to compensate, he began to spend more time with Nancy Lindsay, Norah's daughter, both at Hidcote and at Serre de la Madone. Together they could be seen walking the garden paths, discussing plants, her appearance in sharp contrast to his still dapper attire. She was invariably seen wearing an old pair of once-coloured plimsolls and chain-smoking Turkish cigarettes, held in a much-yellowed short holder.[50] In time Nancy, who had visited Hidcote throughout much of her life, came to know the garden as well as Johnston himself. She had been born in 1896 and, like Johnston and Wharton, had received little or no formal schooling and experienced a lonely and turbulent childhood (Plate 149). She was often left at home with her governess when Norah was away socializing, and just as Lawrence had been smothered by his mother's devotion, Nancy was overwhelmed by her talented and beautiful parent. Her childhood left her desperate to attract attention, and she was forever flying in the face of social convention, alienating strangers and making herself a trial to her friends. But in the gardens at Hidcote she found her retreat, and a place where she discovered an interest in plants. By careful self-education, and Johnston's inspiration, she became a competent botanist and plantswoman. Encouraged by her mentor, Nancy eventually undertook her own plant-hunting expeditions to Turkestan and the remoter parts of the Near East. Johnston's regard for her was perhaps prompted by recognizing certain similarities between them; despite the trials of society, they could escape into their own private botanical worlds. Nancy was only mildly interested in the way a garden was designed, but she shared Johnston's desire always to have the best plants – in form, colour or scent. When his health deteriorated further towards the end of his life, Johnston depended more and more on Nancy's support, and it has been suggested that he came to regard her as the daughter he never had.[51]

Plate 149 Nancy Lindsay as a young woman in 1922.

Inevitably, with his health worsening, Johnston discussed his concern for the future of the gardens. Later Nancy would claim she was the first to persuade him to offer Hidcote to the National Trust, and there are those who believe this to be so.[52] Johnston had no immediate family so that on his death the estate would be sold, perhaps to unsympathetic owners. He had already seen how the Pavillon Colombe had been sold quickly after the death of Edith Wharton, in order to avoid a drain on her estate. In 1945, Peter Lindsay, who had inherited Sutton Courtenay after the death of his father, reached an agreement to sell the Manor House to an old family friend, David Astor, third son of Viscount Astor. Not long after, Johnston was visited by relatives from America whom he had never met before.[53] Under the terms of his mother's will Hidcote was his exclusive property, but he was becoming increasingly pessimistic about the future of the place.

The first mention of the National Trust having a role to play at Hidcote appears in February 1943. James Lees-Milne, by then the Trust's first Secretary for Historic Buildings, recorded in his diary a lunch arranged by Lady Sibyl Colefax, who had been confined to bed with bronchitis, when Norah Lindsay acted as hostess:

> She was wearing a flat, black hat like a pancake on the side of her head, pulled down over one eye. It was adorned by cherry-coloured buttons. Her white frilled blouse had more cherry buttons. She is kittenish, stupid-clever and an amusing talker. On my left was Laurie Johnston. After lunch he took me aside to ask if the National Trust would take over the Hidcote garden without an endowment after the war as he intended to live in the South of France for good.[54]

Lees-Milne, who was noted for his acerbic and not always accurate observations, clearly had a low opinion of Johnston, whom he had described as 'a dull little man, and just as I remember him when I was a child. Mother-ridden. Mrs Winthrop, swathed in grey satin from neck to ankle, would never let him out her sight'. Though this was undoubtedly true, it was rich coming from Lees-Milne who equally adored his own mother, but whose vanity caused her to neglect all her children, leaving him with an overwhelming inferiority complex. In July, Lees-Milne and his father were back at Hidcote and in spite of his opinion of Johnston, he did appreciate the significance of Hidcote and the expertise of its creator. In his diaries he said:

> No reference was made by him to the National Trust. The garden is not only beautiful but remarkable in that it is full of surprises. You are constantly led from one scene to another, into long vistas and little enclosures, which seem infinite. Moreover the total area of this garden does not cover many acres. Surely the twentieth century has produced some remarkable gardens on a small scale. This one is so full of rare plants brought from outlandish places in India and Asia. When my father and Laurie Johnston were absorbed in talk I was tremendously impressed by their profound knowledge of a subject closed to me'. [55]

In 1948 Johnston's achievements at Hidcote were recognized by the Royal Horticultural Society with the award of the Gold Veitch Memorial Medal, 'for his work in connection with the introduction and cultivation of new plants and for the taste and skill he has exercised in garden design'. Johnston was unwell and unable to attend the Society's Annual General Meeting when its major awards were presented, so his medal was accepted by his cousin, Nan Hudson.[56] At the awards ceremony the president, Lord Aberconway, said of Johnston that 'he was a great artist in designing gardens. There is no more beautiful formal garden laid out since the time of the old Palace of Versailles than that designed on quite a small scale, but with exquisite artistry, by Major Lawrence Johnston at Hidcote. Not only that, but that garden is filled, as the earlier gardens were not, with interesting and beautiful plants, some of which he has himself collected in the mountains of China'.[57] The reference to Versailles was appropriate given the influence of French gardens on the early stages of Hidcote's development. It was a measure of Johnston's achievement that not only had he been recognized for having created a most important English garden in the first half of the twentieth century – without the aid of publicity or 'promotion' through articles or books – but of all the gardens created during those years, it was Hidcote

Plate 150 Hidcote Manor: Lawrence Johnston on the Theatre Lawn, shortly before his final departure to the south of France – with his dachshunds around him 'like little mice'.

which was now prompting the question of how gardens of such national significance might be preserved. That was a question made urgent by Johnston's increasing frailty and his desire to leave Hidcote and spend his remaining years in the more congenial climate of the Riviera (Plate 150).

So the possibility of the National Trust assuming responsibility for Hidcote came to the fore. The Trust, however, was in a difficult financial position: it had no gardens in its care at that time, and it was wholly dependent on benefactors and subscriptions from just 6000 members. Johnston in turn had no private capital with which to endow Hidcote, and the income he received from his mother's capital would revert to her estate after his death. The Trust also believed that Hidcote was too remote to attract any substantial number of visitors, and thus very little income could be expected from admission fees. In late spring Lady Colefax sent a note to Lees-Milne urging him to clinch the matter of Hidcote sooner rather than later. She had visited the garden with the actress Vivien Leigh, and reported that Johnston was 'v. seedy with dermatitis', and though 'not gaga ... has no memory'.[58]

In June 1947 Lees-Milne wrote to Johnston informing him that the Trust would be proud to accept Hidcote, but they were worried about the financial position. Harold Nicolson offered to approach Lord Aberconway to find out whether the RHS could give financial support for the upkeep of the garden – Johnston considered five gardeners were needed to maintain the gardens. After Nicolson's meeting with Aberconway, the RHS council members said that they were unable to take on this extra responsibility; but by November the situation had changed. The president proposed that something ought to be done to preserve a few of the outstanding gardens, and he suggested something along the lines of the National Trust being encouraged to look after them. Perhaps this change of approach by Lord Aberconway was prompted by his own realization that he too would shortly have to decide on the future of his great garden at Bodnant. After further discussions, a new Gardens Section of the National Trust was established in February 1948, and given the task of preserving gardens of national importance. 'Only gardens of special design or historic interest, or gardens having collections of plants or trees of value to the Nation either botanically, horticulturally, or scientifically, would be considered.'[59] It was to be financed by 'The Gardens Fund', administered by a committee of members divided between the RHS and the National Trust. The Gardens Committee met for the first time on 23rd March 1948 when it was agreed that Hidcote 'should be one of the first properties to be considered when the Fund has been raised'.[60] In June an article appealing for funds to enable the joint committee to 'accept gardens and provide the specialised care' appeared in *The Times*. It makes interesting reading. It was a testimony to Johnston's skill as a designer, because the 'special correspondent' believed that Hidcote had grown up over the centuries: 'Probably a garden existed here before the dissolution of the monasteries but the many features as they are seen today were initiated when the Manor was rebuilt in the early nineteenth century'.[61] The correspondent was wrong on both facts.

Meanwhile Johnston was still trying anxiously to find a new owner for Hidcote among his friends, and desperate to avoid the taxation that would arise if he continued to live permanently in England. He considered leaving it to Norah Lindsay, but she died in 1948, and Bill Barrington at Nether Lypiatt Manor said he did not want it. Barrington had been devastated by the death of Violet Woodhouse in January of that year, and would stay on at Nether Lypiatt for three more years with her husband Gordon, tending the flower garden and running the farm. Johnston also considered leaving the garden to Ruth Peppercorn, much to the chagrin of Nancy Lindsay.

In June 1948 Lees-Milne returned to Hidcote to find that Lawrence Johnston, apart from some absent-mindedness and loss of memory, was otherwise sane and healthy. Johnston was incensed by a letter he had received from the Trust, and 'had decided no longer to give us Hidcote'. After much discussion and persuasion Johnston agreed to leave the garden to the Trust in his will; on this occasion Lees-Milne described Hidcote as 'a dream of beauty. The old-fashioned rose garden smelled as fragrant as I have always imagined a garden in a French Gothic tapestry might smell'.[62] After much wrangling, a Deed of Gift to the National Trust was finally agreed, which gave Johnston access to Hidcote for the rest of his life and in return, he would make a contribution to its upkeep. He was to remain the uncontrolled supervisor of the gardens, which were to open not more than three times a week, particularly if he was in residence. The Deed was finally signed on 27 August 1948 and in his diary, Lees-Milne wrote a sad epitaph for Johnston and his garden: 'we were conducted

around the garden by the usual route. How often must the old man have done this tour? I think it was a sad occasion for him and I wondered how far he understood he was giving away his precious treasure of a garden. "I have another Hidcote," he murmured, presumably referring to his garden at Mentone'.[63] A month later Johnston left for France with his dogs, two servants, a quantity of plants from Kew and a van load of furniture. His life at Hidcote Manor was at an end (Plates 151 & 152). On Michaelmas Day, 41 years after Johnston and his mother moved to Hidcote, the National Trust took over responsibility for maintaining the gardens, and opening them to the public three days a week. The arrangement was still disadvantageous to the Trust, though, because it was unable to let the manor house while Johnston was alive. As a result, at the end of the first year of its opening to the public, Hidcote ran at a deficit of £1650. In those early years the National Trust itself had an annual deficit of some £1000 to £2000, and this shortfall had to be met from the Gardens Fund.[64]

Plate 151 A view of the south gazebo at Hidcote taken from the Stream garden after Johnston had left, c.1964.

Plate 152 The Pool Garden at Hidcote, c. 1964; the photograph shows Johnston's 'jungle' planting and the topiary drums and peacocks in scale with the garden.

The problem that now arose was how to manage Hidcote in Johnston's absence. Nancy Lindsay was closer to Johnston than anyone else, and in discussions about the transfer, he had made it a condition that she 'should in his absence and purely on his personal behalf act as general supervisor of the garden'. But though she was present at the signing in August, there was no mention of this condition, and Lees-Milne wrote in his diary after the signing: 'Miss Lindsay is like an old witch, very predatory and interfering. She maintains she has been deputed by LJ to supervise the gardens in his absence abroad. We were not overcome with gratitude'[65] (Plate 153). Nancy's awkward nature was causing difficulties, and so the Trust agreed that her involvement should be limited to advice on the purely technical side, and that staff and other administrative matters were not to concern her. But Nancy was not to be deterred, and in October she wrote a long letter to the chairman of the National Trust, Lord Esher, who had been a close friend of her mother, attempting to make clear Johnston's intentions for Hidcote, 'for anyone who is interested'. She wrote that all the previous summer, he had walked and talked 'with me about what was to be seen to, saying, "You must be me, Nancy, and see the gardeners do not forget anything or make mistakes" '. In particular 'he was very much against the idea of installing a grand head gardener, who would "tidy up" the lush and rather jungly effect'.[66] Seeing Hidcote handed over to strangers must have been very difficult for Nancy, but Lord Esher regarded her letter as sinister and advised Lees-Milne that the Gardens Committee must get rid of her. But Nancy continued to send letters, concurring with the decision to appoint Albert Hawkins as Head Gardener, something Johnston had suggested, adding that 'Albert can always refer to me ... I shall be over at Hidcote once a month anyway of course as 'supervisor'.[67]

The difficulties with Nancy Lindsay continued until July 1950 when Johnston returned to Hidcote. It was to be his only visit to the garden after its acquisition by the National Trust and he was upset to see visitors in the garden, commenting that it 'spoils the pleasure of a garden which should be a place of repose and to get away from this world'.[68] By now the effects of his dementia were very evident and, like his mother, he was becoming suspicious of those around him. Robin

Plate 153 Nancy Lindsay in the late 1940s.

Compton of Newby Hall, who had met him, said it was very difficult for friends to communicate with him,[69] and on his departure, to the delight of the Trust, he left instructions that Miss Lindsay was 'to have nothing more to do with the gardens or to stay in the house'. What caused this change is not known, but Major Kenneth Shennan was in no doubt that Johnston had taken an aversion to her and that this 'was the one matter on which he seemed clear in his mind'. Shortly afterwards Nancy was eased off the local garden committee, and its chairman, Major Shennan, the close neighbour and long-standing friend of Johnston, observed that 'she belongs to the past history of Hidcote which we must escape if we are ever to get control of the future'. [70]

There is a persistent story that Nancy took her revenge by burning Johnston's garden notes, planting lists and other papers in the courtyard at the front of the house. Though this is no more than rumour, possibly put about by Lees-Milne, it is just possible she was acting on instructions from Johnston. After all, in this way Edith Wharton had frequently sought to protect those of her Inner Circle from others whom she regarded as unsympathetic and grasping. When her very old friend Walter Berry died, she retrieved and destroyed all the letters she had sent to him; an act of desperation that recalled her childhood when she hid stories and poems from the prying eyes of her mother. Henry James, too, had earlier burnt all the letters he had received from Edith Wharton, fearing exposure to the prying eyes of an ignorant biographer. Perhaps, after being displaced from the garden committee, Nancy Lindsay felt that she could no longer protect Johnston's 'privacy and his legacy' in the way that he would have wanted, and so destroyed his past. If this was the case, it would have been entirely consistent with the wishes of a man who from his childhood onwards, had gone to great lengths to conceal his private life. But it may be that Nancy acted on a whim, for she certainly took many special plants from Hidcote, along with others acquired from Abbotswood and the Oxford Botanic Gardens in order to stock her small garden and nursery at Manor Cottage, Sutton Courtenay. Graham Stuart Thomas observed that 'few people had a better "eye" for a good plant' than Nancy 'or guarded it more tenaciously when they acquired it'.[71]

After Nancy's departure, management of Hidcote became the responsibility of the local gardens committee which included Heather

Muir, Johnston's neighbour at Kiftsgate, chaired by Kenneth Shennan. However, when the secretary of the National Trust visited in 1950, he was of 'the definite impression that the gardens had gone down hill. The grass was unmown, hedges unkempt and the place looks slightly forlorn'. Like all gardens which are the loving creation of one person, Hidcote was suffering from the absence of that guiding hand and the presence, even the interference, of too many well-meaning individuals. Seven years after Hidcote passed to the National Trust the situation was improved by the appointment of Graham Stuart Thomas as the Trust's Garden Advisor. In those early days, when the Trust had few other gardens, Thomas had time to take a direct involvement in securing the future direction of Hidcote Manor gardens. When the gardens committee finally agreed to disband, Shennan added the final epitaph, 'we did our best because of our many nostalgic memories'.[72] In 1956 Johnston's solicitor informed the Trust that, owing to the critically serious condition of the Major's health, there was no longer any possibility of his ever being able to reside at Hidcote again. So Hidcote Manor and its gardens finally passed fully into the hands of the National Trust.

Faced with the financial problems, the National Trust promptly set about clearing the house prior to letting. There is no doubt it was in a difficult position in attempting to run Hidcote as a commercial venture, a task for which the Trust at that time was totally unprepared. But regrettably, the Trust failed to appreciate that the real value of Hidcote resided in both house **and** garden. The only way to understand Johnston and his garden was through the paraphernalia of his life in the form of his hobbies, interests and books. In their haste to save the garden, they cast the man into even greater obscurity. At the end of October his collection of Sèvres and Dresden china, and his Jacobean and Queen Anne furniture, were auctioned along with a library of nearly 500 volumes, many of which were written in or gifted by his friends. Were those books at Hidcote today, they would provide an invaluable insight not only into Johnston's horticultural interests but also his wider literary pursuits; if there had been perhaps a collection of Edith Wharton's novels will never be known. The books were sold for £7-0-0 along with family portraits and Johnston's own paintings. To complete this sad episode, a box of papers, rumoured to have been handed to the Trust, was promptly lost. In its laudable aim of preserving the gardens at Hidcote, the National Trust overlooked its commitment to honour the man who had created them. In 2007 the Trust belatedly acknowledged the value of such material when its Libraries Curator, Mark Purcell, wrote: 'almost every book in our collection has been well read and well loved. There are often touching hand-written inscriptions inside. And we can learn about a person who may not have done anything huge in their lifetime, but through their books they come to life'. Purcell added, 'making sure a library remains ... helps to bring a place back to life'.[73] And in a final footnote, while the Trust was facing up to its problems at Hidcote, plans to hand Nether Lypiatt over to the National Trust fell through, and a year or so later, in 1958, most of Bill Barrington's planting was uprooted when the house and garden was sold out of the family.[74] The chance to compare these two great gardens was lost for ever.

SERRE DE LA MADONE

Plate 154 Lawrence Johnston as a sick old man at Serre de la Madone, with Mme Bottin, daughter of his butler, Alfredo Rebuffo.

People who knew Johnston in those last years, such as the exotic Lesley Blanch, a travel writer and features editor of *Vogue* magazine, described him as lugubrious, a word also used by Alvilde, the wife of James Lees-Milne. Blanch recalled being invited to dinner in the early 1950s, as the only woman present, and remembered a dark garden, a green evening, with many young people. Some of Johnston's friends believed him to be homosexual, though this continues to be refuted strongly by Freda Bottin, the daughter of Alfredo Rebuffo, Johnston's butler for twenty-five years. Moreover, she believed that he entertained only out of good manners and would often feign a headache to escape to the woods. Freda Bottin became very close to Johnston when, for the last three years of his life, he was bedridden (Plate 154). His one regret at the end was that he did not have a title; he told his butler that 'money has no value at all ... it's titles that count'.

In April 1952 a reservoir in the hills behind Menton burst during a ferocious rainstorm. The flood water cut a deep gully causing a massive landslide, which resulted in a great deal of damage to both house and garden. Inside the house, two and a half feet of mud and stones filled the main floor and had to be cleared away by friends. The damage outside was less easily repaired, because the deluge had swept away or buried many trees, plants and walls. Four years later severe frosts caused further damage to many of the valuable plants but, by then, Johnston was unaware of these disasters.

On 27th April 1958 Johnston died at Serre de la Madone. The place was left to Nancy Lindsay but, at the age of 62, she was unable to maintain the garden and lacked the financial resources to ensure its upkeep. When her hopes of living there proved financially impossible, Serre de la Madone was put up for sale in order to pay the inheritance tax. The garden's collection of ornaments and statuary were sold at auction, but some of the pots, as well as the stone bench with its graffiti, made their way to the garden of Johnston's friend Humphrey Waterfield, where they remain at 'Clos du Peyronnet' in Menton. Before the sale Nancy asked the curator of the Cambridge University Botanic Garden to collect whatever plants,

Plate 155 Lawrence Johnston's grave at Mickleton, next to his mother Gertrude Winthrop.

seeds or cuttings he wanted. Twenty years before, the Botanic Gardens had benefited greatly from a magnificent bequest made by Reginald Cory, and Nancy hoped this latter material would provide a memorial to Johnston and his work. Sadly only two plants from that legacy remain, one of which ironically carries the name of *Mahonia x lindsayae* 'Cantab'. It was a strange twist of fate that a mahonia seedling from Serre de la Madone flowered in 1964, and was found to be a hybrid between *M. siamensis* and *M. japonica* – with a scent of hyacinth from the former and of lily of the valley from the latter – and it was named in honour of the garden's then owner, Nancy Lindsay.

When Johnston's will was published, there was very little evidence of his mother's great fortune. Beside bequests to his staff at Menton and former staff at Hidcote, to St. Catherine's Church in Chipping Campden and to Mickleton Church for the upkeep of their graves, the main beneficiary was his cousin, Nan Hudson[75] The family portraits, including one of his great-great grandfather's second wife who, the will said, was the first white child to be born in Baltimore, were to go to the Maryland Historical Society, who declined the bequest,[76] and they too were lost. In *The Times* obituary Vita Sackville-West described Johnston as 'creative', an adjective she said that was rarely applied to gardeners because it was seldom deserved, but which Lawrence Johnston deserved to the full. Her own garden at Sissinghurst, which owed much to Hidcote in spirit at least, had taken two minds to marry together formal design and the exuberance of the carefully co-ordinated

Plate 156 The inscription on Lawrence Johnston's grave.

planting: her husband Harold Nicolson had been responsible for the architectural structure of the garden. Hidcote, by contrast, was the work of a single creative genius, who had transformed the open fields into a horticultural paradise. For Sackville-West, Johnston was no melancholy recluse, rather 'the most generous of friends: "you like that do you? Here, just a moment let me get a trowel" ... and a most charming host, with his swarm of miniature dachshunds running around his ankles like so many mice'.[77] Johnston was buried, as he instructed, next to his mother in the churchyard of Mickleton Parish Church, the inscription on his gravestone reads simply; 'Gifted gardener and horticulturist, deeply loved by his friends' (Plates 155 &156). So like Edith Wharton, Johnston remains forever a part of the country to which he so much wanted to belong, and just as her novels recall a forgotten New York, so Hidcote reminds us of a forgotten age.

NOTES AND REFERENCES

[1]   Lee, H., *Edith Wharton*. Chatto & Windus, London, p. 623.

[2]   In his autobiography, *Another Part of the Wood – a Self Portrait* (John Murray, London, pp. 203-5), Kenneth Clark comments on the complexities of Wharton's character.

[3]   Letter to Jane Clark, 19 July 1932; quoted in Lewis, R.W.B. (ed), *The Letters of Edith Wharton*. Scribner, New York, p. 555.

[4]   Ibid; Letter to Gaillard Lapsley, 28 November 1926, p. 495. Philomène de Lévis-Mirepoix was from one of the leading ducal families of France.

[5]   Lee, op. cit., p. 713.

[6]   *Chicago Tribune, Magazine of Books*, Spring 1962; quoted in Kellog, G., *The Two Lives of Edith Wharton*. Appleton-Century, New York, p. 302.

[7]   Letter to Bernard Berenson, 12 February 1934; quoted in Lewis, op. cit., p. 575.

8   Block, M., *James Lees-Milne Diaries, 1942–1954, Abridged.* John Murray, London, p. 245.

9   Letter to Beatrix Farrand, 6 October 1920; Manzulli, M., ' "Garden Talks": the Correspondence of Edith Wharton and Beatrix Farrand', in Colquitt, C., Goodman, S. and Waid, C., eds, *A Forward Glance – New Essays on Edith Wharton.* Associated University Presses, London, p. 35.

10 Letter to Beatrix Farrand, 25 March 1920; quoted in Manzulli, op. cit., pp. 42–43. Beatrix had married Max Farrand in 1913; he was an accomplished historian and held university posts at Stanford in California, and Yale in Connecticut. He was also the first Director of the Huntington Library at Pasadena, California.

11 Letter to Beatrix Farrand, 23 October 1920; quoted in Manzulli, op. cit., p. 42.

12 Ibid., p. 44.

13 Ibid.

14 Farrand had two gardens – one at the Huntington Library, California, and the other at Reef Point, Maine; she wrote: 'Just as your two Saints, Brice and Claire, vary so do our two places, California and Reef Point. Winter annuals, acacia, iris, oranges, South African bulbs, all thrive themselves in California. Here [Reef Point] sturdy perennials, a few delphiniums, all the heaths ... blueberry, mayflower, lily of the valley, and five foot osmunda ferns thrive. The two problems are so totally unlike that it does not seem as though both of them could be equally horticultural (Letter to Edith Wharton, 20 July 1936, quoted in Manzulli, op. cit., pp. 44–45).

15 Letter to Beatrix Farrand, 7 February 1931; quoted in Manzulli, op. cit., pp. 44–45.

16 Letter to Beatrix Farrand, 4 May 1933; quoted in Manzulli, op. cit., p. 38.

17 Letter to Edith Wharton, 20 July 1936; quoted in Manzulli, op. cit., pp. 37–38. *Iris fulva*, the copper iris, is a Louisiana species found as far north as Ohio and Illinois growing near water.

18 Manzulli, op. cit., p. 45.

19 Quoted in Bratton, D., ed., *Yrs. Ever Affly.* University of Michigan Press, Ann Arbor, p. xv.

20 Ibid., pp. 2–3.

21 Ibid., p. 13.

22 Ibid., p. 42.

23 Page, R., *Education of a Gardener.* Harvill, London, p. 23.

24 Letter to Bernard Berenson, 10 July 1933; quoted in Lewis, op. cit., p. 562.

25 Letter to Dorothy Allhusen, July 1933; quoted in Lee, op. cit., p. 707. Dorothy Allhusen, the daughter of Lady Jeune by her first marriage, was a successful author of cookery books. *A Book of Scents and Dishes*, a collection of recipes from members of aristocratic families, first published in the 1920s, continues to be in print. William Buckler was a lawyer from

Baltimore who served as a diplomat (1902–20). He and his wife became archaeologists (1920–30), specializing in Anatolian studies.

[26] Lee, op. cit., p. 707.

[27] Ibid., p. 708.

[28] Quoted in Lewis, op. cit., p. 586.

[29] Letter to Kenneth Clark, 28 May 1935; quoted in Lewis, op. cit., p. 586.

[30] Bratton, op. cit., p. 35.

[31] Letter to Gaillard Lapsley, 2 April 1936; quoted in Lewis, op. cit., p. 593.

[32] Quoted in Bratton, op. cit., pp. 119–23.

[33] Letter to Louis Bromfield, 11 December 1936; quoted in Kellogg, op. cit., p. 294. *Mis en Bac* refers to a method of packing.

[34] Letter to William Tyler, 16 May 1937; quoted in Lewis, op. cit., p. 605.

[35] Lee, op. cit., p. 743. When Farrand heard of her aunt's death, she wrote: 'we have lost an incomparable friend. We shall find it an empty, queer world without her, and already one feels the void where one could ever before rely on her wisdom, keenness, appreciation, and justice.'

[36] Quoted in Lubbock, P., *Portrait of Edith Wharton*. Jonathan Cape, London, p. 22.

[37] Letter to her sister Madeline, 11 September 1935; quoted in Hayward, A., *Norah Lindsay – the Life and Art of a Garden Designer*. Frances Lincoln, London, p. 192.

[38] Hattersley, R., *Borrowed Time*. Abacus, London, p. 386. John Jacob Astor – a Tory MP who lost a leg during the First World War – purchased *The Times* in 1922 and used the paper to advocate appeasement with Germany.

[39] Letter to Madeline, 23 June 1940; quoted in Hayward, op. cit., p. 228.

[40] Ibid.

[41] Ibid., p. 230.

[42] Ibid., pp. 230–1.

[43] Ibid., p. 231.

[44] Hayward, op. cit., p. 232.

[45] Quoted in Marr, A., *A History of Modern Britain*. Pan Books, London, p. 55.

[46] Ethne Clarke writes that Johnston eventually returned to Serre de la Madone after the Italian surrender in September 1943 (Clarke, E., *Hidcote – the Making of a Garden*. Revised edition. Norton, London & New York, p. 117). Menton was occupied by German troops for a further year until liberation on 8 September 1944.

[47] Personal correspondence with William Waterfield, 13 March 2007.

[48] Clarke, E., *Hidcote*. First edition. Michael Joseph, London, p. 103.

[49] Arnold, C., *Happy as Kings*. Wilton 65, York, p. 86.

[50] Thomas, G. S., *Cuttings from My Garden Notebooks*. John Murray, London, p. 148.

[51] Clarke, 1st ed., p. 77.

52 Personal communication with Roger Phillips.

53 Whitsey, F., *The Garden at Hidcote*. Frances Lincoln, London, p. 28.

54 Lees-Milne, J., *Ancestral Voices*. Chatto and Windus, London, pp. 152–3.

55 Lees-Milne, J., *Diaries 1942–1954*, John Murray, London, p. 46.

56 Annual General Meeting of the Royal Horticultural Society, 17 February 1948.

57 Quoted in Pearson, G., *Hidcote – The Garden and Lawrence Johnston*. National Trust Books, London, p. 46.

58 Ibid., p. 44.

59 Ibid., p. 46.

60 Ibid., p. 47.

61 *The Times*, 29 July 1948.

62 Lees-Milne, *Diaries*, op. cit., p. 349.

63 Ibid., p. 358.

64 'One Hundred Years of Hidcote Manor Gardens'. *Cotswold News*, October 2007.

65 Lees-Milne, Diaries, op. cit., p. 358.

66 Quoted in Pearson, op. cit., pp. 50–1.

67 Clarke, op. cit., p. 121.

68 Whitsey, op. cit., p. 28.

69 Personal communication with the late Robin Compton, Newby Hall.

70 Pearson, op. cit., p. 53.

71 Thomas, op. cit., p. 146.

72 Quoted in Pearson, op. cit., p. 55.

73 The Libraries Curator, National Trust, *The National Trust Magazine*, Autumn 2007.

74 Douglas-Home, J., *Violet*. Harvill Press, London, p. 312.

75 According to Freda Bottin, Johnston left 1,000,000 francs to each member of his staff at Menton, equivalent to £13,200 sterling using the 2010 retail price index. Nan Hudson received £18,500 at 2010 prices.

76 Whitsey, op. cit., p. 28. This may have been Susannah Johnston, née Sith, the second wife of Christopher Johnston (1750–1819), whose family emigrated from Moffat, Scotland, who was born in 1759. He came to Maryland in 1766 and began a career in banking. Johnston married Susannah Sith in 1779 and later, during the American Revolution, enlisted in the Baltimore Light Dragoons, serving under Lafayette's command, taking part in the Yorktown campaign, 1781. In 1795 Johnston was one of the incorporators of the Bank of Baltimore. There is also reference to the Johnstons being Roman Catholic in Scotland (Mackenzie, G., N., *Colonial Families of the United States*, Baltimore 1912; reprinted by the Genealogical Publishing Co., Inc., 1966, 1995).

77 *The Times*, 29 May 1957.

CHAPTER FIFTEEN

AFTERWARDS

The gardens of Edith Wharton and Lawrence Johnston were subject to the same fortunes that beset all gardens once their owners have departed: redesign, neglect, exploitation and restoration. As a result, they provide a valuable insight into what happens after the creative muse departs and, on occasions, well-meaning conservationists take charge.

THE MOUNT

In the autumn of 1911, Edith and Teddy Wharton sold The Mount to Albert and Mary Shattuck, who promptly renamed it 'The White Lodge'. In 1938 the Shattuck heirs sold the property to an elderly couple, Carr Vattel Van Anda, the retired managing editor of *The New York Times*, and his wife, Louise. Then, as so often happens with large houses and estates, The Mount became institutionalized when it was purchased in 1942 by the Foxhollow School for Girls. Although the School generally took care of the fabric, the second floor and attic were converted into a dormitory, but sadly the gardens became overgrown and neglected during this time. Fortunately the School's last headmistress was aware of the significance of The Mount and using her initiative, it was placed on the National Register of Historic Places, in 1976. The following year a Connecticut developer purchased the property and promptly sold it to a theatre group, Shakespeare & Company. In 1980, the Edith Wharton Restoration Inc. (EWR) was founded under financial arrangements devised by the National Trust for Historic Preservation. Unfortunately this arrangement did not stop The Mount's further deterioration, exacerbated by the conflicting interests of the theatre company and the underfunded preservationists. By the time students from the Graduate School of Design from Harvard University undertook a study of the grounds, the gardens had all but disappeared. One of the students, David Bennet,[1] described their condition in February 1982:

> Covered by deep snow with a slick coating of ice and shrouded in thick, gray fog, the place could not have been more gloomy and forlorn. The large, white stucco house seemed overwhelmed by an evergreen thicket on all sides, but below the terrace that

wrapped around the main floor of the house, it was possible to make out a series of terraces defined by arborvitae hedges.

The neglected appearance was made worse by the activities of the theatre company, which Bennet witnessed on a return visit:

> The Mount was occupied by actors and crew of the theatre company that performed on the grounds. Stage sets were being constructed on top of the garden walls and fountains, and the lower branches of the hemlock hedges had been hacked away to make room for port-a-johns. There was no evidence of the lindens along the lime walk. The outlines of this path and other walks were barely discernible in the grass. The stone walls, arches, and pergola of the sunken garden retained a certain faded charm, but the circular pool in the center was cracked, and the dolphin fountain from Wharton's flower garden had been placed here.

The Mount was in urgent need of rescue and this began in 1992 when Stephanie W. Copeland was appointed to head EWR Inc., and charged with the task of overseeing the comprehensive restoration of the buildings and landscape. With a background in theatre production and rescuing ailing theatre companies, Copeland was well-suited to the task of restoring the theatricality of The Mount. Her deputy, Scott Marshall, was a preservationist trained at Columbia University, who had been at The Mount since 1985 and knew the site intimately. Together with John G. Waite Associates, Architects, and the historian Cynthia Zaitzevsky, who was responsible for the cultural landscape survey, Marshall prepared a report setting out the guidelines for future restoration. Most of the buildings – the mansion, stable, gatehouse and greenhouse – had suffered severe deterioration and the gardens were lost to overgrowth. In May 1999 the Federal Save America's Treasures (SAT) program, which channels congressionally appropriated and private funds into preservation projects nationwide, announced a $2.865 million matching grant to EWR. Of the $5.73 million total, $2.5 million went into the landscape restoration. An SAT requirement was that the grant and its matching funds had to be spent 'in very little time', so EWR prepared proposals for 19 landscape restoration projects – later reduced to 11 for financial reasons – which included the lime walk, the flower garden and the walled garden. Susan Child, of Child Associates, Boston, was appointed as landscape architect for the project.

Archaeological digs in 1999, led by a team from the University of Massachusetts at Amherst determined the layout of the original plant beds and pathways, before work began in the summer of 2000 on the extensive reconstruction and restoration of the sunken Italian 'secret garden' with its stone walls and rock-pile fountain (see Frontispiece). Over the next four years, the lime walk, the walled garden, much of the rock garden, the green terraces with boxwood and arborvitae (thuja), the dolphin fountain and the paths and beds for the flower garden were all restored, as well as the installation of a new irrigation system. In 2005 an anonymous grant of $500,000 from a Boston foundation made possible the restoration of the flower garden (Plate 157) and the reconstruction of the trellis-work niche and lattice fence, originally designed by Ogden Codman for the Whartons' Newport home. Plant lists for the gardens at The Mount were developed through extensive research and collaboration among a variety of experts; 'the garden wasn't static during the Wharton years, so we are restoring to an era.'[2] Sun-dependent flowers could no longer thrive in the now-shaded, walled garden, and substitutions had to be made; boxwood was used instead of hemlock, for example, because the latter is now subject to attack by woolly adaelgid (aphis). At the other end of the lime walk, the regeneration of the flower garden required an extensive search; articles, letters and other documentation provided details of Edith

Plate 157 The flower garden at The Mount in 2008, viewed from Edith Wharton's bedroom in the north-east corner of the house. She took endless pleasure from constantly planning new colour arrangements. Codman's trellised arch is just beyond, on the central axis of the garden.

Plate 158 The Mount in 2008: a view of the house from the flower garden, looking towards the rock bank where Edith Wharton planted many native New England shrubs, perennial plants and ferns.

Wharton's designs. Wharton-era photographs of the gardens provided an invaluable reference, and Peter Del Tredici, Director of Harvard's Arnold Arboretum, was able to identify many of the long-forgotten bedding plants.

In four years nearly 50 acres (c. 20 hectares) of the former 113-acre (c. 46 hectares) estate at The Mount were restored (Plate 158), re-creating the original design of a 'calm, well-ordered lifestyle' and from the terrace, the scene 'approximates to the conditions the Whartons experienced during the summer of 1903'.[3] In the intervening years the open landscape of west Massachusetts has become heavily wooded, and the view of Laurel lake is obscured (see Plate 15, page 38). At this stage the next challenge was for EWR Inc. to raise $1 million to establish an endowment for the long-term maintenance of the gardens. In 2008 The Mount was a victim of the financial crisis, not helped by the expensive purchase of part of Edith Wharton's library from a bookseller in York, England (Appendix 1). Faced with the possibility of closure and sale, the Board of Trustees realized that The Mount was not financially viable as an historic house museum, so it was decided to make the house into the Wharton Center for the Written Word. By restructuring the overall debt, and the launch of the 'Save the Mount' campaign in the spring of 2008, the debt was

halved. Today, a diverse programme, which includes outdoor theatre productions, weekly readings of Wharton's works and a Jazz Café – a surprising initiative given Wharton's use of the word 'jazz' as a term of abuse – are all helping to secure the future of The Mount.

THE PAVILLON COLOMBE

At St-Brice, the Pavillon Colombe was hastily sold and the furniture auctioned after Wharton's death. The library was divided between her godson Colin, the young son of Kenneth Clark, and Bill Tyler who received most of the books on architecture, gardens and gardening. Sadly these were destroyed during an air raid in London during the Second World War but the other half, including the few remaining gardening books were returned to The Mount in 2006. The house was bought

Figure 15a An aerial view of the Pavillon Colombe today, showing how little the garden layout has changed from Henri Trésol's plan of 1924 (see Fig. 10b). Lawrence Johnston's formal Blue Garden can be seen to the mid-left part of the photograph.

by the Duc and Duchesse de Talleyrand who refurbished the house extensively and engaged Russell Page to work on the gardens. The Blue Garden made by Edith and Johnnie was retained and filled 'with delphiniums, galtonias, anchusas and *Salvia patens*, and the formal parterre in the middle with Nepeta fassenii and ageratum'. Wharton's favourite blue hibiscus 'Coeleste.' was clipped 'to six feet high like a pyramidal pear tree'. At the Duchess's request, Page added another formal garden, opposite the blue garden, with clipped yews and two fine creamy stone vases, 'filled with garden pinks' surrounded by a frame of silver santolina.[4] After standing empty for a while, the house was bought by its current owners, the Prince and Princess of Liechtenstein, who continue to care lovingly for the garden. An aerial view of the present garden shows how much of Edith Wharton's design remains (Fig. 15a).

SAINTE-CLAIRE

At Hyères, the house and garden at Ste-Claire was less fortunate; the property remained unoccupied throughout the war years until it was finally bought by the town authority. In the 1950s it became a fashionable hotel, but by the late 1970s Ste-Claire was described as empty and decaying with the gardens overgrown and unkempt (Plate 159). Eventually it became the offices of the Parc Nationale de Porquerelles with a modest garden of 6500 square metres around the chateau (Plate 160), renamed the Jardin Exotique Sainte-Claire. Today some of the tiled paths remain but the pool is now filled in (Plate 161). The walk to the tower no longer reveals spring flowers – though they can still be found in the neighbourhood. Elsewhere there are surviving remnants of blue iris and prickly pear. Beyond the perimeter fence of the small garden, Wharton's gardens with their terraces can still be discerned among the rampant acanthus and umbellifers, with abandoned irrigation nozzles protruding forlornly from walls that were so carefully and expensively created (see Plate 104, page 209). Around the tower, Wharton's ivy, *Hedera canariensis variegata*, still clings to the walls, and from the walk to the Villa Noailles and the Jardin St-Bernard (Plates 162 & 163), the view over the red roofs of the old town and beyond to the Îles de Porquerelles is still impressive, in spite of modern developments (Plate 164). The town authorities hope one day to make the whole hillside into a botanical park which would be a fitting tribute to Wharton and de Noailles.

Plate 159 A view of the former Orange Terrace at Ste-Claire in 2007; there was originally a lawn with a line of orange trees here, but the hedge beyond has been allowed to grow into a line of trees.

Plate 160 The entrance to the terrace at Ste-Claire, 2007; now the offices of the Parc National de Porquerelles.

Plate 161 (right) Part of the restored garden at Ste-Claire, 2007; the 'Bassin' has been filled in, and a remnant of the tiled path can be seen.

Plate 162 (left) A view overlooking Edith Wharton's former garden at Ste-Claire in 2007. The turreted roof of the chateau can be seen on the left of the photograph.

Plate 163 (right) The view from the ridge leading to the Villa Noailles.

Plate 164 (left) A corner of the Mediterranean garden, the Jardin St-Bernard, below the Villa Noailles. Familiar to Lawrence Johnston and Edith Wharton, it is a reminder of how Ste-Claire once looked.

HIDCOTE MANOR

Hidcote's fate has been well documented since its acceptance by the National Trust, most recently by Graham Pearson in *Hidcote: the Garden and Lawrence Johnston*. Vita Sackville-West's hope that 'gardeners and garden lovers will visit Hidcote in their thousands' has been more than fulfilled: so much so, that by 1981, James Lees-Milne was prompted to say that 'the crowds are so numerous that I decided I will never turn again to Hidcote'. Today more than 130,000 people visit annually, and it is ironic that in seeking to preserve a very private garden, it has been necessary to make it a very public place. While the National Trust would argue – with every justification – that, by accepting the garden without an endowment, it has been necessary to make Hidcote self-financing through the means of ever-increasing visitor numbers, there is no doubt that what Lees-Milne called 'this dream of beauty', as it was originally conceived, has gone for ever. Despite that loss, Hidcote's popularity has ensured a world-wide influence. An aerial photograph (Fig. 15b) shows the present garden and its surrounds.

Today, Hidcote has to be regarded as very much the Trust's garden. It is immaculately maintained, but it is not entirely the garden Johnston made. It is acknowledged that under the stewardship of Graham Stuart Thomas the planting in the garden was subtly changed: the jungle was tamed and refined into what Noël Kingsbury called 'the classic look of the English garden' (but see Chapter 16). In 2006 the Trust received an anonymous donation of £1.6 million, to be matched by subscriptions, to fund a six-year project aimed at returning the garden to its 1930s heyday. This has seen, among other projects, the restoration of the rockery (Plate 165), the parterre at the front of the house and the replacement of the plant house adjacent to the Lily Pool (Plate 166). This work continues, and the National Trust's vision for the garden over the next decade is 'to create a centre for horticultural education, re-establish Hidcote as a centre of excellence

Figure 15b An aerial view of the current layout of the gardens at Hidcote Manor.

Plate 165 The restored rock bank at Hidcote Manor.

Plate 166 Plate 166 Hidcote Manor: the plant house, whose restoration was completed in 2010.

for horticulture worldwide and ensure it is financially sustainable'. With this aim, it reflects the recommendations of its French 'twin', Johnston's Serre de la Madone (see below).

SERRE DE LA MADONE

In the south of France, Serre de la Madone was bought in 1960 by Sir Evelyn Bingham Baring of banking fame, who widened the driveway and made a new parking area, as well as adding a Japanese garden. In 1967 Serre passed to the Swiss Comte Jacques de Wurstemburger who tried to maintain the garden, at first with four gardeners but finally with only one, which led to its inevitable decline. In 1981 the garden historians Michel Racine and Ernest Boursier-Mougenet found the site in a neglected state and tried unsuccessfully to interest government agencies in the garden. When the neglected garden slid gradually into ruin, developers became interested in purchasing the property; the neighbouring garden of Lady Forres at Villa Mont Agel had already disappeared under ugly orange flats.[5] Concerted efforts by these specialists and others succeeded in having Serre de la Madone listed as an Historic Monument and, as part of a condition for this change of status, an inventory of the plants at Serre was prepared by the botanist Pierre Auge, while the designers Arnaud Maurières and

Plate 167 Serre de la Madone; a view of the house from the central pool, 2007.

Plate 168 Serre de la Madone; a view from the terrace looking over the pools and cool plant house towards the Gorbio valley beyond.

Eric Ossart prepared plans for the garden's restoration. In 1999 the Conservatoire du Littoral succeeded in acquiring the property in agreement with the City of Menton and the Département des Alpes Maritimes. The aim of restoration, based on information gathered from the historical studies and analysis of the present state of the site, was to restore the characteristics of Johnston's original layout, including certain architectural structures and plant compositions (Plates 167 & 168). More recent additions, such as the Japanese garden and car parks, have been removed and land around the house stabilized. This task was closely linked to the management of water flow, which Johnston originally harnessed in a network of steel pipes, sprinklers and taps. By restoring this internal watering system it is hoped to achieve complete independence from the town's water supply.

Gilles Clément, the Conservatoire du Littoral's consultant landscape architect at the time, and Aix-based architect Philippe Deliau, were engaged to consider future use of the garden and, in particular, its conversion into a public space. Clément was very aware that in each of his gardens, Johnston had created a very private and refined place where 'visitors felt they were plunging into a magic new world where time hung suspended'. The question Clément asked himself was, how 'could members of the public hope to glimpse what Serre once was and if so, how could this be achieved?'[6] Having seen the effects of mass tourism at Hidcote and how completely it had destroyed this illusion, Clément wanted to avoid Serre becoming another routine stop on the tourist circuit. He wanted to give visitors the opportunity of spending their time at Serre almost as if at home, or better still as Johnston's guests might have done. His solution was to opt for quality tourism by first limiting the number of visitors in the garden at any one time to 40 people, and a maximum of 15,000 a year, who would be taken round the garden by the gardeners. Income for maintaining the house and garden would be generated by converting the house for its use by artists, musicians and cultural groups:

> Serre de la Madone will now become, with its 'palazzo' and its garden restored, an international centre for rare plants. They will be able to come and to familiarize themselves with trees, climbers, shrubs and flowers new to them, to make out their Latin names, to dream in the garden's green rooms and loggias, to study in the library, to linger on the Boulingrin [lawn], to hear evening concerts, to meet botanists, to take part in seminars and courses ... and of course, to revive themselves in the 'salon de thé'.[7]

Restoration of the planting raises its own problems, for if Serre de la Madone is to recover its former reputation as a great botanical garden, new plants have to be introduced: many of Johnston's own introductions have now become very commonplace, for example *Hypericum 'Hidcote'*. Should the garden become a showcase for newly discovered or 'created' rarities? Another dilemma is the fact that Serre de la Madone was Johnston's winter garden, to be enjoyed from October to March, whereas today's visitors come in summer and expect to see plants of interest. With only five gardeners compared with

Johnston's 12, it will not be possible to re-create the same diversity and density seen in earlier times. So far the planting has focused on genera which do well in the garden, such as pittosporum and hibiscus, as well as others like proteas that have a South African connection. Some of this planting has attracted the criticism that it is too botanical in its arrangement, an echo of Norah Lindsay's lament over Johnston's 'tricked-up' garden.

Implementation and management of the imaginative concept at Serre has been entrusted to a voluntary organisation, The Association for the Protection and Enhancement of Serre de la Madone, which includes respected owners of some of Menton's most important gardens. In September 2000, Hidcote Manor and Serre de la Madone were officially twinned, and while these two gardens are brought back to their former glory, there will be much still to learn from Major Lawrence Johnston's innovative approach to his gardens and his plants, as well as from the contrasting ways in which they are being managed in the twenty-first century.

NOTES AND REFERENCES

[1] David H Bennet, Head, Board of Directors' Grounds Committee at The Mount; senior associate at EDAW Earthasia Ltd in Hong Kong.

[2] Ibid. The students were involved in a Community Assistance Program project, providing design assistance to non-profit organizations. The project at The Mount was funded by the EWR and Shakespeare and Company.

[3] Quoted in Freeman, A., ' A lightning turn around in the Berkshires restores the 100-year-old landscape at Edith Wharton's The Mount. *Landscape Architecture*, September 2003, 90–6.

[4] Page, R., *The Education of a Gardener.* Harvill, London, pp. 19–20.

[5] Jones, L., *Serre de la Madone.* Dexia Editions, Paris, p. 17.

[6] Quoted in Jones, op. cit., pp. 46–7.

[7] The idea of a 'Residence for a Day' was developed by Gilles Clément and Philippe Deliau in *Serre de la Madone; orientations d'aménagement et de gestation.* Conservatoire du Littoral, 1999.

CHAPTER SIXTEEN

CONCLUSIONS AND LEGACIES

The reputations of Edith Wharton and Lawrence Johnston have undergone many changes since their deaths – in diverging ways. Even before her death Edith Wharton was attacked for being 'out of touch with democratic America, snobbish, ladylike and indistinguishable from her subject matter'.[1] It is a criticism which continued to influence her reputation till the end of the twentieth century. After the Second World War, when the last vestiges of the privileged wealthy society she had known were swept away, Wharton was of interest only to literary academics; and when her gardens were lost, so her proficiency as a gardener and garden-maker was overlooked. In the 1990s there was a resurgence of interest in her work, due largely to film adaptations of her novels, *The Age of Innocence* (1993) and *The House of Mirth* (2000). These served indelibly to identify Wharton with the social world and class in which she grew up, and her novels were regarded as stuffy, second-rate and dated. A scattering of books about her houses and gardens were published, however, most notably by Teresa Craig in 1996 [2] and Vivian Russell's updated and illustrated edition of Wharton's *Italian Villas and Their Gardens*.[3] Though her French garden at Hyères has been virtually lost, or at St-Brice changed in private hands, it is with the restoration of The Mount at Lenox in the US in 2002 – recreating in part at least the house and surrounding gardens – that there has been a growing interest in Edith Wharton herself. Today, over seventy years after her death, she has indeed regained an important place in American cultural life. Her words and work still resonate: 'She is still powerful enough to influence, inspire and entertain creative geniuses and ordinary people alike'.[4]

THE ITALIAN-INSPIRED GARDEN

Although Wharton is better known as a novelist, she, along with others such as Charles Platt and her niece Beatrix Farrand, played an important part in transforming the early twentieth-century garden in the United States. It was a pivotal moment in American garden history. During much of the preceding hundred years, the so-called natural style of landscape gardening had been preferred for public parks in particular, a style advocated and executed by the dominant figure of Frederick Law Olmsted. He shared a belief with philosophers such as Ralph Waldo Emerson (1803–82), city fathers, church pastors and many others, that nature had a salutary effect on urban dwellers. They were convinced that the natural style expressed the appropriate political and cultural sentiments of their young democratic republic, and rejected the formal garden and its association with royal and ecclesiastical privilege. However, in the latter part of the nineteenth century, the advent of the American Renaissance, and much travel in Europe by wealthier Americans, brought forward a reappraisal of the formal garden and the prevailing Beaux-Arts architectural style. Fierce debates raged about its suitability in the physical and cultural landscape of America, and it was the authoritative voice of Edith Wharton – as in her scholarly book *Italian Villas and Their Gardens* – which helped to quell this controversy. Subsequently, American landscape designers and their clients reinvented the European formal garden, most significantly by 'combining its architectonic structure with a more informal planting style and a vibrant palette of plant materials, derived from the legacy of colonial and other early American, so-called grandmother's gardens'.[5] The contemporaneous Arts and Crafts movement also influenced the early twentieth-century American formal garden, with its combination of formal and natural elements, and in establishing close ties between

Plate 169 The sunken garden at Filoli; one of the series of garden spaces that open one from another, providing long axial views, in which profuse naturalized plantings of hardy and annual plants contrast with lawns, paving, formal reflecting pools, framed in walls and clipped hedging and punctuated by many narrowly columnar Irish Yews originally grown on the estate from cuttings.

house and garden. This was the case at her house, The Mount, where Wharton also took inspiration from such English writers and designers as Gertrude Jekyll and William Robinson.

The Italianate garden was ideally suited to those of the Gilded Society who had the money to lay out a grand estate and possessed the time to enjoy both house and garden, but it was a style equally applicable to more modest middle-class properties. Its principles were of a close relationship of house to garden, and of garden to natural landscape, with the emphasis on a formal arrangement of garden rooms, linked by axial paths, varied by changing levels, and enriched by statuary and fountains. They were applied in a variety of locations from New England to Florida and west to California. A typical example is Filoli, 25 miles south of San Francisco, built and laid out between 1915 and 1917 for William Bourn (Plate 169).[6]

So by the early part of the twentieth century the Italianate garden had become a national phenomenon in the United States. Its congenial combination of factors led many garden designers, critics, and clients to consider it as the expression of a new Golden Age – but specifically related to the American landscape – whose promise could only be enhanced, it was believed, by improvements in technology, advances in science, and wealth created by the Industrial Revolution and its aftermath.[7] It would not be until the 1930s before this style was challenged by a new generation of landscape architects such as Thomas Church in California, and later by others the most well-known of whom were Garrett Eckbo, Daniel Kiley and James Rose, who had met at Harvard and rebelled against the Beaux-Arts tradition there. They began to explore new ideas of science, art and architecture as sources for a modernist, more pared-down approach to landscape design.

THE CHARACTER OF LAWRENCE JOHNSTON

During the same period the reputation of Lawrence Johnston and Hidcote has undergone a similar change in fortune, but in a more upward trajectory. When first opened, the gardens were largely unknown outside horticultural circles, and Lawrence Johnston himself was presented to the public as a shadowy figure who was shy, reclusive with few friends, dominated by his mother and of dubious sexual orientation. Today Johnston has emerged from the shadows, and though he had an over-attentive mother and was indeed shy, he was far from being a recluse, having an eclectic circle of friends who shared his passion for horticulture and tennis. Behind his apparently diffident manner, Johnston was a generous and cultured man who endeared himself to his friends of both sexes, and especially to his staff; he was a military man, after all, and used to command and the care of his men. So whilst their transatlantic upbringing may have rendered Wharton and Johnston part of 'the most déplacé and useless class on earth', their experiences meant they became what can only be described as worldly; that is to say, experienced, enlightened, cosmopolitan, urbane, cultivated and cultured. And once in England Johnston, in particular, became a part of a coterie that was not just leisured and wealthy, but one which regarded garden-making and gardening as the most respectable pursuit for a country gentleman.

Johnston was a creative visual artist, absorbing ideas of gardens from wherever he went; he had been exposed to French and Italian gardens from an early age and had knowledge of the American Renaissance in art and design. He understood the craft of picture-making: composition, perspective, colour, chiaroscuro and much more. But he was not simply a two-dimensional artist, for Johnston was like a sculptor who is able to visualize the three-dimensional form waiting to be released from the inanimate wood, stone, or in his case, land, with which he worked.

The Making of Hidcote

The garden at Hidcote Manor today has gained worldwide recognition as among the most beautiful, interesting and haunting of twentieth century gardens. To this list should be added 'innovative', for it is a measure of its significance when, nearly sixty years after its creator left, the garden continues to influence and inspire visitors. Johnston too is appreciated as one of the foremost owner-garden designers of the first half of the twentieth century. In recent years Hidcote has been described as the epitome of an Arts and Crafts garden, but it is considerably more than that, as Helena Attlee observed; Hidcote seems:

> ... to develop as a stream of consciousness, an ever-expanding suite of rooms with no perceivable structure. It incorporates Italianate rooms, French parterres, a woodland garden, a stream garden and the skilfully 'borrowed' landscapes of the 18th-century garden. These influences are foreign and far-reaching, yet they are combined to create the archetypal English garden, a blueprint that continues to exert its influence today.[8]

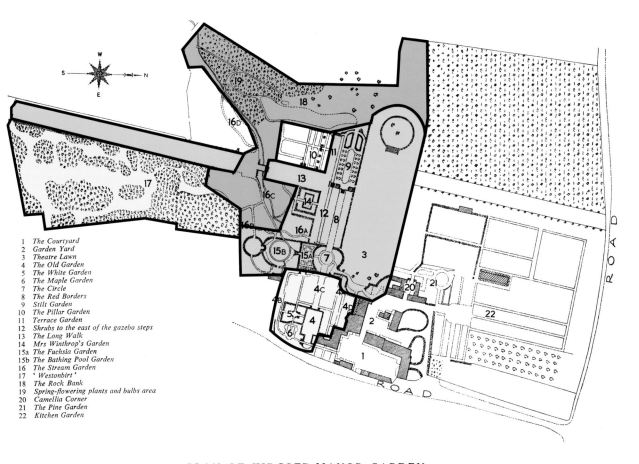

1   The Courtyard
2   Garden Yard
3   Theatre Lawn
4   The Old Garden
5   The White Garden
6   The Maple Garden
7   The Circle
8   The Red Borders
9   Stilt Garden
10 The Pillar Garden
11 Terrace Garden
12 Shrubs to the east of the gazebo steps
13 The Long Walk
14 Mrs Winthrop's Garden
15a The Fuchsia Garden
15b The Bathing Pool Garden
16 The Stream Garden
17 'Westonbirt'
18 The Rock Bank
19 Spring-flowering plants and bulbs area
20 Camellia Corner
21 The Pine Garden
22 Kitchen Garden

PLAN OF HIDCOTE MANOR GARDEN

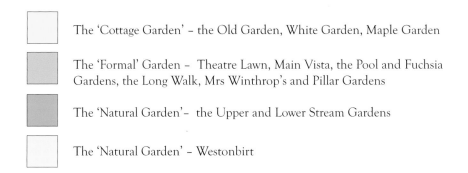

The 'Cottage Garden' – the Old Garden, White Garden, Maple Garden

The 'Formal' Garden – Theatre Lawn, Main Vista, the Pool and Fuchsia Gardens, the Long Walk, Mrs Winthrop's and Pillar Gardens

The 'Natural Garden' – the Upper and Lower Stream Gardens

The 'Natural Garden' – Westonbirt

Figure 16a Hidcote Manor – the four gardens (based on character not chronology of construction).

The reason for its lack of a 'perceivable structure' is because Hidcote's overall layout is complex and can be regarded as four distinct gardens – five if the domestic gardens are included – complementing each other and skilfully drawn together into a unit (Fig. 16a). The Old Garden has all the character of a cottage garden tucked in beside the manor house. Vita Sackville-West wondered whether it would be misleading to call Hidcote a cottage garden on the most glorious scale. She believed

Plate 170 The White Garden: the topiary which Vita Sackville-West said was in the country tradition of smug broody hens, bumpy doves and coy peacocks. This she concluded was right for Hidcote, 'just as it should be; Major Johnston has used the old tradition with taste and restraint'.

it resembled a cottage garden – or a series of cottage gardens – in so far as the plants grow in a jumble, where flowering shrubs mingle with roses, herbaceous plants with bulbous subjects, climbers scrambling over hedges, seedlings coming up where they have chosen to sow themselves.[9] The Old Garden is linked visually to the rest of the garden by the main vista, starting on the Cedar terrace and running through to the Gates of Heaven. The formal gardens are arranged around this central axis. Hedges were used to create a sequence of garden rooms, based deliberately on Italian Renaissance ideals of symmetry and proportion (see Plates 62 & 63).[10]

Johnston was not the first to use hedges to create rooms – it was an idea that was already current when he was creating his garden – but he used them to articulate the spatial arrangement of the garden, creating places where he could experiment with, or without, plants. The views within these spaces were all internal (Fig. 16b), separated from the rest of the garden and which could occasionally be glimpsed over the tall hedges. Links to other parts of the garden were through simple openings in the hedges, 'cut for the convenience of communication', created for its owner alone, 'rather than by the use of walls and gates'[11] (Plate 171). One has only to compare Hidcote with Arts and Crafts gardens designed by Lutyens or Mawson to see what Sackville-West

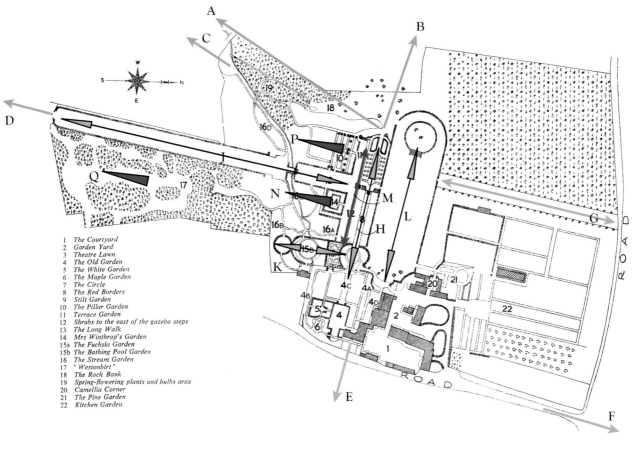

PLAN OF HIDCOTE MANOR GARDEN

Views out of the garden

A.   Towards Chipping Campden

B.   Towards Vale of Evesham (Plate 73)

C & D. Across farmland

Avenues

E.   Front of house towards Hercules (Plate 60)

F.   Huntingdon Elm Avenue

G.   Beech Avenue

Internal Vistas and views

H.   Main Vista - red borders/stilt garden/gates of heaven (Plates 62 & 63)

J.   Long Walk (plate 72)

K.   Pool garden (Plate 65)

L.   Theatre lawn (Plate 70)

M. Spine for lower garden

External Garden Views

N.   from Mrs Winthrop's Garden (Plate 172)

P.   from Pillar Garden (Plate 173)

Q.   in Westonbirt (Plate 94)

Figure 16b Hidcote Manor – *Views and Vistas.*

meant; in those gardens entrances and exits are marked by brick pillars, wooden arches, pergolas and other features all absent from Hidcote. With the main sightlines and themes of the garden established, Johnston undertook the making of the informal part of the garden. A terrace runs below the Main Vista, but is not visible from it, to which other gardens – Mrs Winthrop's and the Pillar Gardens, for example – are attached. These are half-open rooms with external views, so the eye is carried over the stream to the more natural parts of the garden (Plates 172 & 173). In this way the formal elements of the garden are in harmony with the informal, the natural with the architectonic, avoiding any clashes between the two.

There are many reasons for Hidcote's iconic status, but three stand out. First, and undoubtedly the most important, is the visual impact of the Main Vista. It has what in modern parlance can be described as the 'wow' factor, which the Oxford dictionary defines as 'the quality something has of being very impressive or surprising to people' and 'remains in the memory'. It is safe to suggest that without the Main Vista and its twin gazebos, the Stilt Garden and the distant view over the Vale of Evesham, Hidcote would not have achieved its present status. Similar gardens, with rooms and the other features found at Hidcote, but lacking this special ingredient, are often overlooked. The second reason is the exuberance of the planting found throughout the garden, prompting James Fenton to suggest that 'what makes [Hidcote] so English is the planting of each of the enclosures, these rooms, and the snug way the ensemble fits into the landscape'.[12] Until the recent restoration of the garden, much of the planting admired by the public was the work of Graham Stuart Thomas, the National Trust's first Garden Advisor who, while saving the garden's formal structure, also rationalized it and introduced new plants, even to the extent of emphasizing the purple and dusky brown foliage found in the famous red borders (see Plate 62, p.139). The third reason for

Plate 171 The narrow simple openings cut in the hedges to allow access to other 'rooms' in the garden, created not for design purposes but for the convenience its owner alone.

Plate 172 (above) The external view from Mrs Winthrop's Garden, the eye is led to the horizon, so linking the formal garden to the more natural stream garden and beyond.

Plate 173 (above right) The open view from the Pillar Garden.

the garden's success is the esoteric pleasure that comes from the sheer delight and surprise as one passes from one garden, or room, to another, and finding a totally different picture, assemblage of plants or colour theme. Hidcote is the forerunner of the modern flower show with its different show gardens.

There is an aspect of Hidcote, however, which is much closer to the devoutly religious man who made it. The great Renaissance garden of the Villa Lante, near Viterbo in Italy, designed by Jacopo Vignola in the 1550s is another garden of iconic status (Fig. 16c). During the Renaissance gardens had to delight the senses – with the sight and sound of sparkling, tinkling water, the scent of flowers, the taste of fruits and the pleasure of cool shade on a hot afternoon – as well as being an allegory conveying human progression from the chaos of wild nature to an ordered world, in the humanist tradition. At the Villa Lante, Vignola determined the composition of the garden on a single axis, following the natural fall of the land, developing a gradual and nearly imperceptible transition from the woods and nature, to

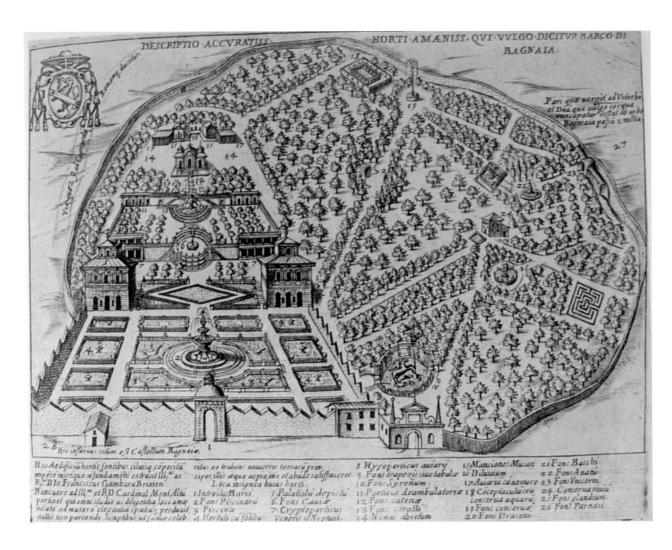

the perfect geometry of a large square parterre. Hidcote has a similar transition, but from symmetry to nature, from the formal to informal, whilst the sensory pleasure of the garden is all around. Perhaps Johnston's greatest achievement, therefore, was to have reinterpreted the Italian Renaissance garden within an English setting. It was after all Johnston himself who described Hidcote as 'a wild garden in a formal setting'.

Figure 16c The Villa Lante di Bagnaia from *Antiqua Urbe Splendor* by Jacobi Lauri, 1612.

NOTES AND REFERENCES

[1] The criticism was made by one of the Pulitzer Prize judges, who clearly disapproved of the prize being awarded to Wharton's novel, *The Age of Innocence*, in 1921; quoted in Lee, H., *Edith Wharton*, Chatto & Windus, London, p. 594.

[2] Craig, T., *Edith Wharton – A House Full of Rooms: Architecture, Interiors, Gardens*. Monacellli Press, New York.

[3] Russell, V., *Edith Wharton's Italian Gardens*. Frances Lincoln, London.

[4] 'Wharton in the 21st century', www.edithwharton.org

[5] Davidson, R. W., 'Opposites Attract: The Garden Art of Charles Platt, Maxfield Parrish, and Edith Wharton', in: Edith Wharton Restoration, ed., *Edith Wharton and the American Garden*. Mount Press, Lenox, MA, p. 62.

[6] Filoli comprises 16 acres (6.5 ha) of formal gardens surrounded by a 654-acre (265 ha) estate. The house was designed by Willis Polk in a free Georgian style; Bruce Porter, an artist-sculptor as well as a landscape designer, collaborated with the Bourns in planning the gardens.

[7] Davidson, op. cit., p. 63.

[8] Attlee, H., *Great Gardens of Britain*. Frances Lincoln, London. Quoted in *Oxford Times*, 7 July 2011.

[9] Sackville-West, V., 'Hidcote Manor'. *J. Royal Horticultural Society*, Vol. 74, No. 11, November 1949, 476–481.

[10] Hobhouse, P., *Flower Gardens*. Frances Lincoln, London, p. 139.

[11] Sackville-West, op. cit.

[12] Fenton, J., 'Tale of the Century'. *The Guardian*, 24 March 2007.

Appendix 1 – Garden Books in Edith Wharton's Libraries

After her death, Wharton's libraries from both her French houses, were divided between Elisina and Royall Tyler's son, William, who was a great personal favourite, and Kenneth Clark, in trust for his son Colin, her godson. Colin Clark, who did not discover his inheritance until 1950 when he was eighteen, mostly received Wharton's works of literature and books inscribed to her by Henry James. Bill Tyler received most of the books on architecture and gardening. By great misfortune these were destroyed by enemy action in London, after he had transferred them from Paris for safe keeping during World War Two. Colin Clark sold his inheritance of 2,600 books in the 1950s and eventually they were purchased by the book dealer and bibliophile George Ramsden of Stone Trough Books in Yorkshire. In December 2005 The Mount's trustees purchased the books for 2.5 million dollars and restored them to the library at Lenox. Among the titles were 26 gardening and botanical books listed below, and though they represented only a small sample, they give a flavour of the breadth and depth of Wharton's interest and study of the subject.

Acloque, A. (1904) *Flore du Sud-est de la France et des Alpes.* J.B. Baillère, Paris.

> Inside is a torn section of an envelope with Ophrys Arachnites (Late Spider Orchid) and O. Bombiliflora (Bumble Bee Orchid) written in Wharton's hand between pp. 630 and 631.
> Hyères bookplate.

Amherst, The Hon. Alicia (Mrs Evelyn Cecil) (1896) *A History of Gardening in England.* Bernard Quaritch, London.

> This was also one of the first gardening books read by Lawrence Johnston, who visited Amherst's home at Lytchett Heath in Dorset.
> Pavillon Colombe bookplate.

Bailey, L. H. (1897) *The Horticulturalist's Rule Book.* Macmillan, New York.

> A very technical and extremely detailed book: evidence of Wharton's serious horticultural study at the outset of her gardening 'career'. Liberty Hyde Bailey was the leading horticulturist of the day, Director of the College of Agriculture at Cornell University, and co-founder of the American Society for Horticultural Science.
> Pavillon Colombe bookplate.

Blomfield, Reginald and Thomas, F. Inigo (1892) *The Formal Garden in England.* 2nd edition with a new preface. Macmillan, London.

> Wharton, like Johnston, shared ideas in common with Blomfield's notion of garden aesthetics and design. In December 1897 she sent a copy of the newly published *The Decoration of Houses* to Blomfield and inscribed it, 'In gratitude for the pleasure of and instruction we have derived from his books'; also signed Ogden Codman Jr. In 1912 Wharton wrote to ask her sister-in-law Mary ('Minnie') Cadwalader Jones to 'thank Trix [Minnie's daughter, Beatrix Farrand] for me and tell her how I rejoice to possess the beautiful Blomfield. I had him on my list, but was waiting to see how *The Reef* sold before giving myself such a sumptuous present, and now have reason to congratulate myself on my prudence'.
>
> Pavillon Colombe bookplate.

Cook, E. T. (1901) *Gardening for Beginners.* Macmillan, London. Preface by Gertrude Jekyll.

> This book, in the series 'From the Country Life Library', was enthusiastically reviewed by the *New York Times* in August 1901, although the reviewer pointed out that the book covered the climate, soil and the peculiarities of England, but that 'a person with a modicum of knowledge will find the book of very great service and one that will save him costly blunders'. 'This,' said the reviewer, 'is particularly true of such persons who are undertaking the beautifying of large grounds. Here ... a hint is as good for Lenox or Newport as for some baronial estate in Surrey'.
>
> Pavillon Colombe bookplate.

Dawson, Sir J. William (1892) *The Geological History of Plants.* Appleton, New York.

> Dawson has been called the grandfather of paleobotany in North America, but throughout his life he maintained a distinctly theological attitude to geology and did not submit to Darwin's theory of human evolution, holding to the view that the human species had made its appearance on earth within recent times.
>
> Land's End and Hyères bookplates.

De Vries, Hugo (1907) *Plant Breeding: comments on the experiments of Nilsson and Burbank.* Open Court Publishing, Chicago.

> Several passages are marked and with substantial annotation as compared with the other books. De Vries was a Dutch botanist and among the first geneticists, defining the word gene and rediscovering Mendel's laws of heredity in the 1890s.
>
> Pavillon Colombe bookplate.

Downing, A. J. (1859) *A Treatise on the Theory and Practice of Landscape Gardening*. Moore, New York.

> This was among the earliest books Wharton read about horticulture, which helped shape her personal philosophy.

Dykes, W. R. (1924) *A Handbook of Garden Irises*. Hopkinson, London.

> Inscribed 'To Edith Wharton from Alice Martineau June 1924'. Wharton wrote the introduction to Martineau's *Gardening in Sunny Lands* (1924), Cobden-Sanderson, London. Marked passages detail the cultivation of specific species and varieties of irises. Wharton evidently exchanged numerous specimens during these decades with her niece Beatrix Farrand. Lawrence Johnston knew William Dykes through the Garden Society, and had an extensive iris border at Hidcote.

Farrer, R. (1922) *The Rainbow Bridge*. Edward Arnold, London. Second Impression with illustrations and maps.

> Reginald Farrer travelled widely in Asia as well as in Europe, and introduced many new plants into cultivation. His lifelong interest in alpine plants, and his observations on their natural occurrence, contributed to his strongly held views on rock-garden design, based upon achieving a more natural appearance. *The Rainbow Bridge* was published posthumously. The book included details of a plant-hunting expedition to Tibet and the Chinese province of Kansu. Farrer's writing was more in the style of a novelist than of a botanist. Wharton marked several passages in the book as if it were a work of literature — none with reference to plants or gardens. The passage on beauty, reflected something which had always been central to Wharton's own life: 'a fanaticism for beauty has always been the real key to my life, and all its happiness and hindrances. So acute is it that one seems to at last merge into something older still and more universal, standing behind beauty; it could not be mere *bien être* or adequate secretions that gave me such unbearably stimulating delight in a group of silly little trees, on top of a silly little hill across the river, against an azure sky in the sunlight.' (p. 335) This transcendental experience summarizes Wharton's own experiences of nature.
>
> Hyères bookplate.

Gray, A. (1858) *Botany for Young People and Common Schools: How Plants Grow.* Iveson, Blakeman, Taylor & Co., New York.

Signed on the flyleaf, 'Edith Wharton Pencraig Cottage 1887', this was probably among the first gardening books in her library, written by one of the most important American botanists of the 19th century. Gray was Professor of Botany at Harvard University from 1842 to 1892 and, besides being a staunch supporter of Charles Darwin, unified the taxonomic knowledge of North American plants.
Pavillon Colombe bookplate.

Holme, Charles, ed. (1911) *The Gardens of England in the Northern Counties.* The Studio, London.

Unidentified inscription 'Edith from Simon 1936'. Holmes was a leading figure in the Arts and Crafts Movement and a founder of *The Studio.* His garden at Upton Grey had been designed by Gertrude Jekyll.

Huntingdon, Annie Oakes (1902) *Studies of Trees in Winter: A Description of the Deciduous Trees of North-eastern America.* Knight & Millet, Boston.

Introduction by Charles Sprague Sargent with photographs by the author and coloured plates by Mary S Morse depicting the winter buds of some thirty trees. The *New York Times* said the author's commentary was as original as the subject, and that she was more interested in the economic value of the tree and their history than their literature.
Pavillon Colombe bookplate.

Jahandiez, Emile & Albert, Abel (1908) *Catalogue des Plantes Vasculaires du Département du Var.* Klincksieck, Paris.

The unopened book was inscribed to 'Madame Edith Wharton from Emile Jahandiez'. During her time at Hyères, Wharton, together with Vicomte Charles de Noailles, often visited the nearby nursery of the Jahandiez brothers at Carqueiranne, who specialized in succulents which featured strongly in the planting at Ste-Claire.

Jekyll, Gertrude (1901) *Lilies for English Gardens.* Scribner, New York.

Species ticked, passages marked and a small annotation by Wharton. Lilies were grown at The Mount and the ticked species may indicate varieties she liked or actually planted.

Jekyll, Gertrude & Mawley, Edward (1902) *Roses for English Gardens.*
Scribner, New York.
> A sentence advocating the planting of pink China Roses with rosemary bushes at the foot of a 'rather warm wall' was marked.
> Pavillon Colombe bookplate.

Jekyll, Gertrude (1921) *Colour Schemes for the Flower Garden.* 5th edition.
Country Life, London.
> Wharton was a great admirer of Jekyll's work and at both The Mount and the Pavillion Colombe, she arranged annuals and perennials in the broad sweeps advocated by the English designer. In the chapter on The June Garden, Wharton marked pp 118–119, where Jekyll discusses her plans for iris and lupin borders.

Le Blond, Mrs Aubrey (1912) *The Old Gardens of Italy: How to Visit Them.*
John Lane, London.
> This was one of the many books on Italian gardens that followed the publication of Wharton's treatise, *Italian Villas and Their Gardens* (1904). Mrs Barnaby acknowledges this in the introduction, stating that Wharton's book 'has proved more helpful and inspiring to the writer than any other'. The author's own achievements were as remarkable as those of Edith Wharton. She had been born into an upper-class Irish family as Elizabeth Hawkins Whitshed. She moved to Switzerland after the death of her father for her health, pioneered mountain climbing at a time when it was an unheard of activity for women, and wrote several books about her experiences.
> Pavillon Colombe bookplate.

Lee, Vernon (1897) *Limbo and Other Essays.* Grant Richards, London.
> Vernon Lee was an inspiration to Wharton, who wrote in her autobiography, *A Backward Glance* (1934), that Lee 'was the first highly cultivated and brilliant woman [she] had ever known', and that Lee's works on Italy were among her 'best-loved companions of the road'. Vernon Lee was the pseudonym of Violet Paget, a strong advocate of the Aesthetic Movement, who lived near Florence. She wrote extensively and was a friend and colleague of Henry James. Wharton dedicated *Italian Villas and Their Gardens* to 'Vernon Lee who, better than anyone else, has understood and interpreted the garden-magic of Italy'.
> Hyères bookplate.

Martineau, Mrs Philip (1924) *The Secrets of Many Gardens*. Williams and Norgate, London.

> Inscribed 'Edith with love from one gardener to another. Alice Martineau 1924'. Wharton wrote an introduction for Martineau's *Gardening in Sunny Lands* (1924). In this book Wharton marked passages on *Cyclamen europeum* and *C. neapolitanum*, including the suggestion that the latter should be planted so that its leaves can provide a backdrop to spring-flowering bulbs such as scillas, snowdrops and *Narcissus Nanus* (p. 39). Also marked is a passage stating that 'Wind [which was underlined] is a great enemy to a rock garden and needs to be guarded against, if not by the contour of the land, then by shelter belts of suitable nature, not laurels or other greedy fellows' (p. 67) – a practice successfully adopted at Hidcote Manor by Lawrence Johnston.

McDonald, Alexander (pseudonym for R. W. Dickson) (1807) *Complete Dictionary of Gardening*, 2 vols. Printed for George Kearsley, 46 Fleet Street, by R. Taylor and Co. 38 Shoe Lane, London. 60 hand-coloured engravings by F. Sansom after Sydenham Edwards, and other engraved plates.

> Full calf spines of elaborately decorated gilt with red and black morocco labels. Many of the engravings of flowers, drawn by Sydenham Edwards who had been trained by William Curtis, were of American plants. Pavillon Colombe bookplate.

Nicholson, George, ed. (1887) *The Illustrated Dictionary of Plants*. Gills, London. 9 volumes including 2 supplements of 1900-01.

> The title page described it as a practical and scientific encyclopaedia of horticulture for gardeners and botanists. Written largely by Nicholson, a distinguished Curator of Kew Gardens, it was a standard reference work for more than fifty years. Among the subjects that would have interested Wharton was Nicholson's interest in native flora and his promotion of the perennial-only garden. Markings were made next to various species. Pavillon Colombe bookplate.

Parsons, Frances Theodora (1900) *How to Know the Ferns*. Scribner, New York.

> Pavillon Colombe bookplate.

Parsons, Frances Theodora (1902) *According to the Seasons: Talks about the Flowers in the Order of Their Appearance in the Woods and Fields.* Scribner, New York. Colour Plates by Elsie Louise Shaw.

> The cover design for both of Parsons' books was by Margaret Armstrong, an important Arts and Crafts book designer who designed the dust jackets for Wharton's *Italian Backgrounds* (1905) and *In Morocco* (1920). Parsons was a leading American botanist whose books were immensely popular. Wharton shared her interest in native plants, wherever she was, and incorporated wild flowers and ferns in her gardens, often collecting them from the surrounding countryside.

Robinson, William (1883) *The Wild Garden.* John Murray, London. 3rd edition illustrated by Alfred Parsons.

> Signed 'Edith Wharton 1888'. Various species ticked.
> Pavillon Colombe bookplate.

Robinson, William (1901) *The English Flower Garden and Home Grounds.* John Murray, London.

> It is interesting that Wharton had both of Robinson's books and Blomfield's *The Formal Garden in England*, which together articulated the opposing sides of the debate about informal versus formal gardens. As an American, Wharton, like Johnston, was above such domestic quarrels, and was able to harmonize both approaches in her gardens. Markings were made against various species listed.
> Pavillon Colombe bookplate.

(The catalogue was prepared by Betsy Anderson with annotations added by the author)

Appendix 2 – Chronology

Date	Edith Wharton (EW) – née Jones	Lawrence Johnston (LJ)
1862	Edith Newbold Jones born 24 January in New York to George Frederic & Lucretia Rhinelander Jones. Elder brothers Frederic ('Freddie') 16 & Henry ('Harry') 11.	–
1866	Jones family moves to Europe.	–
1870	Freddie Jones marries Mary ('Minnie') Rawles of Philadelphia: parents of Beatrix Farrand.	Elliott Johnston marries Gertrude Waterbury & move to Paris.
1871	–	Lawrence Waterbury Johnston born 12 October in Paris. Family shuttles between Europe and US.
1872	Jones family returns to New York & lives on 23rd St.	Elliott, Jr born in Switzerland.
1875	–	Johnston family returns to New York & lives on 35th St., Murray Hill district.
1879	Edith 'comes out' in New York society.	–
1880	George Jones ill; family returns to Europe – London, Cannes & Italy. Edith introduced to Ruskin's books about Italian art & architecture.	–
1882	George Jones dies in Nice; Edith & her mother return to New York.	LJ's father 'disappears'.
1883	–	LJ's brother Elliott dies.

1885	Edith marries Edward ('Teddy') Wharton: live at Pencraig Cottage, Newport, Rhode Island. Travel to Europe each February spending several months in Italy.	Many American expatriates settle in the Cotswolds, including actress Mary Anderson and husband Antonio de Navarro & artists Frank Millet, Edwin Abbey, & English artist Alfred Parsons.
1886	EW meets the architect Ogden Codman in Boston.	–
1887	EW begins a friendship with Egerton Leigh Winthrop, which lasts 30 years. He becomes her cultural mentor.	Gertrude Johnston marries Charles Francis ('Frank') Winthrop (second cousin once removed to E.L. Winthrop) in London. Return to Frank's home in Paris. LJ educated in France. Gertrude spends season in USA & travels in Europe, occasionally accompanied by LJ.
		–
1890	Whartons purchase 'Lands End', Newport; EW engages Codman to work on house & garden.	
1893	–	LJ comes to England & enrolls in a 'crammer' at Little Shelford, near Cambridge.
1894	–	LJ enters Trinity College, Cambridge University, to read history; friends with Reginald Cory (Dyffryn), Hon. Bill Barrington (later Nether Lypiatt). Enrolled in Architecture Department at Columbia College, New York.
1895	–	Travels to US, listed as 'engineer'.
1897	–	Graduates with 2rd class degree from Cambridge.

1898	EW & Codman collaborate in architecture and style; write *The Decoration of Houses*.	Frank Winthrop dies leaving Gertrude very wealthy. LJ becomes student farmer on Laing estate at New Etal, Northumberland.
1899	EW discovers Lenox, Massachusetts.	2nd Boer War (1899–1902).
1900	–	LJ enlists in Northumberland Hussars after taking British citizenship (Jan); embarks for South Africa (Feb).
1901	EW buys Laurel Farm, Lenox.	LJ promoted to rank of 2nd Lieutenant, then Lieutenant. Mark Fenwick buys Abbotswood, Gloucestershire.
1902	'The Mount' built at Lenox, designed by Francis L. Hoppin. EW's niece, Beatrix Jones (later Farrand) advises on the landscape. Writes first novel, *The Valley of Decision*.	Boers surrender (May). LJ returns to England (Aug); resumes farming & meets Mark Fenwick, brother-in-law of army friend George Savile Clayton.
1903	EW accepts commission from *Century Magazine* for articles on Italian gardens; later published as *Italian Villas and Their Gardens*.	–
1904	Whartons purchase their first motor car; EW's fascination with France begins. Friendship with Henry James starts.	–
1905	EW writes *The House of Mirth*.	LJ joins the Royal Horticultural Society.
1906	EW rents apartment in rue de Varenne, Paris, from George Vanderbilt. Paris becomes her second home.	Reggie Cory begins the alterations to Dyffryn with Thomas Mawson.

1907	Whartons settle into rue de Varenne for the winter. EW meets Morton Fullerton with whom she has an affair. Returns to The Mount in May.	Mrs Winthrop buys Hidcote Manor. LJ (probably) meets Norah Lindsay at Stanway or Sutton Courtenay.
1908	EW visits England and until First World War considers settling there. Establishes a circle of female friends including some expatriate Americans such as the Astors at Cliveden. Others are Lady Wemyss, Lady Jeune and Mary Hunter.	Work begins at Hidcote in Arts & Crafts style similar to Alfred Parsons' work.
1909	EW moves to Hôtel Crillon, Paris. Harry Jones finds 53 rue de Varenne. Spends summer in England staying some weeks with Henry James and Howard Sturgis, and with Lady Wemyss at Stanway where she meets John Hugh-Smith and Robert Norton. These four, with Walter Berry and Gaillard Lapsley, become her 'Inner Circle' of male friends.	LJ promoted to Captain.
1910	Moves into 53 rue de Varenne, her French home till 1920. Writes *Ethan Frome* and other major works in Paris.	Expands his group of gardening friends: Mark Fenwick (Abbotswood), George Simpson-Haywood (Icomb), Hon. Robert ('Bobbie') James (St Nicholas, N. Yorks) & Hon. Bill Barrington.
1911	EW returns to The Mount and spends her last summer there. Her Inner Circle advise departure, as Teddy impossible to live with. Returns to France.	Receives Award of Merit at RHS flower show for Hidcote strain of *Primula pulverentula*.
1912	Sale of The Mount completed; bought by Albert and Mary Shattuck and renamed 'The White Lodge'. After the sale EW never returns there.	Gertrude Winthrop expresses a desire to leave Hidcote and move to Bath.

1913	(16 April) EW divorced from Teddy. Considers buying Coopersale House, near Epping, but decides to live permanently in France, though visits the US 60 times up to 1924.	LJ travels to Egypt & Italy. Attends cavalry officers' course at Aldershot; promoted to Major. Joins Boodle's club in London.
1914	First World War. EW begins charitable work. Rents 'Stocks' in the Chilterns, England. Returns to Paris in October and is fully engaged in war work & campaign to bring USA into the war.	LJ recalled to Northumberland Hussars as officer in charge of transport. Embarks for Belgium with 7th Division, British Expeditionary Force; wounded in first Battle of Ypres.
1915	Sets up 'Children of Flanders' charity for refugees in Paris and ferries supplies to to the war zone. Publishes *Fighting France* based on articles for *Scribner's Magazine*.	–
1916	EW awarded the Légion d'Honneur for her war work.	LJ returns to France as Second in Command of his regiment before Somme offensive.
1917	–	LJ in temporary command of Northumberland Hussars. Returns to Staff College in England but health not good.
1918	EW buys the Pavillon Colombe at St-Brice-sous-Forêt, north of Paris, wintering at Hyères near Toulon in the south.	Liaison Officer with French Army in France. On sick leave in August.
1919	Leases Ste-Claire, Hyères, and writes *Age of Innocence* there (published 1920), for which she receives the Pulitzer Prize for Literature.	LJ recuperates in south of France (Jan), and is discharged from active service (March). Returns to Hidcote; visited by Prince of Wales.

1920	Starts restoration of St-Brice and Ste-Claire; remaking of the gardens begins.	After reorganization, LJ becomes Second in Command of Northumberland Hussars (Yeomanry). Norah Lindsay and husband separate; she is obliged to become a professional garden designer.
1921	–	Gertrude Winthrop suffering from dementia. LJ proposed as a member of The Garden Society.
1922	Visits the major gardens on Cap Ferrat.	Retires from the Army (Nov). Appoints Frank Adams as Head Gardener, who has important horticultural influence on Hidcote; likewise Norah Lindsay who is a frequent guest. Plant-collecting in the Alpes Maritimes.
1923	Lady Colefax and LJ have lunch at Ste-Claire; EW also visited there by Alice Martineau, author of *Gardening in Sunny Lands*.	Bill Barrington moves to Nether Lypiatt, Gloucestershire.
1924	Henri Trésol prepares plans for St-Brice. LJ helps design a 'blue' garden – is referred to as EW's 'new and very nice gardening friend' in a letter to Berenson.	Visits Menton with his mother; buys first parcel of land, 'Les Moulins' in the Val de Gorbio, renamed 'Serre de la Madone'.
1925	EW visits Serre in March; together with LJ visits Lady Forres at Mont Agel & the Hanburys at La Mortola; also many nurseries. Makes first visit to Hidcote to see LJ's 'incomparable garden'.	–

1926	–	Mrs Winthrop dies: buried in Mickleton churchyard, Gloucestershire. LJ now sole owner of Hidcote. Part sponsors Kingdon-Ward's expedition to Burma.
1927	EW purchases Ste-Claire, Hyères.	Plant-hunting expedition to South Africa with Cherry Ingram, Reggie Cory and George Taylor of Kew.
1928	–	Solo expedition to Kenya; climbs Mount Kilimanjaro.
1929	Stock market crash in America. Garden at Ste-Claire wrecked by extreme cold; EW has nervous collapse & severe chill from which she nearly dies. Travels to England in July and stays at Hidcote to recuperate in LJ's 'tormentingly perfect garden'. Appoints Joseph, ablest of her gardeners in October.	Sends plants to Royal Botanic Garden, Edinburgh, propagated by Frank Adams from plant-hunting expeditions. Organizes sponsors for George Forrest's expedition to Yunnan, China; contributes £500.
1930	–	Sails for Rangoon with Forrest in November.
1931	Suffers first stroke when at Ste-Claire. Meets Louis and Mary Bromfield at Senlis in June.	LJ becomes seriously ill at Bhamo; abandons the trip in Chengdu, Yunnan; returns to France via Ceylon.
1932	EW spends part of every summer in England including Hidcote, until 1936. LJ a regular visitor at St-Brice & Ste-Claire, often with Norah Lindsay.	Continues to sponsor plant-collecting expeditions and revisits the Alps and Alpes Maritimes; also Morocco with Will Ingwersen. Serre visited by Prince of Wales. Royal Botanic Garden, Edinburgh, sends seeds from Forrest expedition to Hidcote. Friendship with Ruth Peppercorn of Cheltenham.

1933	EW's health deteriorates; enjoys a long rest at Hidcote.	–
1934	–	French Government taxes property and overseas assets of residents; affects LJ's finances.
1935	–	LJ survives bronchial pneumonia when staying with Philip Sassoon.
1936	Lady Wemyss makes final visit to St-Brice. EW makes final visit to England. With LJ makes last trip to Senlis; travels to Ste-Claire in September via Serre for the last time.	Lady Wemyss visits Serre.
1937	EW dies at St-Brice on 11 August; buried in the American (Protestant) cemetery at Versailles. Lady Wemyss also dies.	–
1938	Robert Norton, member of EW's Inner Circle and friend of LJ, dies.	LJ's Head Gardener at Hidcote, Frank Adams, dies aged 49.
1939	–	Start of Second World War. LJ travels to Serre in the autumn.
1940	–	Italians invade south of France. LJ escapes via Marseilles. Serre de la Madone used as billet by occupying troops.
1942	The Mount becomes Foxhollow School for Girls.	First mention of the National Trust having a role at Hidcote after LJ's death.
1945	–	Mark Fenwick dies. Sutton Courtenay sold to David Astor; house and garden remodelled; again by Brenda Colvin in 1960.

1948	Duc & Duchesse de Talleyrand purchase Pavillon Colombe. Russell Page engaged to redesign the gardens.	RHS awards the Gold Veitch Memorial Medal; LJ too ill to attend presentation – accepted by his cousin, Nan Hudson. Norah Lindsay dies. Deed of Gift of Hidcote to the National Trust signed. LJ departs Hidcote for Serre. Nancy Lindsay acts as supervisor at Hidcote till 1950.
1949	Gaillard Lapsley dies.	Local Gardens Committee appointed, chaired by LJ's friend, Major Kenneth Shennan, to oversee the Hidcote Garden.
1950	–	LJ makes last visit to Hidcote – suffering from dementia.
1955	Ste-Claire taken over by Hyères Municipal Council.	LJ bed-ridden. Graham Stuart Thomas is appointed Gardens Officer for the National Trust.
1956	–	National Trust, informed that LJ no longer able to visit Hidcote, begins to clear the house and sell the contents. Gardens Committee disbands. Graham Stuart Thomas has sole responsibility for Hidcote gardens.
1958	–	LJ dies at Serre de la Madone on 27 April, buried at Mickleton Church next to his mother. Serre left to Nancy Lindsay, who cannot afford its upkeep; property & contents sold to pay inheritance taxes. National Trust unable to take on Nether Lypiatt; Bill Barrington's planting ripped out.
1959	Beatrix Farrand dies.	Nan Hudson dies.
1960	–	Bill Barrington & Bobbie James die.

Appendix 3 – Gardens to Visit

UNITED STATES

The Mount
2 Plunkett Street • Lenox,
Massachusetts 01240-0974
General Info call 413-551-5111
www. edithwharton.org/visit/

ENGLAND & WALES

Hidcote Manor Garden
Hidcote Bartrim,
    nr Chipping Campden
Gloucestershire GL55 6LR
www.nationaltrust.org.uk/hidcote

Abbotswood
Stow-on-the-Wold, Cheltenham
Gloucestershire GL54 1LE
Tel:01451 830173

Cothay Manor and Gardens
Greenham, Nr. Wellington
Somerset TA21 OJR
www. cothaymanor.co.uk

Dyffryn Gardens
St Nicholas
Vale of Glamorgan CF5 6SU
Wales
www.dyffryngardens.org.uk

Kiftsgate Court Gardens
Chipping Campden
Gloucestershire GL55 6LW
www.kiftsgate.co.uk

Luggers Hall
Springfield Lane, Broadway
Worcestershire WR12 7BT
www.luggershall.com

FRANCE

Le Parc Sainte-Claire
Avenue Edith Wharton
83400 Hyères
Tel : 04 94 00 78 65

Le Parc Saint-Bernard
Montée de Noailles
83400 Hyères
Tel : 04 94 00 78 65

Serre de la Madone
74 Route de Gorbio
06500 Menton
www.serredelamadone.com

ITALY

La Mortola
Amici dei Giardini Botanici Hanbury
c/o Arch. Italo Muratore
Corso Repubblica, n. 2
18039 Ventimiglia IM
www.amicihanbury.com/
menu_english
Tel: +39 0184 35 11 26

BIBLIOGRAPHY

Sources for Edith Wharton:

Auchincloss, L., (1972) *Edith Wharton – a woman in her time*. Michael Joseph, London.

Benstock, S., (1994) *No Gifts from Chance*. Scribner, New York.

Collas, P. & Villedary, E., (2002) *Edith Wharton's French Riviera*. Flammarion, Paris.

Colquitt, C., Goodman, S. & Waid, C., eds (1999) *A Forward Glance – New Essays on Edith Wharton*. University of Delaware Press/Associated University Presses, Pennsylvania.

Craig, T., (1996) *Edith Wharton: a house full of rooms, architecture, interiors and gardens*. Monacelli, New York.

Dwight, E., (1994) *Edith Wharton – an extraordinary life*. Abrams, New York.

'E.C'., (1928) 'A Riviera Garden Sainte-Claire le Chateau, Hyères', *Country Life*, 3 November.

Edith Wharton Restoration, ed., (2009) *Edith Wharton and the American Garden*. Lenox, MA.

Freeman, A., (2003) 'A lightning turn around in the Berkshires restores the 100-year-old landscape at Edith Wharton's The Mount'. *Landscape Architecture*, September.

Fryer, J., (1986) *Felicitous Space*. University of North Carolina Press, Chapel Hill.

Goodman, S., (1994) *Edith Wharton's Inner Circle*. University of Texas Press, Austin.

Goodman, S., (1990) *Edith Wharton's Women – Friends & Rivals*. University Press of New England, Lebanon, New Hampshire.

Karson, R., (2007) *A Genius For Place*. University of Massachusetts Press, Amherst.

Kellog, G., (1965) *The Two Lives of Edith Wharton*. Appleton-Century, New York.

Lee, H., (2007) *Edith Wharton*. Chatto & Windus, London.

Lewis, R.W.B., (1975) *Edith Wharton: a biography*. Constable, London.

Lewis, R.W.B., ed., (1988) *The Letters of Edith Wharton*. Scribner, New York.

Lubbock, P., (1947) *Portrait of Edith Wharton*. Jonathan Cape, London.

Martineau, A., (1924) *Gardening in Sunny Lands*. Cobden-Sanderson, London.

Russell, V., (1997) *Edith Wharton's Italian Gardens*. Frances Lincoln, London.

Wegener, F., ed., (1998) *Edith Wharton: the Uncollected Critical Writings*. Princeton University Press.

Wharton, E., (1934) *A Backward Glance*. Appleton Century, New York/ Constable, London.

Novels by Edith Wharton quoted from:

Ethan Frome. (1911) Scribner, New York. (2000) Wordsworth Classics, London.

The Age of Innocence. (1920) Appleton, New York/Virago, London.

The House of Mirth. (1905) Scribner, New York. (1990) /Virago, London.

The Touchstone. (1900) Scribner, New York/pagebypage books.com

Twilight Sleep. (1927) Appleton, New York.

Sources for Lawrence Johnston:

Clarke, E., (1989) *Hidcote.* Michael Joseph, London.

—— (2009) *Hidcote.* Revised edition. Norton, London & New York.

de Navarro, M., (1936) *A Few More Memories.* Hutchinson, London.

Fretwell, K., (2000) 'The Real Major Johnston Revealed'. *Country Life,* 9 March, 194 (10), 118-21.

Hayward, A., (2007) *Norah Lindsay – the Life and Art of a Garden Designer.* Frances Lincoln, London.

Lees-Milne, J., (2006) *Diaries 1942–1954.* John Murray, London.

Lees-Milne, J., (1975) *Ancestral Voices.* Chatto and Windus, London.

Mowl, T., (2002) *Historic Gardens of Gloucestershire.* Tempus, Stroud.

Johnson [sic], Lawrence (1929) 'Some Flowering Plants of Kilimanjaro'. *The New Flora and Fauna,* Vol. 11, No. 5, October.

Jones, L., (2003) *Serre de la Madone.* Actes Sud, Arles.

Pearson, G., (2007) *Hidcote – The Garden and Lawrence Johnston.* National Trust Books, London.

Pavord, A., (1993) *Hidcote Manor Gardens.* The National Trust, London.

Pease, H., ed., (1924) *The History of the Northumberland (Hussars) Yeomanry.* Constable, London.

Sackville-West, V., (1949) 'Hidcote Manor'. *J. Royal Horticultural Society,* Vol.74, No. 11 November.

Stirling, G., (1953) 'Serre de la Madone'. *J. Royal Horticultural Society,* April.

Thomas, G. S., (1979) *Gardens of the National Trust.* Weidenfeld & Nicolson, London.

The Times, 7 July 1911.

Tipping, H. A., (1930) 'Hidcote Manor, Gloucestershire: the seat of Mr. Lawrence Johnston'. *Country Life,* Vol. 67, 22 February.

—— (1930) 'Early Summer at Hidcote Manor, Gloucestershire: the seat of Mr. Lawrence Johnston'. *Country Life,* Vol. 68, 29 February.

Whitsey, F., 'A Passion for Planting'. *Daily Telegraph,* 21 July 2007.

Whitsey, F., (2007) *The Garden at Hidcote.* Frances Lincoln, London.

Other Sources:

Abdy, S. and Gere, C., (1984) *The Souls*. Sidgwick and Jackson, London.

Alfrey, N., (2004) 'On Garden Colour', in *The Art of the Garden*. Tate Publishing, London.

Allan, M., (1982) *William Robinson 1898–1935*. Faber, London.

Anderson, E. B., (1973) *Seven Gardens or Sixty years of Gardening*. Michael Joseph, London.

Arnold, C., (Orde, L., ed.) (1994) *Happy as Kings – the Story of the Fenwicks of Abbotswood 1905–1945*. Wilton 65, Bishop Wilton, York.

Baron, W., (1977) *Miss Ethel Sands and Her Circle*. Peter Owen, London.

Bennet, J. H., (1870) *Winter & Spring on the Shores of the Mediterranean*. Churchill, London.

Benson, E. F., (1984) *Queen Lucia*. Black Swan, London.

Berenson, B., (1963) *Sunset & Twilight – the Last Diaries, 1947–1958*. Harcourt, Brace & World, New York.

Berger, R., (1997) 'Kitty Lloyd Jones: Lady Gardener and Nurserywoman'. *Garden History*, Vol. 25, no.1, Summer 1997.

Bisgrove, R., (1992) *The Gardens of Gertrude Jekyll*. Frances Lincoln, London.

—— (2008) *William Robinson – The Wild Gardener*. Frances Lincoln, London.

Block, M., (2008) *James Lees-Milne Diaries, 1942–1954*. Abridged. John Murray, London.

Bradley-Hole, K., (2002) 'Cothay Manor Gardens'. *Country Life*, 196 (31), 1 August.

Bradley-Hole, K., (2004) *Lost Gardens of England*. Aurum Press, London.

Bratton, D., ed., (2001) *Yrs Ever Affly*. University of Michigan Press, Ann Arbor.

Brown, J., (1995) *Beatrix – the Gardening Life of Beatrix Jones Farrand*. Viking, New York & London.

—— (1990) *Eminent Gardeners*. Viking, London.

—— (1999) *The English Garden through the Twentieth Century*. Garden Art Press, Woodbridge.

Brown, M., (2004) *1914*. Pan, London.

Clark, K., (1974) *Another Part of the Wood – a Self Portrait*. John Murray, London.

Cooper, D., (1984) *The Rainbow Comes & Goes: Part 1 of Diana Cooper Autobiography*. Carroll & Graf, New York.

Douglas-Home, J., (1996) *Violet – the Life and Loves of Violet Woodhouse*. Harvill Press, London.

Edmunds, J. E., (1929) *Military Operations in France & Belgium – 1914, Vol. 2*. Macmillan, London.

Emmet, A., (1996) *So Fine a Prospect: Historic New England Gardens*. University Press of New England, Lebanon, New Hampshire.

Farrer, J.M., (2005) *Mary Anderson*. Gutenberg E-Book, #14758.

Farrer, R., (1910) *Among the Hills*. Headley Brothers, London.

Gerrish, H., (2011) *Edwardian Country Life – The Story of H. Avray Tipping*. Frances Lincoln, London.

Greggio, S., (2002) *La Côte d'Azur des Jardins*. Editions Ouest-France, Rennes.

Hadfield, M., (1960) *Gardening in Britain*. Hutchinson, London.

Hattersley, R., (2008) *Borrowed Time*. Abacus, London.

Hewitt, B., (1997) *The Crocus King – E. A. Bowles of Myddleton House*. Touchwood Books, London.

Hitchmough, W., (1997) *Arts and Crafts Gardens*. Pavilion Books, London.

Hobhouse, P., (1991) *Flower Gardens*. Frances Lincoln, London.

Hussey, C., (1927) 'Cold Ashton Manor'. *Country Life*, 21 February.

—— (1929) 'Cothay Manor'. *Country Life*, 29 October.

—— (1934) 'Nether Lypiatt'. *Country Life*, Vol. 75, 19 May.

—— (1946) 'Nelson Cottage, Cheltenham'. *Country Life*, Vol. C 2589, 30 August.

Hyams, E., (1964) *The English Garden*. Thames & Hudson, London.

Ingram, C., (1970) *A Garden of Memories*. Witherby, London.

James, R.J., ed., (1996) *Chips: The Diaries of Sir Henry Channon*. Orion, London.

Jekyll, G. & Weaver, L., (1914) *Gardens for Small Country Houses*. Country Life, London.

Kennedy, E. J., (1916) *The Immortal Seventh Division*. Hodder & Stoughton, London.

Lees-Milne. J.,(1975) *Ancestral Voices*. Chatto & Windus, London.

—— (1980) *Harold Nicolson 1886–1929*. Chatto & Windus, London.

Lindsay, N., (1904) 'Sutton Courtney'. *Country Life*.

Lucas, E., (1921) *Edwin Austin Abbey, Royal Academician*. Vol. 1. Methuen, London.

Mako, M., (2006) 'Painting With Nature in Broadway, Worcestershire.' *Garden History*, Vol. 34, no.1.

Marr, A., (2008) *A History of Modern Britain*. Pan Books, London.

Massachusetts Horticultural Society, (1992) *Keeping Eden*. Bullfinch Press; Little, Brown and Company, London.

Mawson, T. H., (1907) *The Art and Craft of Garden Making*. Batsford, London.

—— (1927) *The Life and Work of an English Landscape Architect*. Batsford, London.

McLean, B., (2004) *George Forrest: Plant Hunter*. Antique Collectors Club, Woodbridge.

Moore, A., (2004) *La Mortola*. Cadogan Guides, London.

Morgan, K. N., (1988) *Charles Platt: the Artist as Architect*. MIT Press, Cambridge, Massachusetts & London.

Morseburg, J., (undated) *The American Renaissance*. Morseburg Galleries, Hollywood, California.

National Trust (2007) 'The Libraries Curator'. *The National Trust Magazine*, Autumn.

de Navarro, M., (1936) *A Few More Memories*. Hutchinson, London

Nicholson, S., (1992) *Nymans*. Tempus, Stroud in association with National Trust.

Nicolson, J., (2007) *The Perfect Summer: Dancing into Shadow. England in 1911*. John Murray, London.

Norwich, J. J., (2005) *The Duff Cooper Diaries, 1915–1951*. Weidenfeld & Nicolson, London.

Ottewill, D., (1989) *The Edwardian Garden*. Yale University Press, New Haven & London.

Page, R., (1962) *Education of a Gardener*. Harvill Press, London.

Parsons, A., (1896) *Notes in Japan*. Harper, New York.

Piebenga, S. and Toomer, S., (2007) 'Westonbirt Arboretum: from private, nineteenth estate collection to national arboretum'. *Garden History*, Vol. 35, supplement 2.

Quest-Ritson, C., (1992) *The English Garden Abroad*. Viking, London.

Richardson, T., (2005) *English Gardens in the Twentieth Century*. Aurum Press, London.

Rogers, E. B., (1987) *Rebuilding Central Park*. MIT Press, Cambridge, Massachusetts.

Schinz, M. and van Zuylen, G., (1991) *The Gardens of Russell Page*. Stewart, Tabori & Chang, New York; reprinted (2008), Frances Lincoln, London.

Sitwell, O., (1948) *Left Hand Right Hand. Vol. 3, Great Morning*. Macmillan, London.

—— (1948) *Left Hand Right Hand. Vol. 5, Noble Essences*. Macmillan, London.

Stansky, P., (2003) *Sassoon: The Worlds of Philip and Sybil*. Yale University Press, London.

Stephensen, L. S., (2007) *Garden Design in Denmark – G. N. Brandt and the Early Decades of the Twentieth Century*. Packard, Chichester.

Tankard, J., (1993) *Gardens of the Arts and Craft Movement*. Abrams, New York.

Thomas, G. S., (1984) *The Art of Planting*. Dent for National Trust, London.

—— (1997) *Cuttings from My Garden Notebooks*. John Murray, London.

Torode, S., (1993) *Duffryn – an Edwardian Garden*. Glamorgan Record Office, Cardiff.

Treib, M., ed., (1998) *Modern Landscape Architecture*. MIT Press, Cambridge, Massachusetts & London.

Turner, J., ed., (1996) *The Grove Dictionary of Art*. Oxford University Press.

Venn, J. S., (1947) *Alumni Cantabrigienses*, Part 11, Vol. 1V. Cambridge University Press.

Vilmorin, H. de (1893) *Flowers of the French Riviera*. Spottiswoode, London.

Waymark, J., (2009) *Thomas Mawson – Life, Gardens & Landscapes*. Frances Lincoln, London.

Wilson, A. N., (2002) *The Victorians*. Arrow Books, London.

List of Illustrations, sources and credits

Plate Number:

Frontispiece   View of The Mount from the walled Italian Garden. Author's photograph.

1   Part of the Ramble in Central Park, New York c.1905. Library of Congress Prints & Photographic Division.

2   Stone pines in the Piazza di Siena, Borghese Gardens. Wikipedia, Howard Hudson.

3   Interior of the Jones' brownstone house on West 23rd Street, New York c. 1884. Beinecke Rare Books and Manuscripts Library, Yale University.

4   The Tuileries, Paris, in 1871. McCormick Library of Special Collections, Northwestern University.

5   Fifth Avenue at 42nd Street, New York, c. 1883. Library of Congress Prints & Photographic Division.

6   A portrait of Edith Jones, c.1881 by Edward Harrison May. Collection of the American Academy of Arts and Letters, New York City.

7   Edward 'Teddy' Wharton with the dogs. Beinecke Rare Books and Manuscripts Library, Yale University.

8   Edith Wharton riding 'Fatty', c. 1885. Courtesy, Lilly Library, Indiana University, Bloomington, Indiana.

9   Egerton Leigh Winthrop, by John Singer Sargent, c. 1901. The Knickerbocker Club, New York.

10   Ogden Codman. Society for the Preservation of New England Antiquities – Historic New England, Boston.

11   Land's End, Newport, Rhode Island. Beinecke Rare Books and Manuscripts Library, Yale University.

12   A birds-eye view of the Chicago's World Columbian Exposition, 1893. Library of Congress Prints and Photographic Division.

13   a) Belton House, Lincolnshire. Wikipedia/National Trust.

b) The Mount, summer c. 1910. Beinecke Rare Books and Manuscripts Library, Yale University.

14   The Mount – the front entrance. Author's photograph.

15   a) A view of Laurel Lake, c. 1910. Beinecke Rare Books and Manuscripts Library, Yale University.

b) The same view in 2008. Author's photograph.

16   A view of The Mount. Author's photograph.

17   The Mount – the entrance drive designed by Beatrix Jones (Farrand). Author's photograph.

18   Beatrix Jones (Farrand) as a young woman. Beatrix Jones Farrand Collection (1955-2) Environmental Design archives, University of California, Berkeley.

19   Edith Wharton. Beinecke Rare Books and Manuscripts Library, Yale University.

20   The Mount – the restored greenhouse, 2008. Author's photograph.

21   Caprarola – the Catena d'Aqua. ATG-Oxford.

22   Maxfield Parrish's illustration of the Villa Gamberaia in *Italian Villas and Their Gardens c.* 1904. Minneapolis Institute of Arts, Bequest of Margaret B. Hawks, 84.35.

23   a) An advertisement for the Pope-Hartford motor car purchased by Teddy Wharton; b) Motoring at The Mount, 1904. Lilly Library, Indiana University, Bloomington, Indiana.

24   The Mount, Lenox, *c.* 1906. Beinecke Rare Books & Manuscripts Library, Yale University.

25   The enigmatic and alluring Morton Fullerton. Beinecke Rare Books & Manuscripts Library, Yale University.

26   Paris, 53 rue de Varenne. Author's photograph.

27   Paris, 53 rue de Varenne. Author's photograph.

28   A cartoon of Nan Hudson, from W. Baron, *Miss Ethel Sands & her Circle.* Peter Owen Ltd, London.

29   Trinity College, Cambridge University, *c.* 1890s. Trinity College Library. University of Cambridge.

30   Reginald Cory. Royal Horticultural Society, Lindley Library, London.

31   Lawrence Johnston and his mother, Gertrude Winthrop *c.* 1890s. Micklefield Womens' Institute.

32   New Etal, Northumberland *c.* 1910. archives@northumberland.gov.uk

33   An officer of the Northumberland Hussars. Author's photograph/Discovery Museum, Newcastle upon Tyne.

34   The Riding School of the Northumberland Hussars, Newcastle upon Tyne. 'A Soldier's Life' exhibition, Discovery Museum, Newcastle upon Tyne.

35   'Night send-off – departure of Imperial Yeomanry from Liverpool', February 1900. National Maritime Museum, Greenwich, London.

36   The Northumberland Hussars at Otley summer camp, 1914. 'A Soldier's Life' exhibition, Discovery Museum, Newcastle upon Tyne.

37   Officers of the Northumberland Hussars at Rothbury summer camp in 1902. 'A Soldier's Life' exhibition, Discovery Museum, Newcastle upon Tyne.

38   Mark Fenwick and his wife Molly (née Clayton) at the time of their marriage; from C. Arnold, *Happy as Kings – the Story of the Fenwicks of Abbotswood*, courtesy of Mr & Mrs M. Fox.

39   Abbotswood, Stow-on-the-Wold. Author's photograph.

40   Abbotswood, Stow-on-the-Wold – the lower spring garden. Author's photograph.

41 The Village Green, Broadway by Alfred Parsons; from *Harper's New Monthly Magazine* 1889. Making of America Archive, Cornell University.

42 Mary Anderson de Navarro, *c.* 1894. National Portrait Gallery, London.

43 Court Farm, Broadway, *c.* 1936, from M. de Navarro, *A Few More Memories*, Hutchinson, London.

44 Alfred Parsons – from 'Our Artists in Europe', *Harper's New Monthly Magazine*, 1889. Making of America Archive, Cornell University.

45 'A Garden at Broadway', by Alfred Parsons from William Robinson's magazine, *The Garden*, April 1893.

46 An aerial view of Luggers Hall, Alfred Parsons's home at Broadway. Catalogue, 'The Art of the Garden', Tate Britain, London, 2004. Photo © Marcus Leith & Andrew Dunkley.

47 Stanway House. Photo: Phillip Halling.

48 Mary Constance Charteris (née Wyndham), Lady Elcho, Countess of Wemyss, *c.* 1925, with Arthur James Balfour, 1st Earl Balfour, the former Prime Minister (1902–05). National Portrait Gallery, London.

49 A portrait of Adele Capell, Countess of Essex *c.*1892 by Edward Hughes. Watford Museum.

50 Cliveden – part of the Borghese Terrace. National Trust Picture Library, Swindon.

51 Mary Jeune, later Lady St Helier; from Mary Hare, 'History of Arlington Manor', web page.

52 Arlington Manor, near Newbury; from Mary Hare, 'History of Arlington Manor', web page.

53 Mary Hunter, charcoal drawing by John Singer Sargent *c.* 1908. Memorial Art Gallery, University of Rochester, New York.

54 Hill Hall, Theydon Mount. Country Life Picture Library, London.

55 Ellen Willmott. www.commonweeder.com

56 Warley Place, Essex. gardenpaintingsart.blogspot.com

57 Henry James, *c.* 1905; from Patten, W. ed, *Short Story Classics (American)*, Vol. 3. Collier, New York.

58 Howard Sturgis with a friend at 'Qu'acre'. Beinecke Rare Books and Manuscripts Library, Yale University.

59 Hidcote Manor. Author's photograph/National Trust.

60 Hidcote Manor – Johnston's use of perspective. Author's photograph/ National Trust.

61 Hidcote Manor – the Phlox (now White) Garden *c.* 1915; a Lumière Brothers Autochrome by Archibald Renfrew.

62 Hidcote Manor – the main vista and red borders. Author's photograph/ National Trust.

63 Hidcote Manor – the main vista seen from the red borders. Author's photograph/National Trust.

64   Lawrence Johnston and his gardeners in the Old Garden at Hidcote. National Trust at Hidcote.

65   Hidcote Manor – a) Fuchsia Garden and original Pool Garden *c.* 1907–14. National Trust at Hidcote; b) the Fuchsia Garden today. Author's photograph/National Trust.

66   Hidcote Manor – Mrs Winthrop's Garden. Author's photograph/National Trust.

67   Hidcote Manor – the Stream Garden. Author's photograph/National Trust.

68   Hidcote Manor – the Stream Garden in spring. Author's photograph/National Trust.

69   The fish pond, Wrest; from R. Blomfield, *The Formal Garden in England*, 1915. Macmillan, London.

70   Hidcote Manor – the Theatre Lawn. National Trust Picture Library, Swindon.

71   Hidcote Manor – the North Gazebo. Author's photograph/National Trust.

72   Hidcote Manor – the Long Walk seen from the South Gazebo. Author's photograph/National Trust.

73   Hidcote Manor – view of the Vale of Evesham and Bredon Hill. Author's photograph/National Trust.

74   The Northumberland Hussars on the Zillebeke Road, moving up to Ypres, October 1914. Imperial War Museum, London.

75   Mary Anderson as 'America', from M. de Navarro, *A Few More Memories*. Hutchinson, London.

76   Edith Wharton with Walter Berry meeting French troops. Beinecke Rare Books and Manuscripts Library, Yale University.

77   Edith Wharton visiting the ruins of a village. Beinecke Rare Books and Manuscripts Library, Yale University.

78   Horses of the officers, Northumberland Hussars, at Etri Cour, October 1917. Imperial War Museum, London.

79   The street façade of the Pavillon Colombe at St-Brice-sous-Forêt. Beinecke Rare Books and Manuscripts Library, Yale University.

80   The Château Ste-Claire at Hyères. Beinecke Rare Books and Manuscripts Library, Yale University.

81   a) The Hon. Robert ('Bobbie') James. © *The Gardener's Chronicle*, 1961; courtesy of the RHS Lindley Library, London; b) Bobbie James, Norah Lindsay & Lawrence Johnston. James family collection, courtesy of Ursula Westbury.

82   Gertrude Winthrop. National Trust Picture Library, Swindon.

83   Norah Lindsay (two photos). David Lindsay family collection.

84   Sutton Courtenay. Country Life Picture Library, London.

85   A study of flowers by Lawrence Johnston. National Trust Picture Library, Swindon.

86   Heather Muir created the garden at Kiftsgate after 1920, inspired and helped by Lawrence Johnston. Courtesy of Anne Chambers, Kiftsgate.

87   Violet Woodhouse and her ménage à trois, from J. Douglas-Home, *Violet – the Life and Loves of Violet Woodhouse*. Harvill Press, London.

88   Ethel Sands in her London house at The Vale, Chelsea, *c.* 1922, from W. Baron, *Miss Ethel Sands and Her Circle*. Peter Owen Ltd, London.

89   Nan Hudson at Newington *c.* 1908, from W. Baron, *Miss Ethel Sands and Her Circle*. Peter Owen Ltd, London.

90   Lawrence Johnston with his head gardener Frank Adams. Source unknown; from, E. Clarke, *Hidcote*. Michael Joseph, London.

91   Hidcote Manor – the main vista, *c.* 1929. Country Life Picture Library, London.

92   Hidcote Manor – the herbaceous borders *c.* 1929. Country Life Picture Library, London.

93   Hidcote Manor – the Pillar Garden *c.* 1960s; from E. Hyams, *The English Garden*. Thames & Hudson, London.

94   Hidcote Manor – a) 'Picturesque' principles in 'Westonbirt'. Author's photograph/National Trust; b) Holford Ride at Westonbirt Arboretum. Forestry Commission Picture Library.

95   Pavillon Colombe – rear view of the house. Beinecke Rare Books and Manuscripts Library, Yale University.

96   Pavillon Colombe – the terrace. Courtesy, Lilly Library, Indiana University, Bloomington, Indiana.

97   Pavillon Colombe – the pool. Beinecke Rare Books and Manuscripts Library, Yale University.

98   Abbotswood – the Blue Garden, designed by Edwin Lutyens. Author's photograph.

99   Pavillon Colombe – the Blue Garden. Beinecke Rare Books and Manuscripts Library, Yale University.

100   Pavillon Colombe – Edith Wharton in the Rose garden. Beinecke Rare Books and Manuscripts Library, Yale University.

101   Château Sainte-Claire at Hyères. Courtesy, Lilly Library, Indiana University, Bloomington, Indiana.

102   A view of Ste-Claire from the old town of Hyères. Author's photograph.

103   Ste-Claire – a view from the terrace. Author's photograph.

104   Ste-Claire – the unkempt garden in 2007. Author's photograph.

105   The terrace at Ste-Claire with its plane trees. Courtesy, Lilly Library, Indiana University, Bloomington, Indiana.

106   *Buddleja madagascarensis*. Author's photograph.

107   Ste-Claire – the terrace with cyprus trees. Courtesy, Lilly Library, Indiana University, Bloomington, Indiana.

108   The walk to the tower at Ste-Claire. Courtesy, Lilly Library, Indiana University, Bloomington, Indiana.

109   Part of the restored garden at Ste-Claire. Author's photograph.

110   Hyères – Robert Norton sketching. Beinecke Rare Books and Manuscripts Library, Yale University.

111   Edith Wharton picnicking with Robert Norton and Gaillard Lapsley. Courtesy, Lilly Library, Indiana University, Bloomington, Indiana.

112   Serre de la Madone – the dining room. Southhill Chattels Trust, ref. W/H39/9.

113   Serre de la Madone – the living room. Southhill Chattels Trust, ref. W/H39/9

114   Serre de la Madone – the main entrance c. 1930. Southhill Chattels Trust, ref. W/H39/9

115   Serre de la Madone – the main axis looking towards the house. Southhill Chattels Trust, ref. W/H39/9.

116   Serre de la Madone – one of the terracotta sphinxes. Author's photograph.

117   Serre de la Madone – the fishponds on the central axis. Southhill Chattels Trust, ref. W/H39/9.

118   Serre de la Madone – the blue-tiled loggia. Southhill Chattels Trust, ref. W/H39/9.

119   La Mortola. Author's photograph.

120   Charles de Noailles' Villa St-Bernard. Author's photograph.

121   Villa St-Bernard – the cubist garden by Gabriel Guevrekian, c. 1927. Author's photograph.

122   The former upper garden at Ste-Claire. Author's photograph.

123   South Africa. Source unknown; from C. Ingram, *A Garden of Memories*. Witherby, London.

124   *Senecio johnstonii*. 'Information/picture from 7summits.com © Harry Kikstra'.

125   George Forrest. Forrest Family Archive, via Antique Collectors' Club, Woodbridge.

126   *Jasminum polyanthemum*. Author's photograph.

127   *Mahonia siamensis* at Serre de la Madone. Author's photograph.

128   *Hypericum forrestii*. Author's photograph.

129   Le Bois des Moutiers, Varengeville-sur-Mer, Normandy. Author's photograph.

130   Lawrence Johnston. Source unknown; from G. S. Thomas, *Gardens of the National Trust*. Weidenfeld & Nicolson, London.

131   Gertrude Jekyll at Deanery Garden, Sonning. English Heritage. NMR Picture Library, Swindon.

132   Lady Sybil Colefax with Cecil Beaton. National Portrait Gallery, London.

133   Reginald Cooper. Source unknown; from *The Garden*, Vol. 125, 2000.

134 Cothay Manor. Author's photograph.

135 Cothay Manor – garden rooms in the Hidcote style. Author's photograph.

136 Little Moreton Hall, Cheshire. Country Life Picture Library, London.

137 Philip Sassoon, *c.* 1929. National Portrait Gallery, London.

138 Trent Park, Hertfordshire. Country Life Picture Library, London.

139 Nelson Cottage, Cheltenham. Country Life Picture Library, London.

140 Nelson Cottage, Cheltenham – painting of a magnolia. Country Life Picture Library, London.

141 The Feast of the Assumption at the Pavillon Colombe. Beinecke Rare Books and Manuscripts Library, Yale University.

142 Beatrix Farrand in later life. Environmental Design Archives, University of California, Berkeley; courtesy of Jane Brown.

143 Irises at Ste-Claire in 2007. Author's photograph.

144 Hyères: Edith Wharton on the terrace at Ste-Claire. Beinecke Rare Books and Manuscripts Library, Yale University.

145 The Vicomte Charles de Noailles. © Michael Warren, Epicurius Images Ltd, Ipswich.

146 Pavillon Colombe – the last photograph of Edith Wharton *c.* July 1937. Courtesy, Lilly Library, Indiana University, Bloomington, Indiana.

147 Edith Wharton's grave in the Cimetière des Gonards, Versailles. © K. Baptiste.

148 Mark Fenwick and other members of the RHS Chelsea Show Committee, 1930. Royal Horticultural Society Lindley Library, London.

149 Nancy Lindsay as a young woman in 1922. David Lindsay Family Collection.

150 Hidcote – Lawrence Johnston on the Theatre Lawn. Source unknown; from A. Pavord, *Hidcote Manor Gardens,* National Trust.

151 Hidcote – a view of the south gazebo from the Stream garden. *c.* 1964. Source unknown; from E. Hyams, *The English Garden*. Thames & Hudson, London.

152 Hidcote – the Pool Garden, *c.* 1964. Source unknown; from E. Hyams, *The English Garden*. Thames & Hudson, London.

153 Nancy Lindsay in the late 1940s. David Lindsay Family Collection.

154 Lawrence Johnston at Serre de la Madone, with Mme Freda Bottin. Rebuffo Family collection/KEO Films, London.

155 Lawrence Johnston's grave at Mickleton. Author's photograph.

156 Inscription on Lawrence Johnston's grave. Author's photograph.

157 The Mount – the flower garden 2008. Author's photograph.

158 The Mount – the house from the flower garden. Author's photograph.

159 Ste-Claire – the former Orange Terrace, 2007. Author's photograph.

160 Ste-Claire – the entrance to the terrace, 2007. Author's photograph.

161 Ste-Claire – part of the restored garden, 2007. Author's photograph.

Figures

13a   Plan of the Deanery, Sonning, designed by Edwin Lutyens. Environmental Design Archives, University of California, Berkeley.

15a   Aerial view of the Pavillon Colombe today. © Google 2011.

15b   Aerial view of the current layout of Hidcote Manor gardens. © Google 2011.

16a   Hidcote Manor Garden – the four gardens. Author's diagram based on the plan in the National Trust Guide, 1965.

16b   Hidcote Manor Garden – Views and Vistas. Author's diagram based on the plan in the National Trust Guide, 1965.

16c   The Villa Lante; from J. Lauri, *Antiqua Urbe Splendor*, 1612.

Every effort to find the sources and copyright holders, if appropriate, of photographs and figures has been made. The Author and editor apologize for any unintentional errors or omissions.

Maps

1   The Eastern seaboard of the United States.

2   Northumberland.

3   The Cotswolds.

4   The First Battle of Ypres, 1914.

5   The Côte d'Azur showing the location of Edith Wharton and Lawrence Johnston's gardens.

6   Lawrence Johnston's plant-collecting journey in Burma and China, 1930–1.

INDEX

Abbreviations: EW for Edith Wharton, LJ for Lawrence Johnston, n for note or reference, Pl. for Plate. Dates of birth and death are included only for key or influential people.